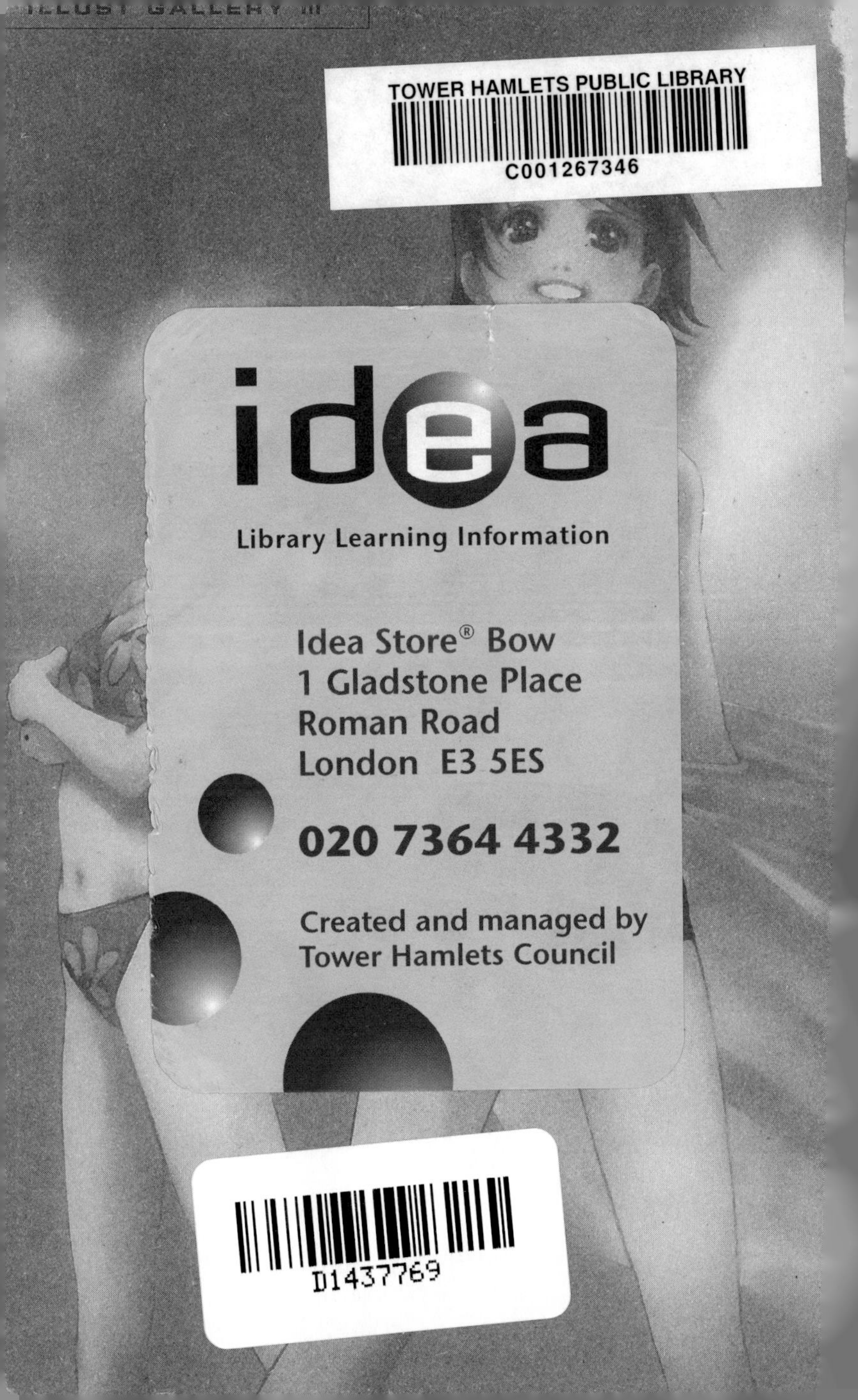
ILLUST GALLERY III

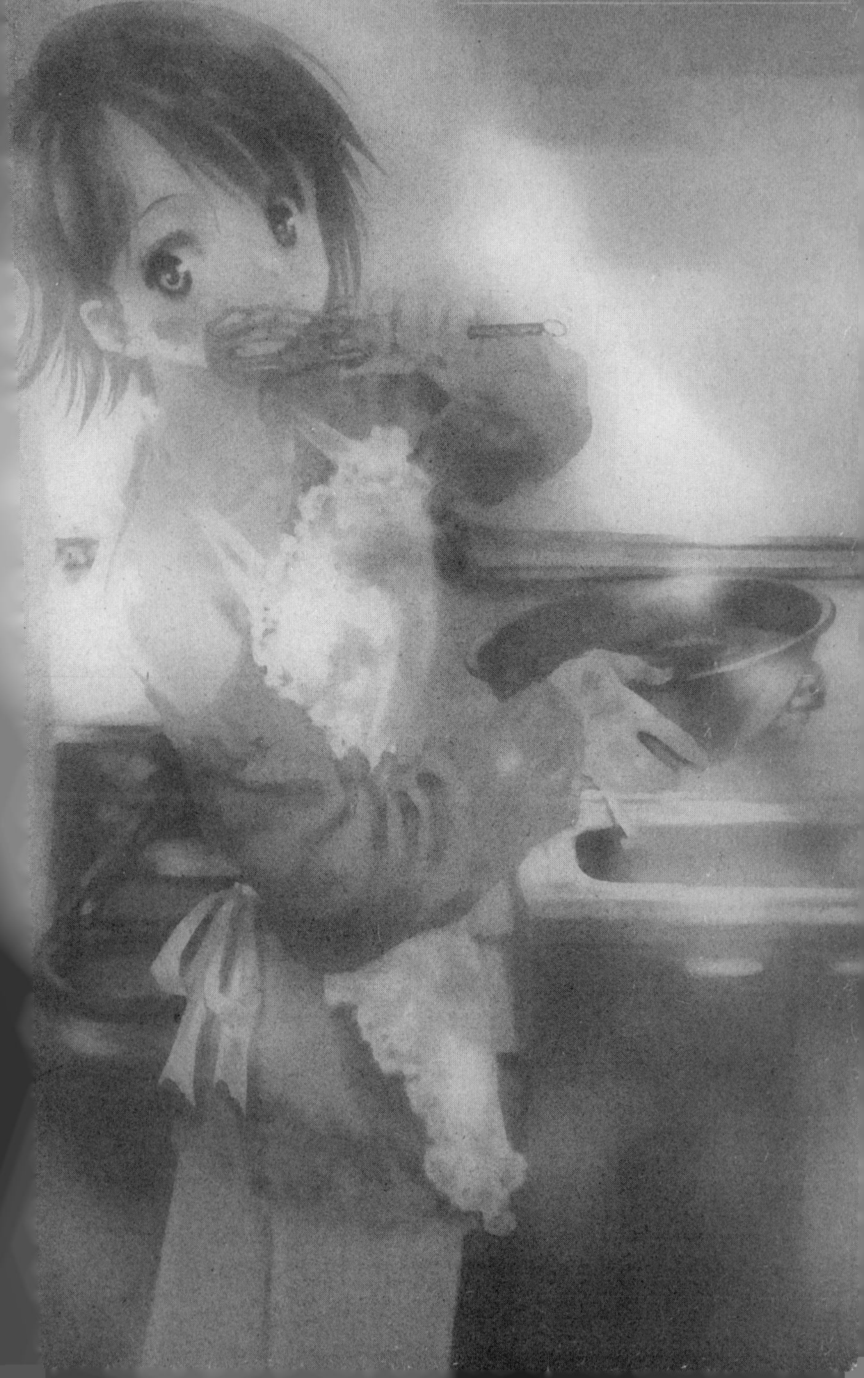

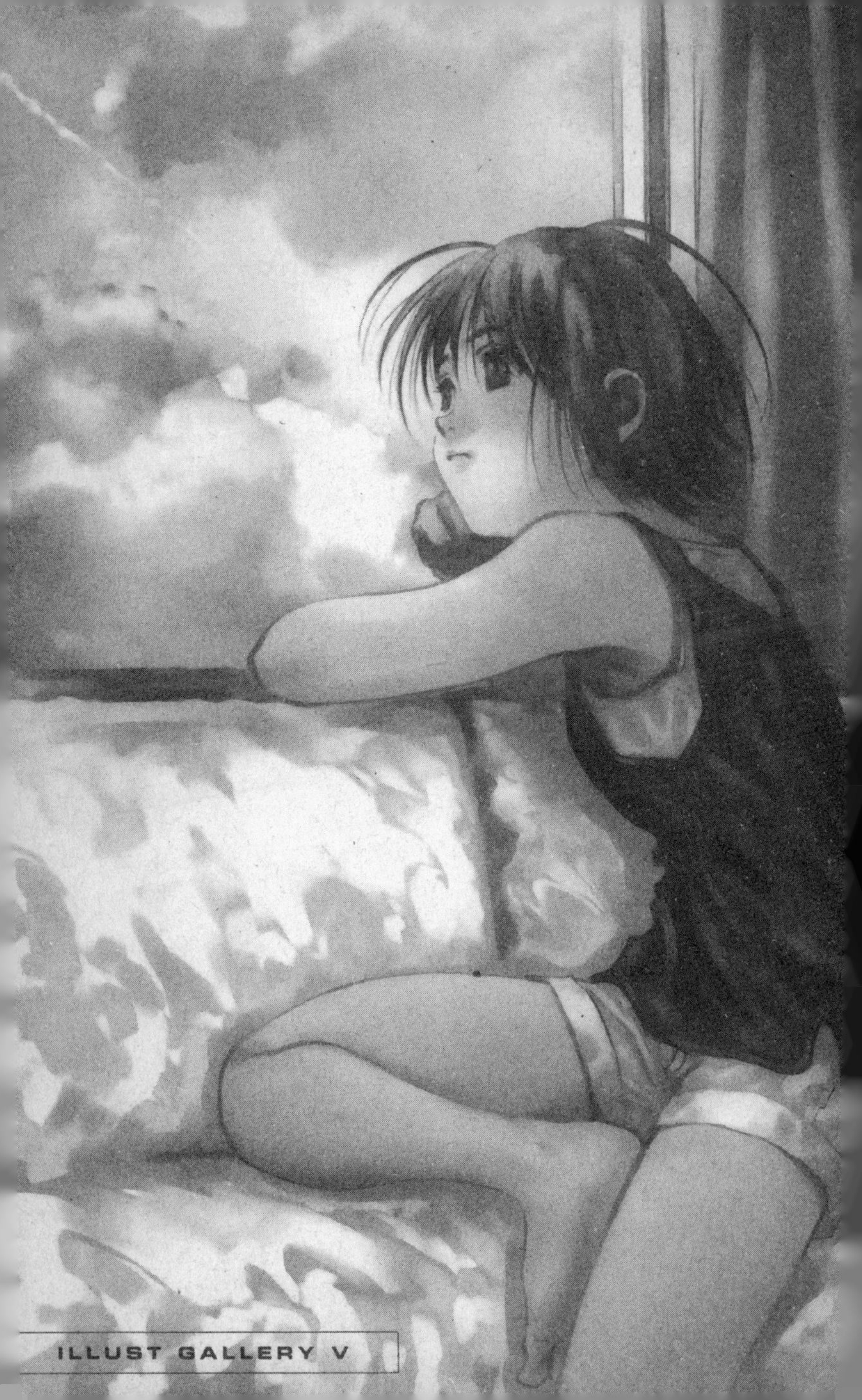

ILLUST GALLERY V

TGM-79C (SPACE SPECIFICATION)

MECHANIC DESIGN

Yoshinori Sayama

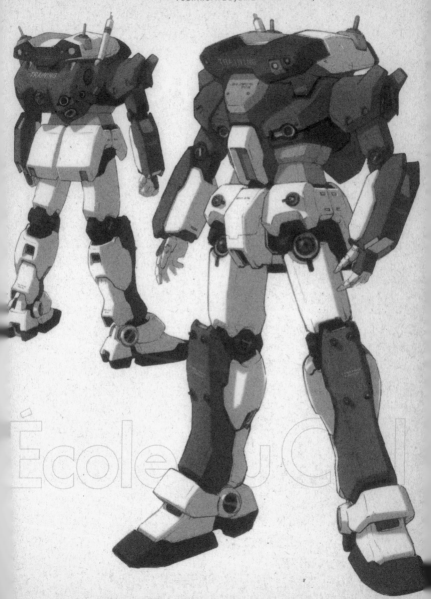

Mobile Suit Gundam
École du Ciel
天 空 の 学 校

Volume 2

By
Haruhiko Mikimoto

HAMBURG // LONDON // LOS ANGELES // TOKYO

Mobile Suit Gundam École du Ciel Volume 2

Written and Illustrated by Haruhiko Mikimoto
Gundam Series Created by Hajime Yatate & Yoshiyuki Tomino
Mechanic Design by Yoshinori Sayama
Produced by OUTASIGHT

Translation - Ikoi Hiroe
English Adaptation - Ikoi Hiroe and Paul Morrissey
Copy Editor - Hope Donovan
Retouch and Lettering - Jose Macasocol, Jr. and Alyson Stetz
Production Artist - Jose Macasocol, Jr.
Cover Design - Raymond Makowski

Editor - Paul Morrissey
Digital Imaging Manager - Chris Buford
Production Managers - Jennifer Miller and Mutsumi Miyazaki
Managing Editor - Lindsey Johnston
VP of Production - Ron Klamert
Publisher and E.I.C. - Mike Kiley
President and C.O.O. - John Parker
C.E.O. - Stuart Levy

A  Manga

TOKYOPOP Inc.
5900 Wilshire Blvd. Suite 2000
Los Angeles, CA 90036

E-mail: info@TOKYOPOP.com
Come visit us online at www.TOKYOPOP.com

MOBILE SUIT GUNDAM ÉCOLE DU CIEL 2
© HARUHIKO MIKIMOTO 2003
© SOTSU AGENCY• SUNRISE
First published in Japan in 2003 by
KADOKAWA SHOTEN PUBLISHING CO., LTD., Tokyo.
English translation rights arranged with
KADOKAWA SHOTEN PUBLISHING CO., LTD., Tokyo
through TUTTLE–MORI AGENCY, INC., Tokyo.
English text copyright © 2006 TOKYOPOP Inc.

All rights reserved. No portion of this book may be reproduced or transmitted in any form or by any means without written permission from the copyright holders. This manga is a work of fiction. Any resemblance to actual events or locales or persons, living or dead, is entirely coincidental.

ISBN: 1-59532-852-1

First TOKYOPOP printing: January 2006
10 9 8 7 6 5 4 3 2 1
Printed in the USA

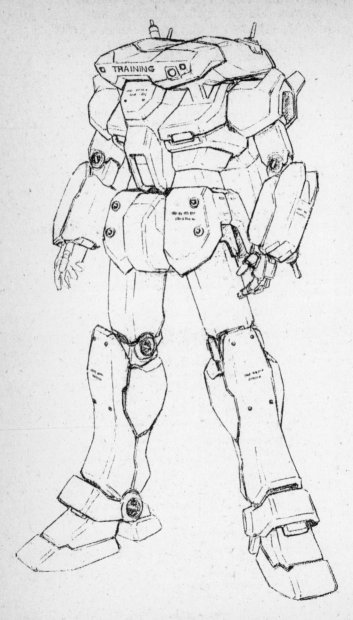

Editor's note: To see a Universal Century timeline and a glossary of terms,
visit http://www.gundamofficial.com/worlds/uc/index.html

Previously In... Mobile Suit Gundam École du Ciel

天空の学校

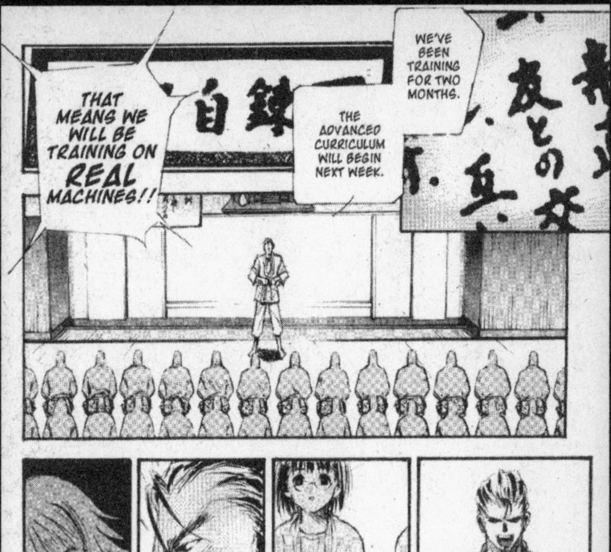

WE'VE BEEN TRAINING FOR TWO MONTHS.
THE ADVANCED CURRICULUM WILL BEGIN NEXT WEEK.
THAT MEANS WE WILL BE TRAINING ON REAL MACHINES!!
HOWEVER, THOSE THAT DO NOT HAVE PASSING SCORES IN COMBAT BASICS... WILL NOT MOVE FORWARD.
WE HAVE ONE LOSER.
THAT'S YOU...
...ASUNA ELMARIT!!

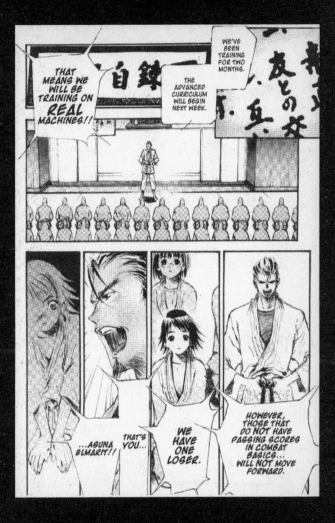

The year is 0085 of the Universal Century. Asuna Elmarit is a struggling student at École du Ciel--the Earth Federation's Mobile Suit military academy. Life isn't easy for Asuna. Teachers and students alike belittle her lackluster abilities, and her father--a brilliant Zeon professor--is currently a fugitive suspected of war crimes.

Previously In... Mobile Suit Gundam École du Ciel

天 空 の 学 校

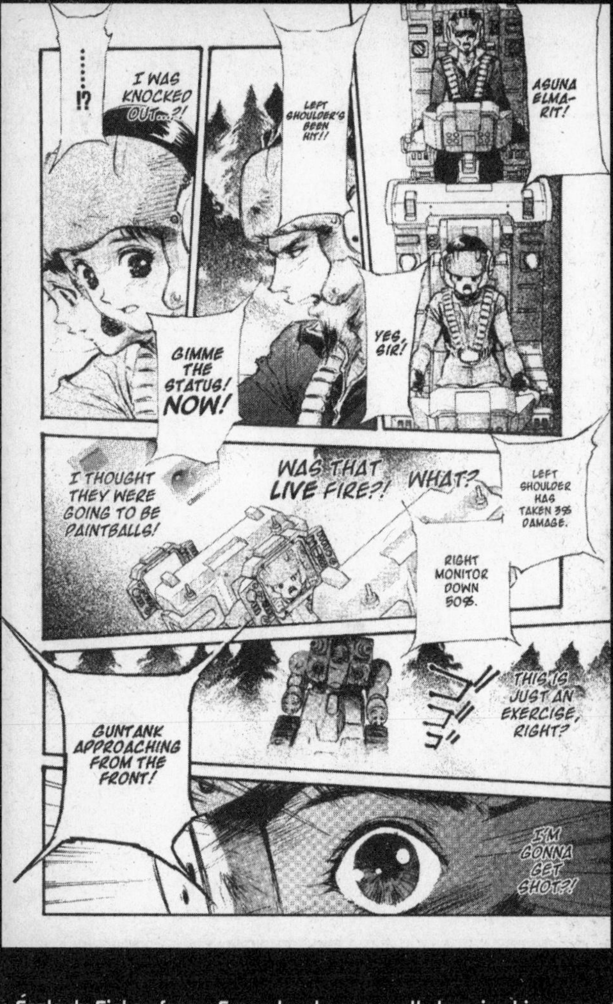
ASUNA ELMA-RIT!
YES, SIR!
LEFT SHOULDER'S BEEN HIT!!
GIMME THE STATUS! NOW!
......!?
I WAS KNOCKED OUT...?!
LEFT SHOULDER HAS TAKEN 3% DAMAGE.
RIGHT MONITOR DOWN 50%.
WHAT?
WAS THAT LIVE FIRE?!
I THOUGHT THEY WERE GOING TO BE PAINTBALLS!
THIS IS JUST AN EXERCISE, RIGHT?
GUNTANK APPROACHING FROM THE FRONT!
I'M GONNA GET SHOT?!

However, École du Ciel professor Forma has been secretly keeping his eye on Asuna, reporting his observations to "the council"--a shadowy group that created École du Ciel in order to develop and seek out potential Newtypes--humans gifted with superhuman powers of intuition and awareness. The council dreams of harnessing Newtype abilities for military purposes. During a routine battle simulation, Asuna and Professor Yahagi are startled when they find themselves shelled by live rounds of ammo! Yahagi miraculously saves the day, and students begin to spread a rumor that Yahagi is a Newtype...

Mobile Suit Gundom École du Ciel

天空の学校

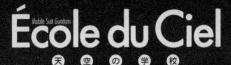

CONTENTS

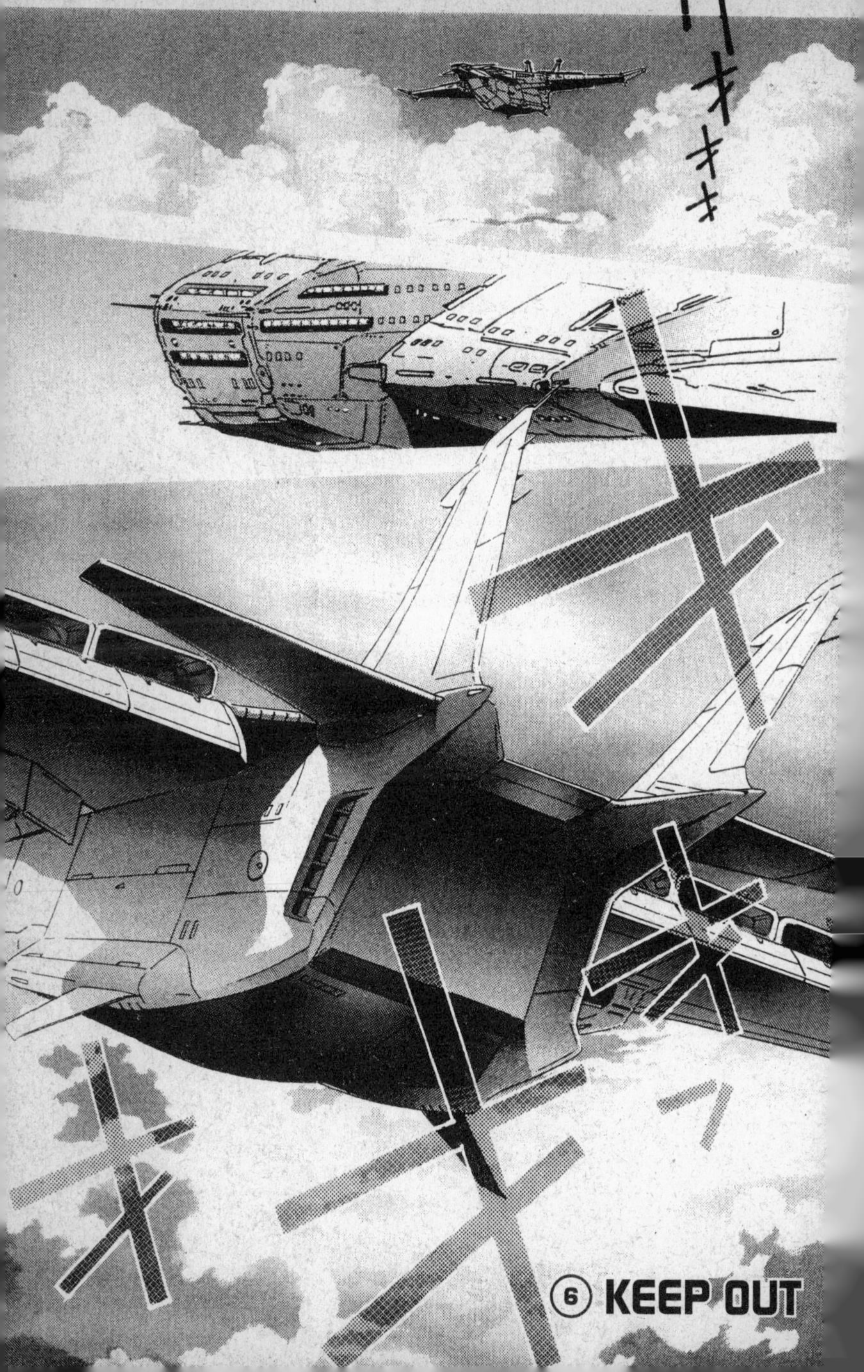
⑥ KEEP OUT

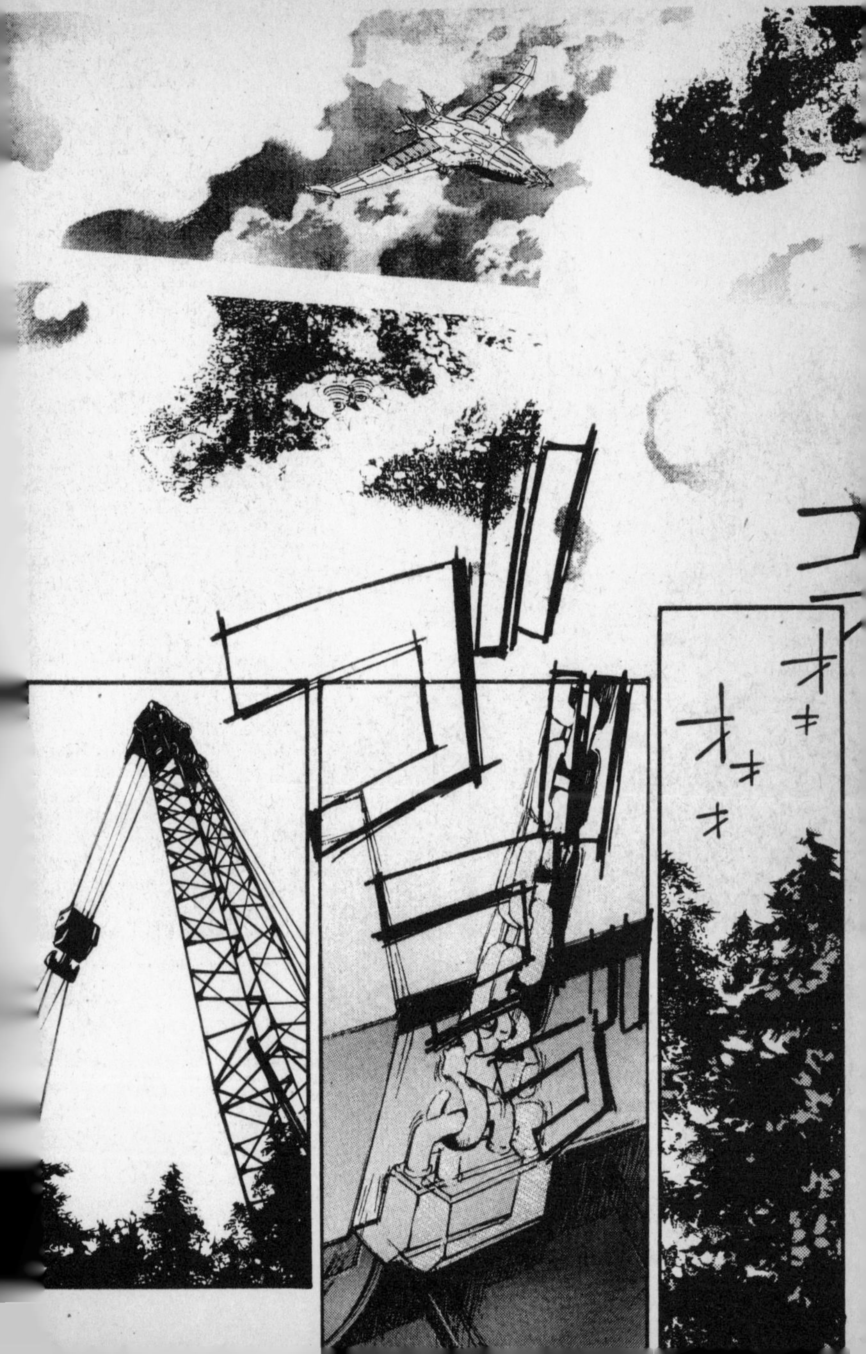
オォ
オォォ

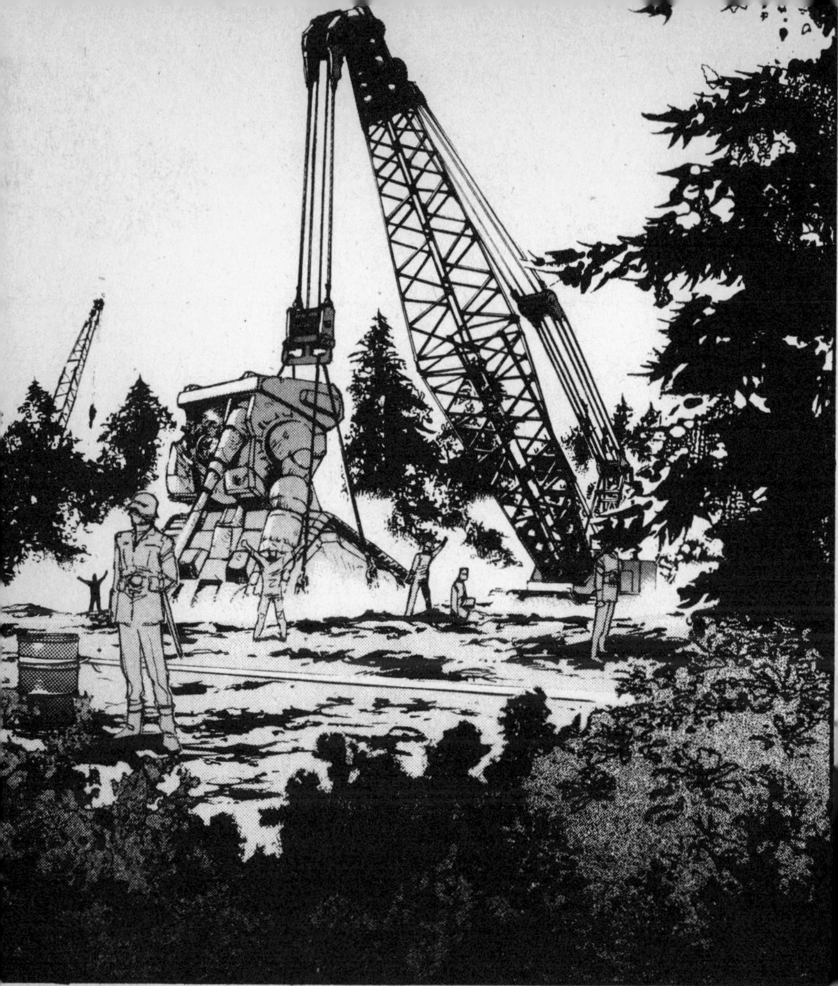

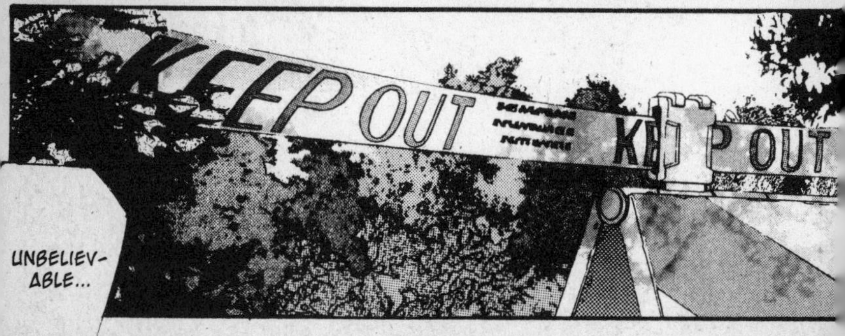
KEEP OUT
UNBELIEV-
ABLE...

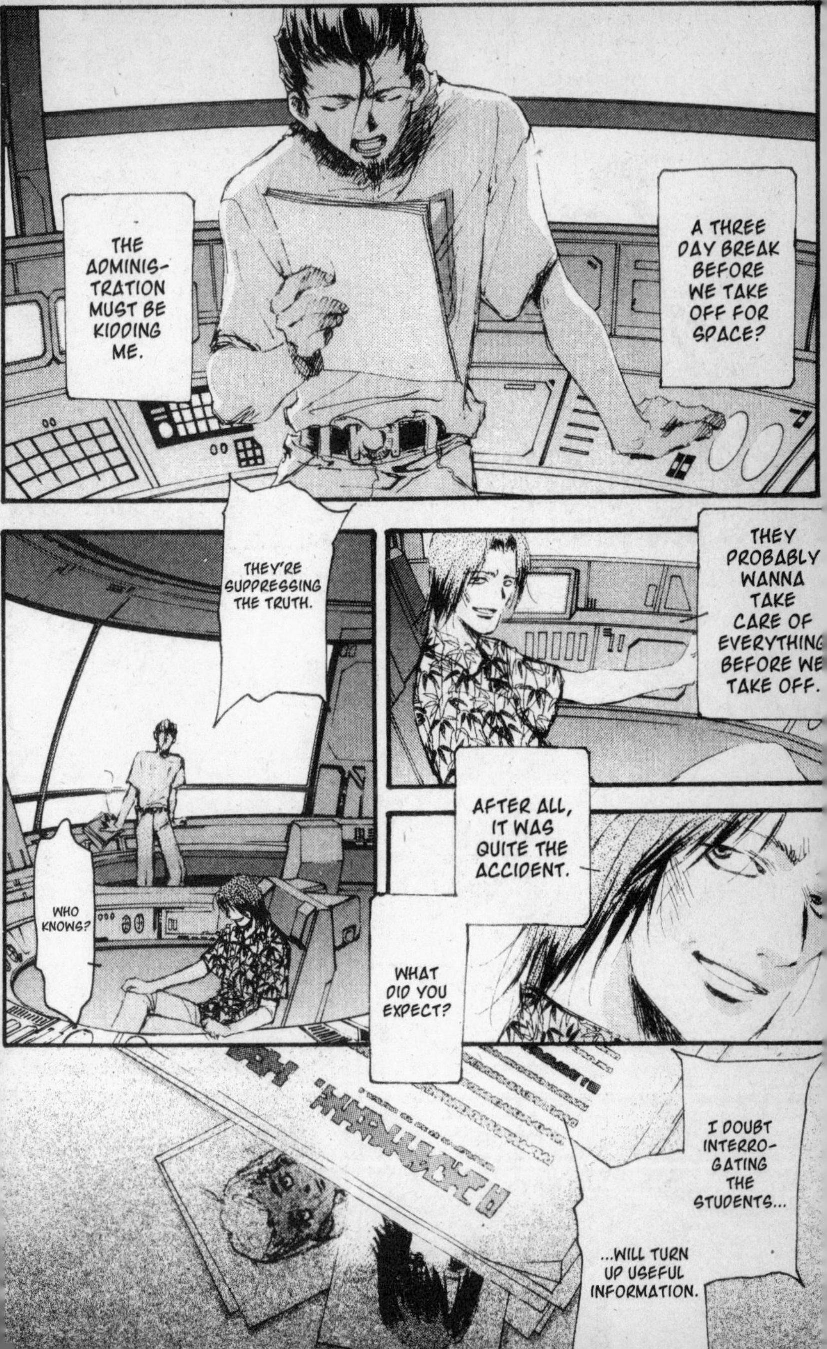
A THREE DAY BREAK BEFORE WE TAKE OFF FOR SPACE?
THE ADMINIS-TRATION MUST BE KIDDING ME.
THEY PROBABLY WANNA TAKE CARE OF EVERYTHING BEFORE WE TAKE OFF.
AFTER ALL, IT WAS QUITE THE ACCIDENT.
WHAT DID YOU EXPECT?
THEY'RE SUPPRESSING THE TRUTH.
WHO KNOWS?
I DOUBT INTERRO-GATING THE STUDENTS...
...WILL TURN UP USEFUL INFORMATION.

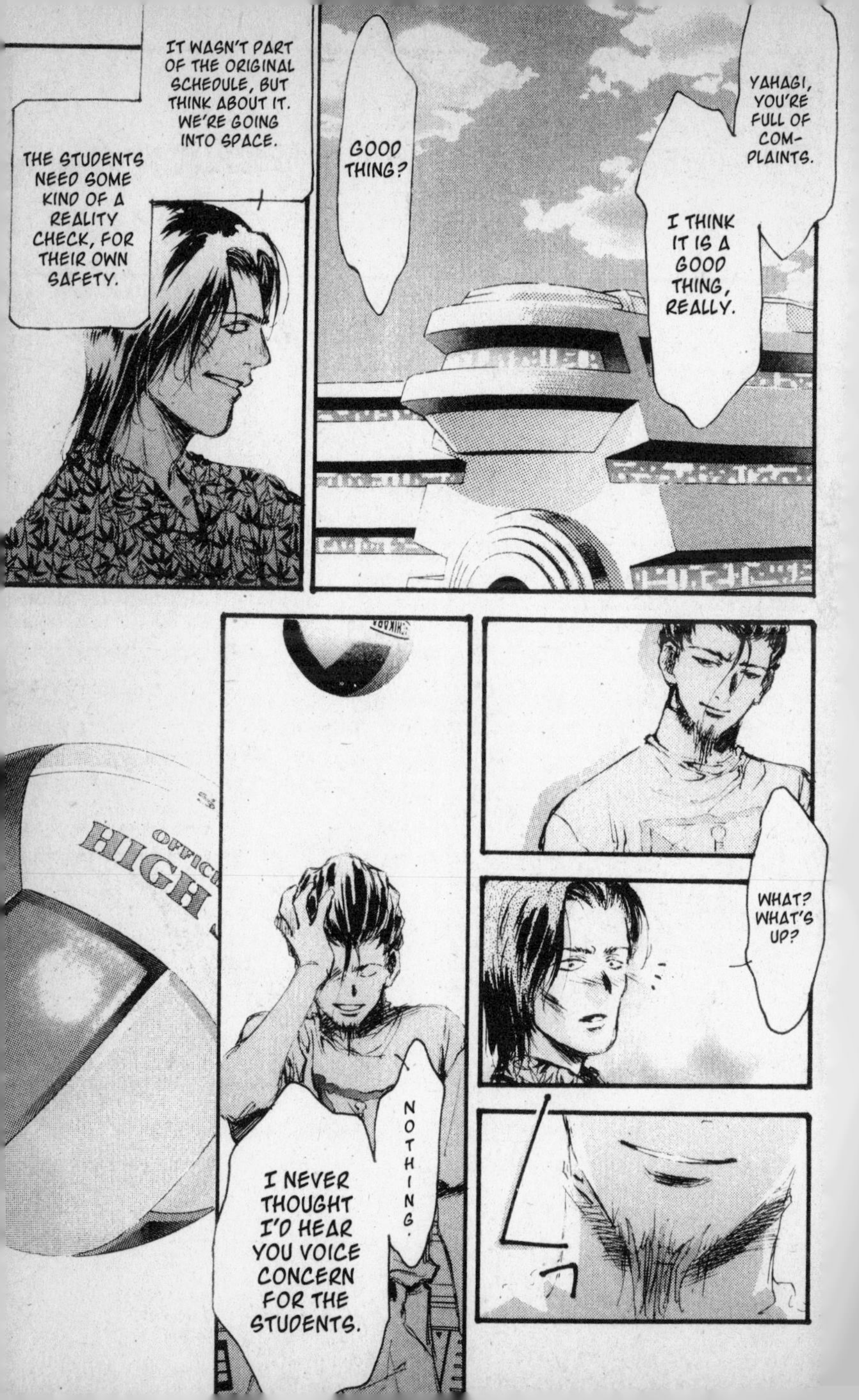
YAHAGI, YOU'RE FULL OF COM-PLAINTS.
I THINK IT IS A GOOD THING, REALLY.
GOOD THING?
IT WASN'T PART OF THE ORIGINAL SCHEDULE, BUT THINK ABOUT IT. WE'RE GOING INTO SPACE.
THE STUDENTS NEED SOME KIND OF A REALITY CHECK, FOR THEIR OWN SAFETY.
WHAT? WHAT'S UP?
NOTHING.
I NEVER THOUGHT I'D HEAR YOU VOICE CONCERN FOR THE STUDENTS.

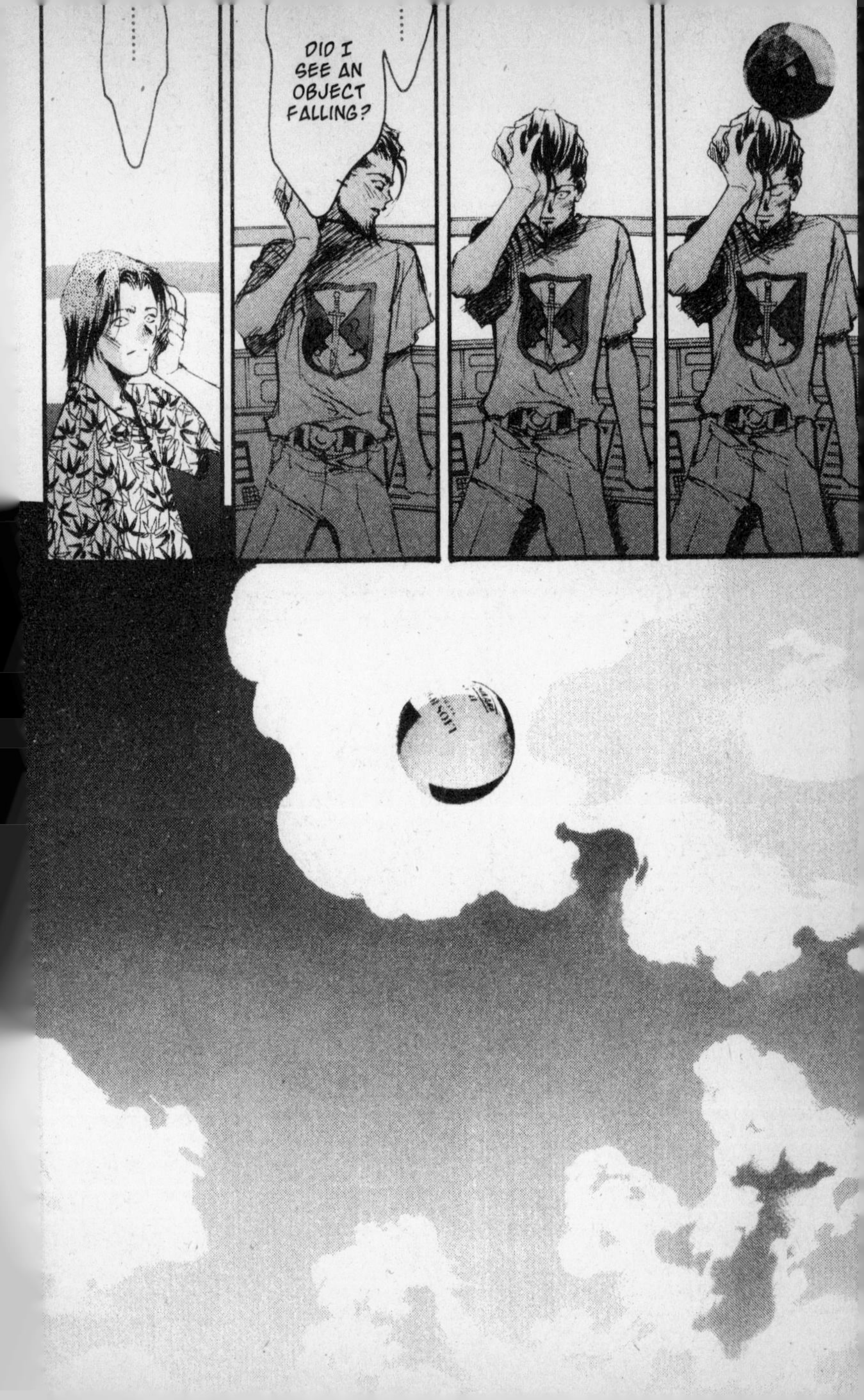
....
DID I SEE AN OBJECT FALLING?
....

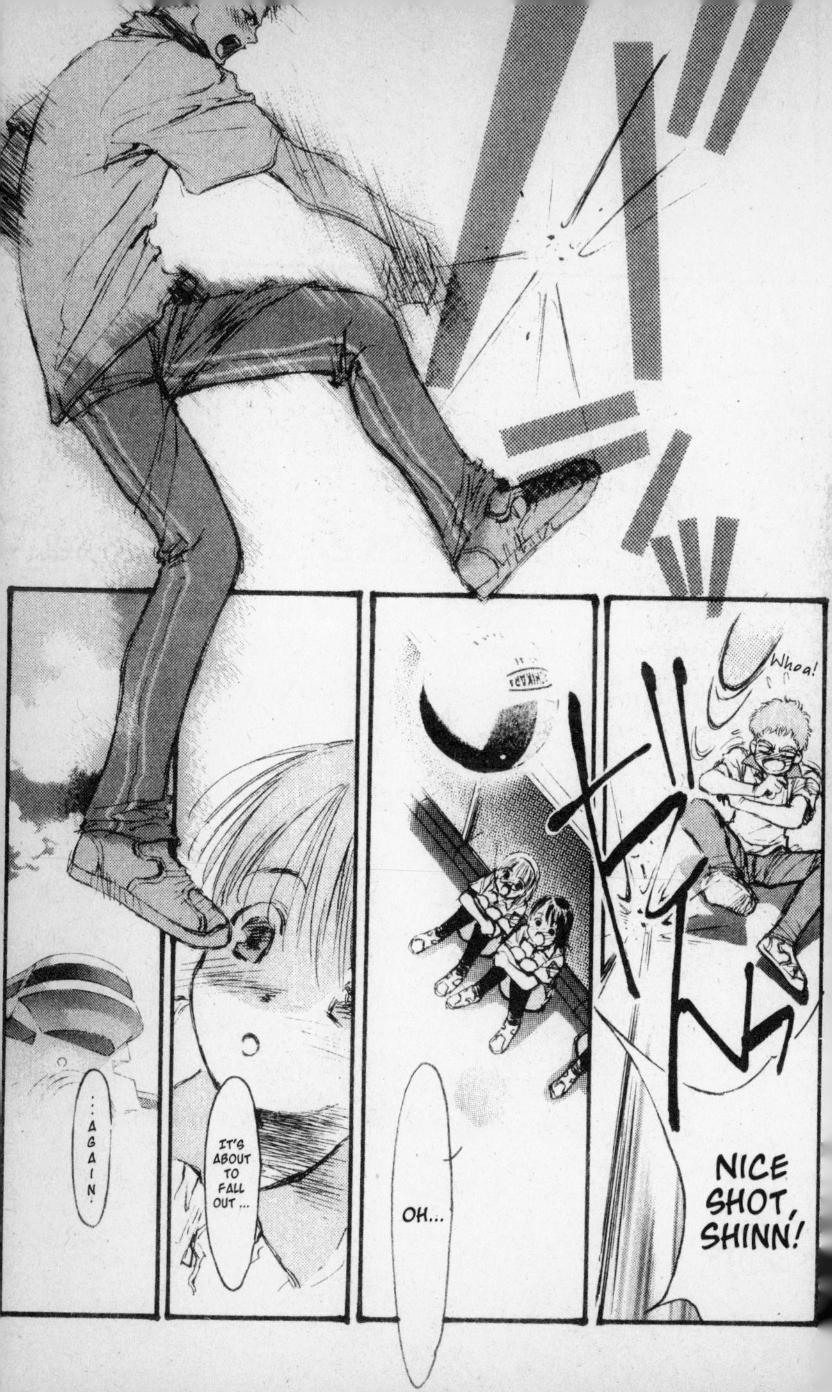
Whoa!
NICE SHOT, SHINN!
OH...
IT'S ABOUT TO FALL OUT ...
...AGAIN.

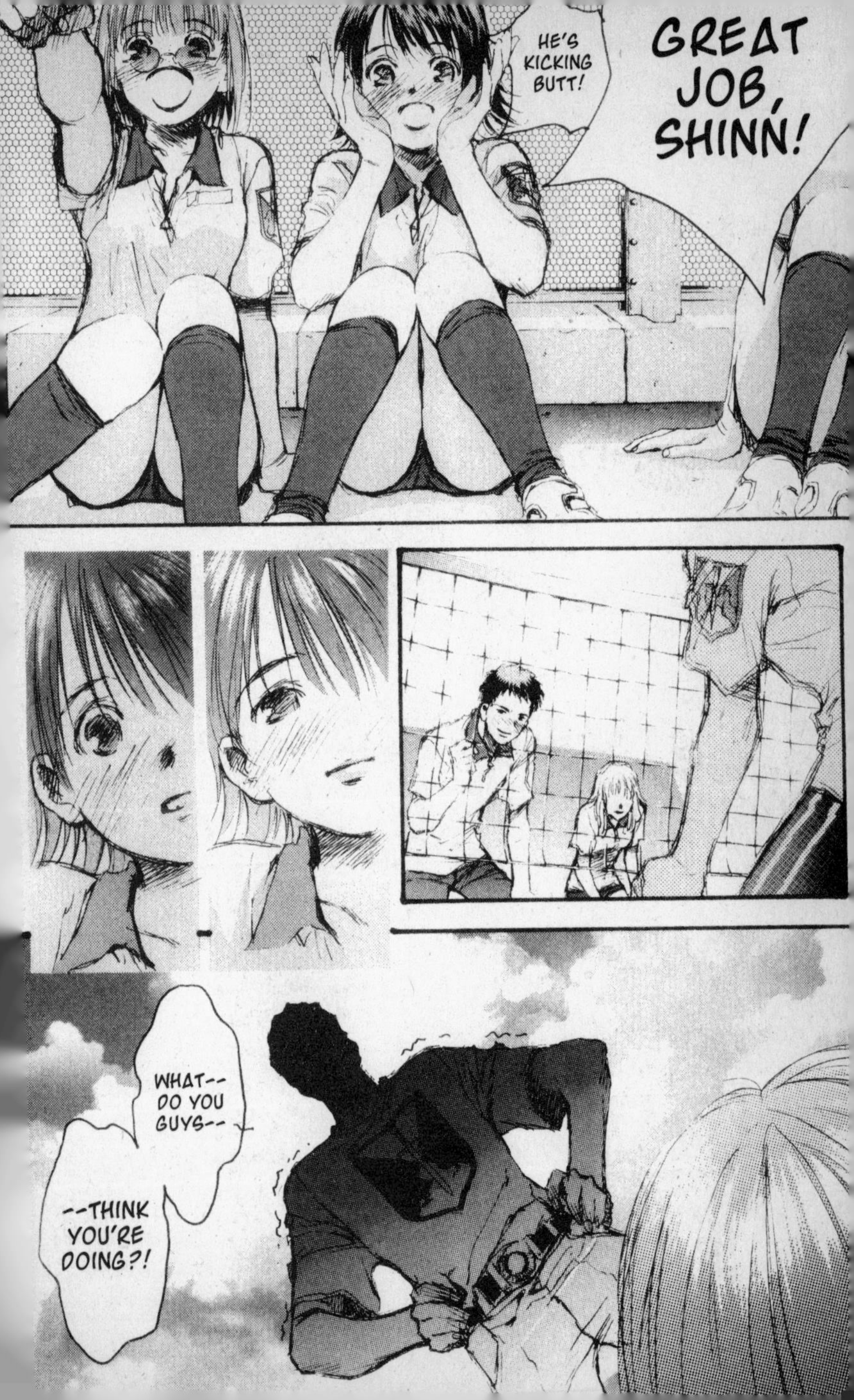
GREAT JOB, SHINN!
HE'S KICKING BUTT!
WHAT-- DO YOU GUYS--
--THINK YOU'RE DOING?!

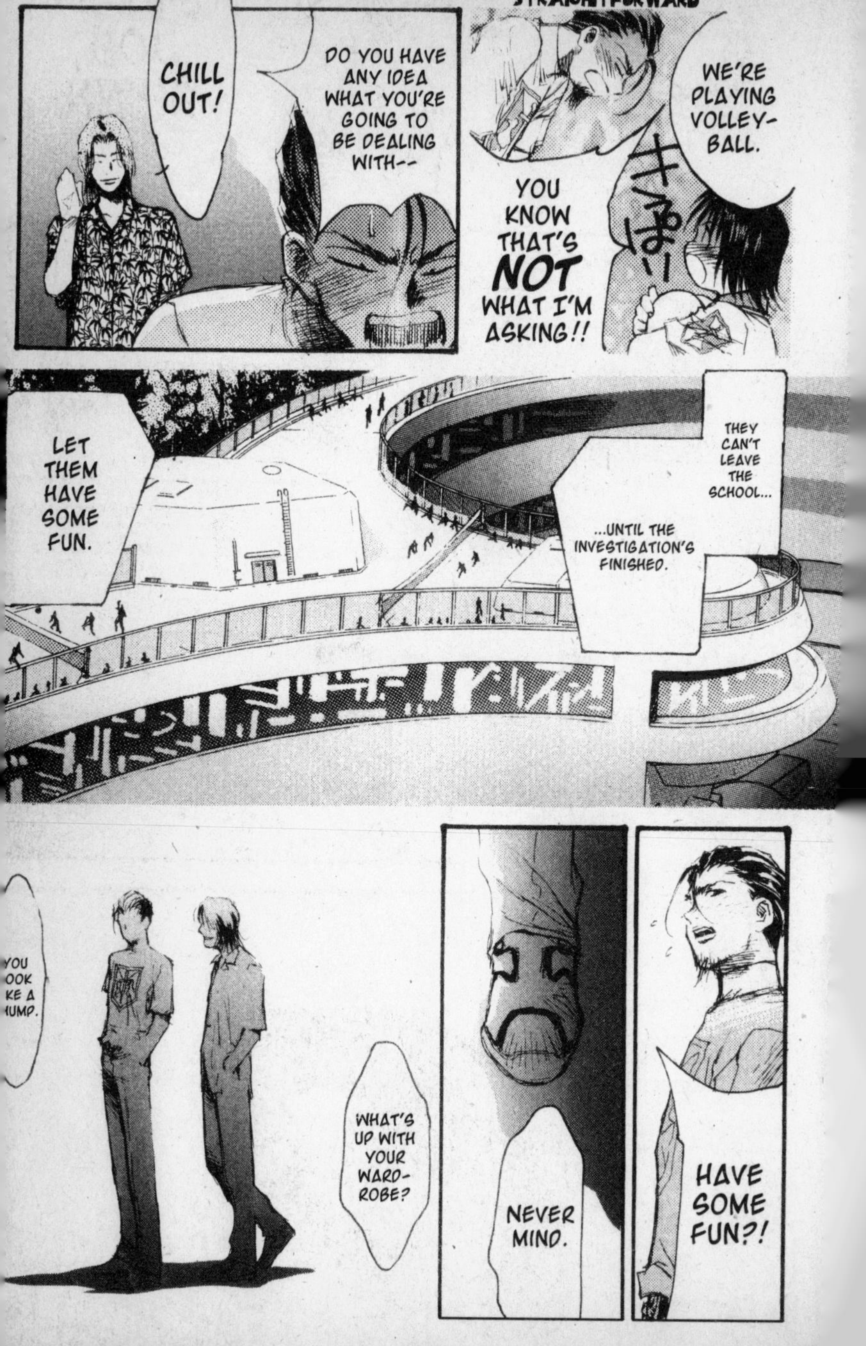
WE'RE PLAYING VOLLEY-BALL.
YOU KNOW THAT'S **NOT** WHAT I'M ASKING!!
DO YOU HAVE ANY IDEA WHAT YOU'RE GOING TO BE DEALING WITH--
CHILL OUT!
THEY CAN'T LEAVE THE SCHOOL...
...UNTIL THE INVESTIGATION'S FINISHED.
LET THEM HAVE SOME FUN.
HAVE SOME FUN?!
NEVER MIND.
WHAT'S UP WITH YOUR WARD-ROBE?
YOU OOK KE A HUMP.

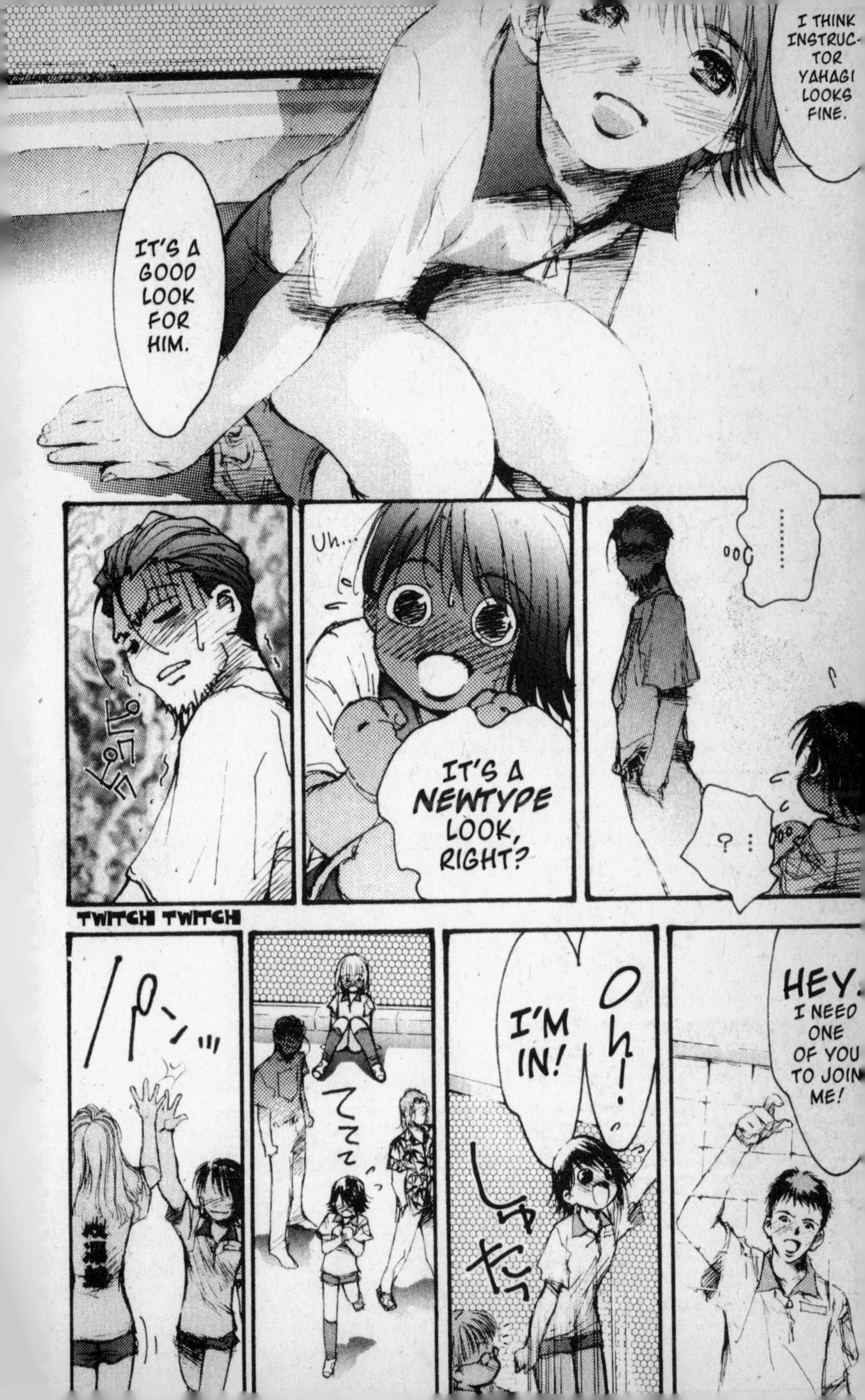
I THINK INSTRUCTOR YAHAGI LOOKS FINE.
IT'S A GOOD LOOK FOR HIM.
......
?...
Uh...
IT'S A NEWTYPE LOOK, RIGHT?
TWITCH TWITCH
HEY. I NEED ONE OF YOU TO JOIN ME!
Oh!
I'M IN!

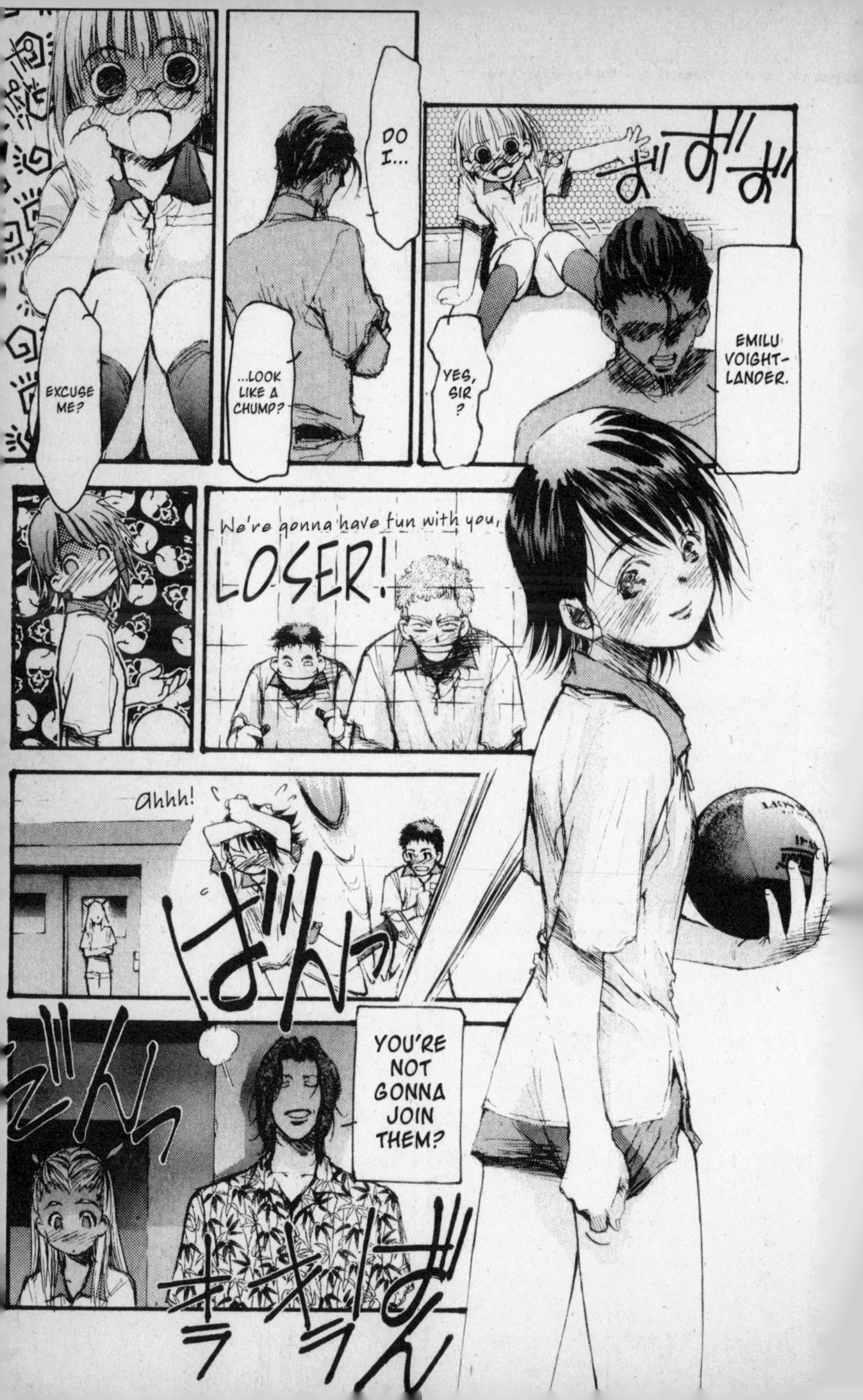
EMILU VOIGHT-LANDER.
YES, SIR?
DO I...
...LOOK LIKE A CHUMP?
EXCUSE ME?
We're gonna have fun with you, LOSER!
ahhh!
YOU'RE NOT GONNA JOIN THEM?

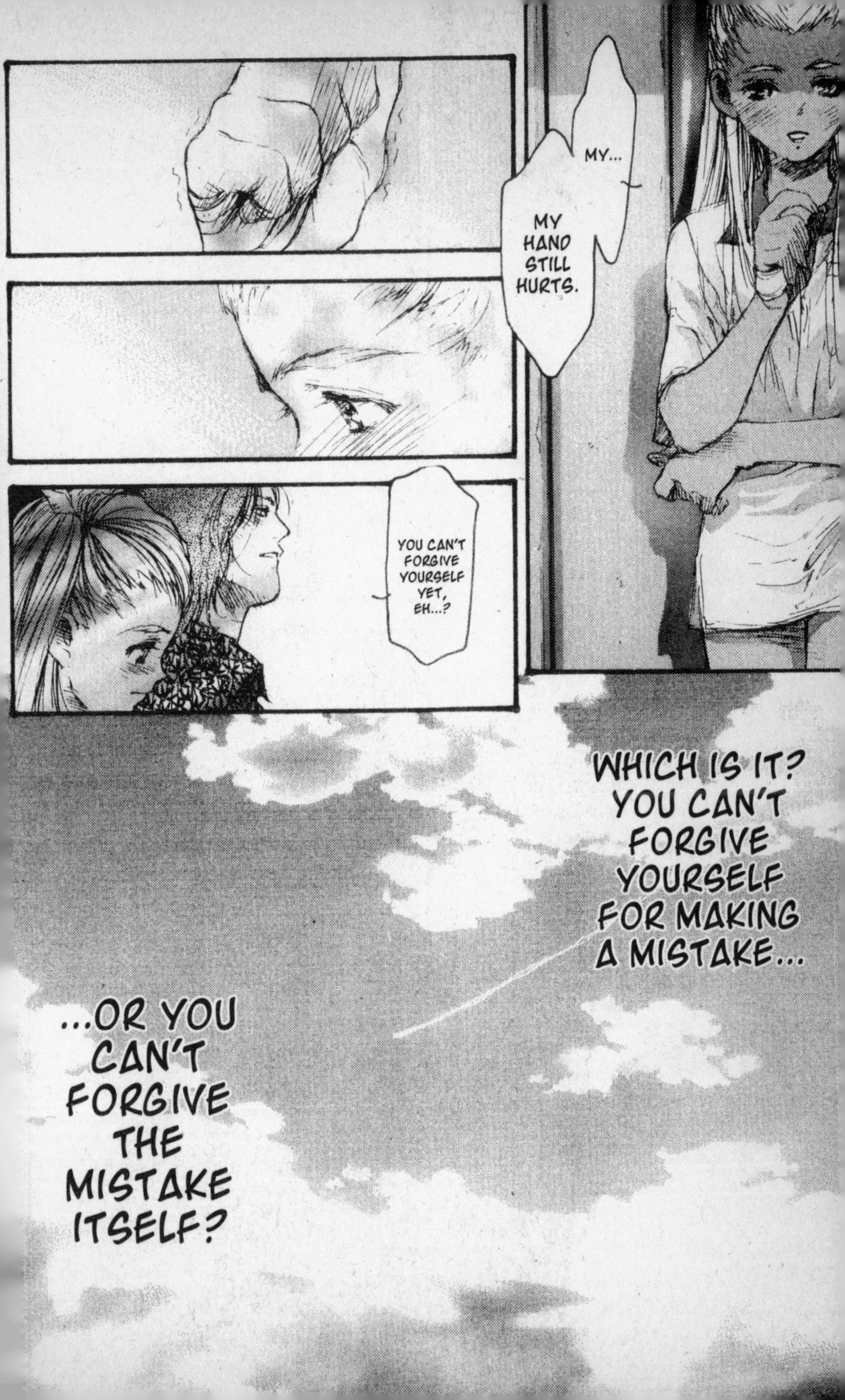
MY...
MY HAND STILL HURTS.
YOU CAN'T FORGIVE YOURSELF YET, EH...?
WHICH IS IT? YOU CAN'T FORGIVE YOURSELF FOR MAKING A MISTAKE...
...OR YOU CAN'T FORGIVE THE MISTAKE ITSELF?

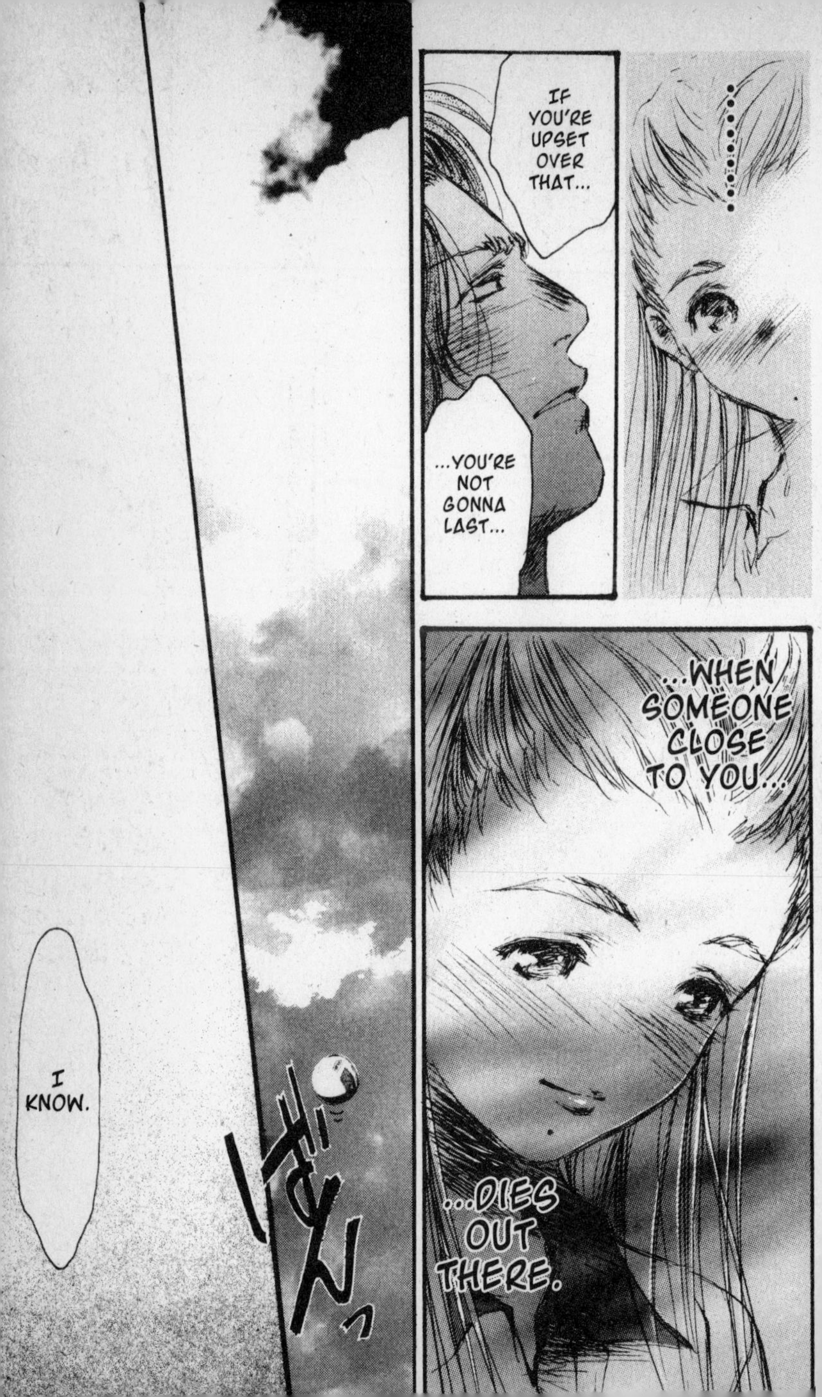
......
IF YOU'RE UPSET OVER THAT...
...YOU'RE NOT GONNA LAST...
...WHEN SOMEONE CLOSE TO YOU...
...DIES OUT THERE.
I KNOW.

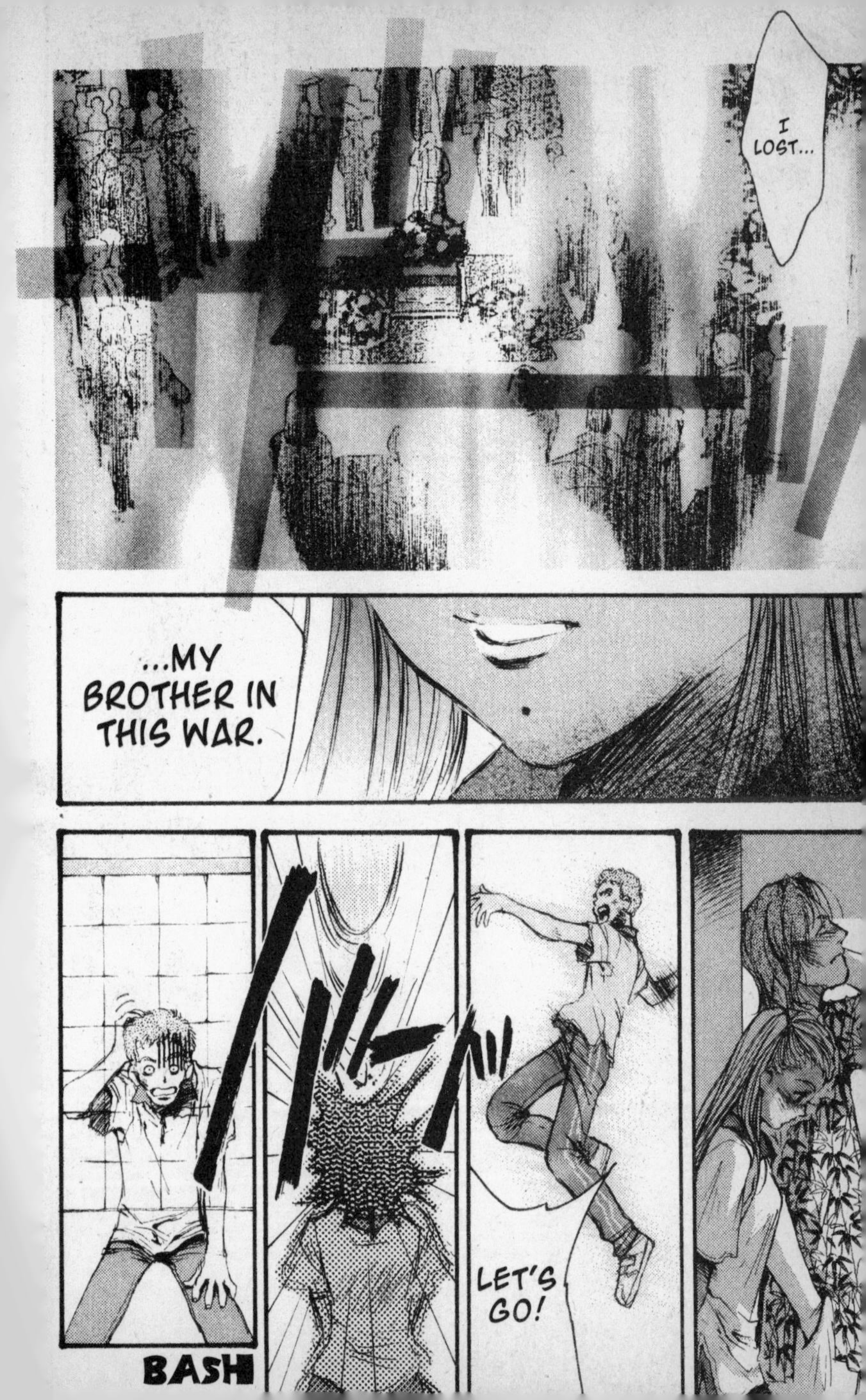

I LOST...
...MY BROTHER IN THIS WAR.
LET'S GO!
BASH

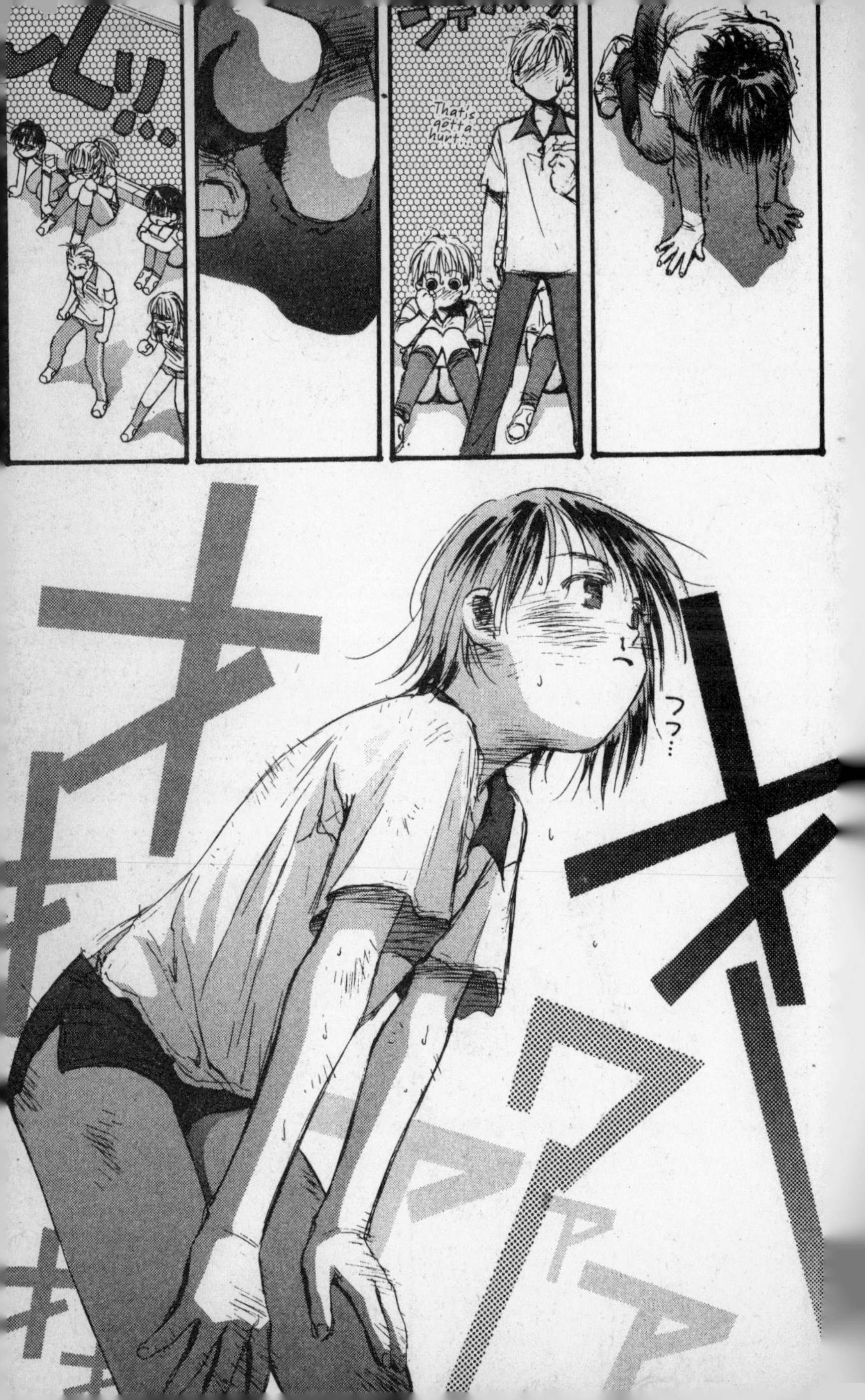
That's gotta hurt...
フフ…

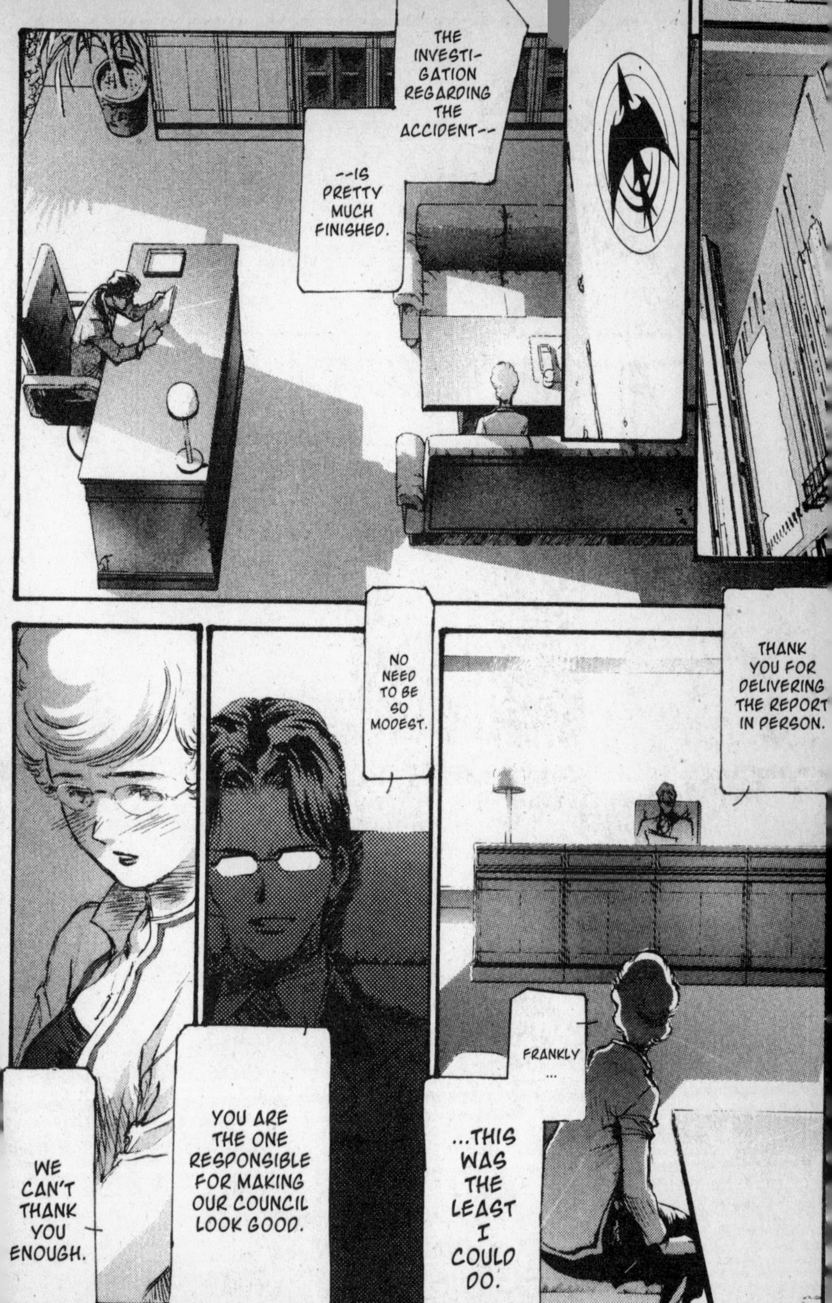
THE INVESTIGATION REGARDING THE ACCIDENT--
--IS PRETTY MUCH FINISHED.
THANK YOU FOR DELIVERING THE REPORT IN PERSON.
FRANKLY...
...THIS WAS THE LEAST I COULD DO.
NO NEED TO BE SO MODEST.
YOU ARE THE ONE RESPONSIBLE FOR MAKING OUR COUNCIL LOOK GOOD.
WE CAN'T THANK YOU ENOUGH.

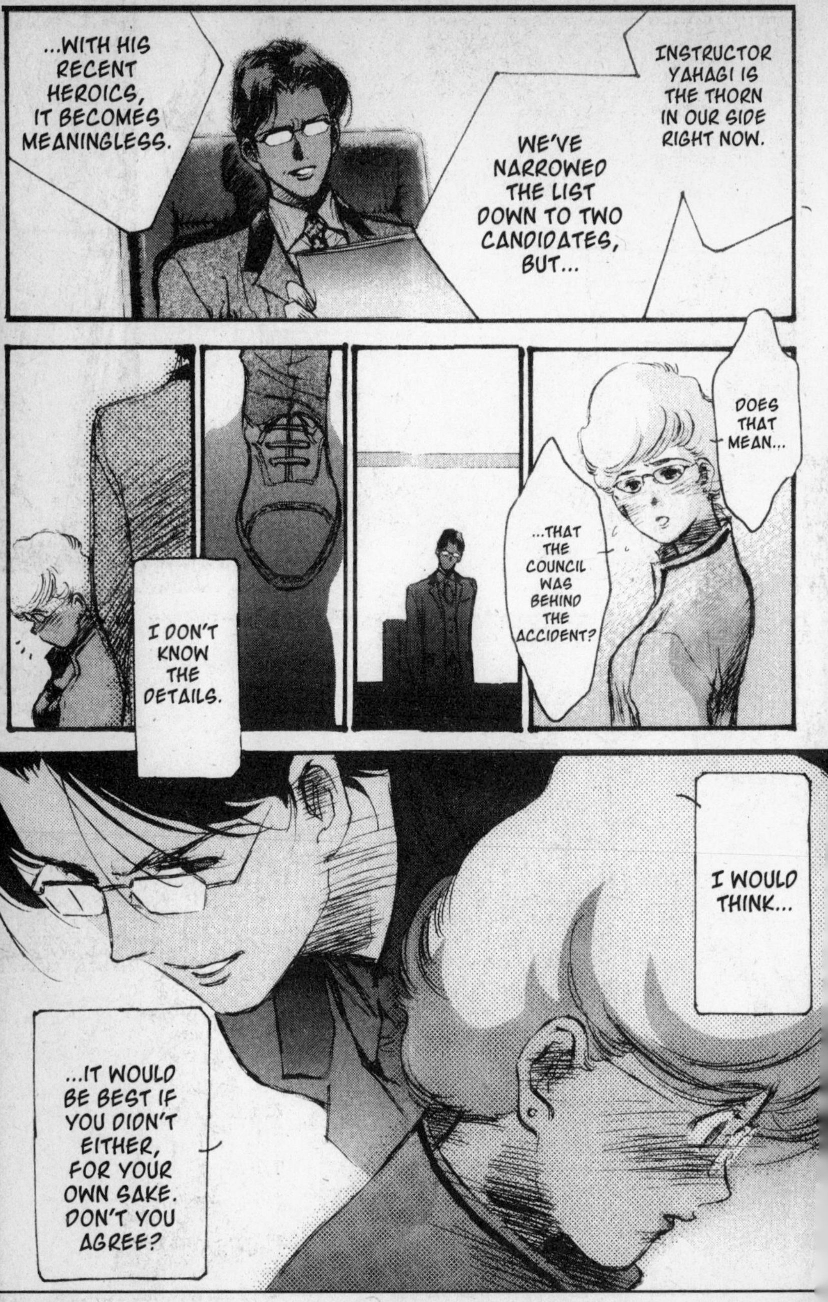
INSTRUCTOR YAHAGI IS THE THORN IN OUR SIDE RIGHT NOW.
WE'VE NARROWED THE LIST DOWN TO TWO CANDIDATES, BUT...
...WITH HIS RECENT HEROICS, IT BECOMES MEANINGLESS.
DOES THAT MEAN...
...THAT THE COUNCIL WAS BEHIND THE ACCIDENT?
I DON'T KNOW THE DETAILS.
I WOULD THINK...
...IT WOULD BE BEST IF YOU DIDN'T EITHER, FOR YOUR OWN SAKE. DON'T YOU AGREE?

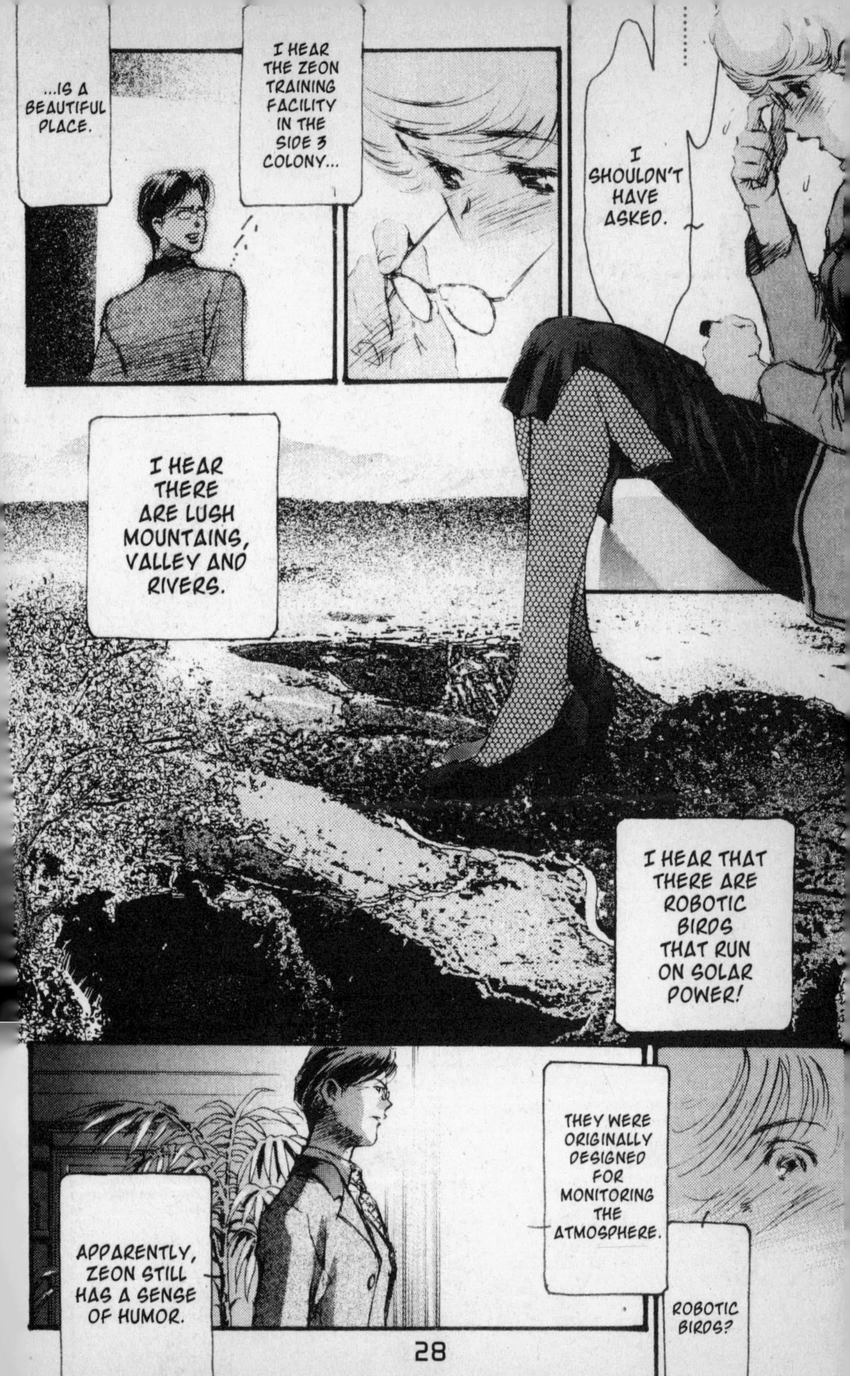
I SHOULDN'T HAVE ASKED.
I HEAR THE ZEON TRAINING FACILITY IN THE SIDE 3 COLONY...
...IS A BEAUTIFUL PLACE.
I HEAR THERE ARE LUSH MOUNTAINS, VALLEY AND RIVERS.
I HEAR THAT THERE ARE ROBOTIC BIRDS THAT RUN ON SOLAR POWER!
ROBOTIC BIRDS?
THEY WERE ORIGINALLY DESIGNED FOR MONITORING THE ATMOSPHERE.
APPARENTLY, ZEON STILL HAS A SENSE OF HUMOR.

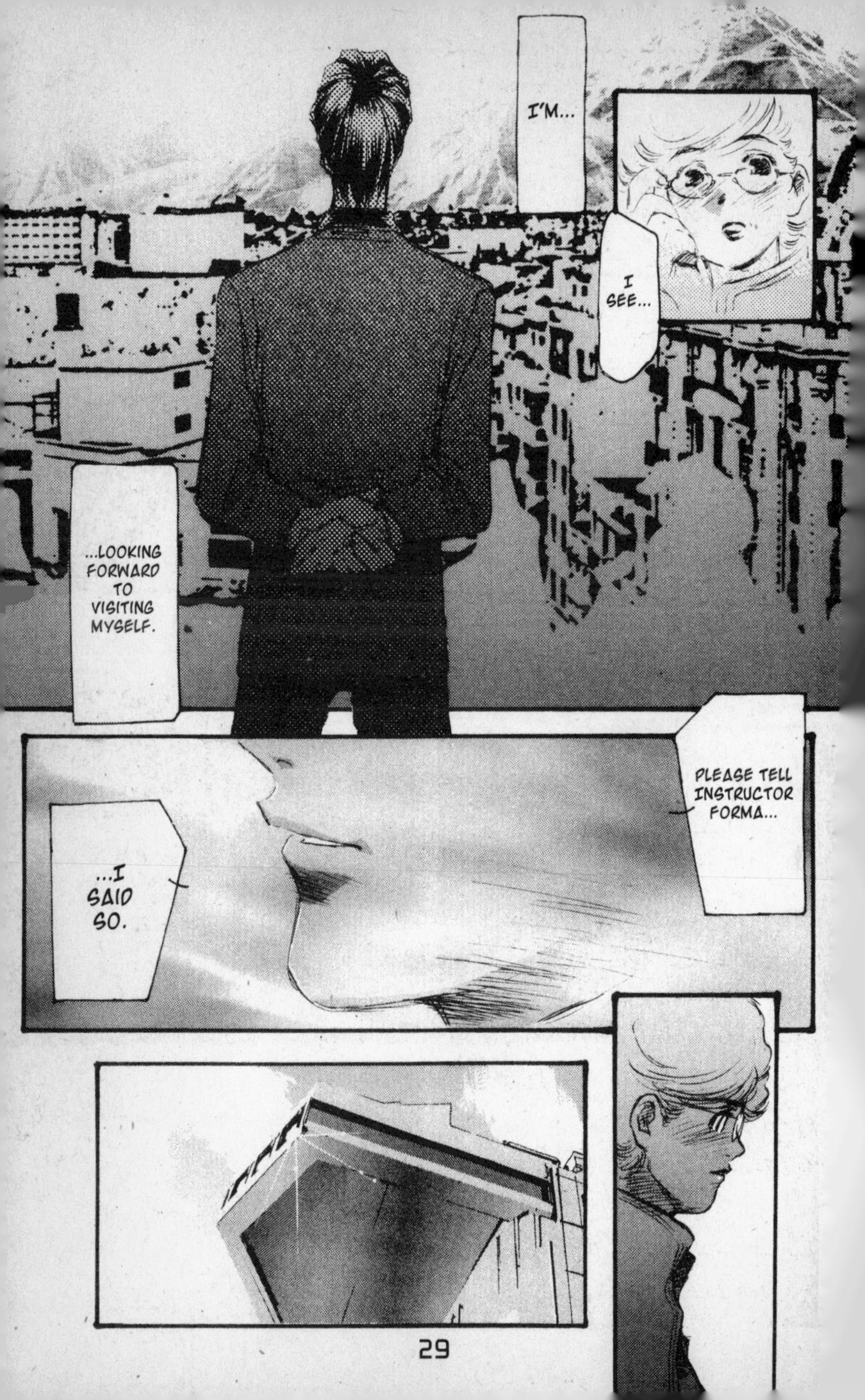
I'M...
I SEE...
...LOOKING FORWARD TO VISITING MYSELF.
PLEASE TELL INSTRUCTOR FORMA...
...I SAID SO.

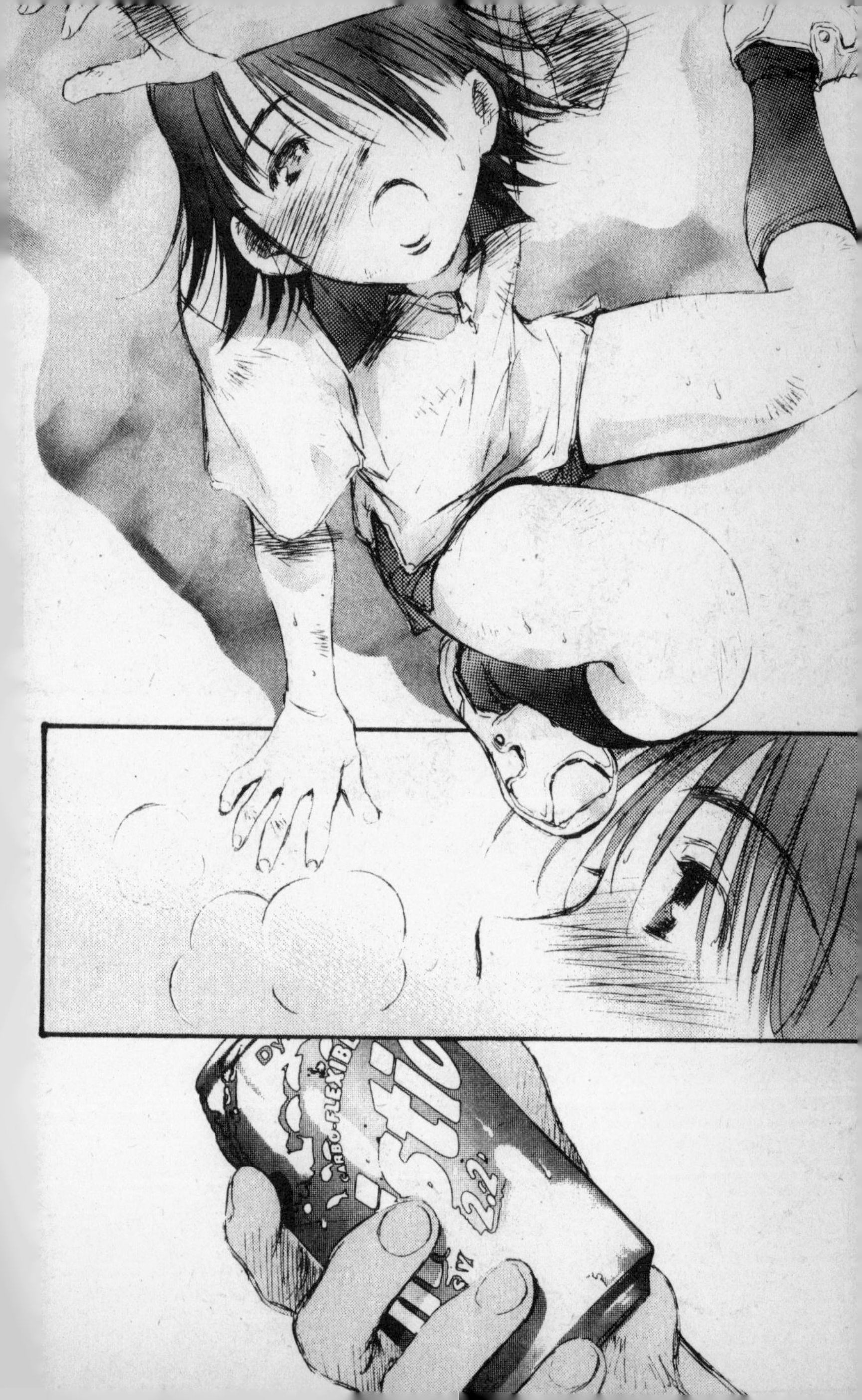

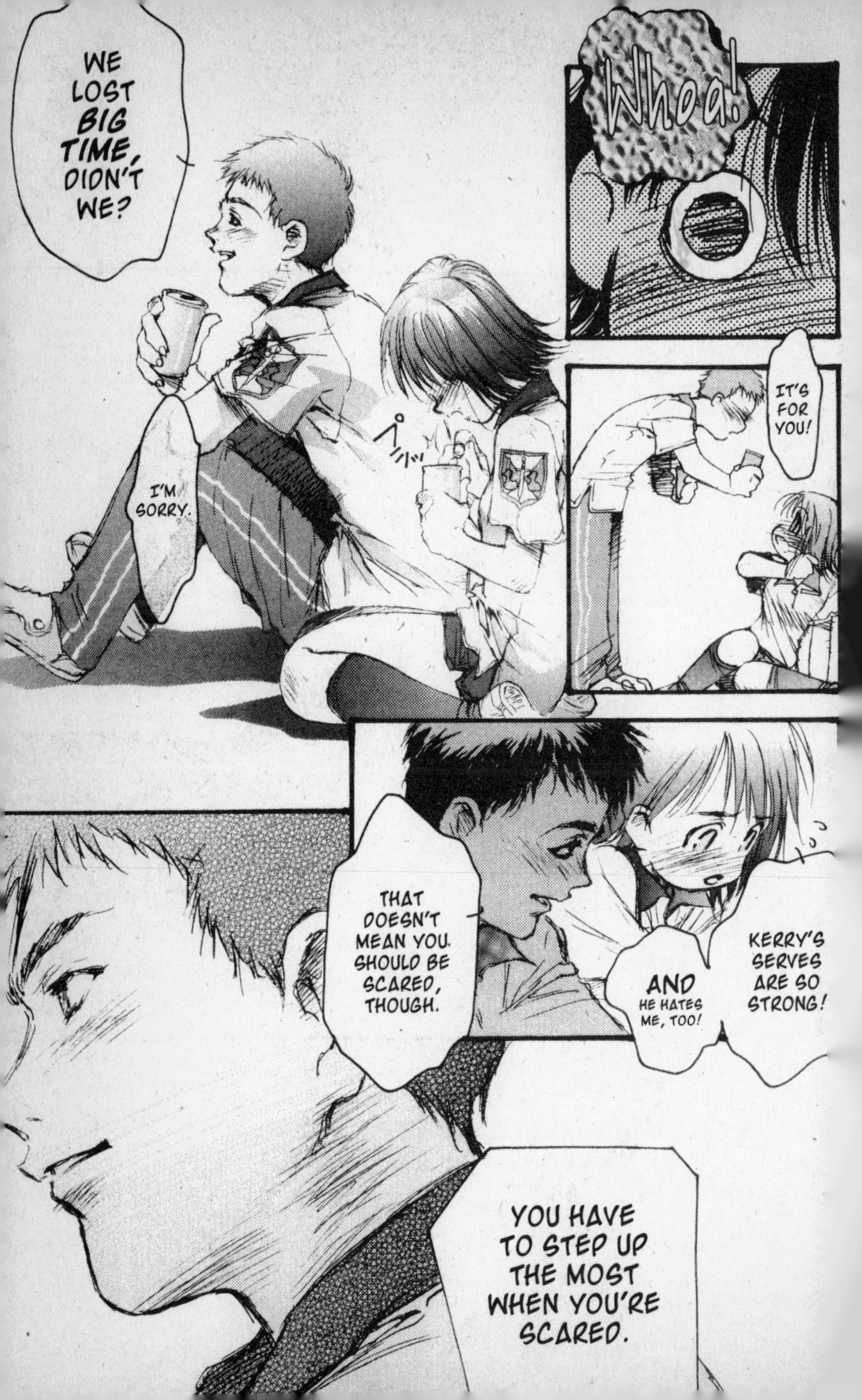
Whoa!
IT'S FOR YOU!
WE LOST BIG TIME, DIDN'T WE?
I'M SORRY.
KERRY'S SERVES ARE SO STRONG!
AND HE HATES ME, TOO!
THAT DOESN'T MEAN YOU SHOULD BE SCARED, THOUGH.
YOU HAVE TO STEP UP THE MOST WHEN YOU'RE MOST SCARED.

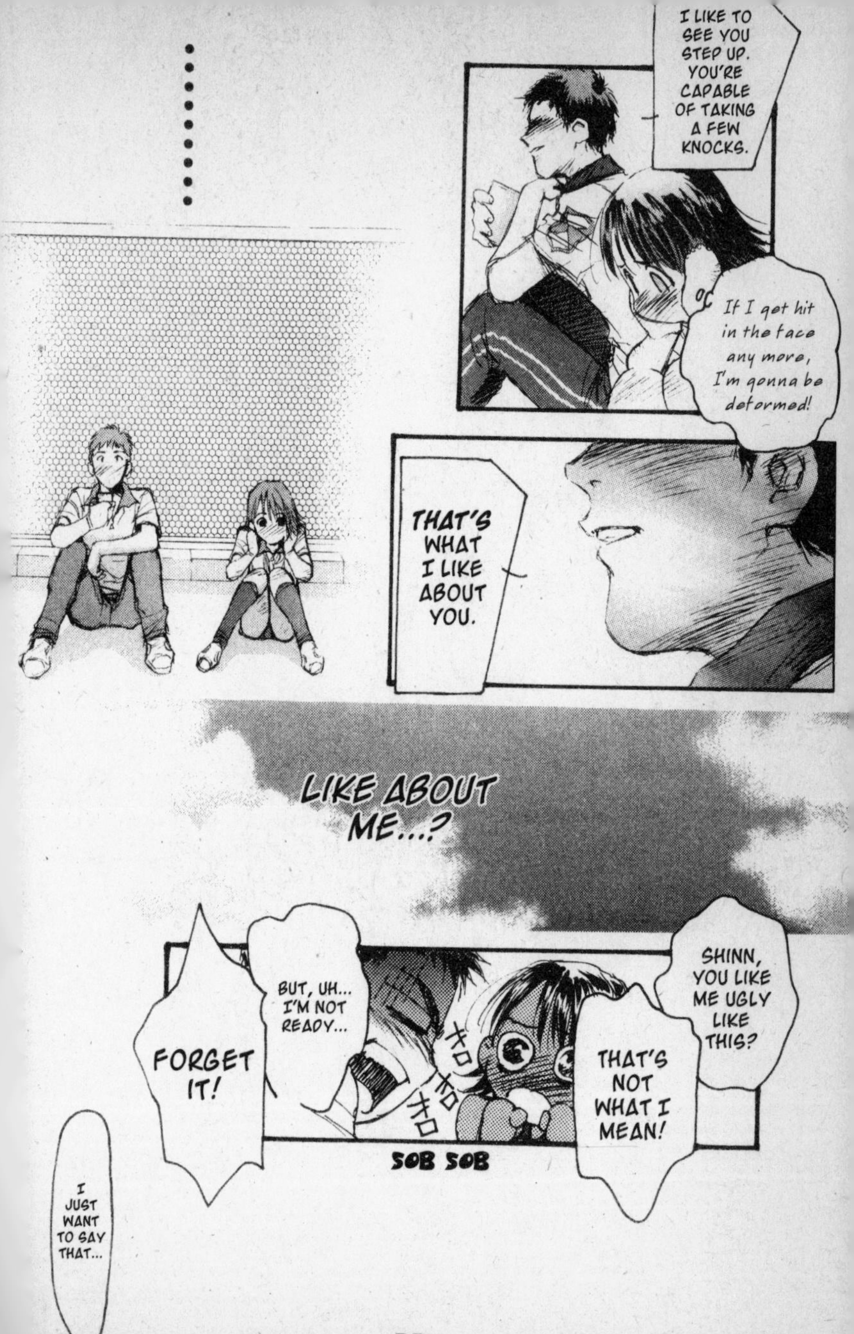
I LIKE TO SEE YOU STEP UP. YOU'RE CAPABLE OF TAKING A FEW KNOCKS.
If I get hit in the face any more, I'm gonna be deformed!
THAT'S WHAT I LIKE ABOUT YOU.
LIKE ABOUT ME...?
SHINN, YOU LIKE ME UGLY LIKE THIS?
THAT'S NOT WHAT I MEAN!
BUT, UH... I'M NOT READY...
FORGET IT!
SOB SOB
I JUST WANT TO SAY THAT...

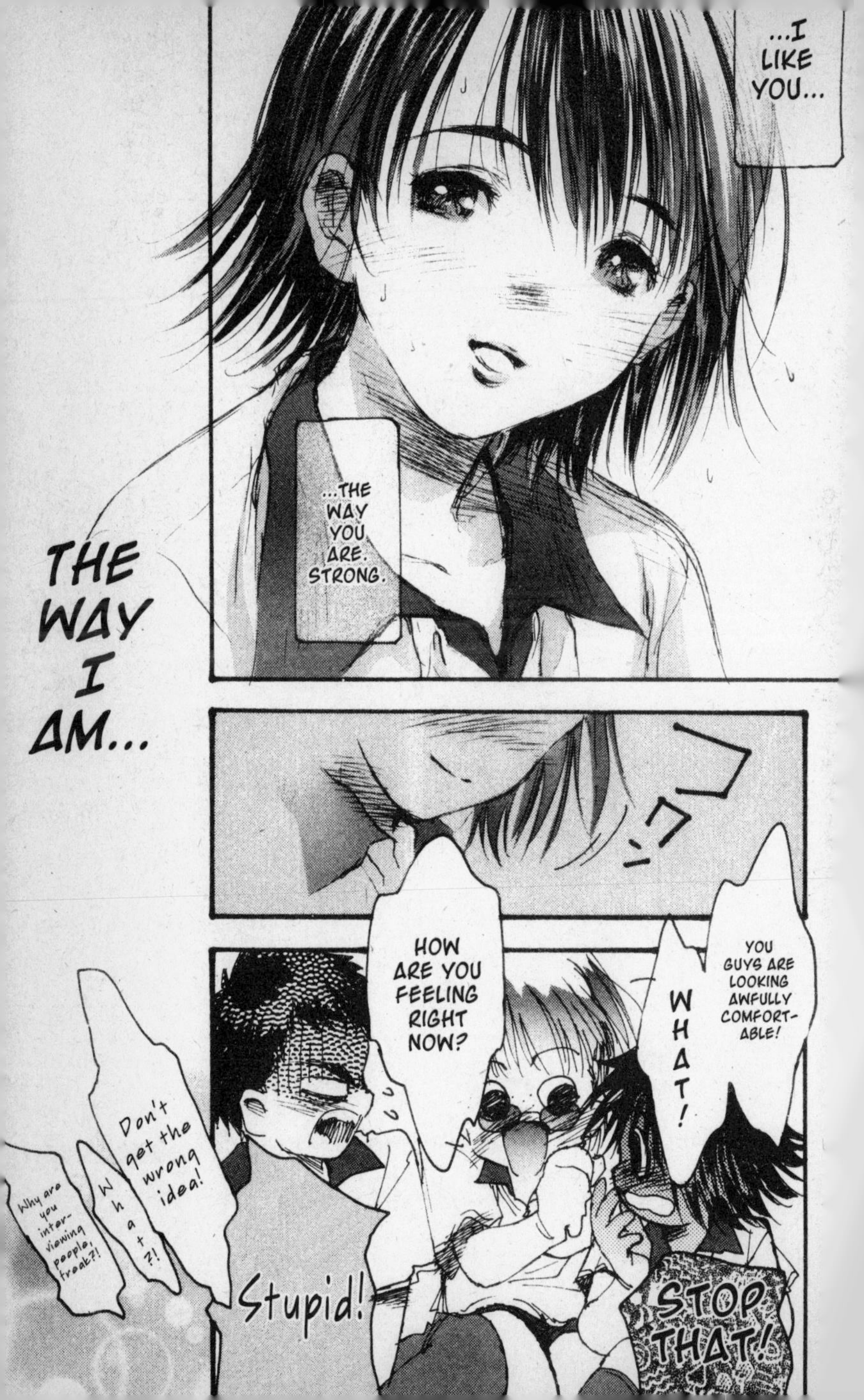
...I LIKE YOU...
...THE WAY YOU ARE. STRONG.
THE WAY I AM...
YOU GUYS ARE LOOKING AWFULLY COMFORTABLE!
WHAT!
HOW ARE YOU FEELING RIGHT NOW?
Don't get the wrong idea!
What?!
Why are you interviewing people, freak?!
STOP THAT!
Stupid!

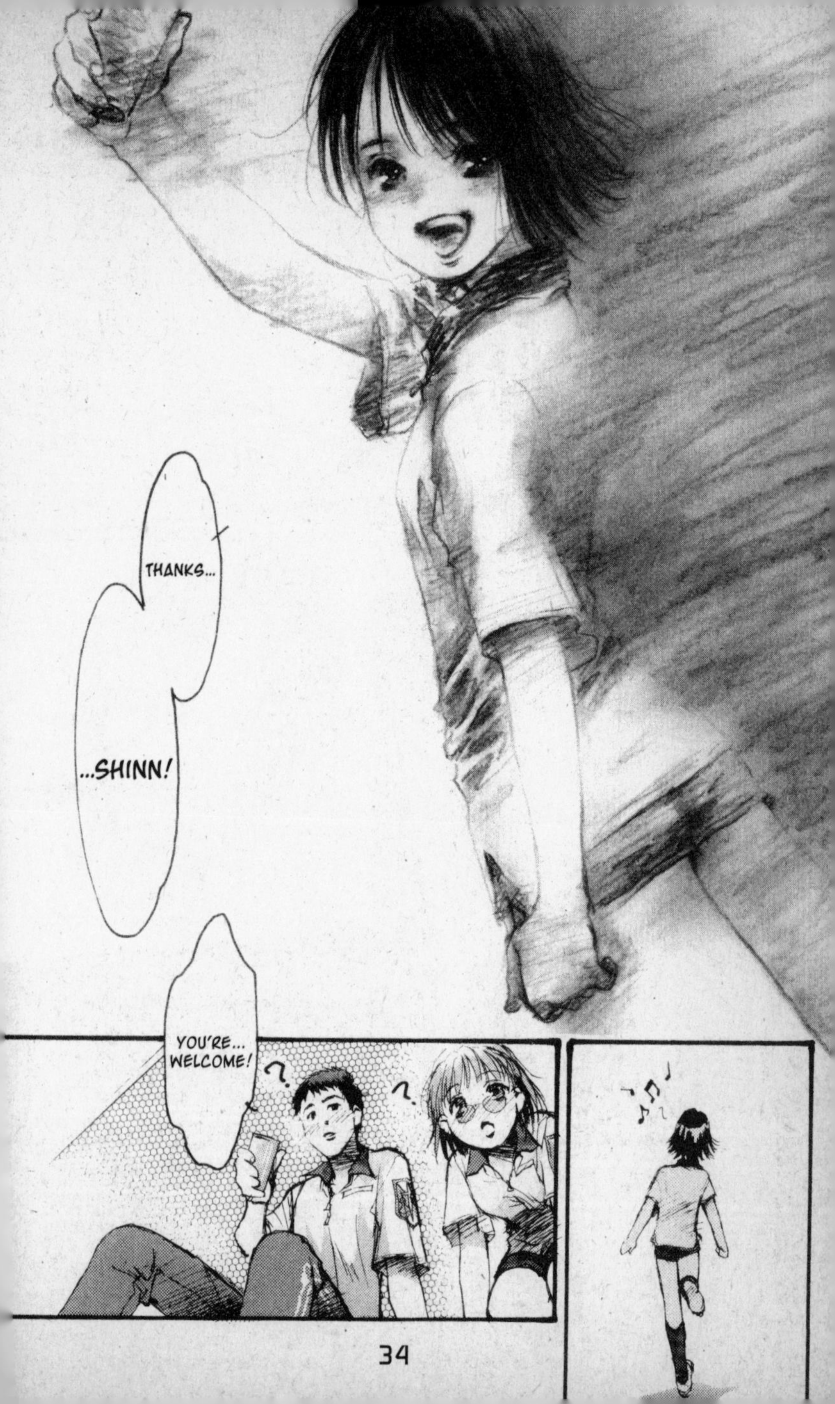
THANKS...
...SHINN!
YOU'RE... WELCOME!

CHARACTER FILE:01

Asuna Elmarit

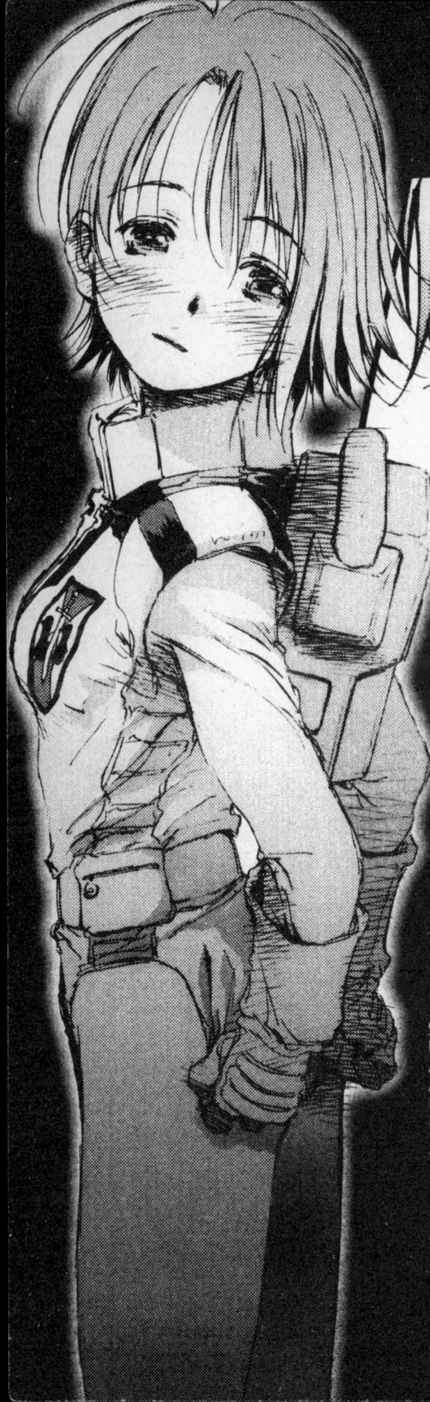

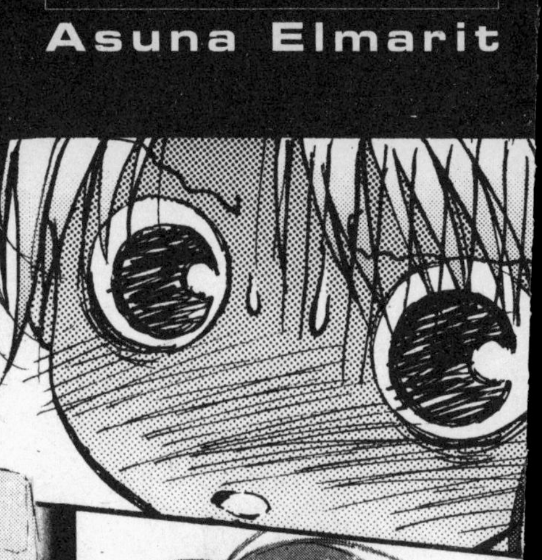

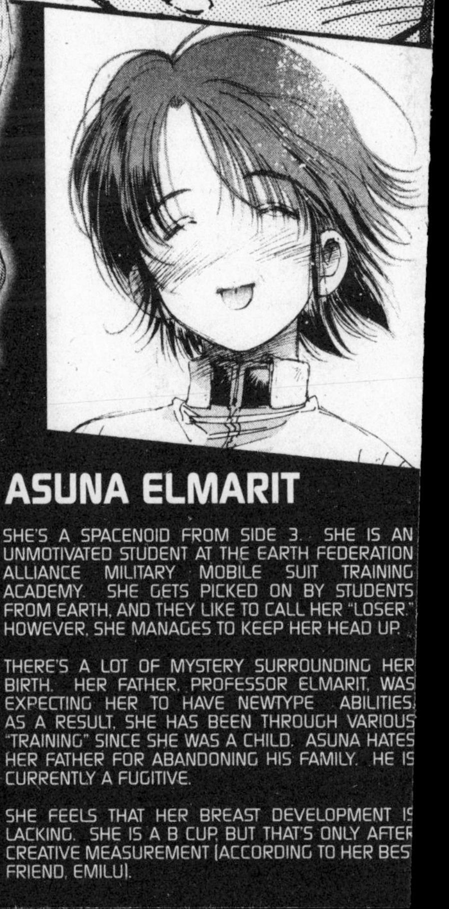

ASUNA ELMARIT

SHE'S A SPACENOID FROM SIDE 3. SHE IS AN UNMOTIVATED STUDENT AT THE EARTH FEDERATION ALLIANCE MILITARY MOBILE SUIT TRAINING ACADEMY. SHE GETS PICKED ON BY STUDENTS FROM EARTH, AND THEY LIKE TO CALL HER "LOSER." HOWEVER, SHE MANAGES TO KEEP HER HEAD UP.

THERE'S A LOT OF MYSTERY SURROUNDING HER BIRTH. HER FATHER, PROFESSOR ELMARIT, WAS EXPECTING HER TO HAVE NEWTYPE ABILITIES. AS A RESULT, SHE HAS BEEN THROUGH VARIOUS "TRAINING" SINCE SHE WAS A CHILD. ASUNA HATES HER FATHER FOR ABANDONING HIS FAMILY. HE IS CURRENTLY A FUGITIVE.

SHE FEELS THAT HER BREAST DEVELOPMENT IS LACKING. SHE IS A B CUP, BUT THAT'S ONLY AFTER CREATIVE MEASUREMENT (ACCORDING TO HER BEST FRIEND, EMILU).

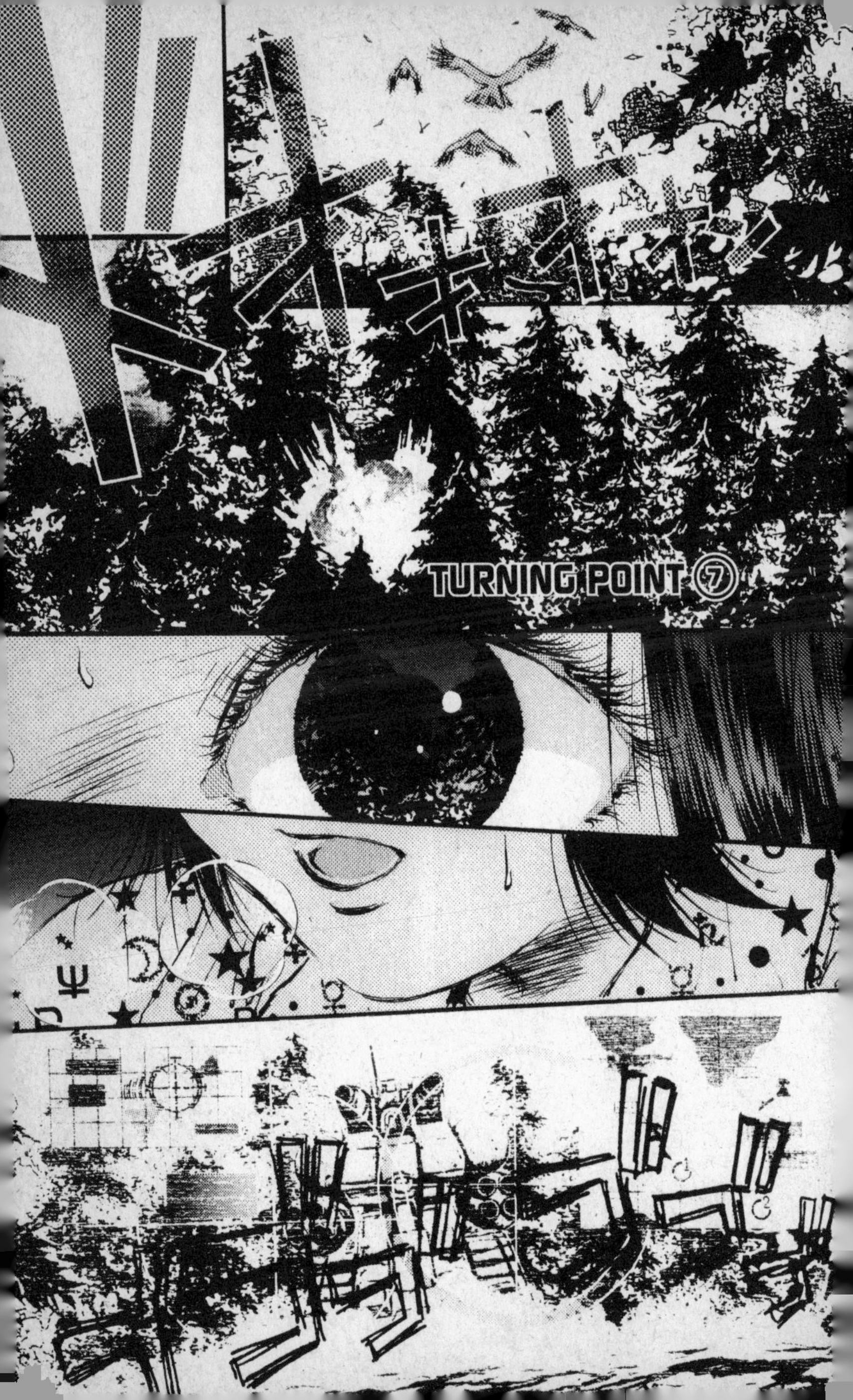

TURNING POINT ⑦

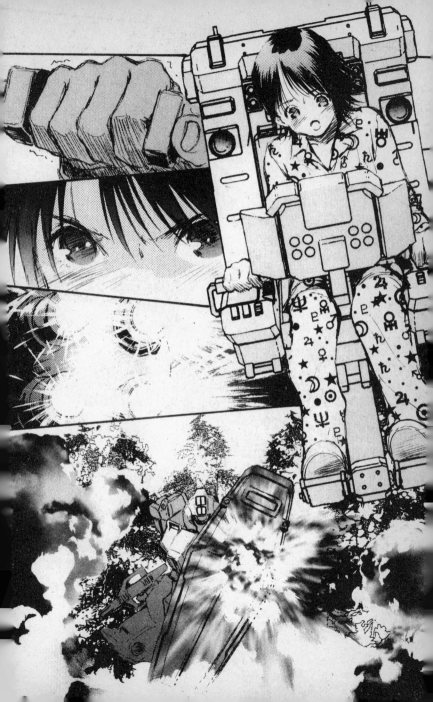

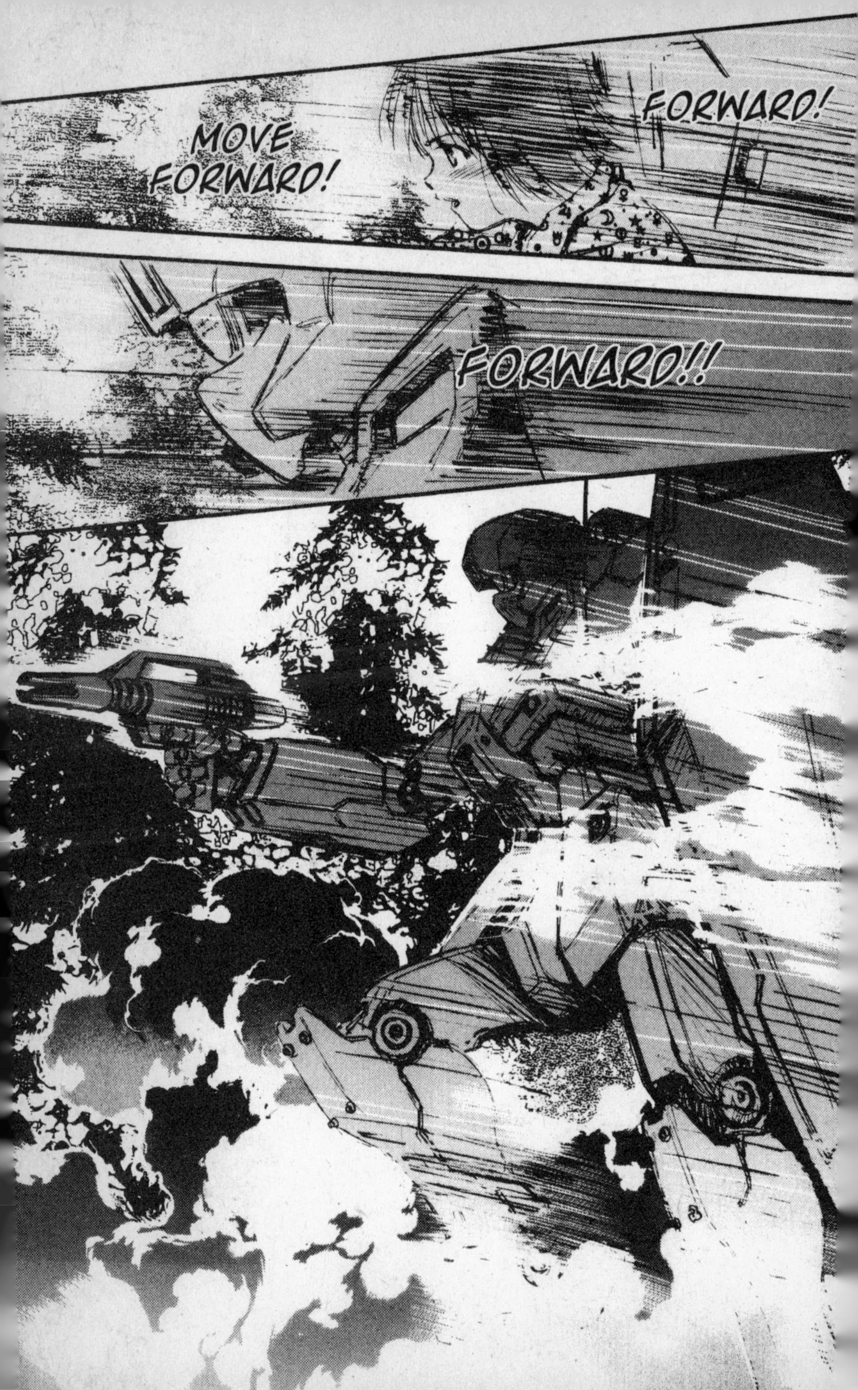
FORWARD!
MOVE FORWARD!
FORWARD!!

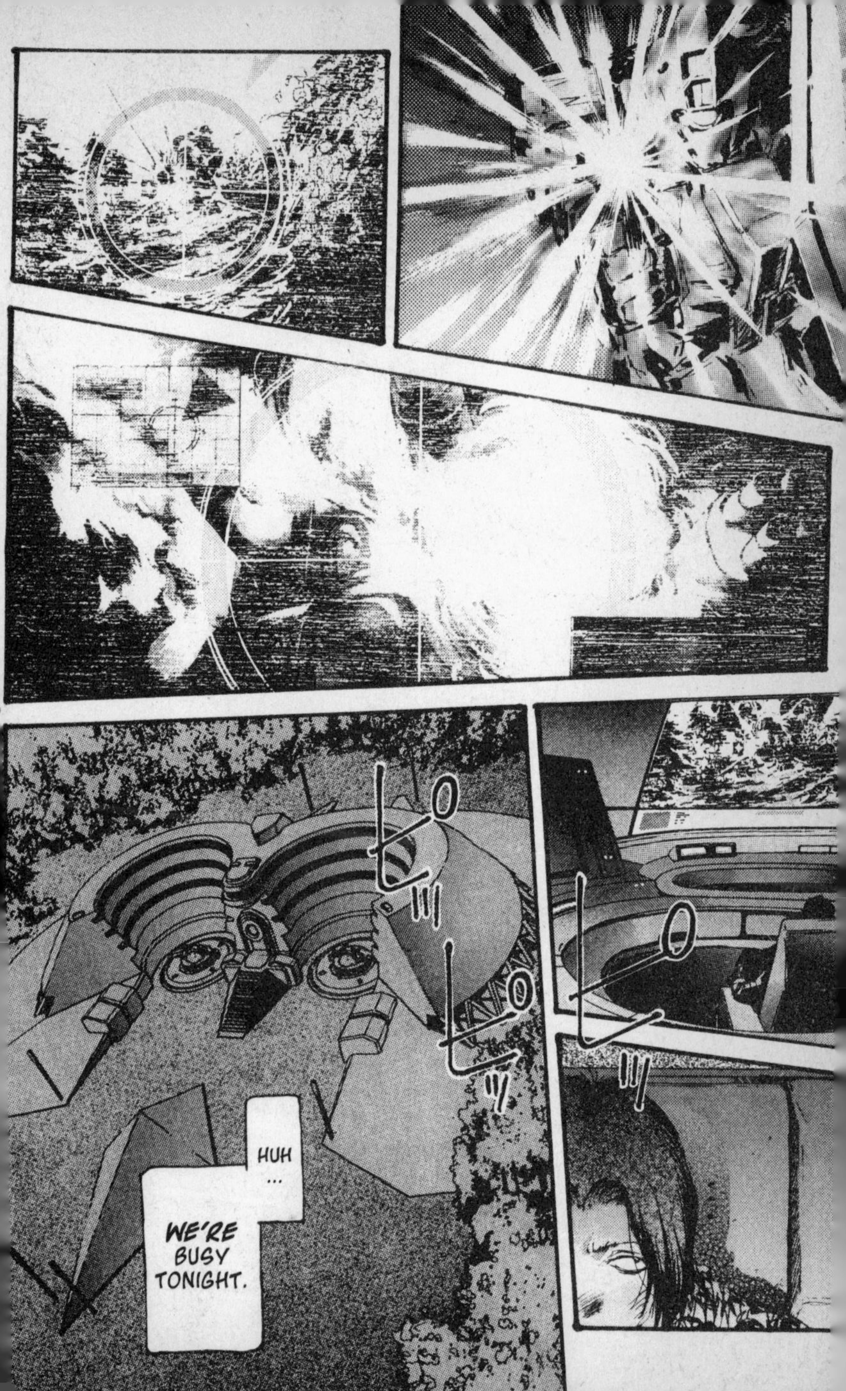
HUH ...
WE'RE BUSY TONIGHT.

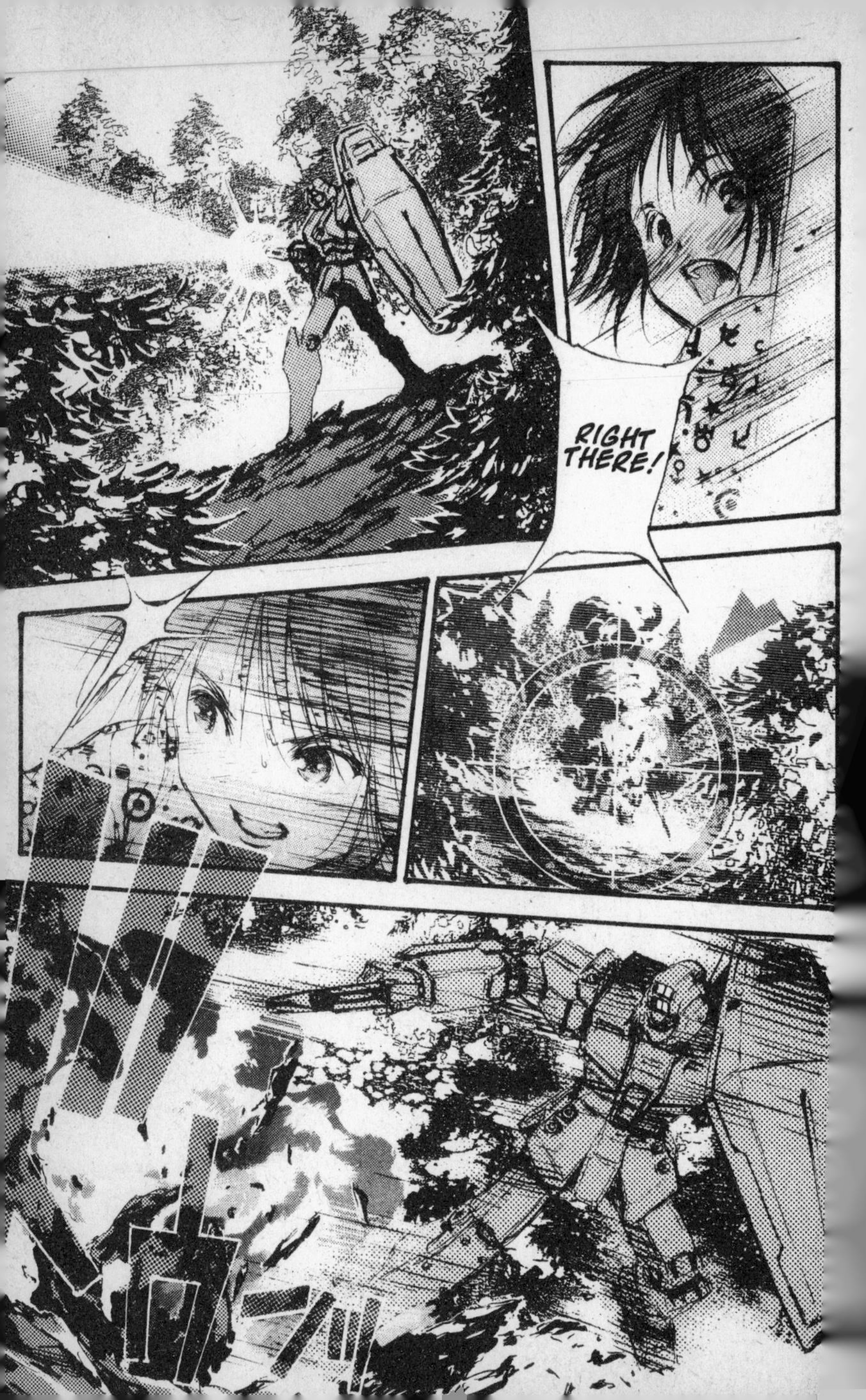
RIGHT THERE!

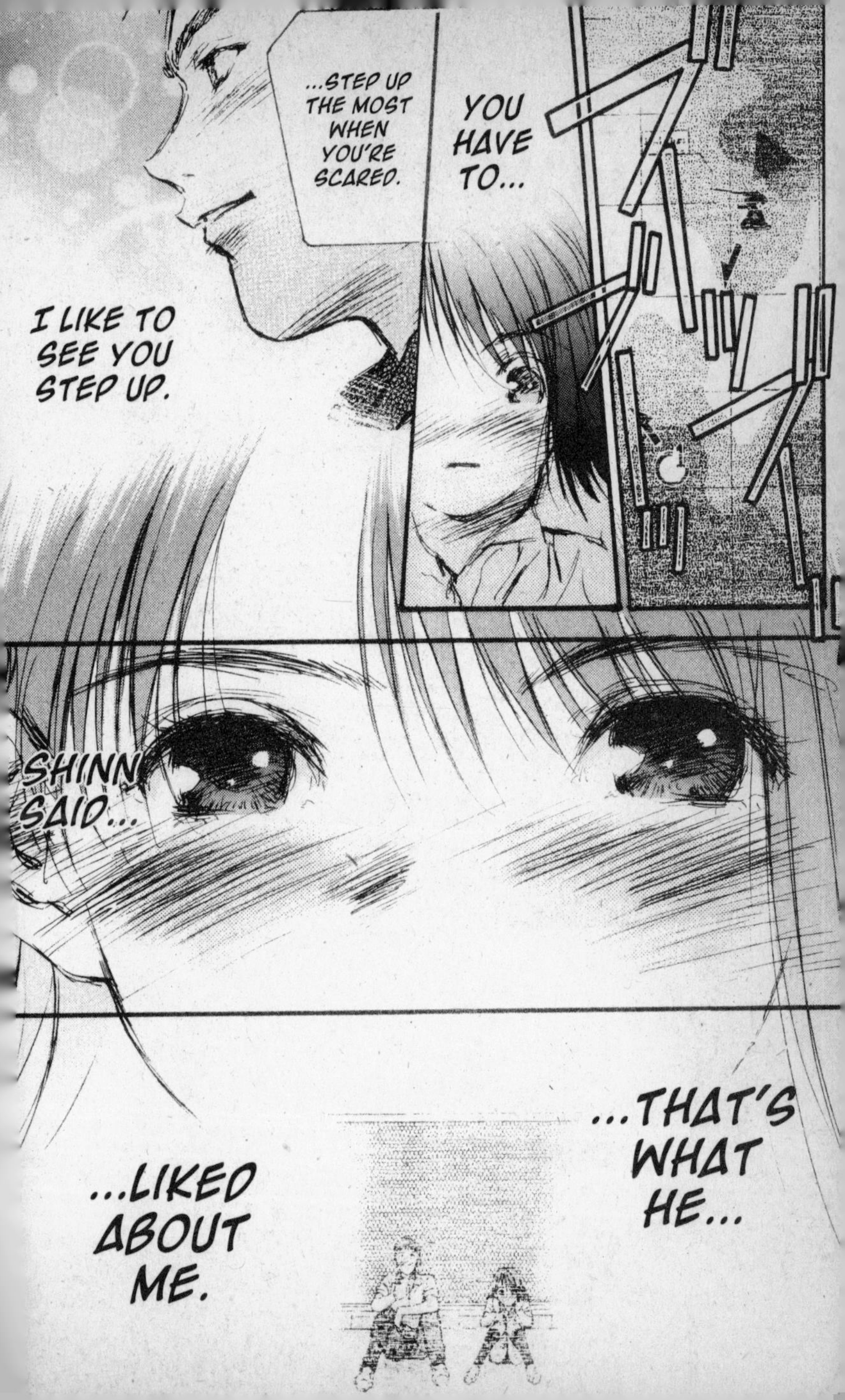
YOU HAVE TO...
...STEP UP THE MOST WHEN YOU'RE SCARED.
I LIKE TO SEE YOU STEP UP.
SHINN SAID...
...THAT'S WHAT HE...
...LIKED ABOUT ME.

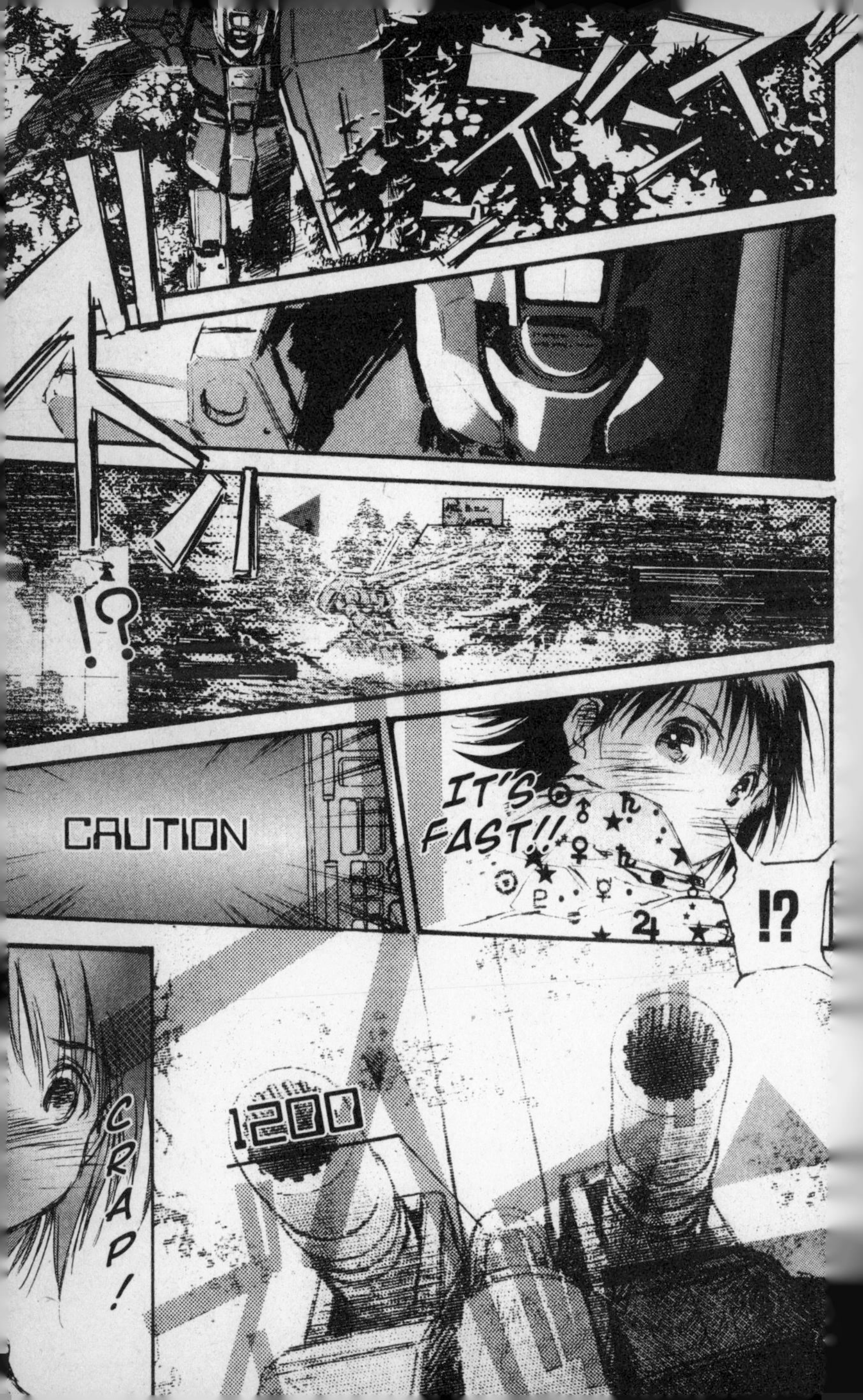
!?
!?
IT'S FAST!!
CAUTION
1200
CRAP!

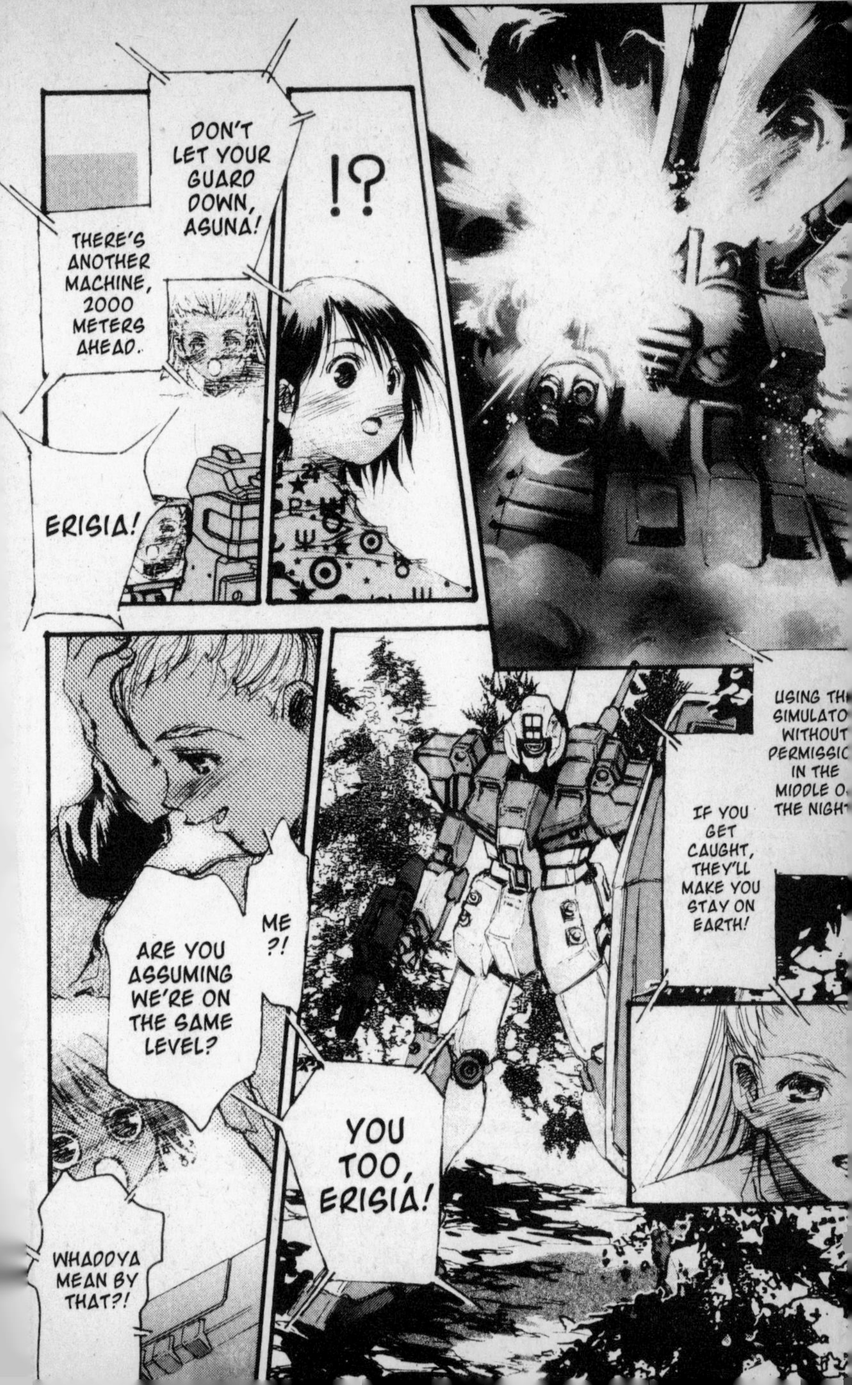
!?
DON'T LET YOUR GUARD DOWN, ASUNA!
THERE'S ANOTHER MACHINE, 2000 METERS AHEAD..
ERISIA!
USING TH SIMULATO WITHOUT PERMISSIC IN THE MIDDLE O THE NIGH
IF YOU GET CAUGHT, THEY'LL MAKE YOU STAY ON EARTH!
YOU TOO, ERISIA!
ME ?!
ARE YOU ASSUMING WE'RE ON THE SAME LEVEL?
WHADDYA MEAN BY THAT?!

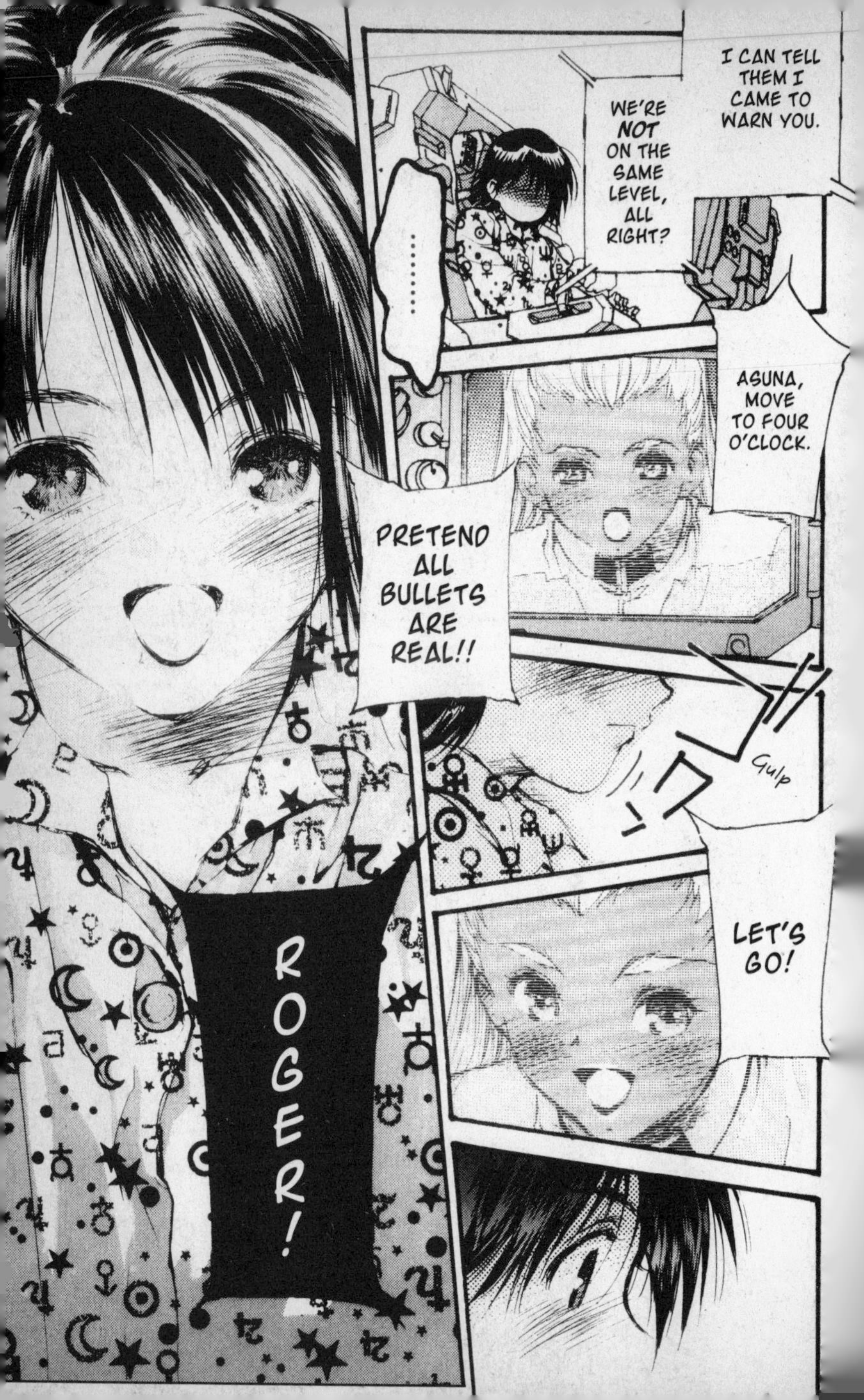
I CAN TELL THEM I CAME TO WARN YOU.
WE'RE *NOT* ON THE SAME LEVEL, ALL RIGHT?
......
ASUNA, MOVE TO FOUR O'CLOCK.
PRETEND ALL BULLETS ARE REAL!!
Gulp
LET'S GO!
ROGER!

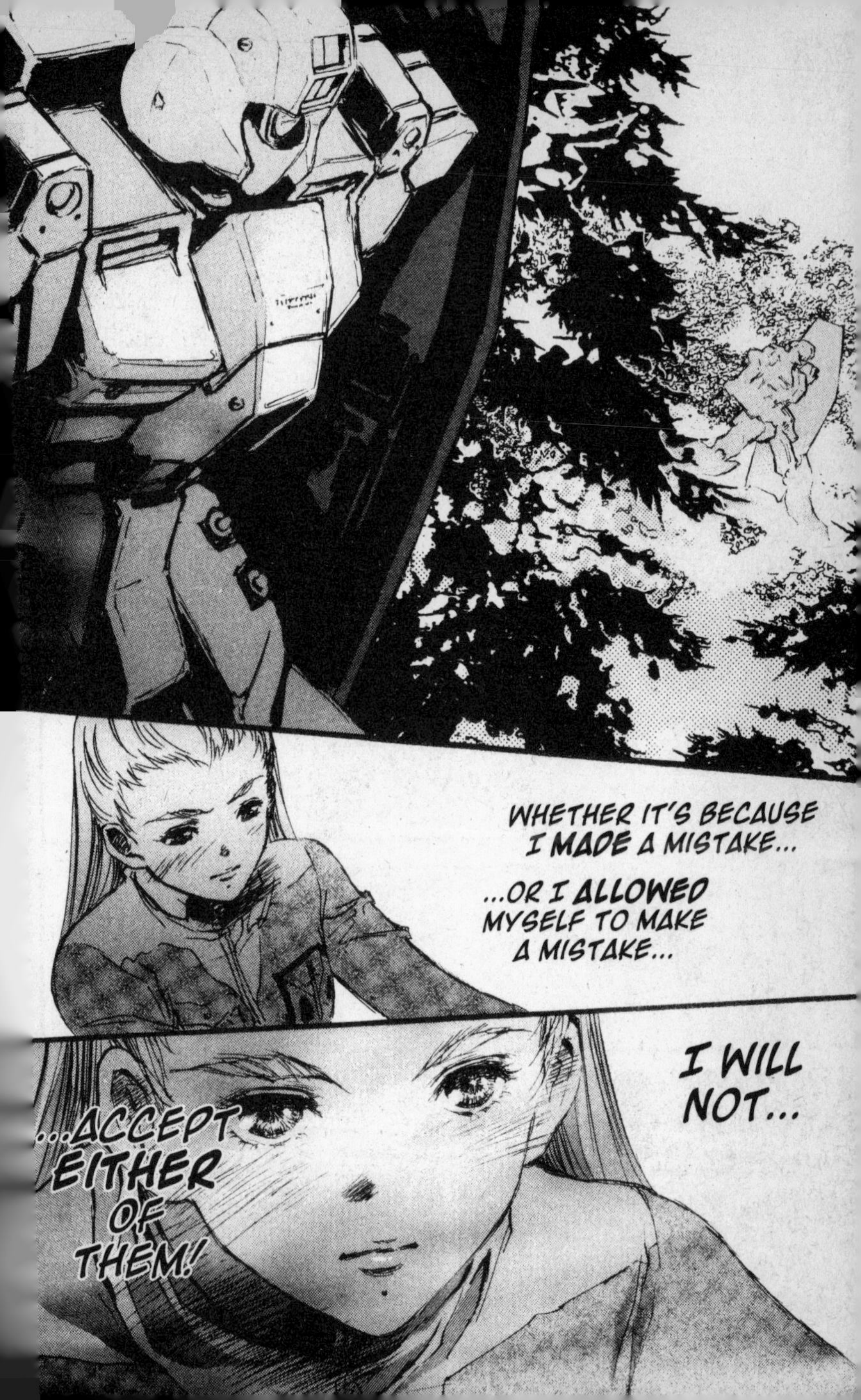
WHETHER IT'S BECAUSE I MADE A MISTAKE...
...OR I ALLOWED MYSELF TO MAKE A MISTAKE...
I WILL NOT...
...ACCEPT EITHER OF THEM!

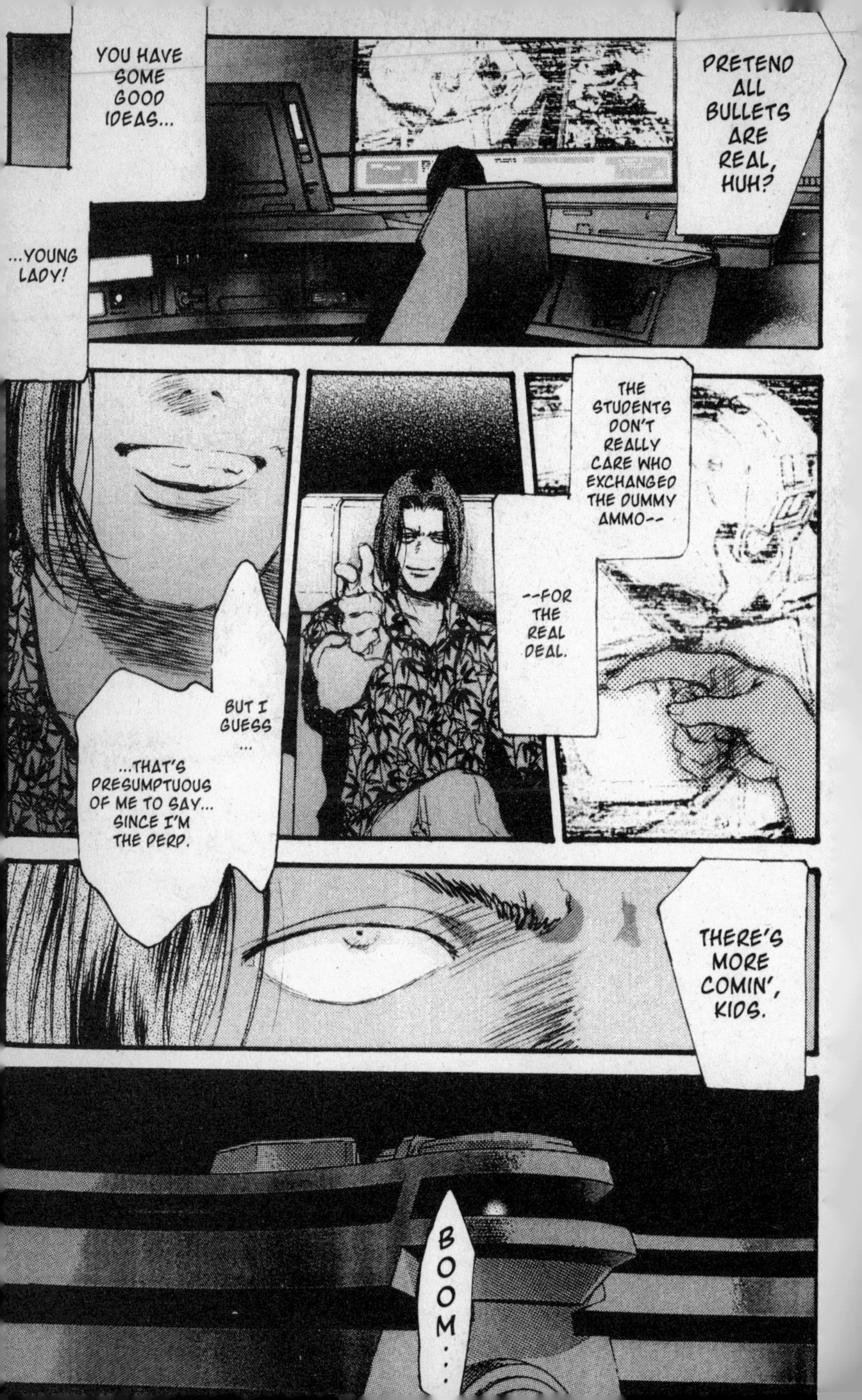
PRETEND ALL BULLETS ARE REAL, HUH?
YOU HAVE SOME GOOD IDEAS...
...YOUNG LADY!
THE STUDENTS DON'T REALLY CARE WHO EXCHANGED THE DUMMY AMMO--
--FOR THE REAL DEAL.
BUT I GUESS ...
...THAT'S PRESUMPTUOUS OF ME TO SAY... SINCE I'M THE PERP.
THERE'S MORE COMIN', KIDS.
BOOM...

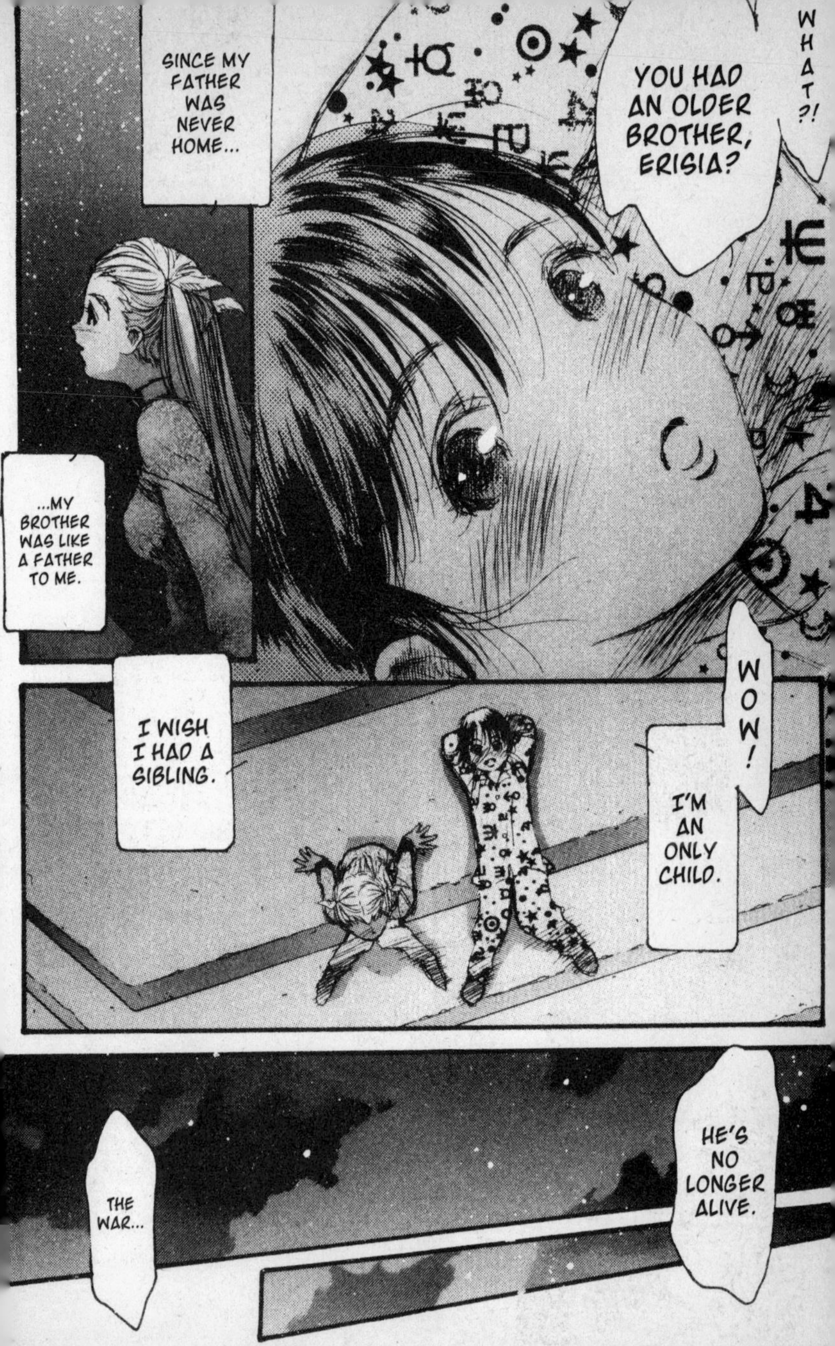
WHAT?!
YOU HAD AN OLDER BROTHER, ERISIA?
SINCE MY FATHER WAS NEVER HOME...
...MY BROTHER WAS LIKE A FATHER TO ME.
WOW!
I'M AN ONLY CHILD.
I WISH I HAD A SIBLING.
HE'S NO LONGER ALIVE.
THE WAR...

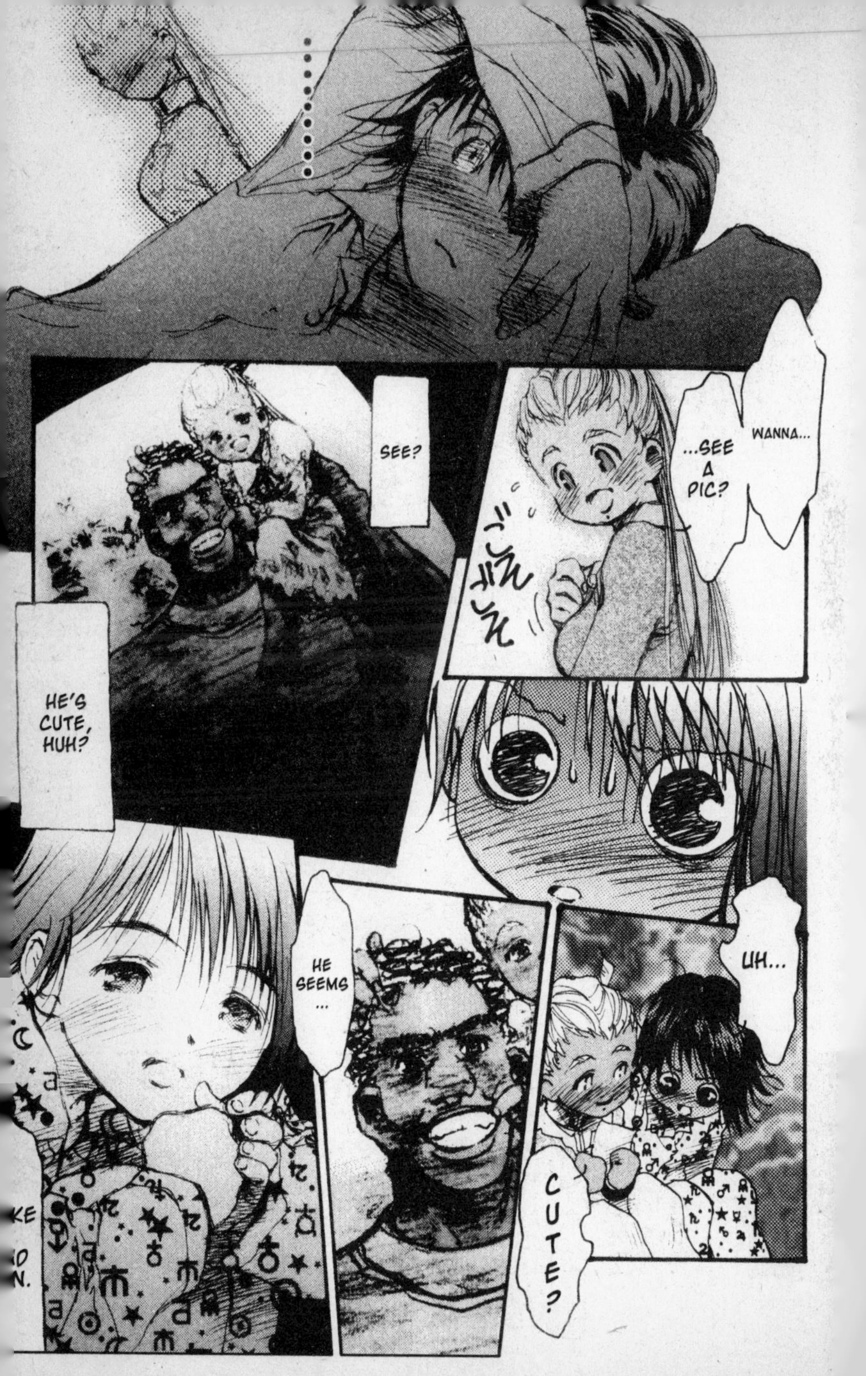
WANNA...
...SEE A PIC?
SEE?
HE'S CUTE, HUH?
UH...
CUTE?
HE SEEMS ...

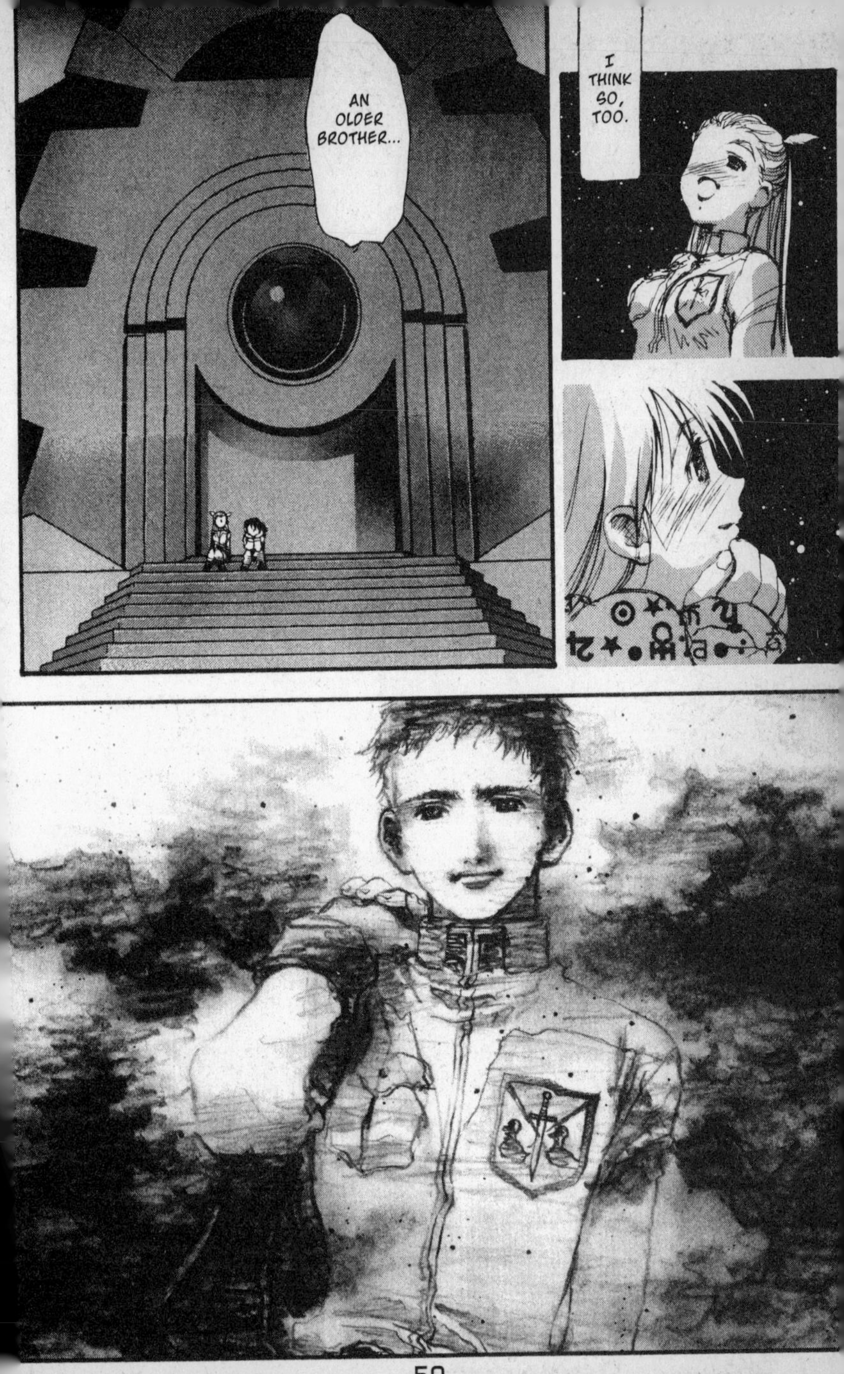
I THINK SO, TOO.
AN OLDER BROTHER...

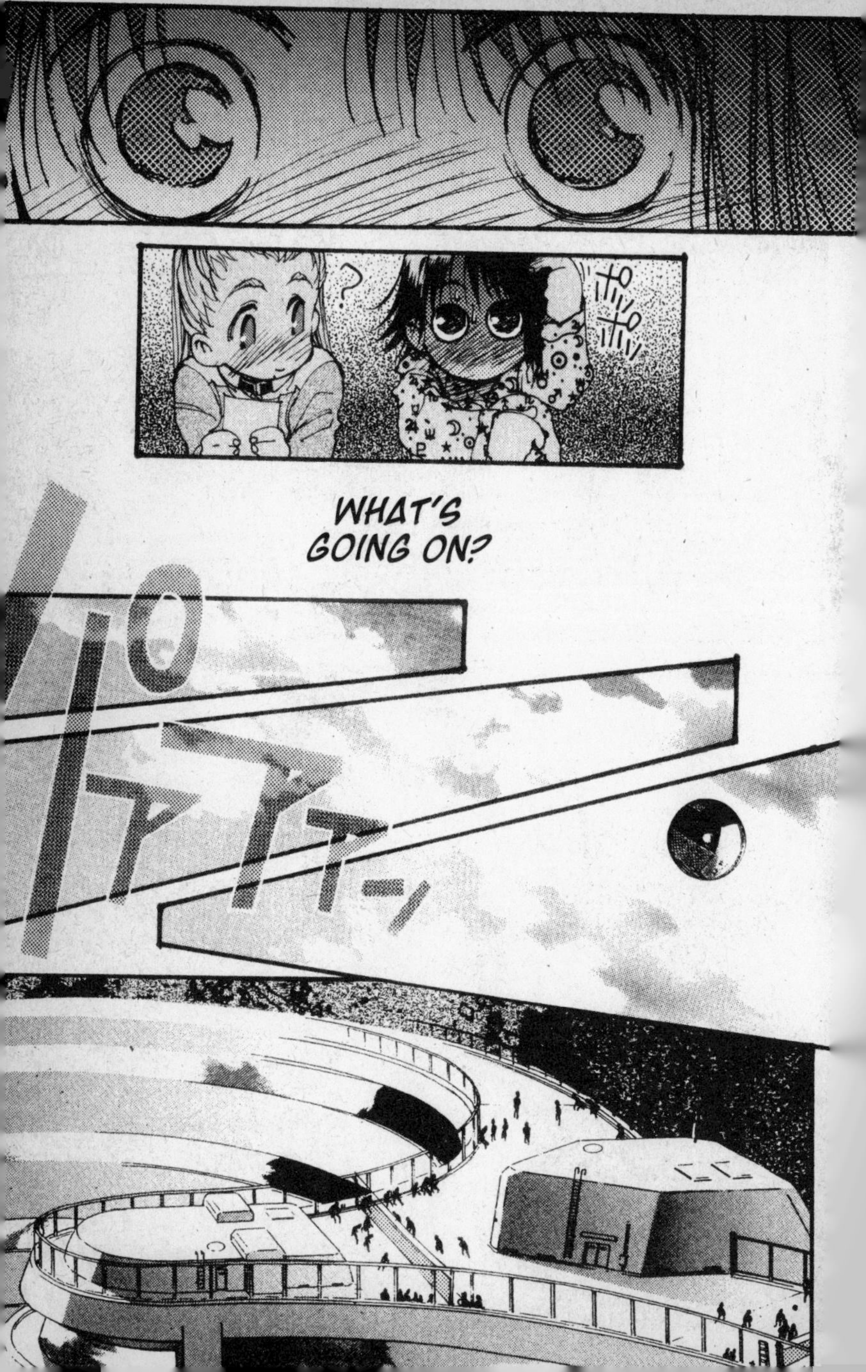
WHAT'S GOING ON?

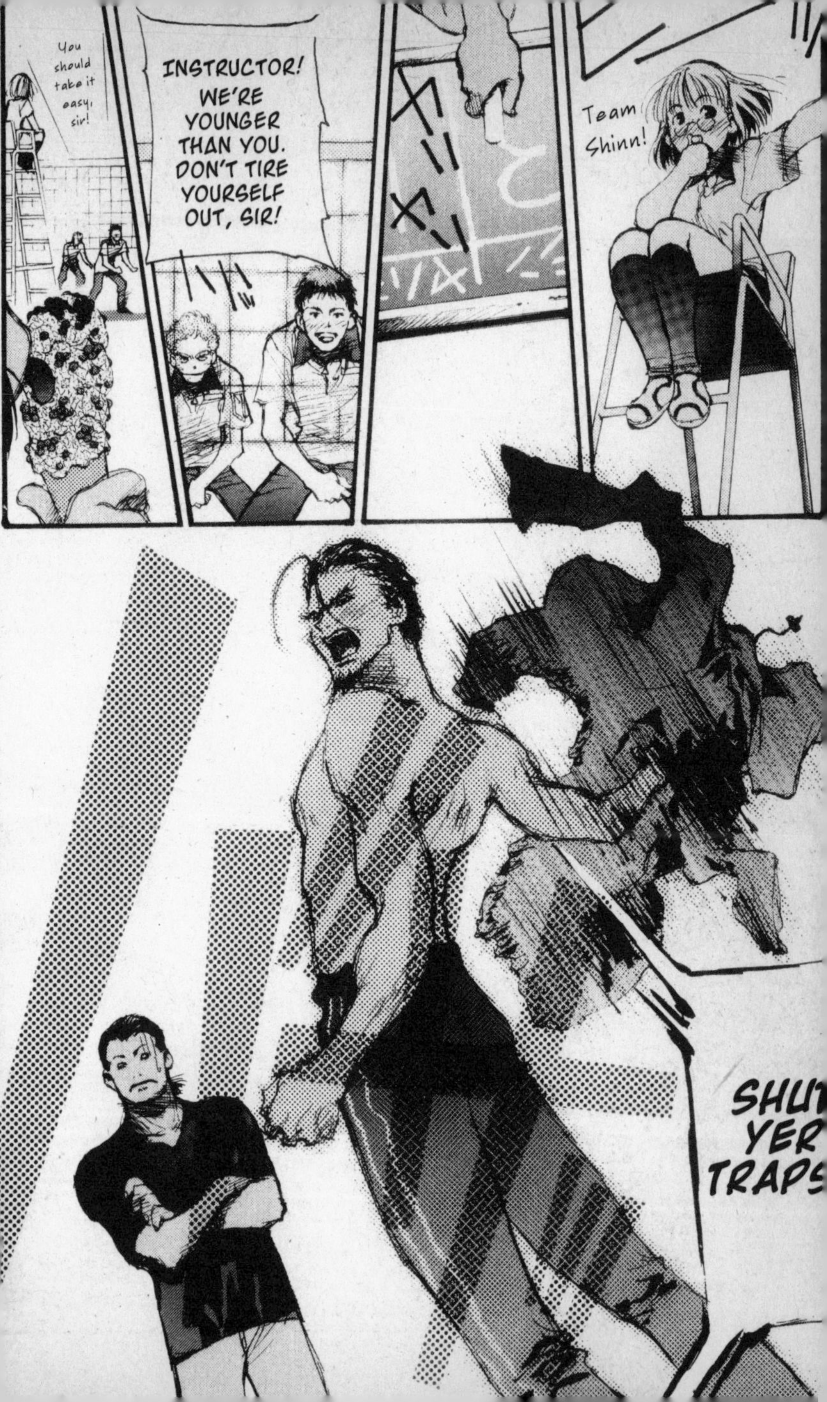
Team Shinn!
INSTRUCTOR! WE'RE YOUNGER THAN YOU. DON'T TIRE YOURSELF OUT, SIR!
You should take it easy, sir!
SHUT YER TRAPS

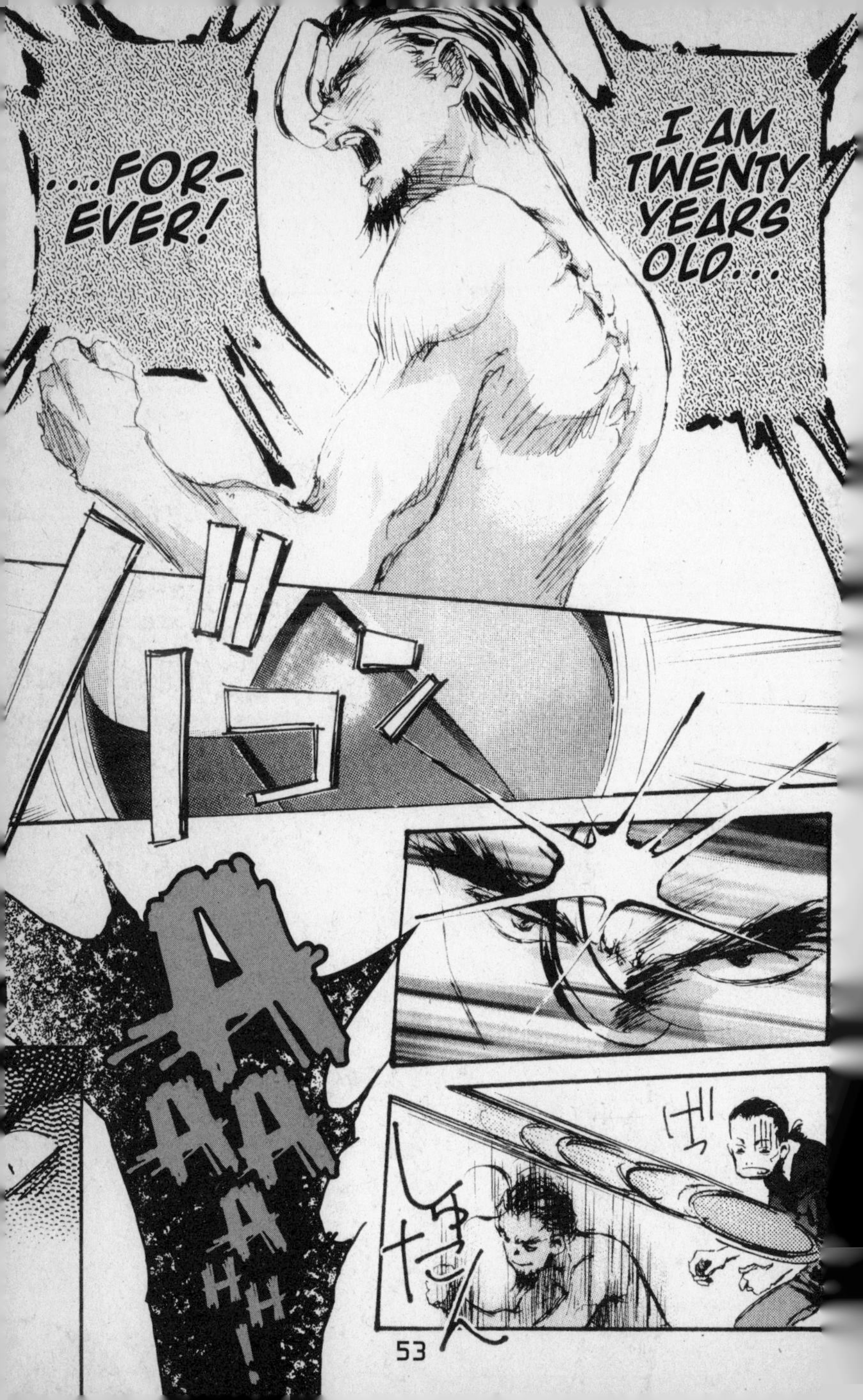
I AM TWENTY YEARS OLD...
...FOR-EVER!
AAAAHHH!

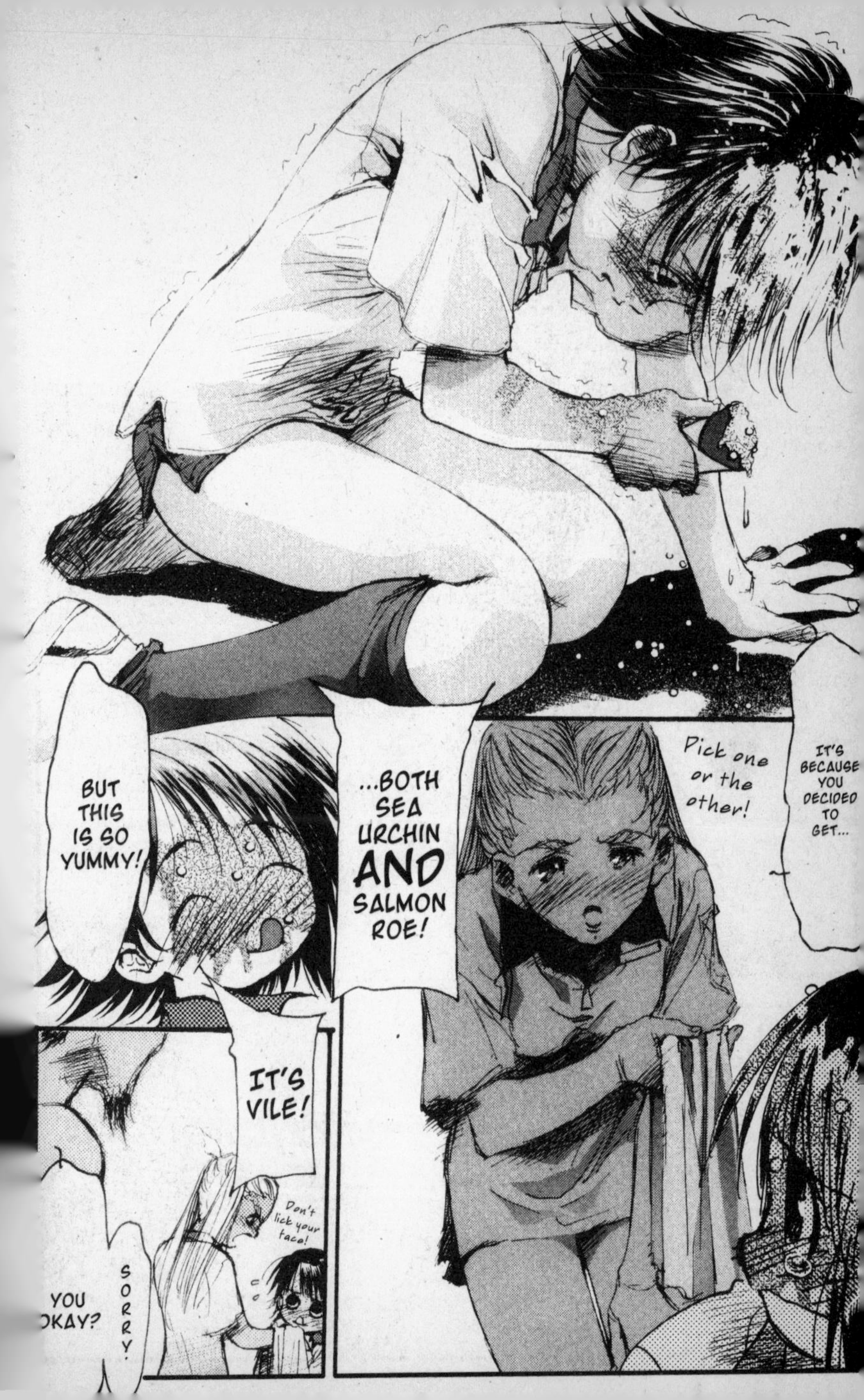
IT'S BECAUSE YOU DECIDED TO GET...
Pick one or the other!
...BOTH SEA URCHIN AND SALMON ROE!
BUT THIS IS SO YUMMY!
IT'S VILE!
Don't lick your face!
SORRY.
YOU OKAY?

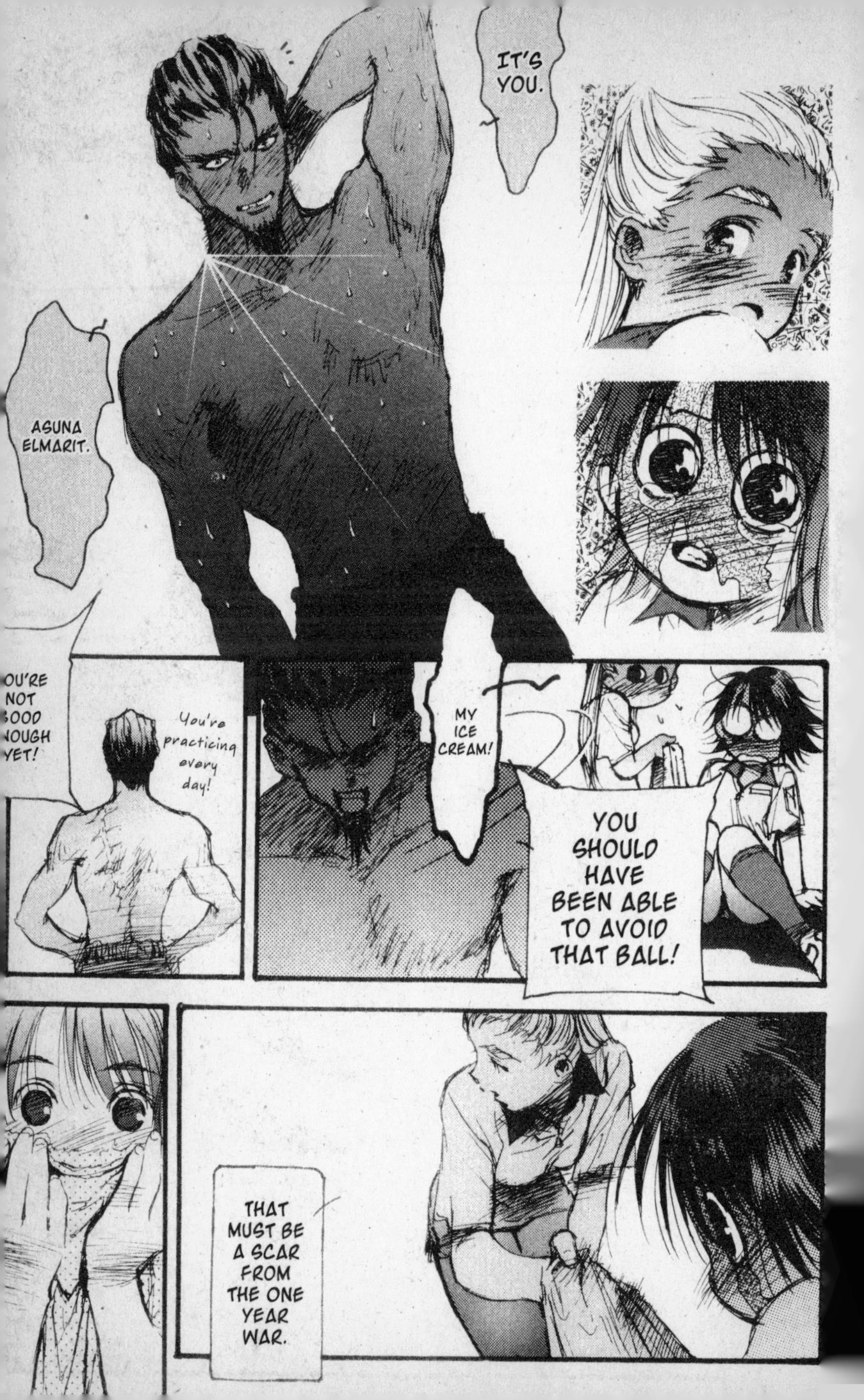
IT'S YOU.
ASUNA ELMARIT.
YOU SHOULD HAVE BEEN ABLE TO AVOID THAT BALL!
MY ICE CREAM!
You're practicing every day!
OU'RE NOT OOD NOUGH YET!
THAT MUST BE A SCAR FROM THE ONE YEAR WAR.

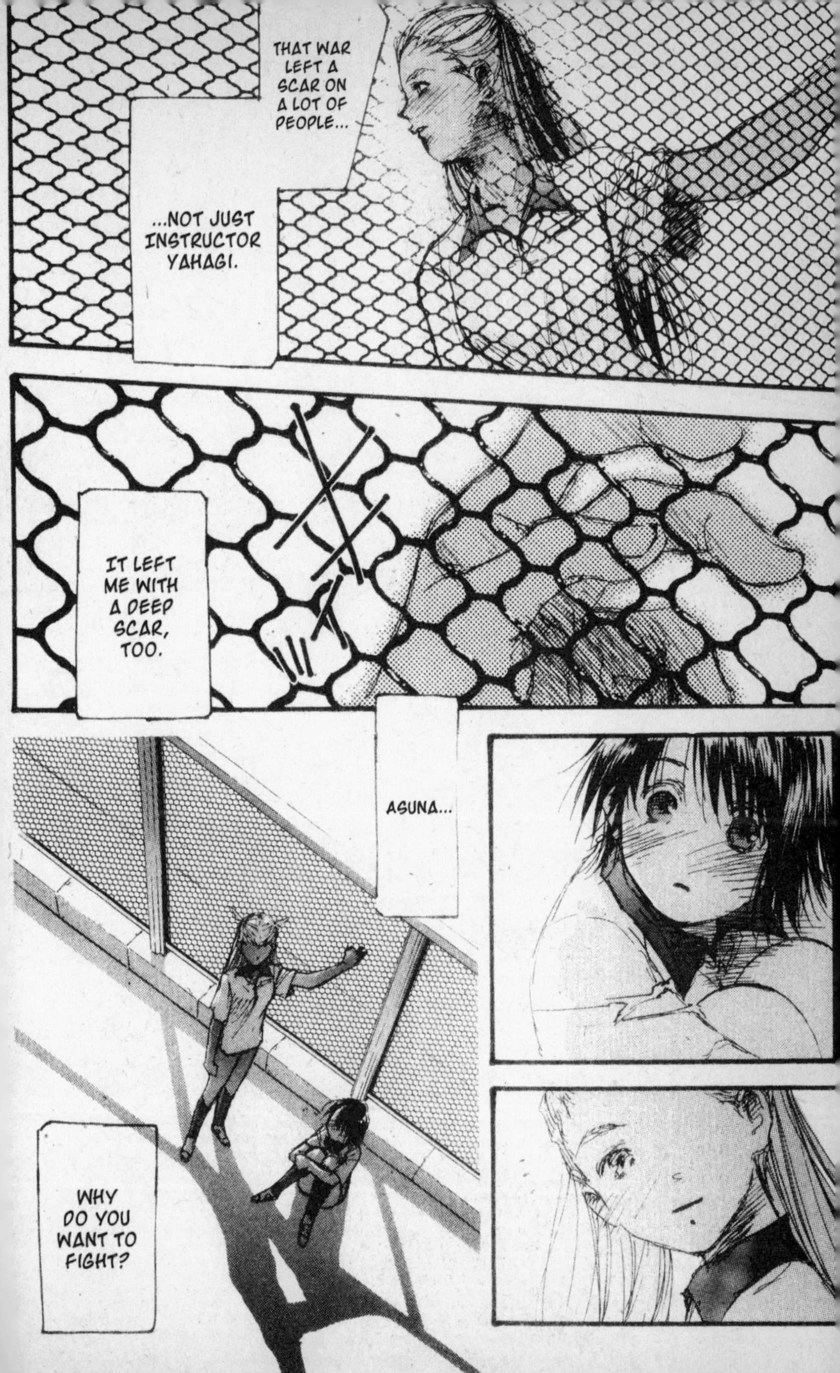
THAT WAR LEFT A SCAR ON A LOT OF PEOPLE...
...NOT JUST INSTRUCTOR YAHAGI.
IT LEFT ME WITH A DEEP SCAR, TOO.
ASUNA...
WHY DO YOU WANT TO FIGHT?

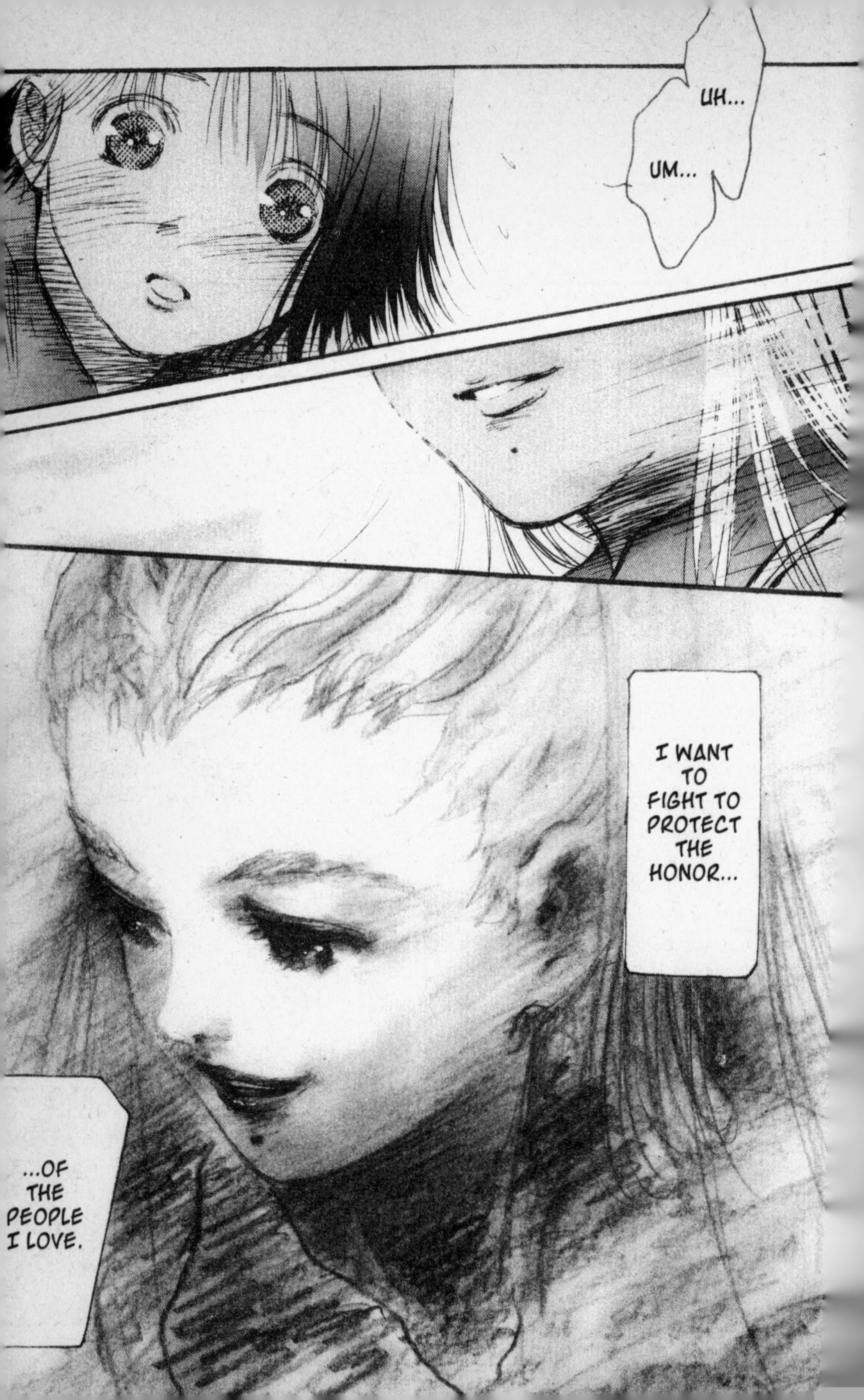
UH...
UM...
I WANT TO FIGHT TO PROTECT THE HONOR...
...OF THE PEOPLE I LOVE.

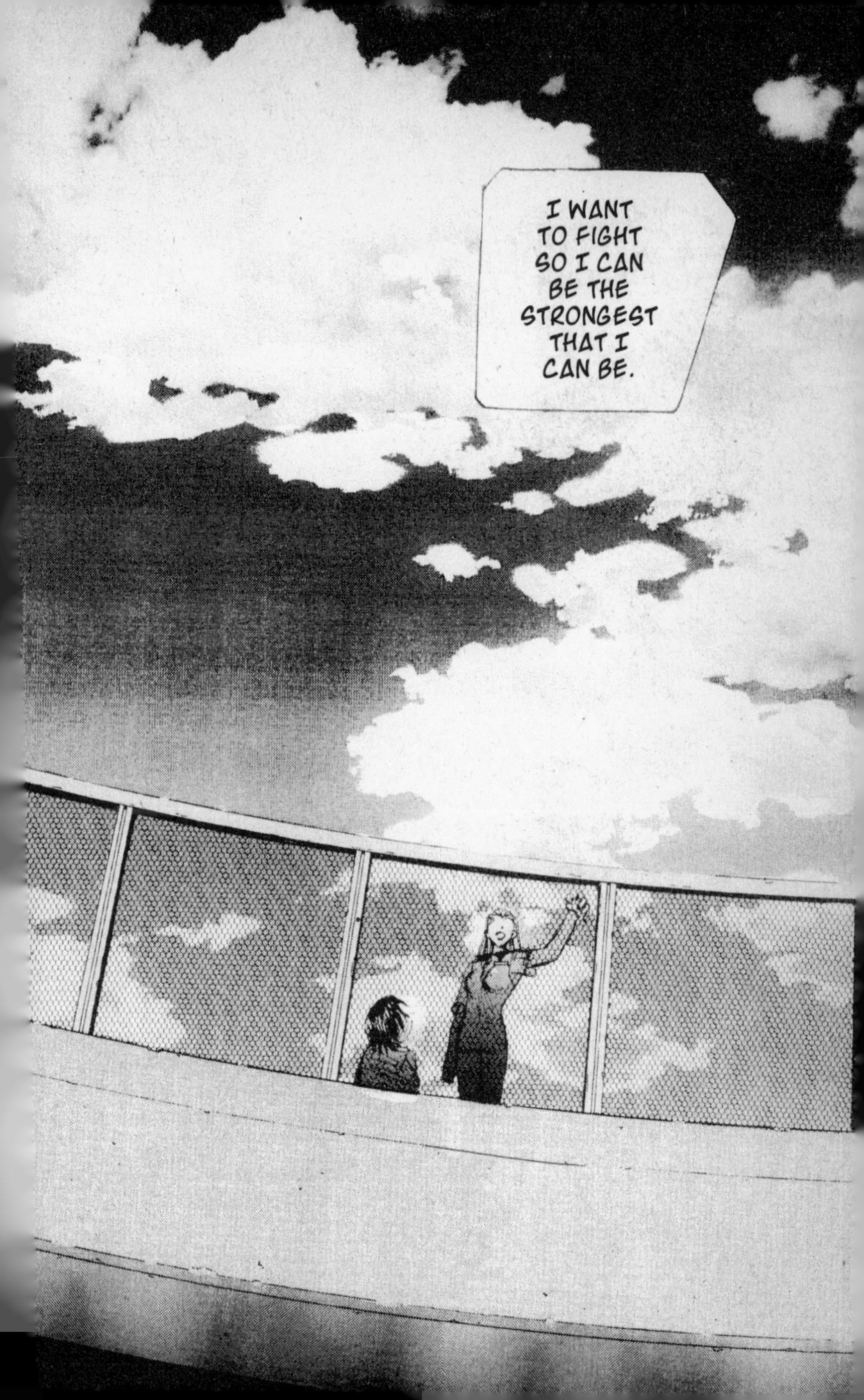
I WANT TO FIGHT SO I CAN BE THE STRONGEST THAT I CAN BE.

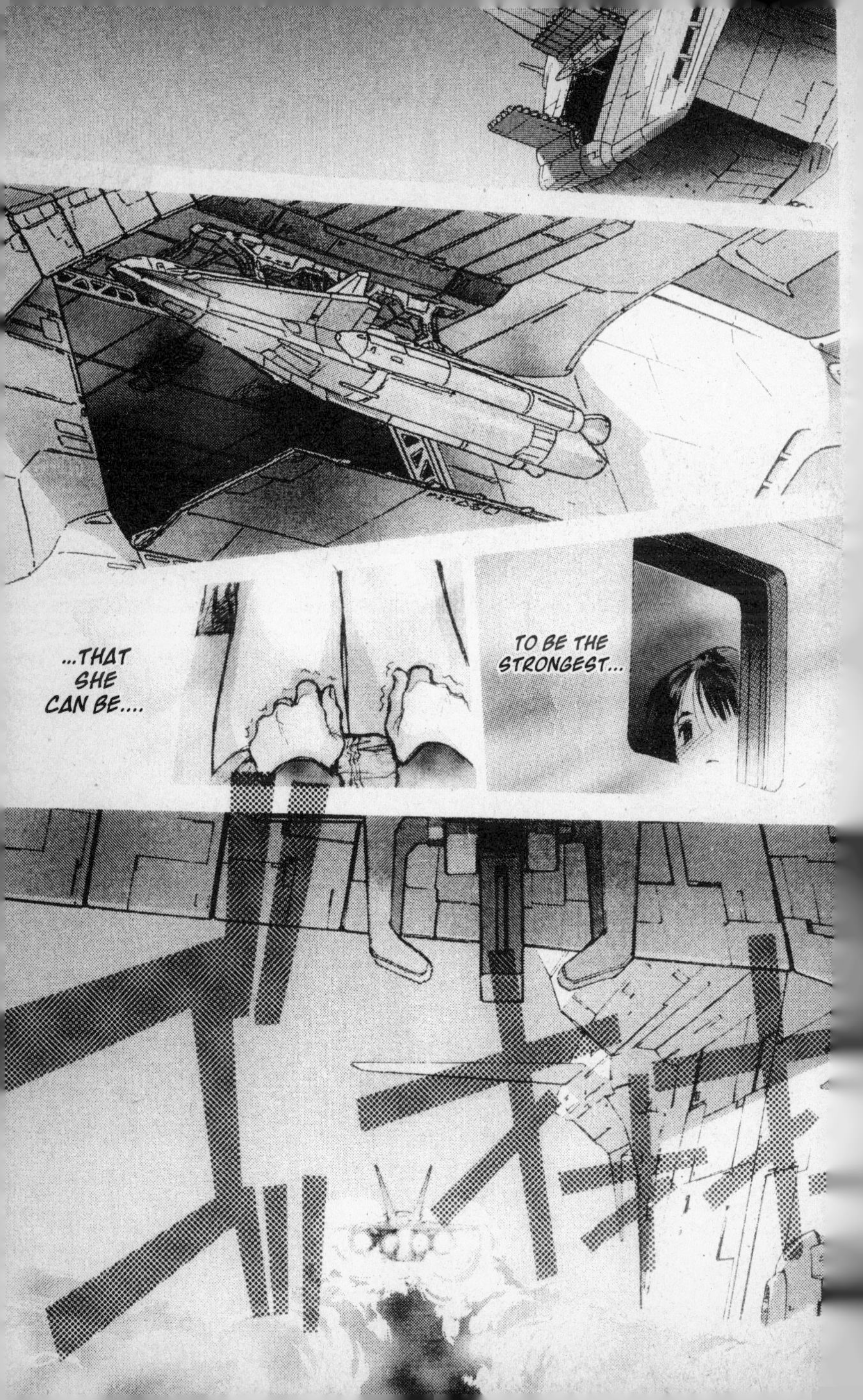
TO BE THE STRONGEST...
...THAT SHE CAN BE....

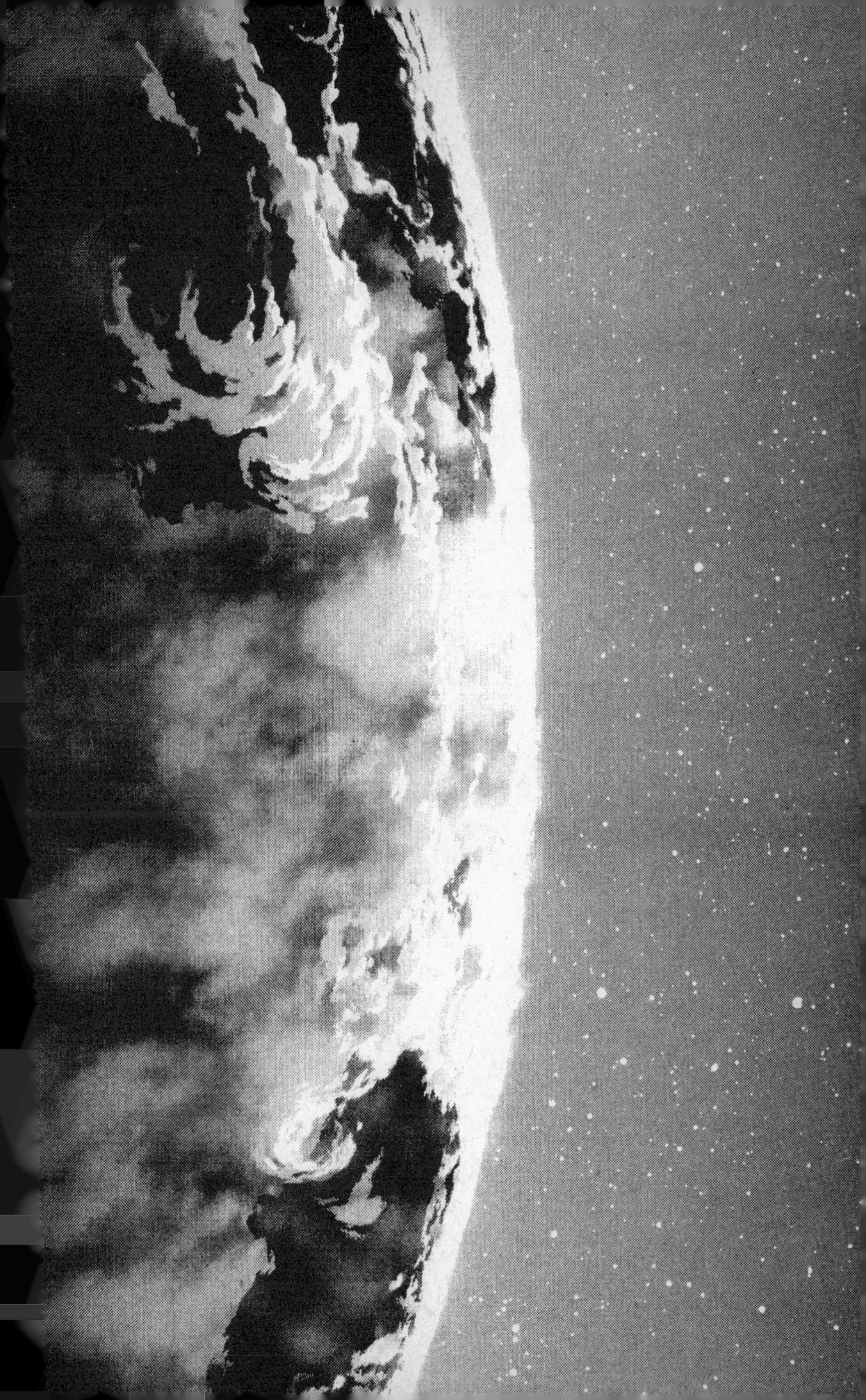

CHARACTER FILE:02

Erisia Nocton

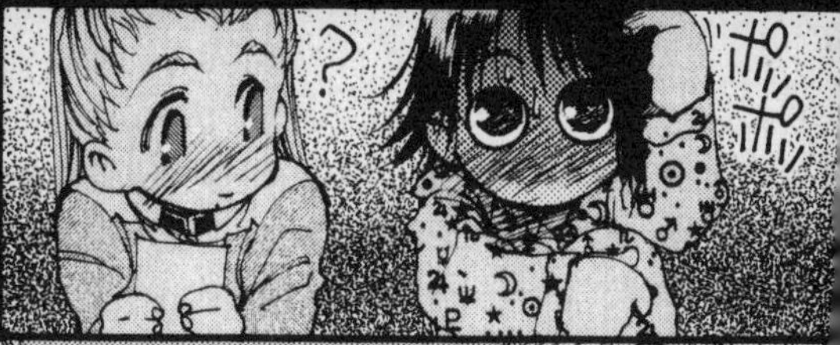

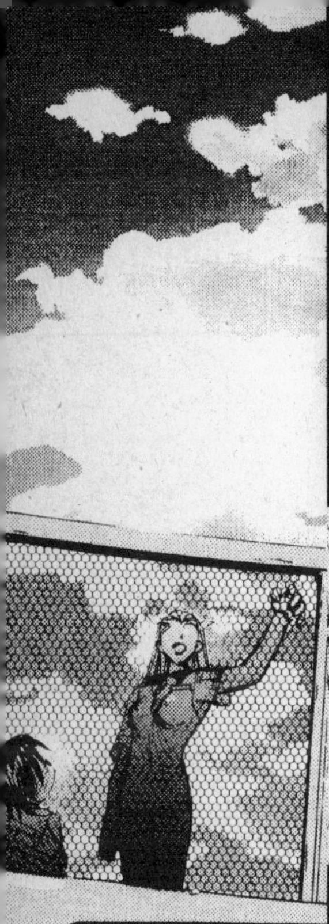

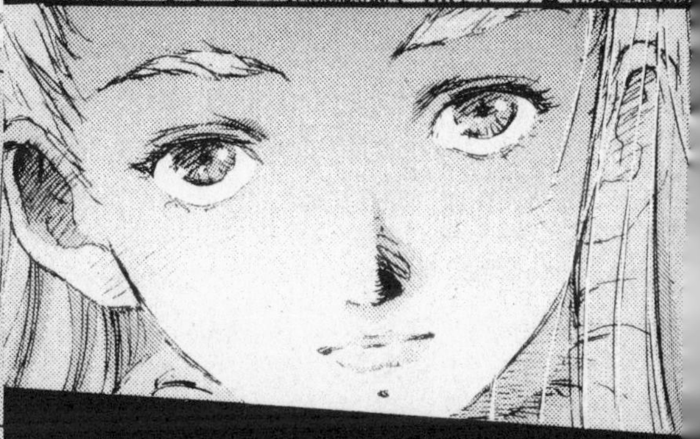

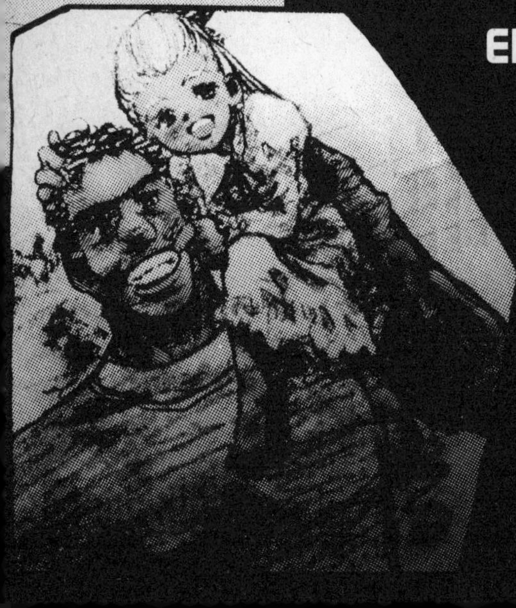

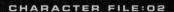

ERISIA NOCTON

HER FATHER OWNED A COMPANY THAT SUPPLIED MILITARY ELECTRONICS. BORN ON EARTH INTO AN ELITE, WEALTHY FAMILY. AT ÉCOLE DU CIEL, SHE WAS THE TOP OF HER CLASS IN EVERY SUBJECT UNTIL THE LIVE EXERCISE. MANY PEOPLE, INCLUDING THE TITANS TASKFORCE AND OTHERS IN THE MILITARY, HAVE HIGH EXPECTATIONS FOR HER.

IN A SIMULATOR, SHE WON AGAINST ASUNA IN 2 MINUTES AND 18 SECONDS. HOWEVER, ASUNA WAS ABLE TO "LOCK ON" TO HER. AS A RESULT, SHE HAS BEEN WATCHING ASUNA EVER SINCE. SHE LOST HER BELOVED BROTHER IN THE ONE YEAR WAR.

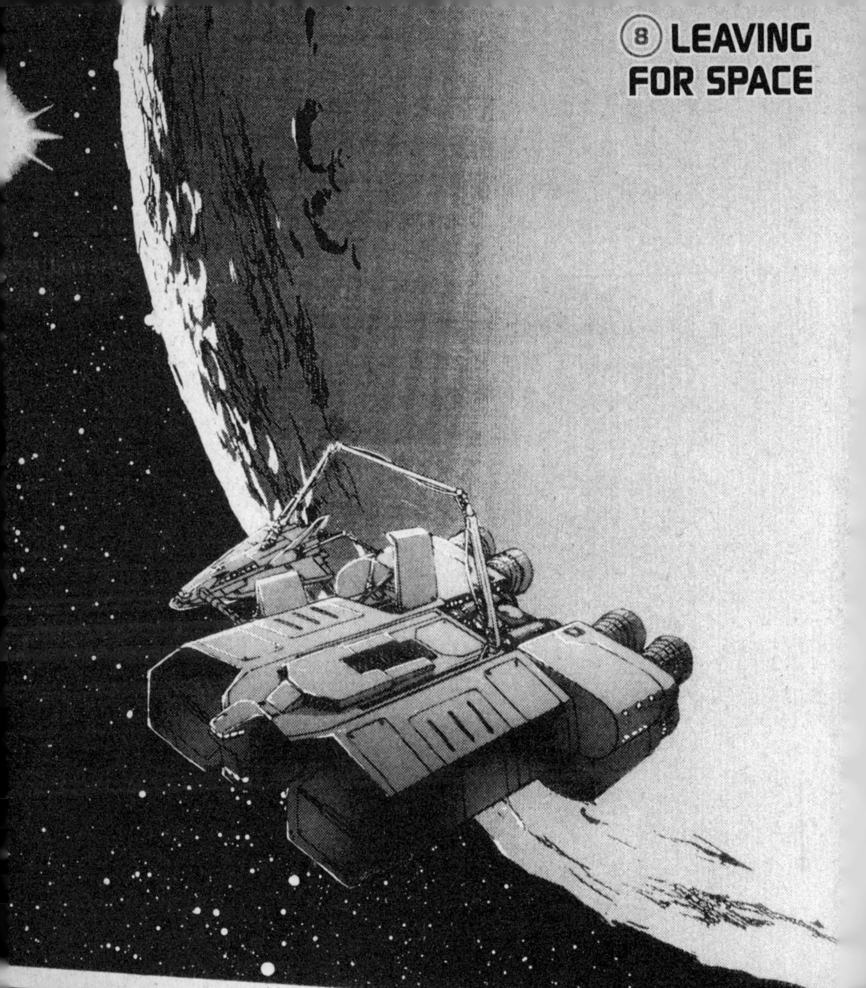
8 LEAVING FOR SPACE
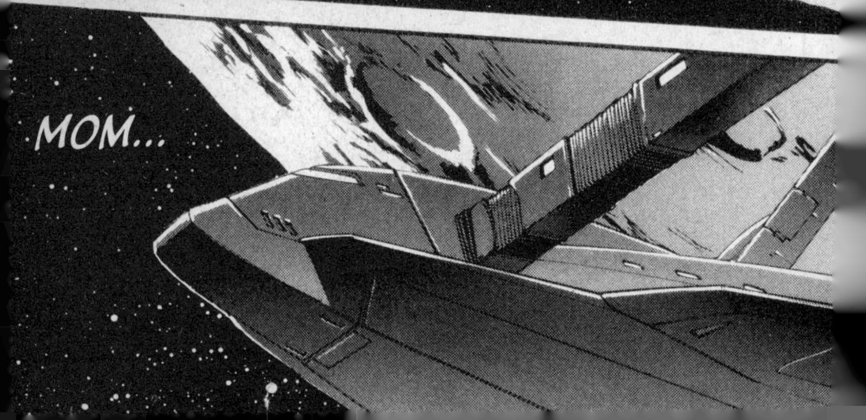
MOM...

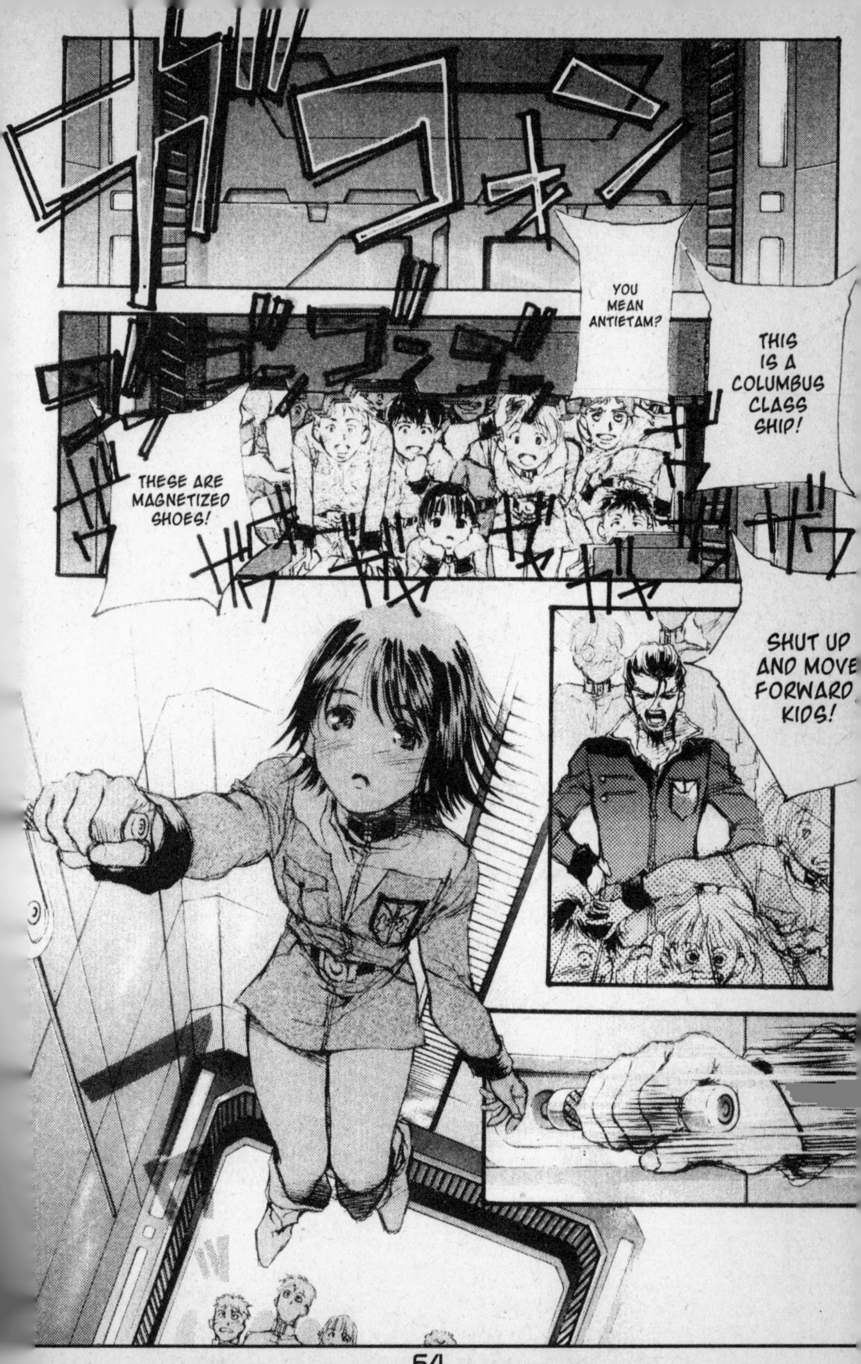
THIS IS A COLUMBUS CLASS SHIP!
YOU MEAN ANTIETAM?
THESE ARE MAGNETIZED SHOES!
SHUT UP AND MOVE FORWARD KIDS!

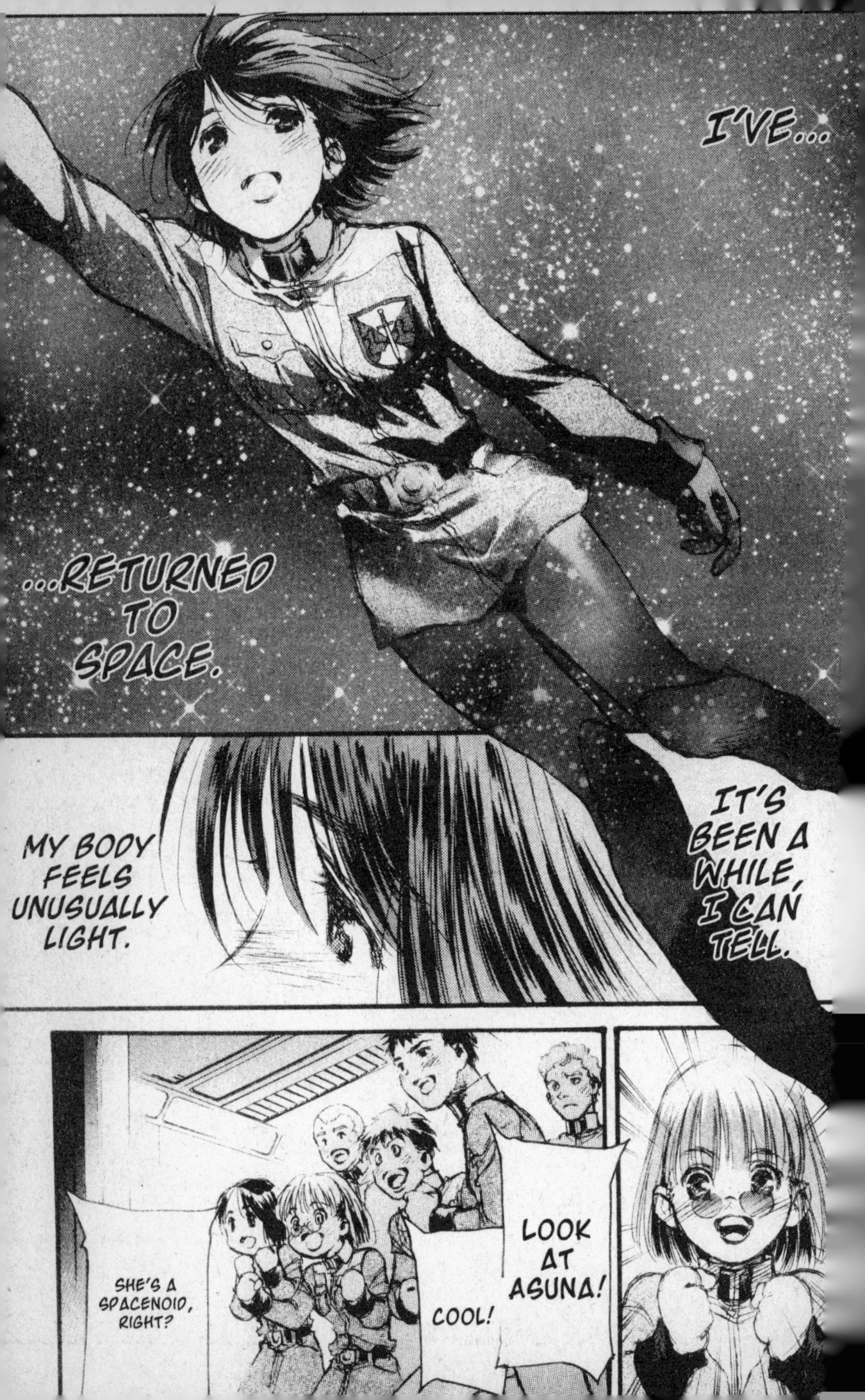
I'VE...
...RETURNED TO SPACE.
IT'S BEEN A WHILE, I CAN TELL.
MY BODY FEELS UNUSUALLY LIGHT.
LOOK AT ASUNA!
COOL!
SHE'S A SPACENOID, RIGHT?

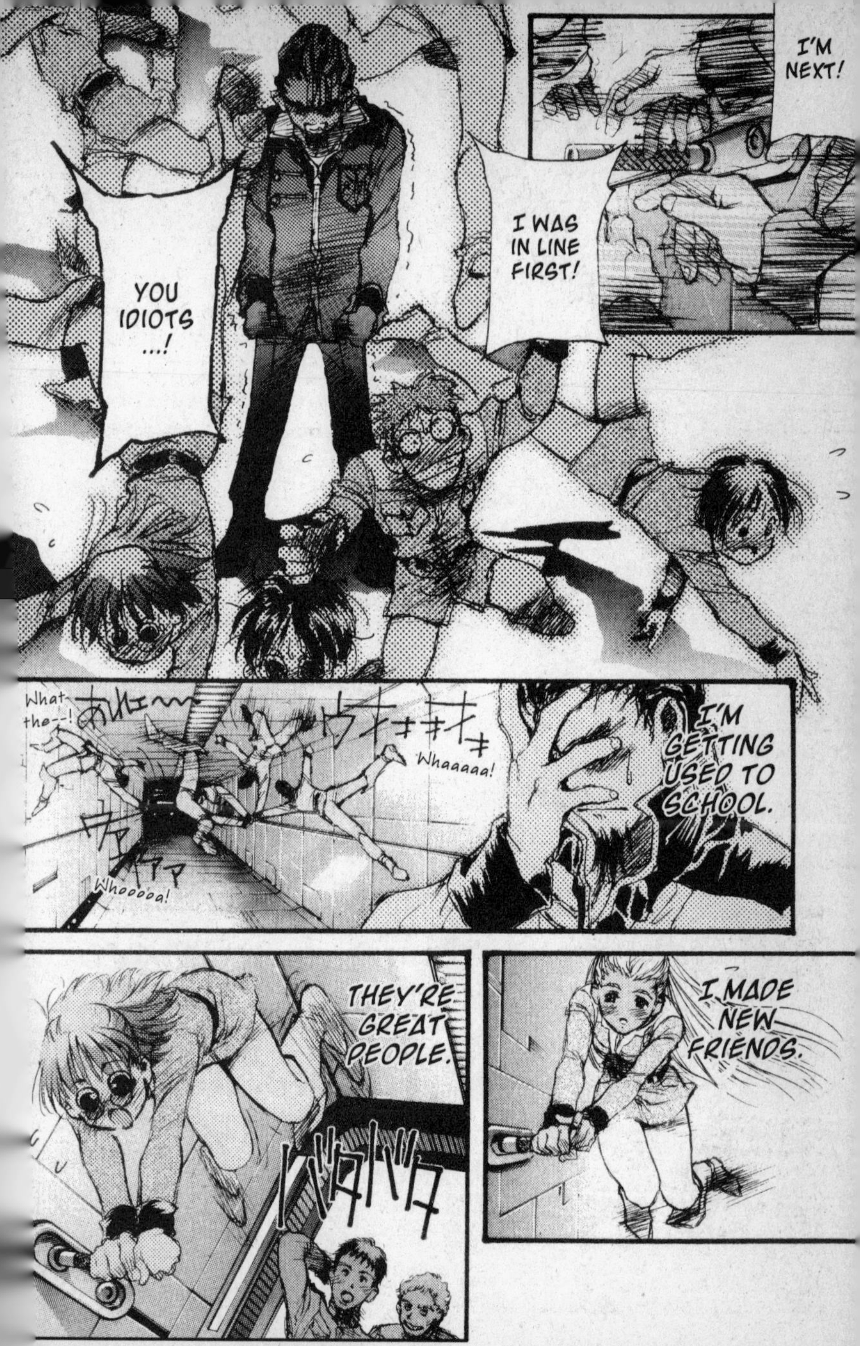
I'M NEXT!
I WAS IN LINE FIRST!
YOU IDIOTS ...!
I'M GETTING USED TO SCHOOL.
Whaaaaa!
What the--!
Whoooa!
I MADE NEW FRIENDS.
THEY'RE GREAT PEOPLE.

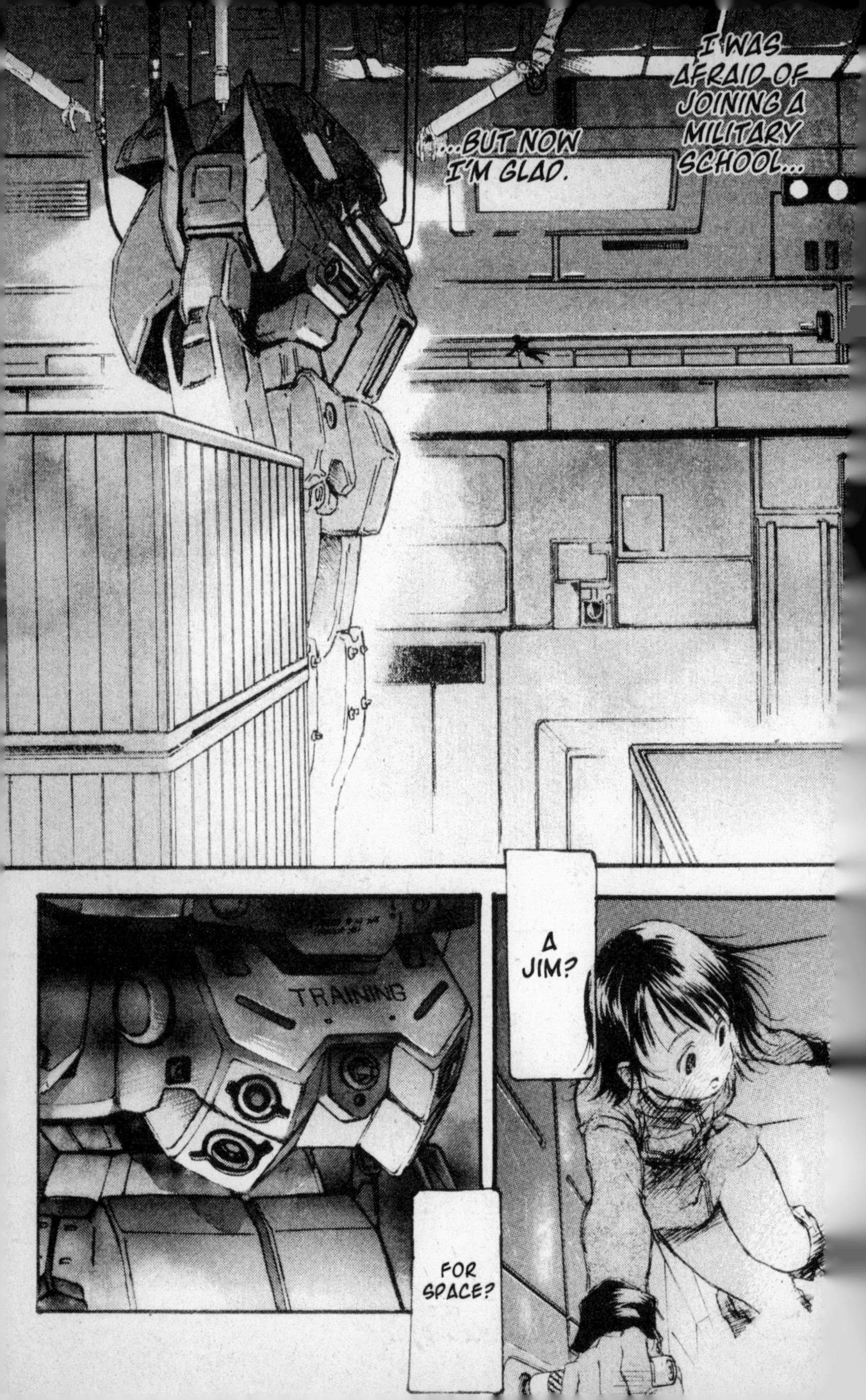
I WAS AFRAID OF JOINING A MILITARY SCHOOL...
...BUT NOW I'M GLAD.
A JIM?
FOR SPACE?
TRAINING

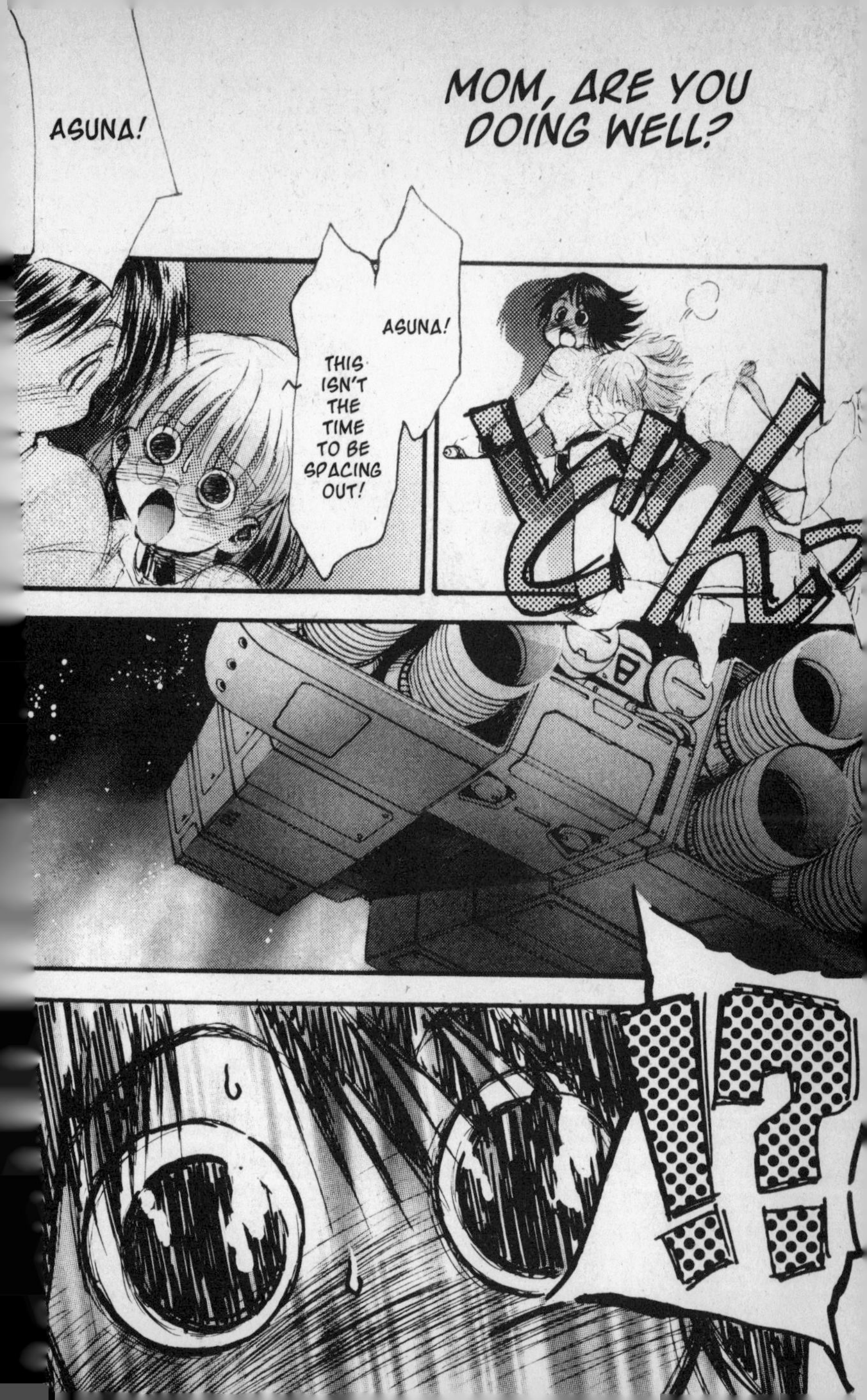
MOM, ARE YOU DOING WELL?
ASUNA!
ASUNA!
THIS ISN'T THE TIME TO BE SPACING OUT!
!?

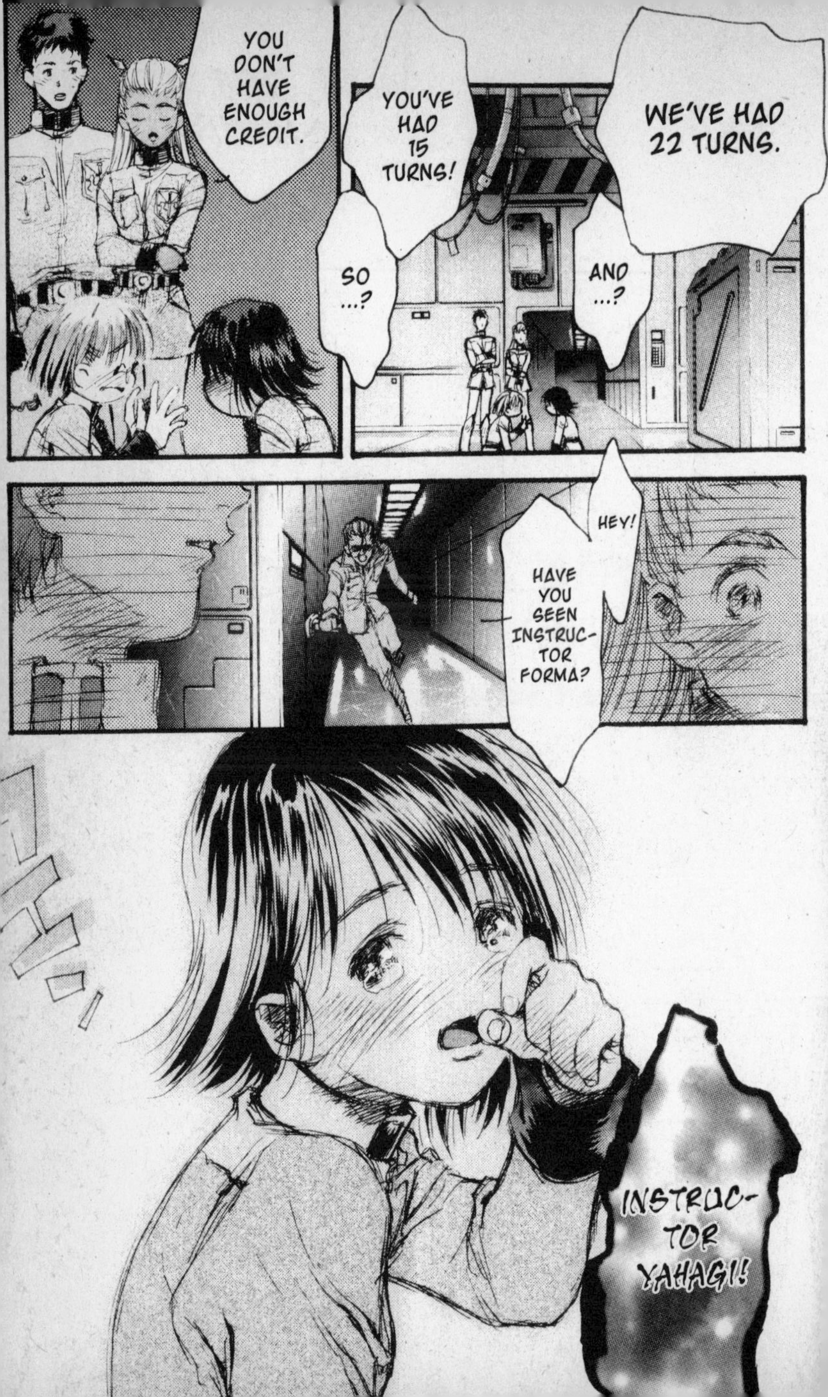
WE'VE HAD 22 TURNS.
YOU'VE HAD 15 TURNS!
AND ...?
SO ...?
YOU DON'T HAVE ENOUGH CREDIT.
HEY!
HAVE YOU SEEN INSTRUC-TOR FORMA?
INSTRUC-TOR YAHAGI!

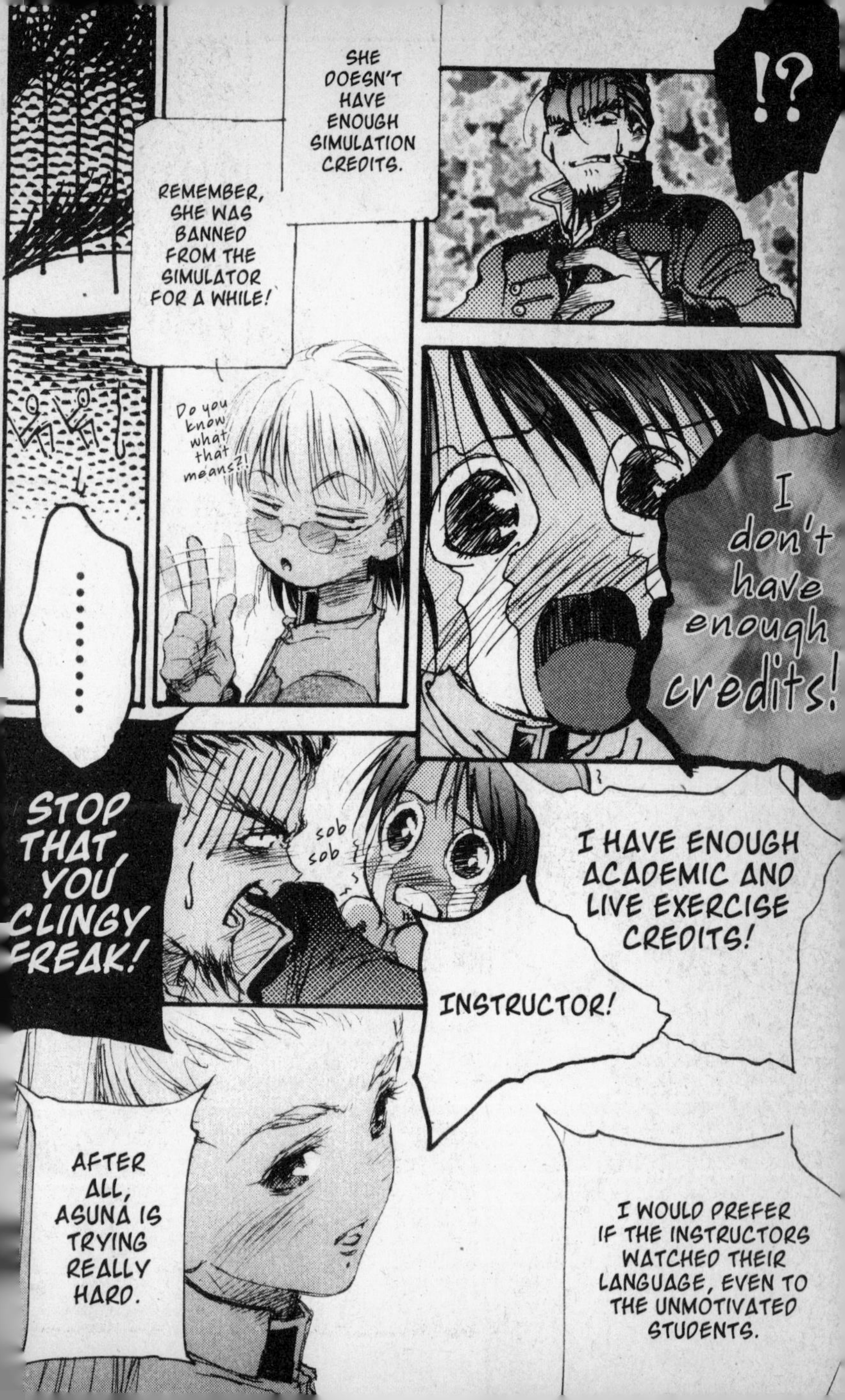
!?
SHE DOESN'T HAVE ENOUGH SIMULATION CREDITS.
REMEMBER, SHE WAS BANNED FROM THE SIMULATOR FOR A WHILE!
Do you know what that means?!
I don't have enough credits!
......
I HAVE ENOUGH ACADEMIC AND LIVE EXERCISE CREDITS!
sob sob
STOP THAT, YOU CLINGY FREAK!
INSTRUCTOR!
I WOULD PREFER IF THE INSTRUCTORS WATCHED THEIR LANGUAGE, EVEN TO THE UNMOTIVATED STUDENTS.
AFTER ALL, ASUNA IS TRYING REALLY HARD.

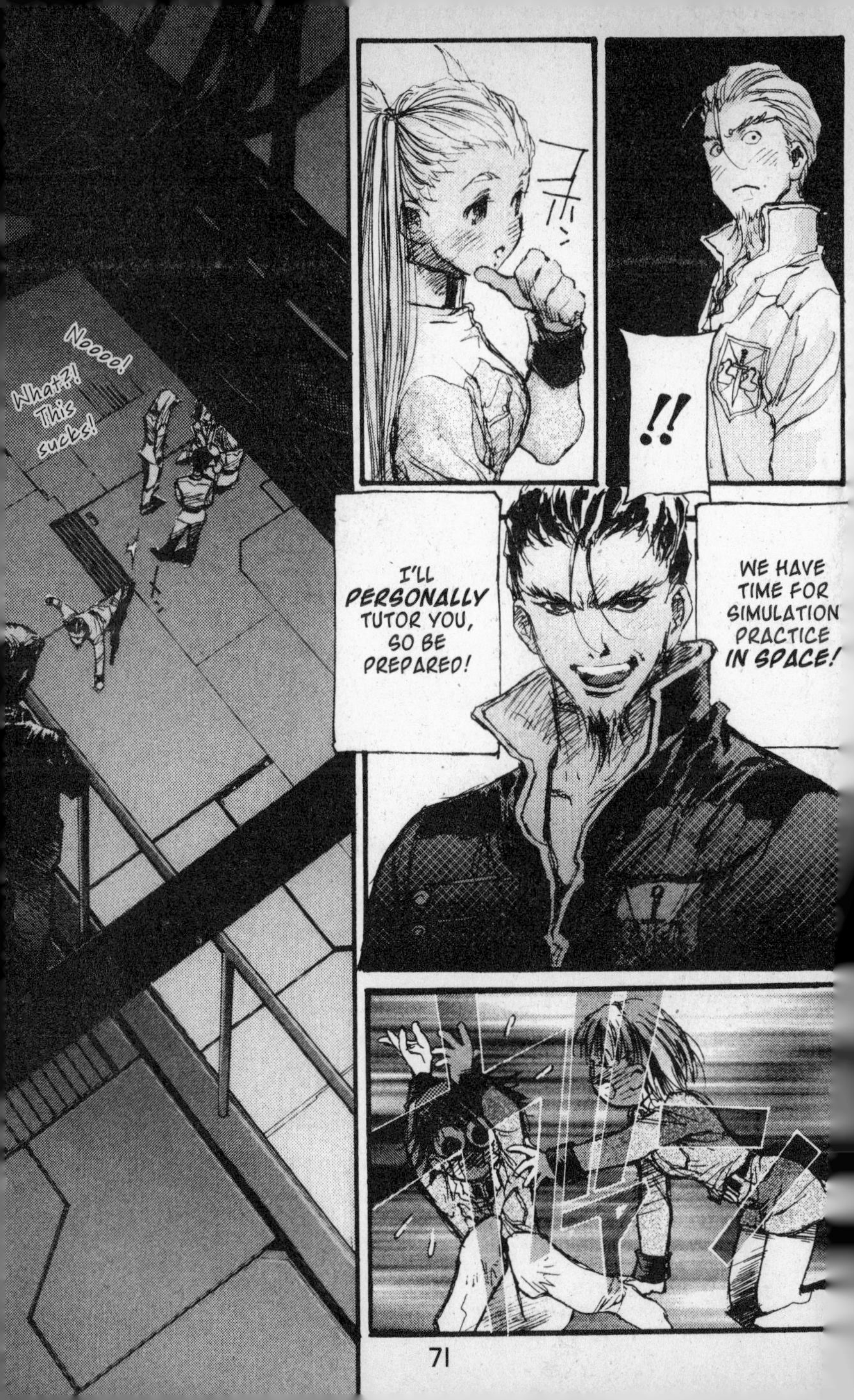
!!
WE HAVE TIME FOR SIMULATION PRACTICE IN SPACE!
I'LL PERSONALLY TUTOR YOU, SO BE PREPARED!
Noooo!
What?! This sucks!

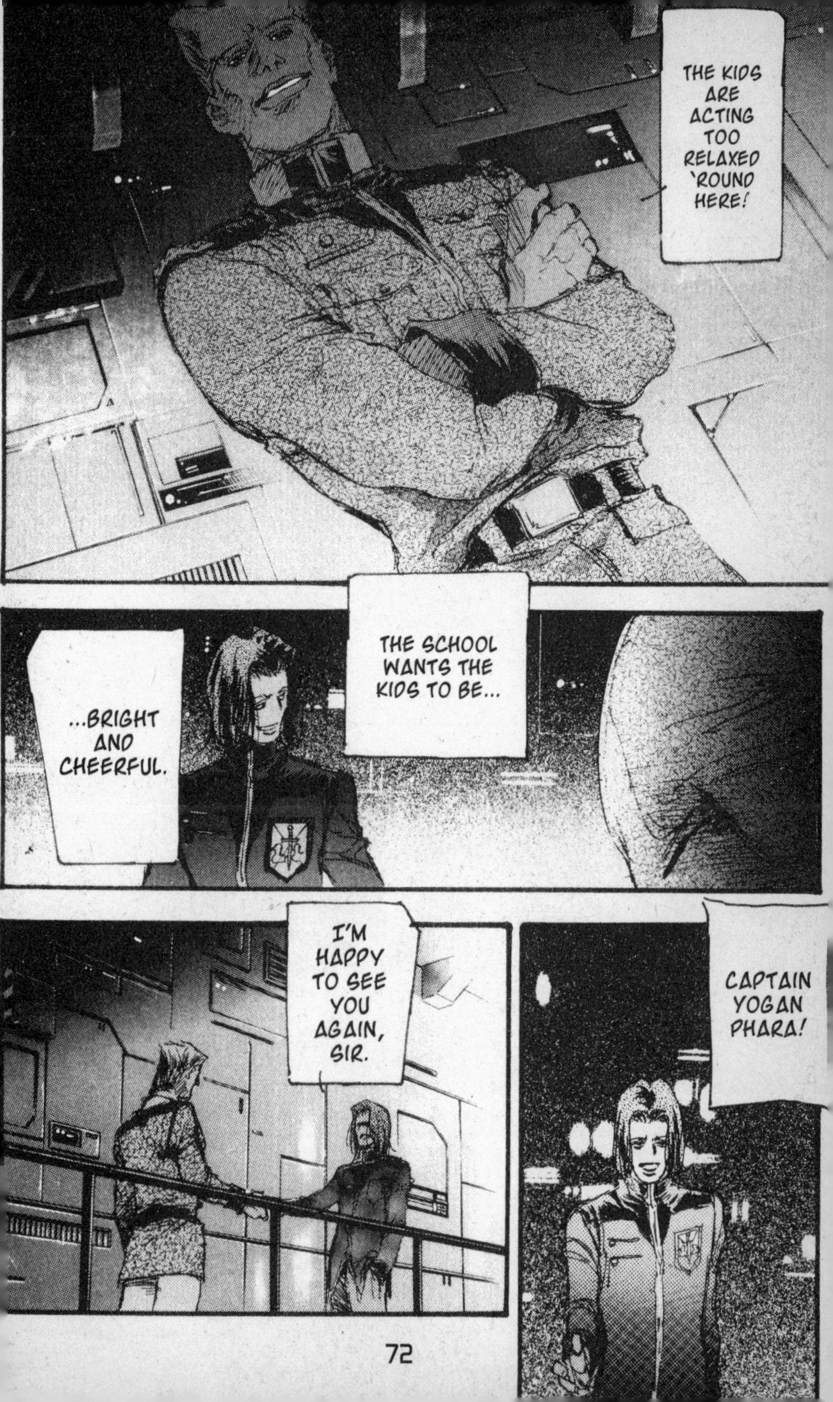
THE KIDS ARE ACTING TOO RELAXED 'ROUND HERE!
THE SCHOOL WANTS THE KIDS TO BE...
...BRIGHT AND CHEERFUL.
CAPTAIN YOGAN PHARA!
I'M HAPPY TO SEE YOU AGAIN, SIR.

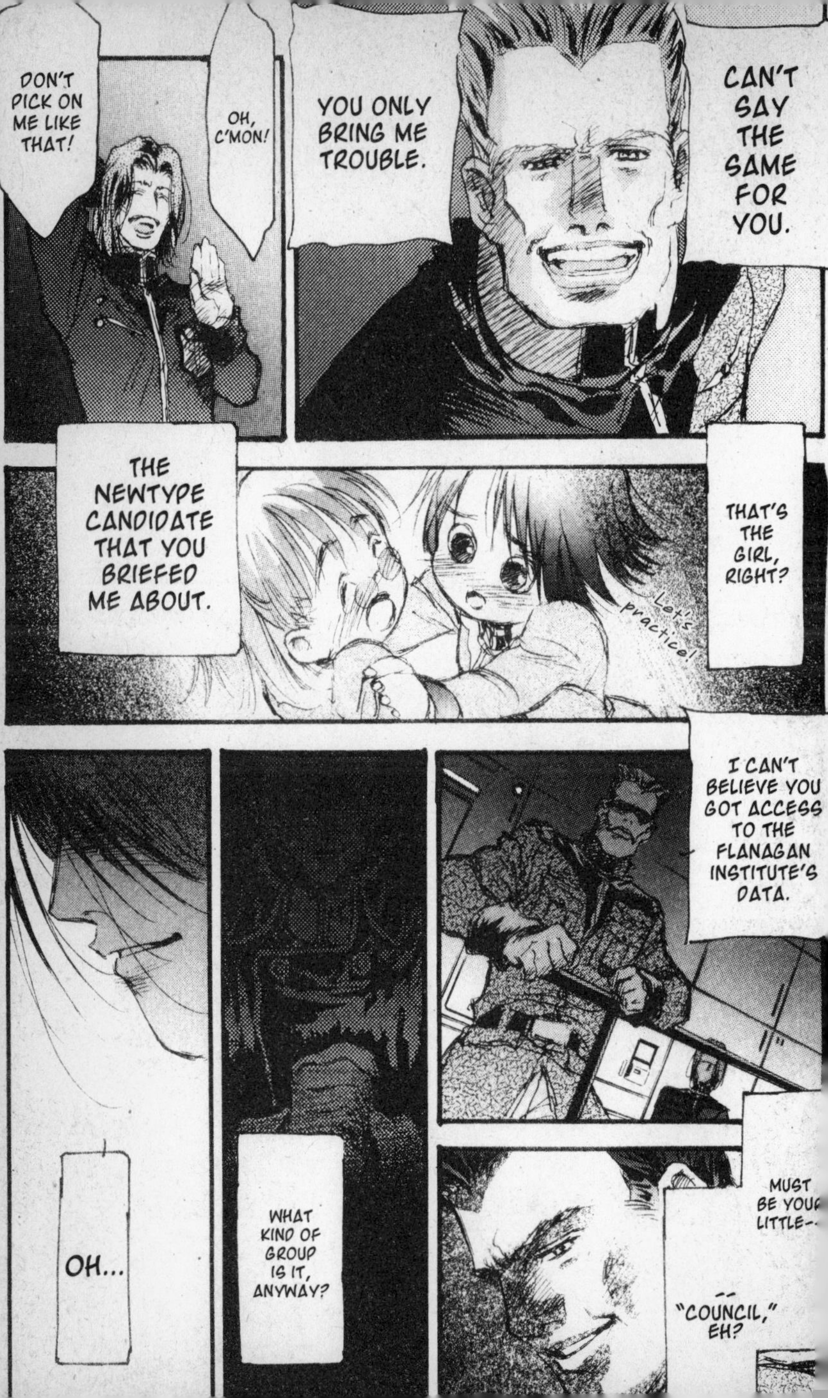
CAN'T SAY THE SAME FOR YOU.
YOU ONLY BRING ME TROUBLE.
OH, C'MON!
DON'T PICK ON ME LIKE THAT!
THAT'S THE GIRL, RIGHT?
Let's practice!
THE NEWTYPE CANDIDATE THAT YOU BRIEFED ME ABOUT.
I CAN'T BELIEVE YOU GOT ACCESS TO THE FLANAGAN INSTITUTE'S DATA.
MUST BE YOUR LITTLE--
--"COUNCIL," EH?
WHAT KIND OF GROUP IS IT, ANYWAY?
OH...

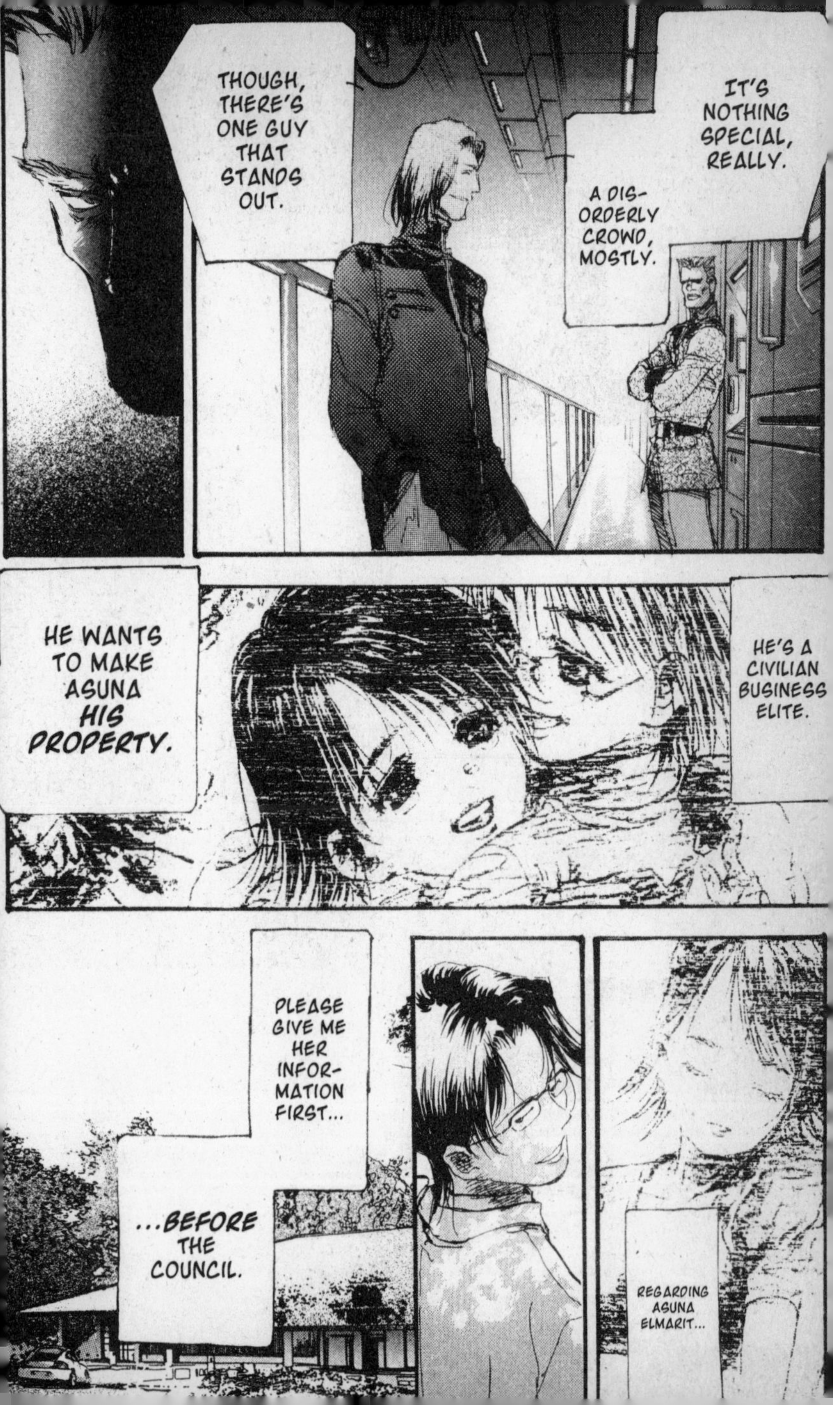
IT'S NOTHING SPECIAL, REALLY.
A DIS-ORDERLY CROWD, MOSTLY.
THOUGH, THERE'S ONE GUY THAT STANDS OUT.
HE'S A CIVILIAN BUSINESS ELITE.
HE WANTS TO MAKE ASUNA **HIS PROPERTY.**
REGARDING ASUNA ELMARIT...
PLEASE GIVE ME HER INFOR-MATION FIRST...
...**BEFORE** THE COUNCIL.

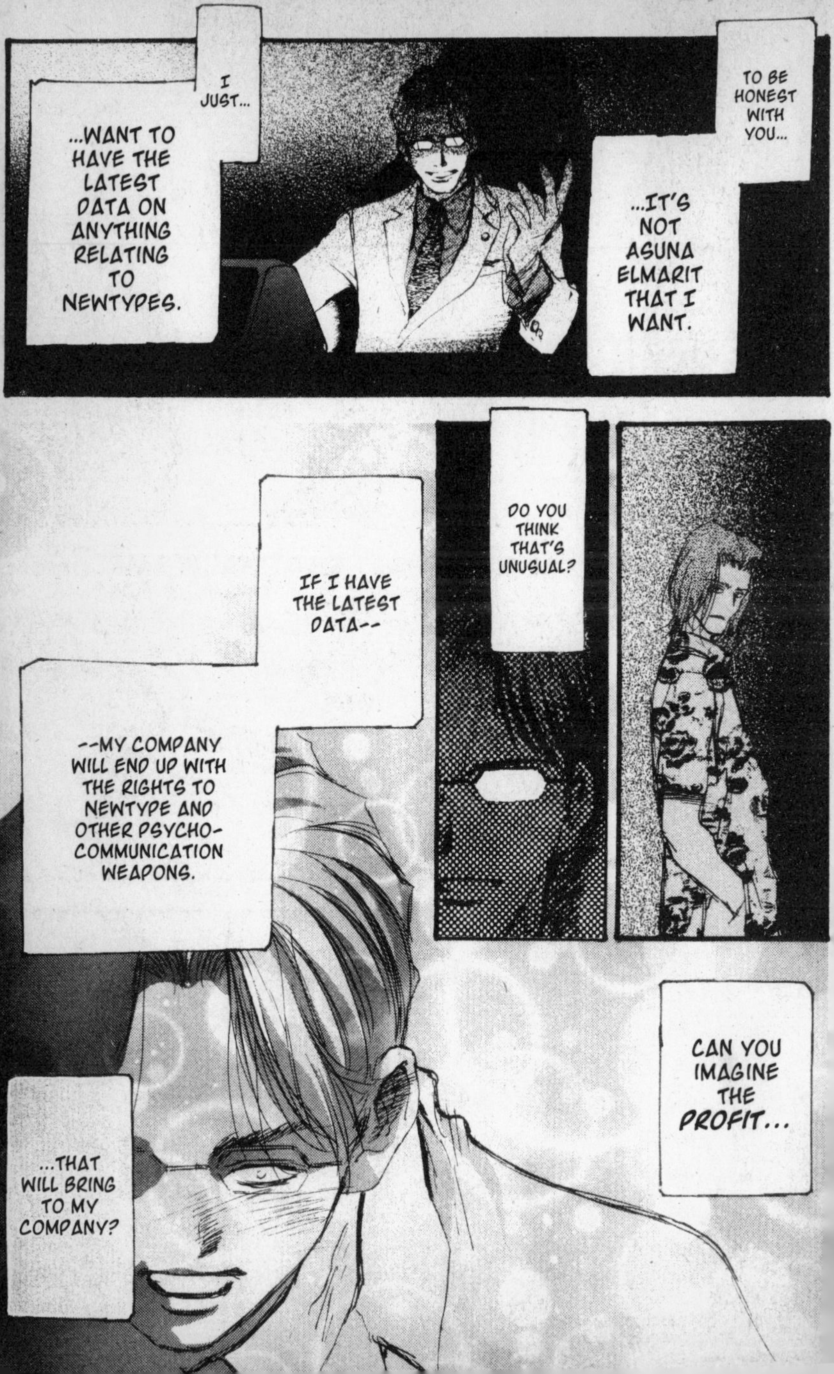
TO BE HONEST WITH YOU...
...IT'S NOT ASUNA ELMARIT THAT I WANT.
I JUST...
...WANT TO HAVE THE LATEST DATA ON ANYTHING RELATING TO NEWTYPES.
DO YOU THINK THAT'S UNUSUAL?
IF I HAVE THE LATEST DATA--
--MY COMPANY WILL END UP WITH THE RIGHTS TO NEWTYPE AND OTHER PSYCHO-COMMUNICATION WEAPONS.
CAN YOU IMAGINE THE *PROFIT*...
...THAT WILL BRING TO MY COMPANY?

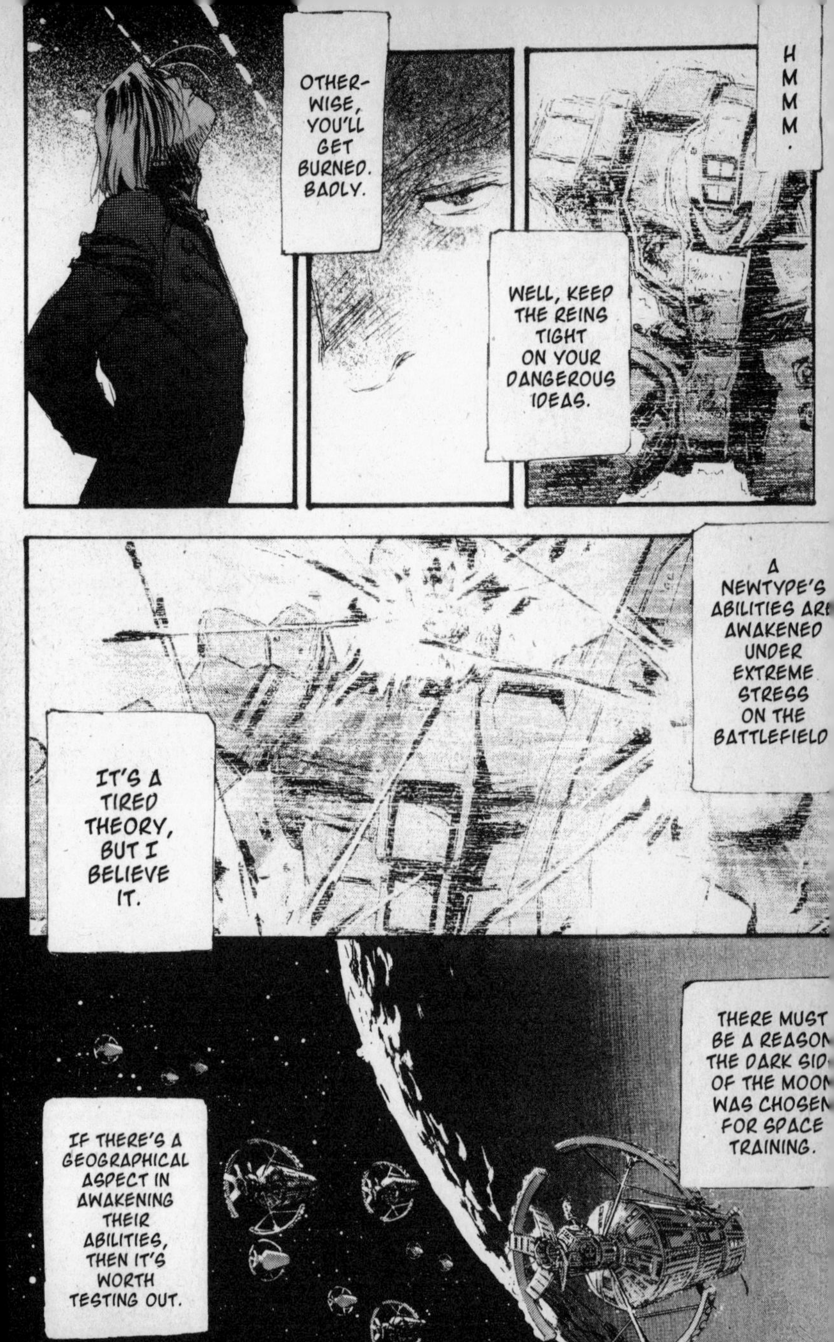
HMMM.
WELL, KEEP THE REINS TIGHT ON YOUR DANGEROUS IDEAS.
OTHER-WISE, YOU'LL GET BURNED. BADLY.
A NEWTYPE'S ABILITIES AR AWAKENED UNDER EXTREME STRESS ON THE BATTLEFIELD
IT'S A TIRED THEORY, BUT I BELIEVE IT.
THERE MUST BE A REASO THE DARK SID OF THE MOO WAS CHOSE FOR SPACE TRAINING.
IF THERE'S A GEOGRAPHICAL ASPECT IN AWAKENING THEIR ABILITIES, THEN IT'S WORTH TESTING OUT.

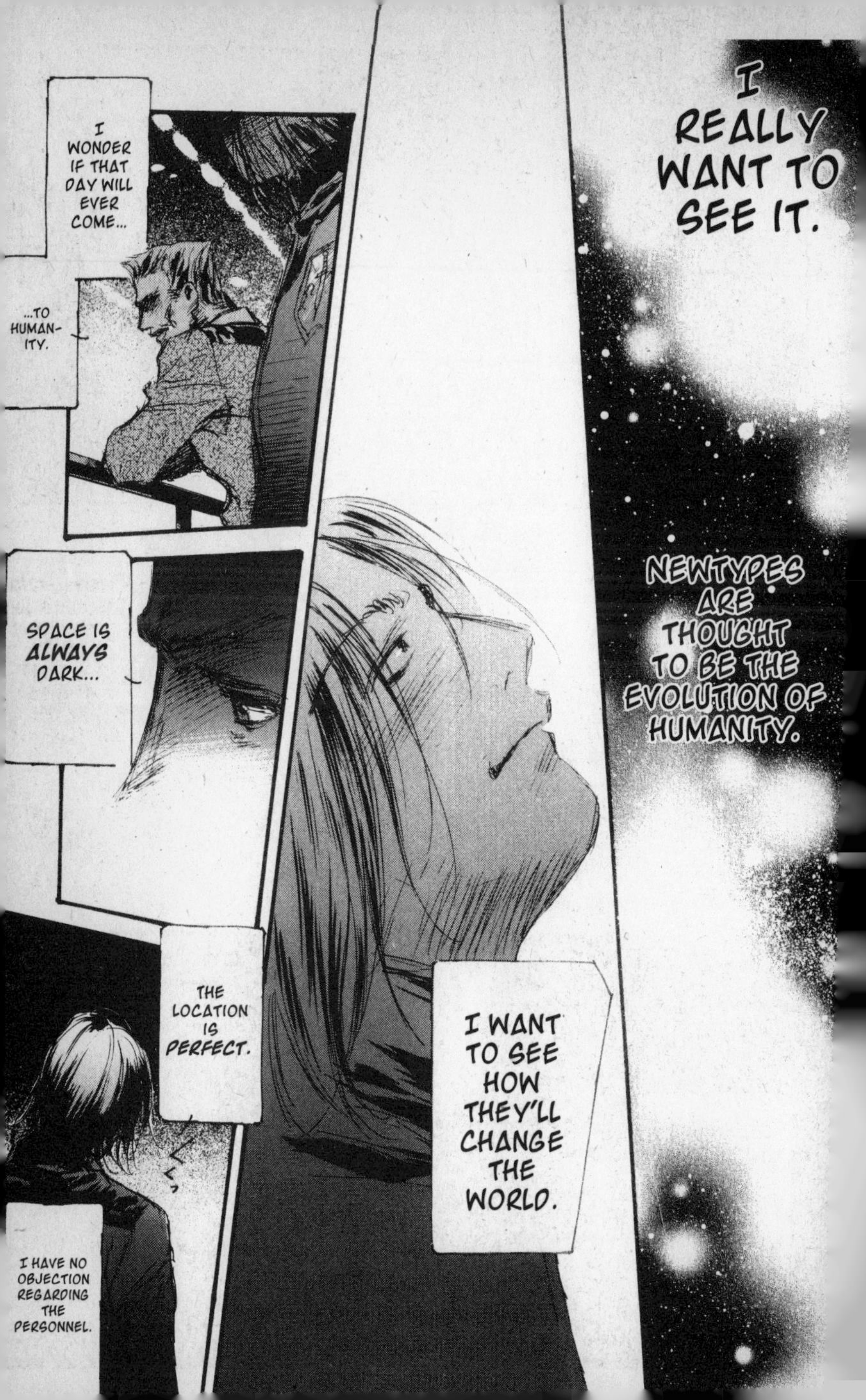
I REALLY WANT TO SEE IT.
NEWTYPES ARE THOUGHT TO BE THE EVOLUTION OF HUMANITY.
I WANT TO SEE HOW THEY'LL CHANGE THE WORLD.
I WONDER IF THAT DAY WILL EVER COME...
...TO HUMAN-ITY.
SPACE IS ALWAYS DARK...
THE LOCATION IS PERFECT.
I HAVE NO OBJECTION REGARDING THE PERSONNEL.

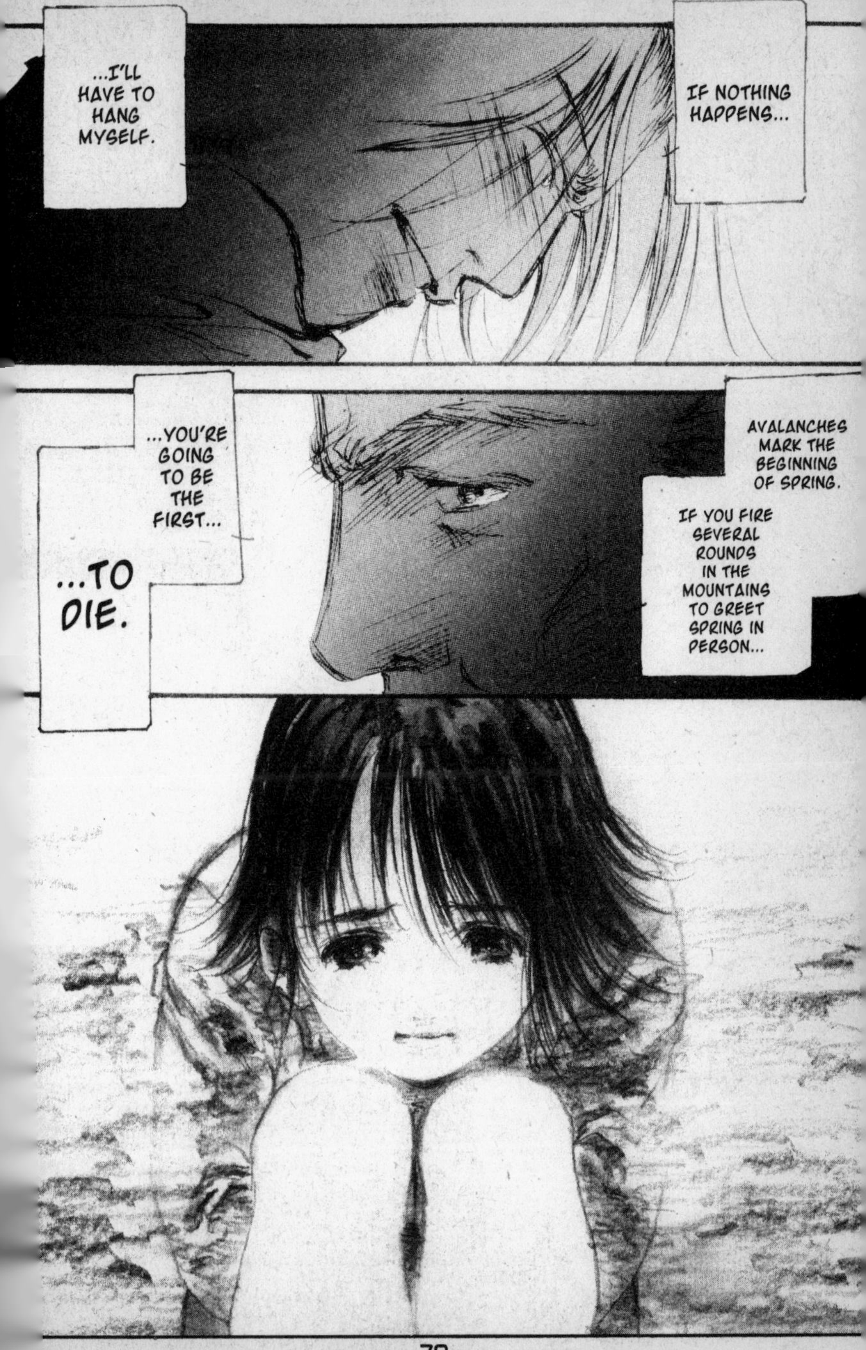
IF NOTHING HAPPENS...
...I'LL HAVE TO HANG MYSELF.
AVALANCHES MARK THE BEGINNING OF SPRING.
IF YOU FIRE SEVERAL ROUNDS IN THE MOUNTAINS TO GREET SPRING IN PERSON...
...YOU'RE GOING TO BE THE FIRST...
...TO DIE.

CHARACTER FILE:03

Emilu Voigtlander

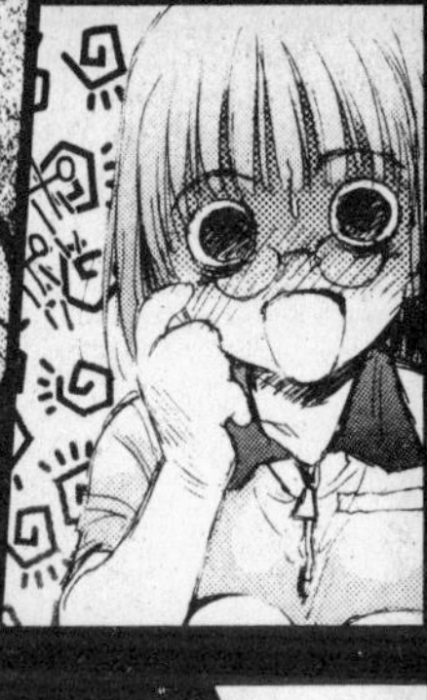

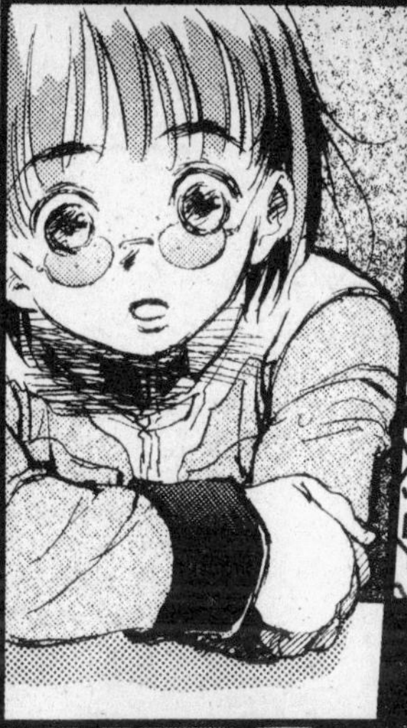

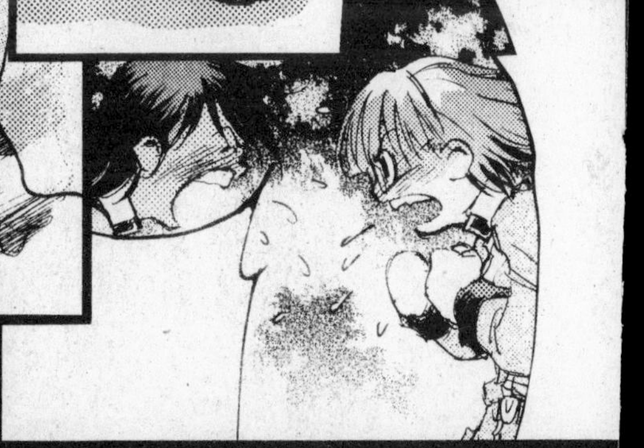

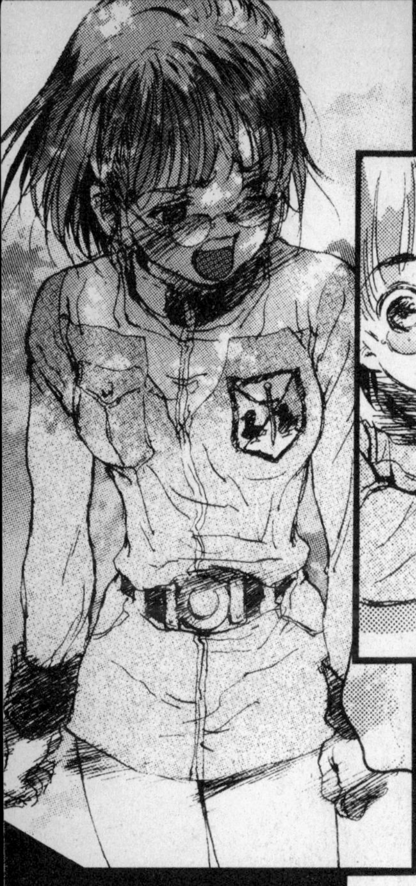

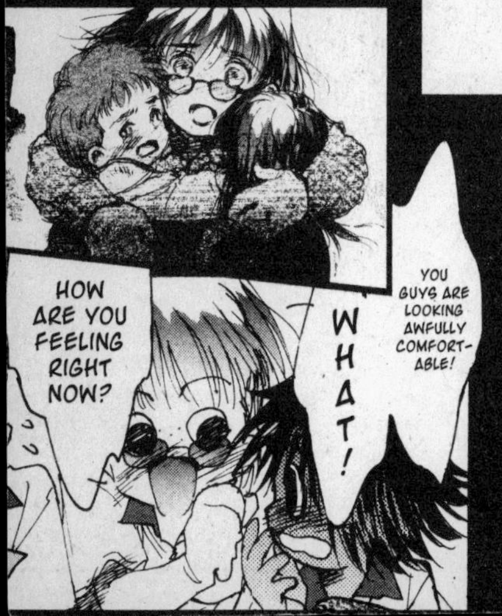
YOU GUYS ARE LOOKING AWFULLY COMFORT-ABLE!
WHAT!
HOW ARE YOU FEELING RIGHT NOW?

EMILU VOIGHTLANDER

AT FIRST, SHE DISLIKED ASUNA DUE TO ASUNA'S ZEON BACKGROUND. HOWEVER, THEY HAVE BECOME BEST FRIENDS. THEY LIVE IN THE SAME DORM, AND SHE'S ASUNA'S ROOMMATE.

SHE TRIES TO HELP OUT ASUNA BY TRAINING WITH HER IN THE MORNING. SHE ALSO TRIES TO GENTLY PUSH ASUNA TO PURSUE HER FIRST LOVE, SHINN. EMILUE IS A SWEETHEART WITH MATERNAL QUALITIES.

WHILE SHE SEEMS LIKE A HAPPY-GO-LUCKY GIRL, SHE LOST HER PARENTS IN THE ONE YEAR WAR. SHE ENTERED ÉCOLE DU CIEL IN THE HOPES THAT SHE WOULD BE ABLE TO TAKE CARE OF HER YOUNGER SIBLINGS.

SHE LOOKS YOUNG, BUT SHE IS OLDER THAN ASUNA.

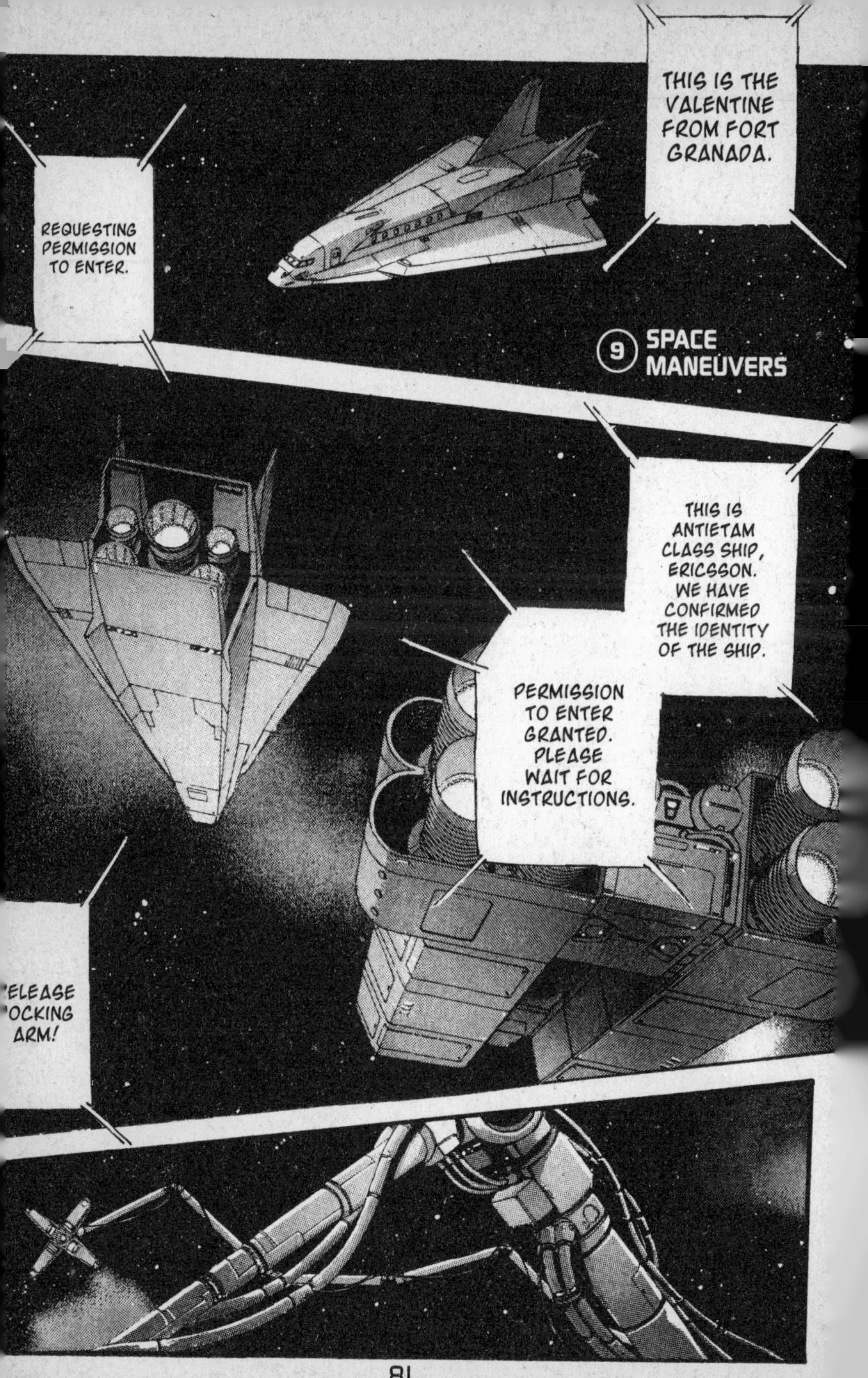
THIS IS THE VALENTINE FROM FORT GRANADA.
REQUESTING PERMISSION TO ENTER.
9 SPACE MANEUVERS
THIS IS ANTIETAM CLASS SHIP, ERICSSON. WE HAVE CONFIRMED THE IDENTITY OF THE SHIP.
PERMISSION TO ENTER GRANTED. PLEASE WAIT FOR INSTRUCTIONS.
ELEASE OCKING ARM!

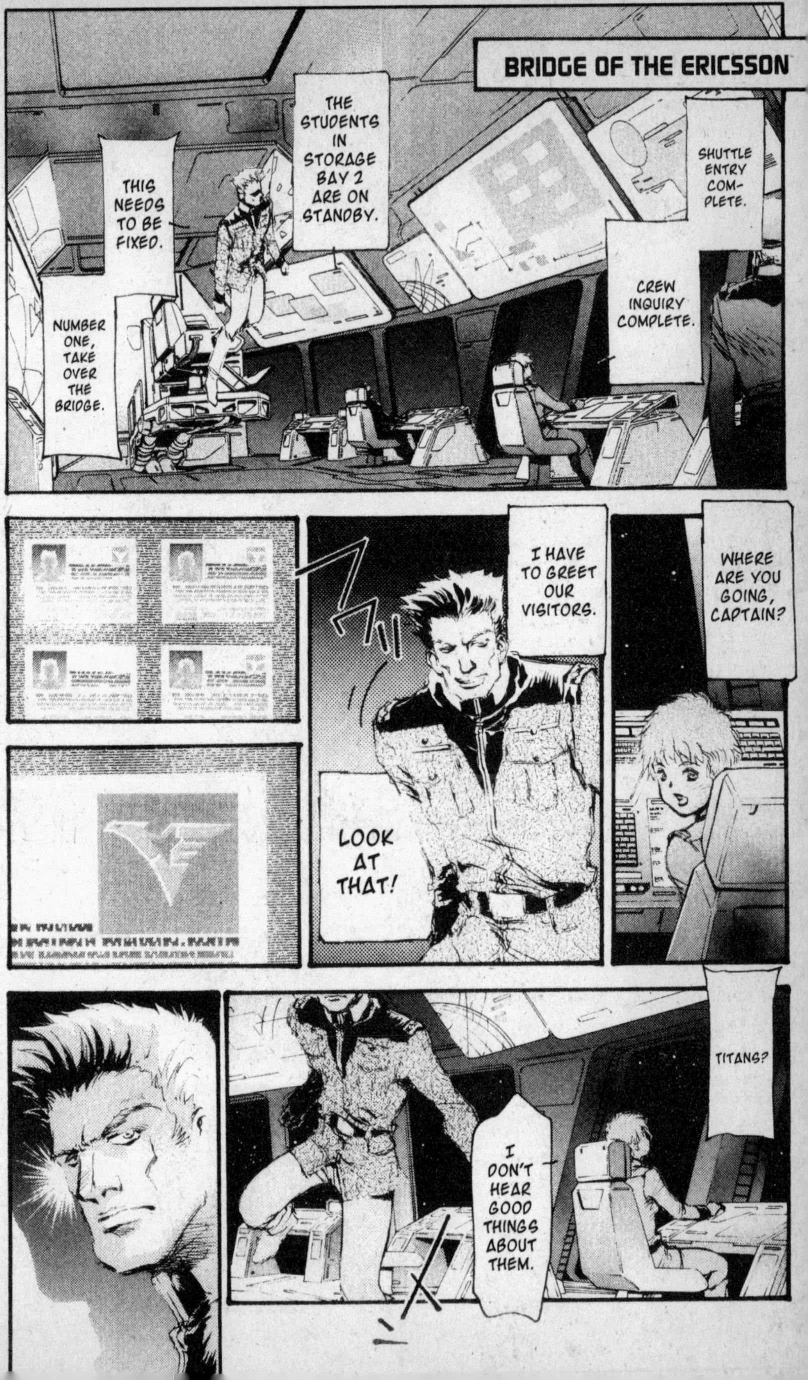
BRIDGE OF THE ERICSSON
SHUTTLE ENTRY COMPLETE.
CREW INQUIRY COMPLETE.
THE STUDENTS IN STORAGE BAY 2 ARE ON STANDBY.
THIS NEEDS TO BE FIXED.
NUMBER ONE, TAKE OVER THE BRIDGE.
WHERE ARE YOU GOING, CAPTAIN?
I HAVE TO GREET OUR VISITORS.
LOOK AT THAT!
TITANS?
I DON'T HEAR GOOD THINGS ABOUT THEM.

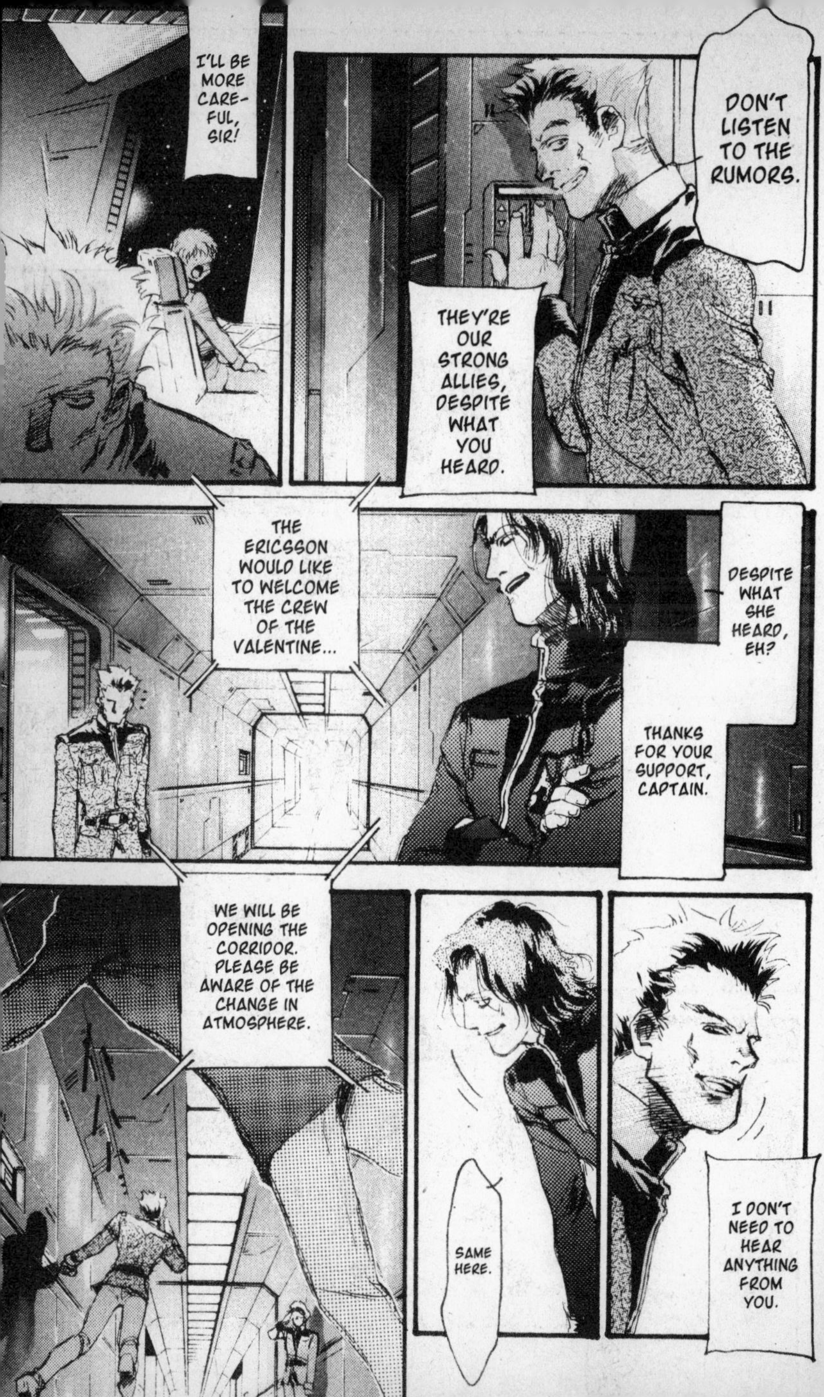
DON'T LISTEN TO THE RUMORS.
THEY'RE OUR STRONG ALLIES, DESPITE WHAT YOU HEARD.
I'LL BE MORE CARE-FUL, SIR!
DESPITE WHAT SHE HEARD, EH?
THANKS FOR YOUR SUPPORT, CAPTAIN.
THE ERICSSON WOULD LIKE TO WELCOME THE CREW OF THE VALENTINE...
I DON'T NEED TO HEAR ANYTHING FROM YOU.
SAME HERE.
WE WILL BE OPENING THE CORRIDOR. PLEASE BE AWARE OF THE CHANGE IN ATMOSPHERE.

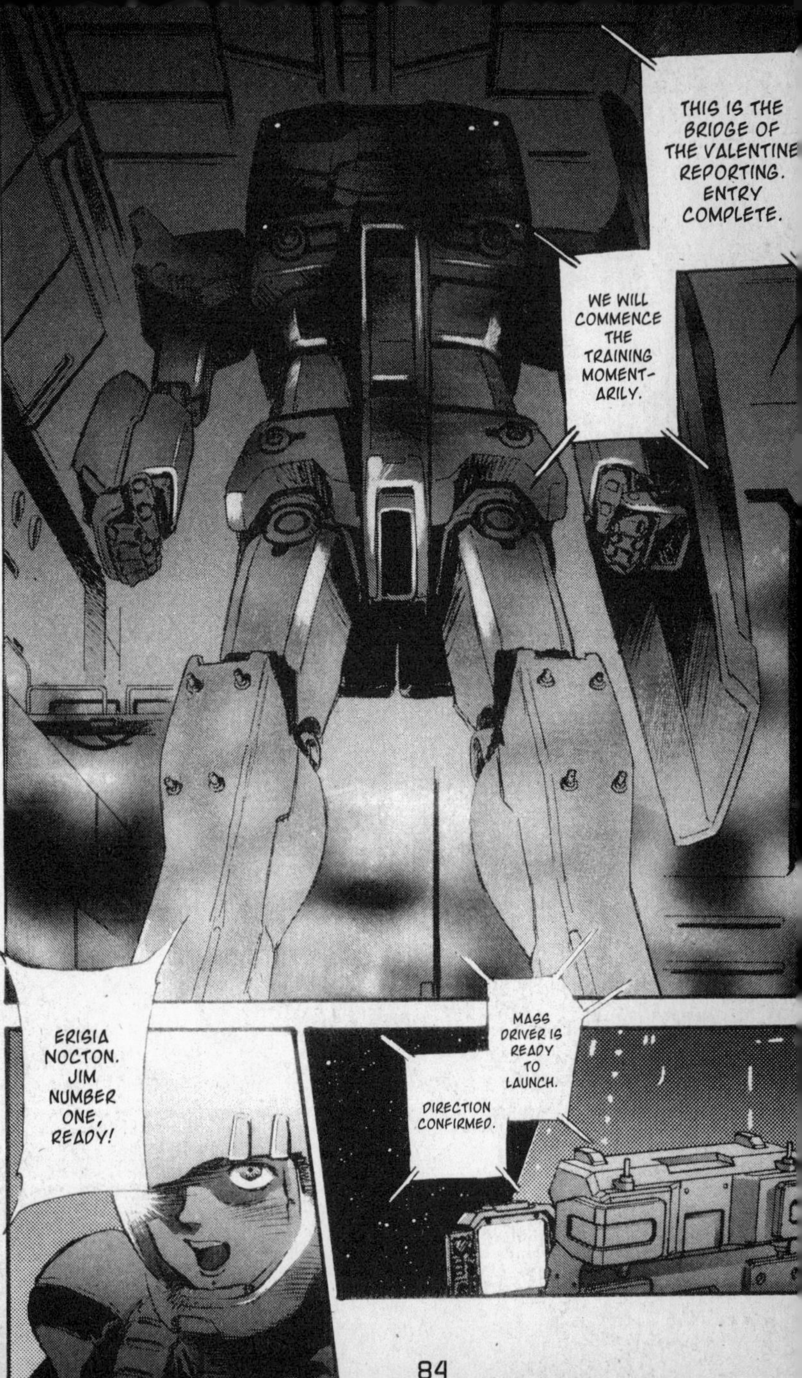
THIS IS THE BRIDGE OF THE VALENTINE REPORTING. ENTRY COMPLETE.
WE WILL COMMENCE THE TRAINING MOMENT-ARILY.
MASS DRIVER IS READY TO LAUNCH.
DIRECTION CONFIRMED.
ERISIA NOCTON. JIM NUMBER ONE, READY!

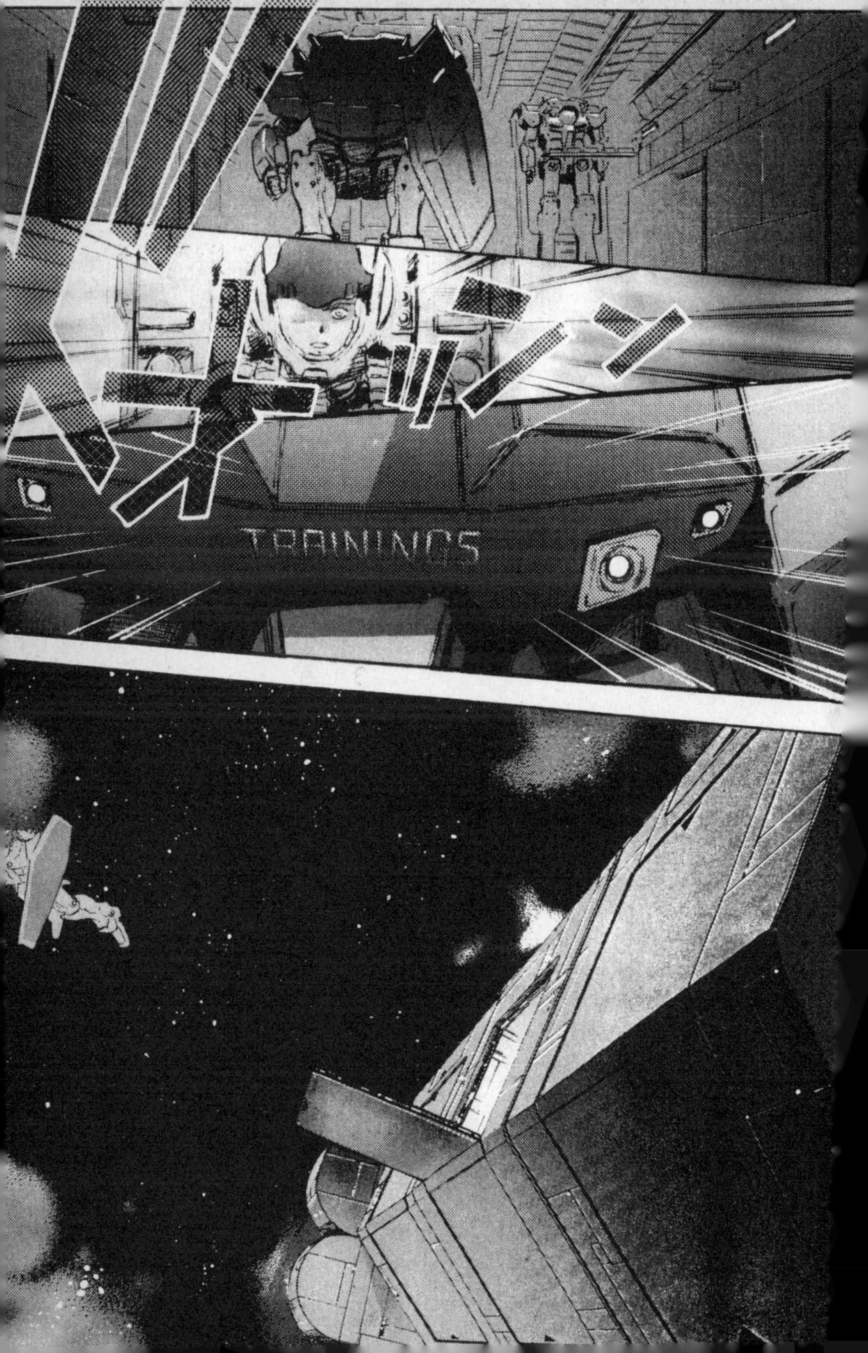
TRAININGS

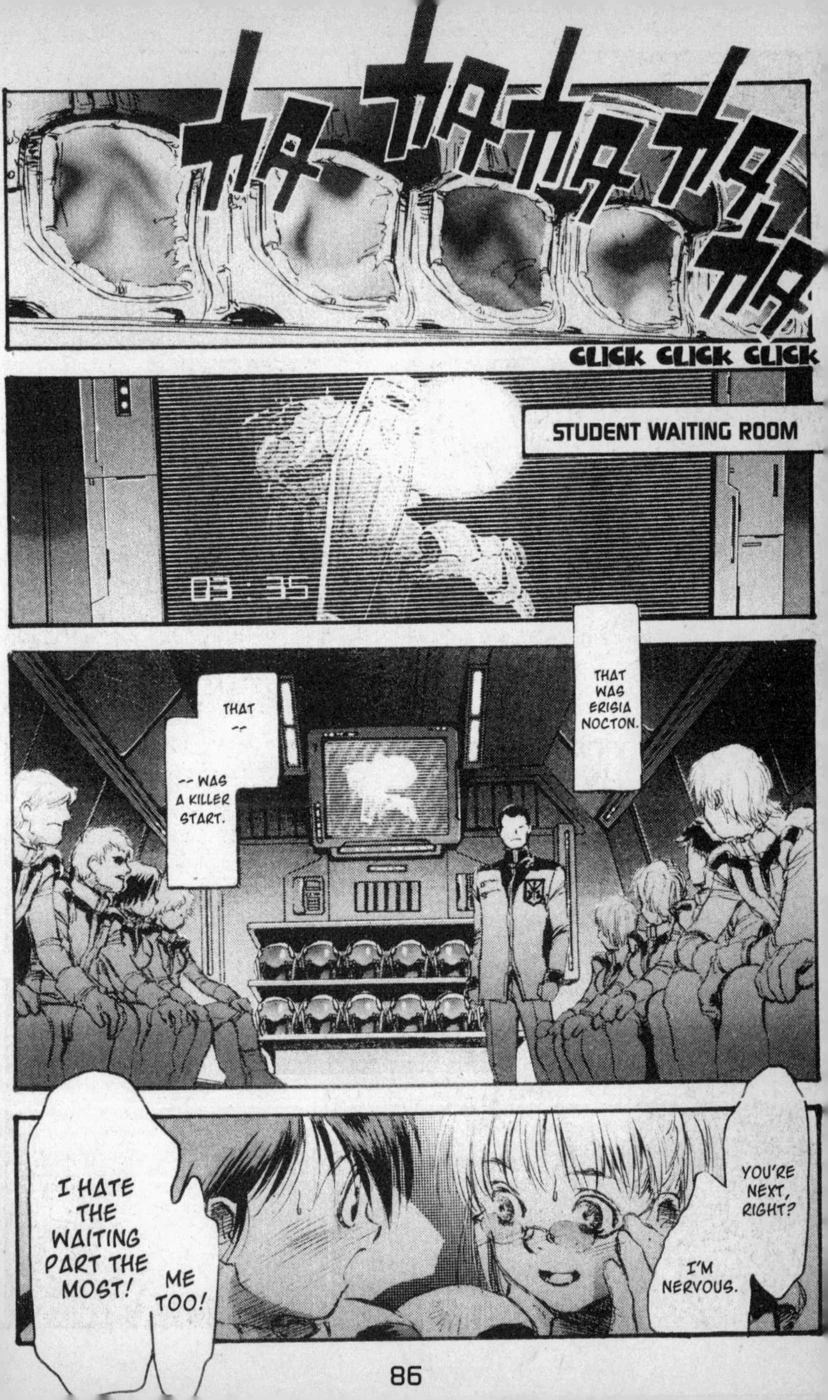
カタカタカタカタカタ
CLICK CLICK CLICK
STUDENT WAITING ROOM
03:35
THAT WAS ERISIA NOCTON.
THAT --
-- WAS A KILLER START.
YOU'RE NEXT, RIGHT?
I'M NERVOUS.
I HATE THE WAITING PART THE MOST!
ME TOO!

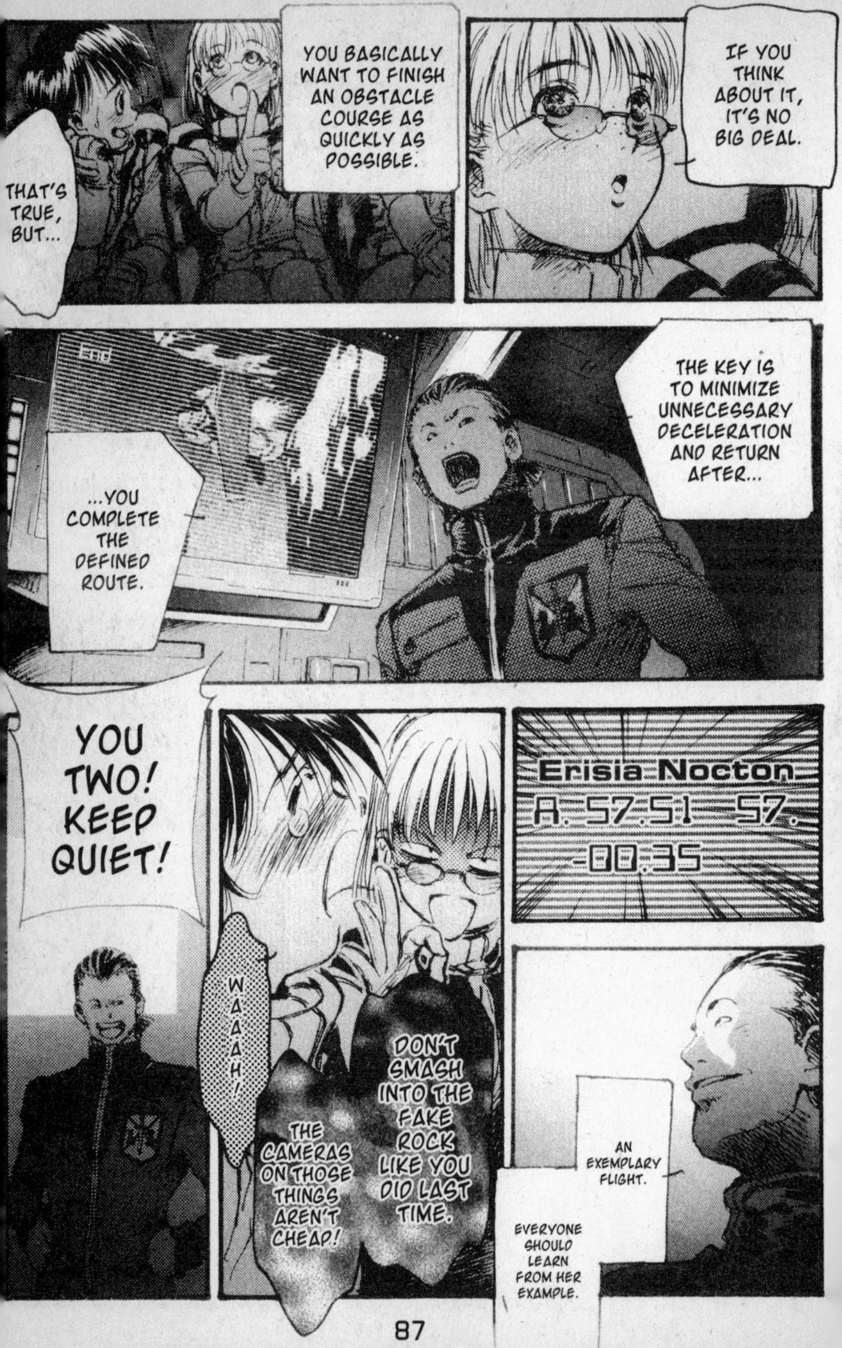
IF YOU THINK ABOUT IT, IT'S NO BIG DEAL.
YOU BASICALLY WANT TO FINISH AN OBSTACLE COURSE AS QUICKLY AS POSSIBLE.
THAT'S TRUE, BUT...
THE KEY IS TO MINIMIZE UNNECESSARY DECELERATION AND RETURN AFTER...
...YOU COMPLETE THE DEFINED ROUTE.
Erisia Nocton
A. 57.51 57.
-00.35
AN EXEMPLARY FLIGHT.
EVERYONE SHOULD LEARN FROM HER EXAMPLE.
WAAAAH!
DON'T SMASH INTO THE FAKE ROCK LIKE YOU DID LAST TIME.
THE CAMERAS ON THOSE THINGS AREN'T CHEAP!
YOU TWO! KEEP QUIET!

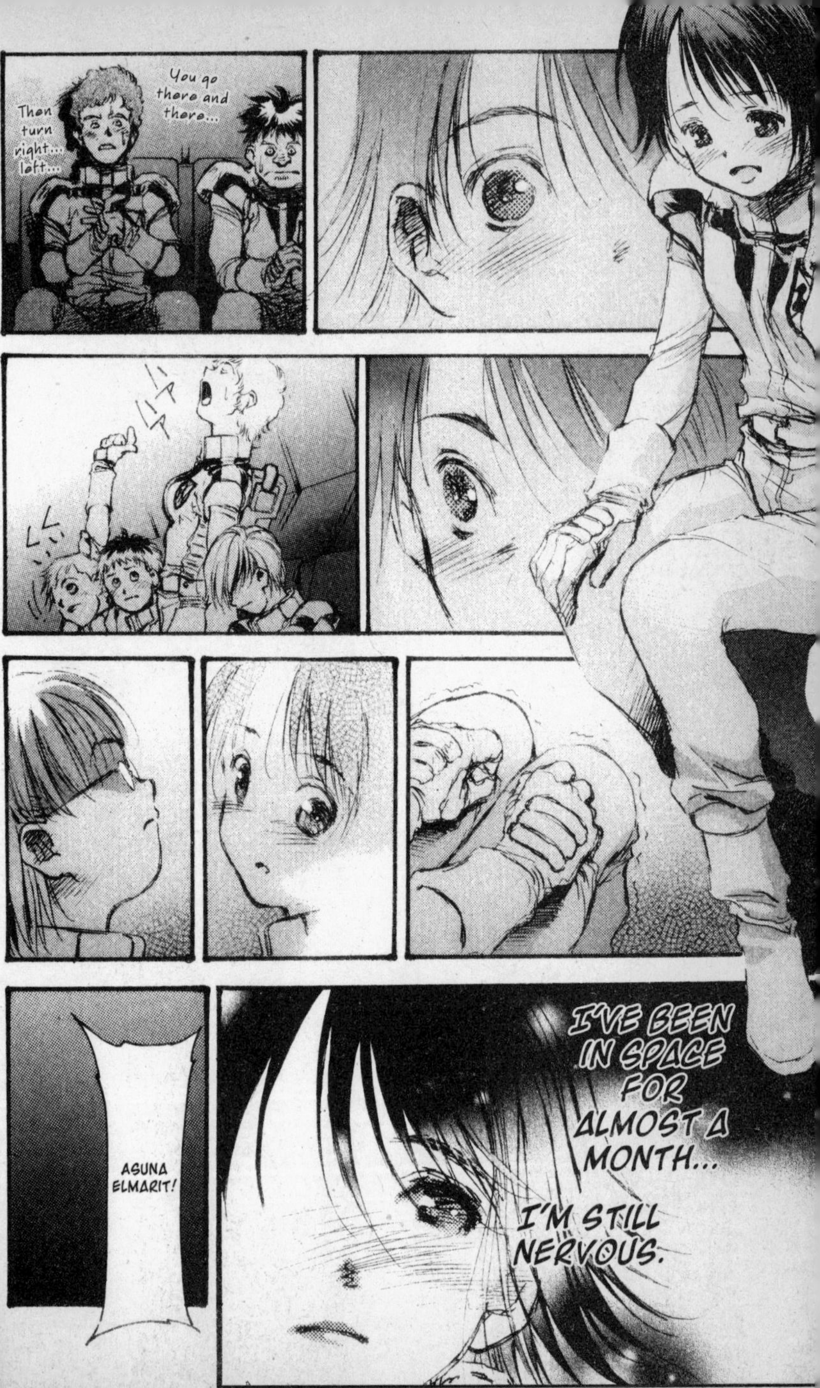
You go there and there...
Then turn right... left...
I'VE BEEN IN SPACE FOR ALMOST A MONTH...
I'M STILL NERVOUS.
ASUNA ELMARIT!

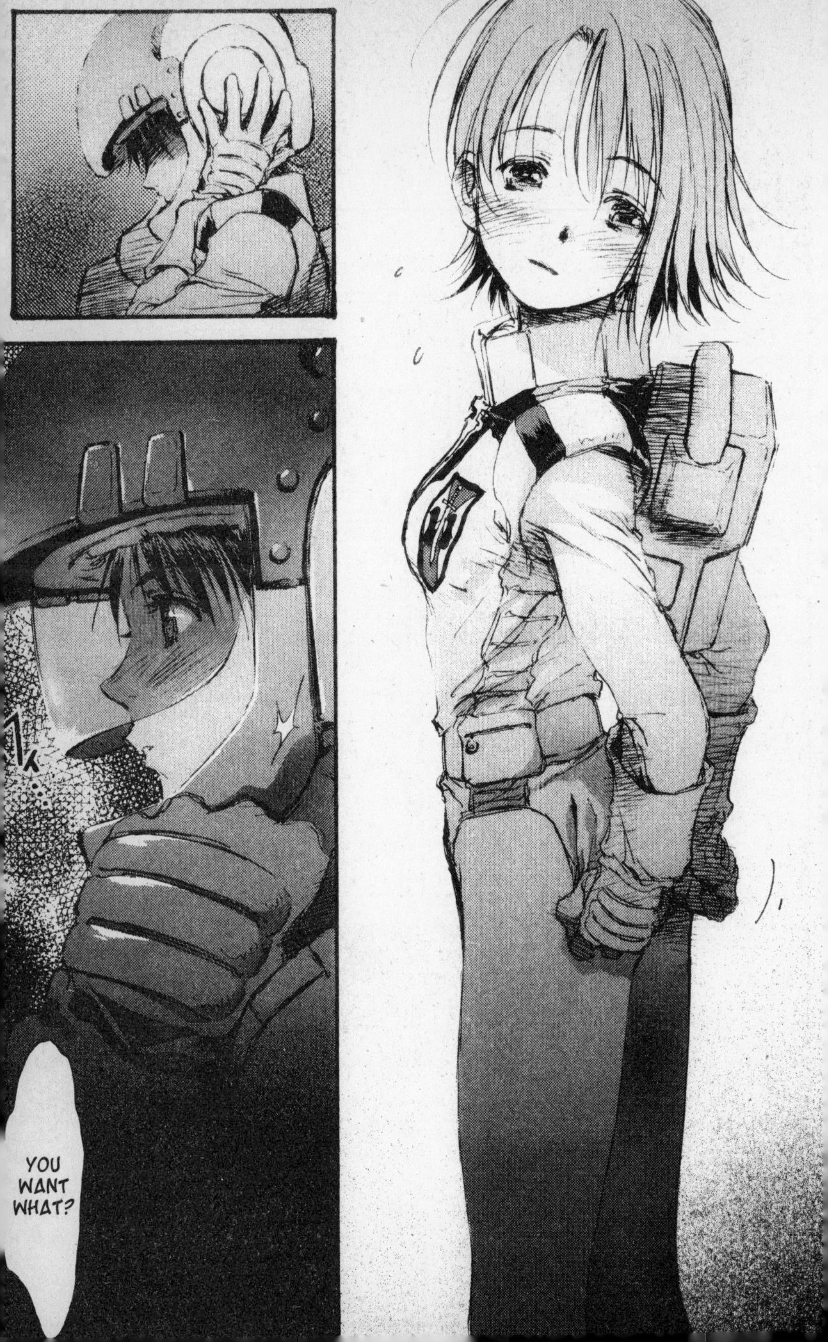
YOU WANT WHAT?

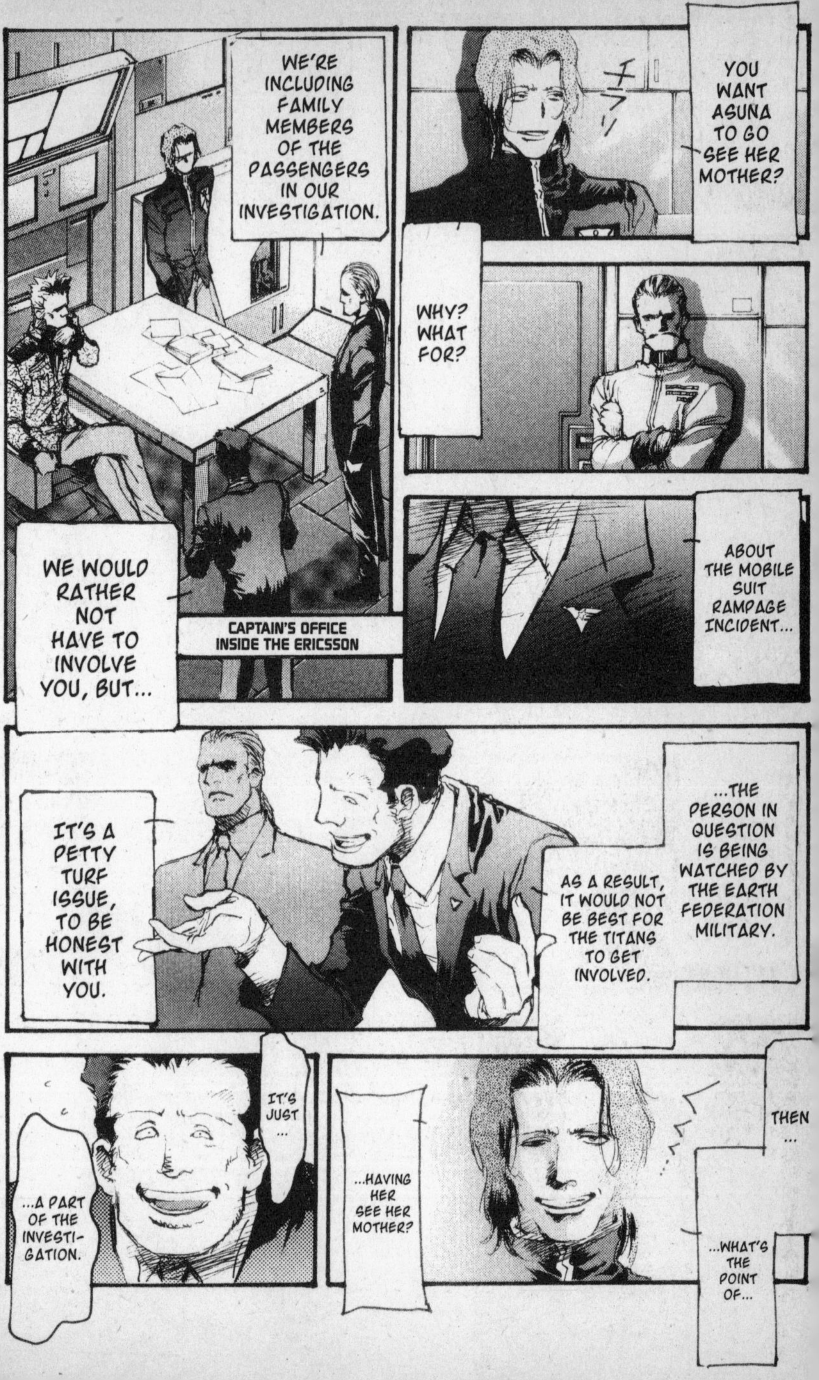
YOU WANT ASUNA TO GO SEE HER MOTHER?
WHY? WHAT FOR?
ABOUT THE MOBILE SUIT RAMPAGE INCIDENT...
WE'RE INCLUDING FAMILY MEMBERS OF THE PASSENGERS IN OUR INVESTIGATION.
WE WOULD RATHER NOT HAVE TO INVOLVE YOU, BUT...
CAPTAIN'S OFFICE INSIDE THE ERICSSON
...THE PERSON IN QUESTION IS BEING WATCHED BY THE EARTH FEDERATION MILITARY.
AS A RESULT, IT WOULD NOT BE BEST FOR THE TITANS TO GET INVOLVED.
IT'S A PETTY TURF ISSUE, TO BE HONEST WITH YOU.
THEN ...
...WHAT'S THE POINT OF...
...HAVING HER SEE HER MOTHER?
IT'S JUST ...
...A PART OF THE INVESTI-GATION.

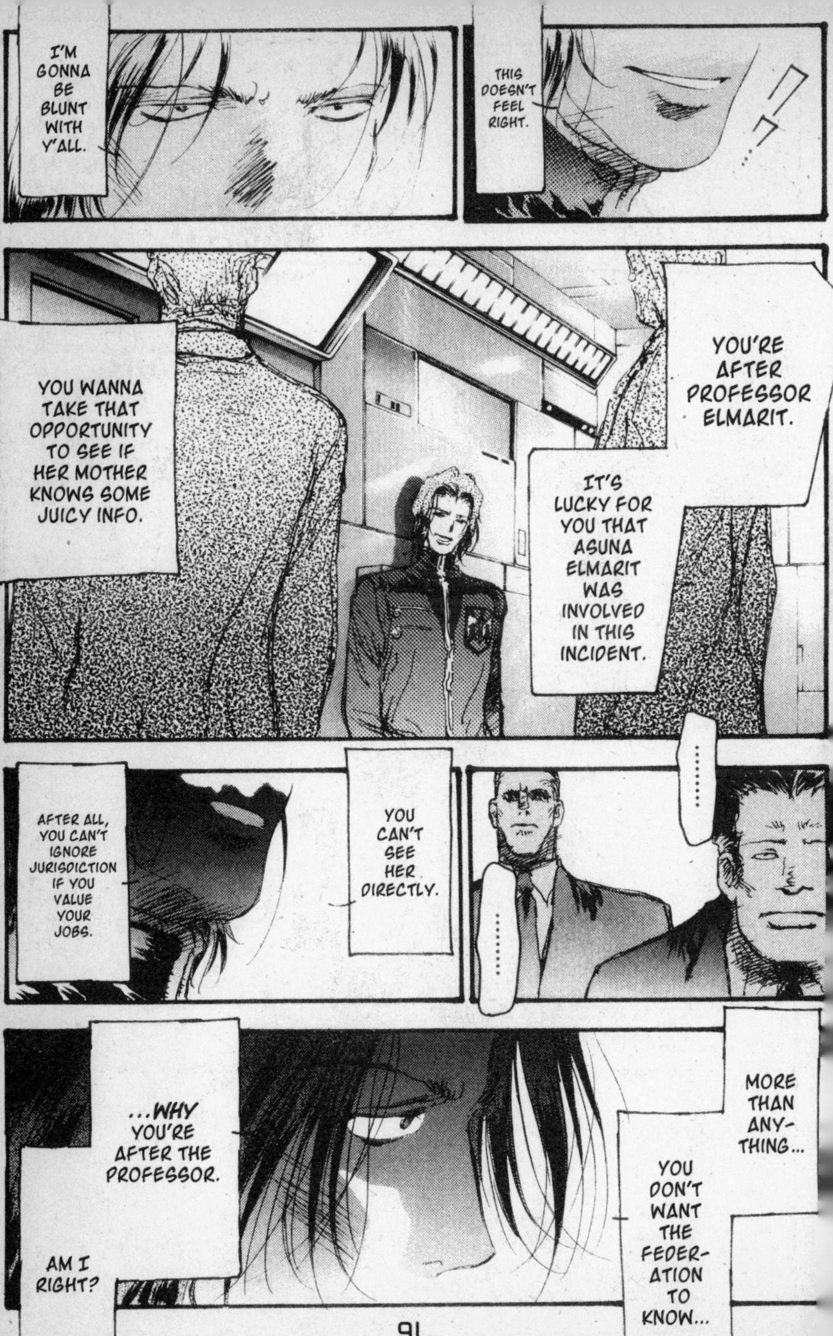
THIS DOESN'T FEEL RIGHT.
I'M GONNA BE BLUNT WITH Y'ALL.
YOU'RE AFTER PROFESSOR ELMARIT.
IT'S LUCKY FOR YOU THAT ASUNA ELMARIT WAS INVOLVED IN THIS INCIDENT.
YOU WANNA TAKE THAT OPPORTUNITY TO SEE IF HER MOTHER KNOWS SOME JUICY INFO.
......
......
YOU CAN'T SEE HER DIRECTLY.
AFTER ALL, YOU CAN'T IGNORE JURISDICTION IF YOU VALUE YOUR JOBS.
MORE THAN ANYTHING...
YOU DON'T WANT THE FEDERATION TO KNOW...
...WHY YOU'RE AFTER THE PROFESSOR.
AM I RIGHT?

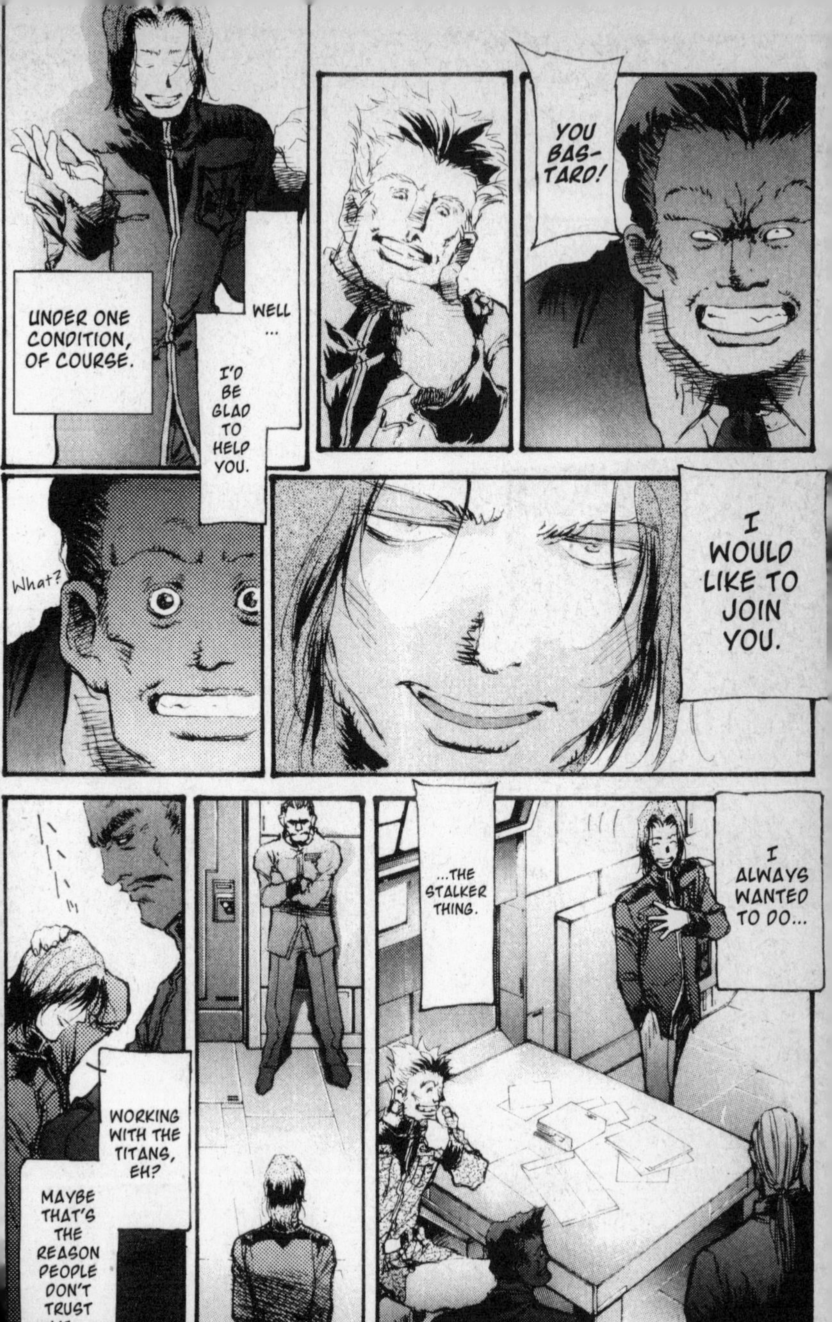
YOU BAS-TARD!
WELL ... I'D BE GLAD TO HELP YOU.
UNDER ONE CONDITION, OF COURSE.
I WOULD LIKE TO JOIN YOU.
What?
I ALWAYS WANTED TO DO...
...THE STALKER THING.
WORKING WITH THE TITANS, EH?
MAYBE THAT'S THE REASON PEOPLE DON'T TRUST ME...

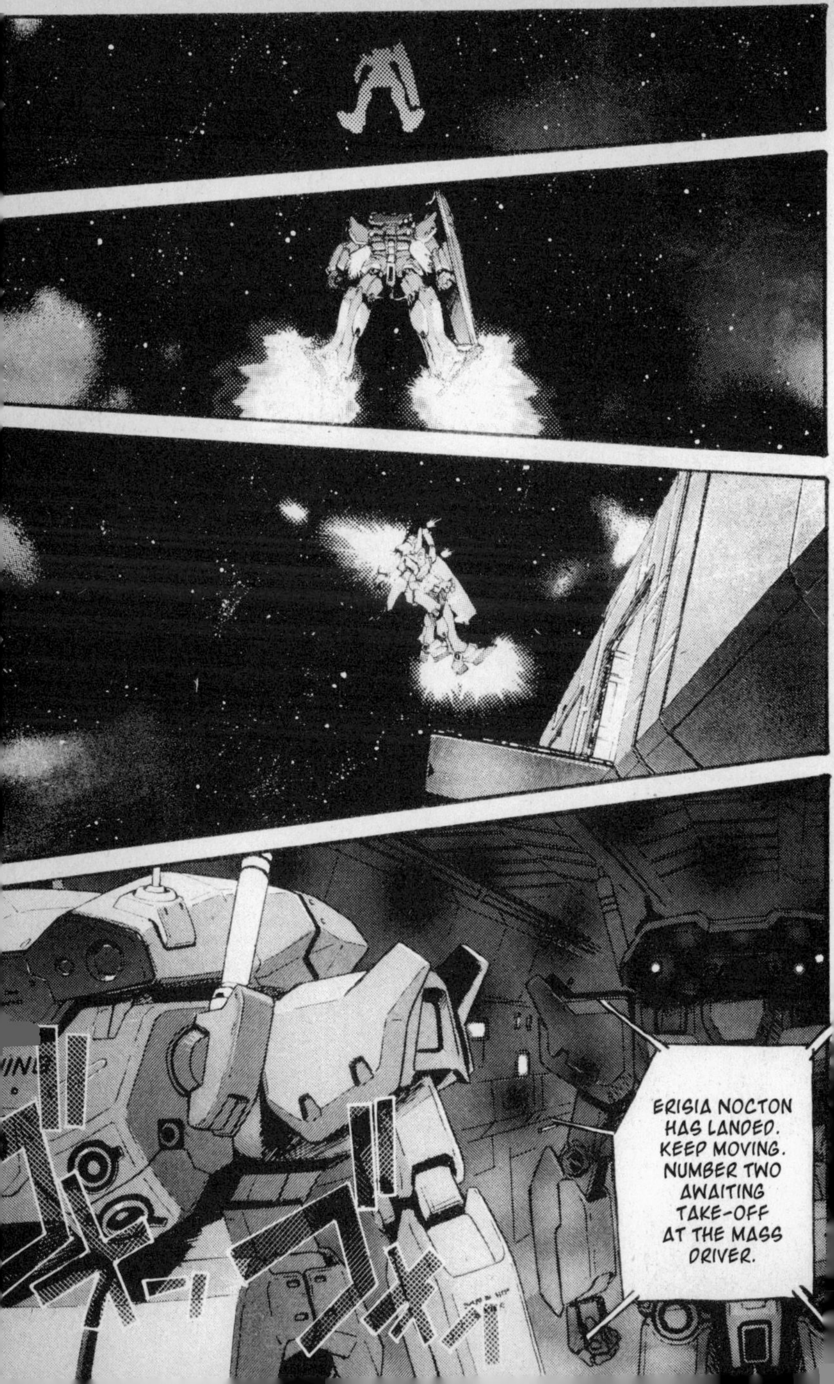
ERISIA NOCTON HAS LANDED. KEEP MOVING. NUMBER TWO AWAITING TAKE-OFF AT THE MASS DRIVER.

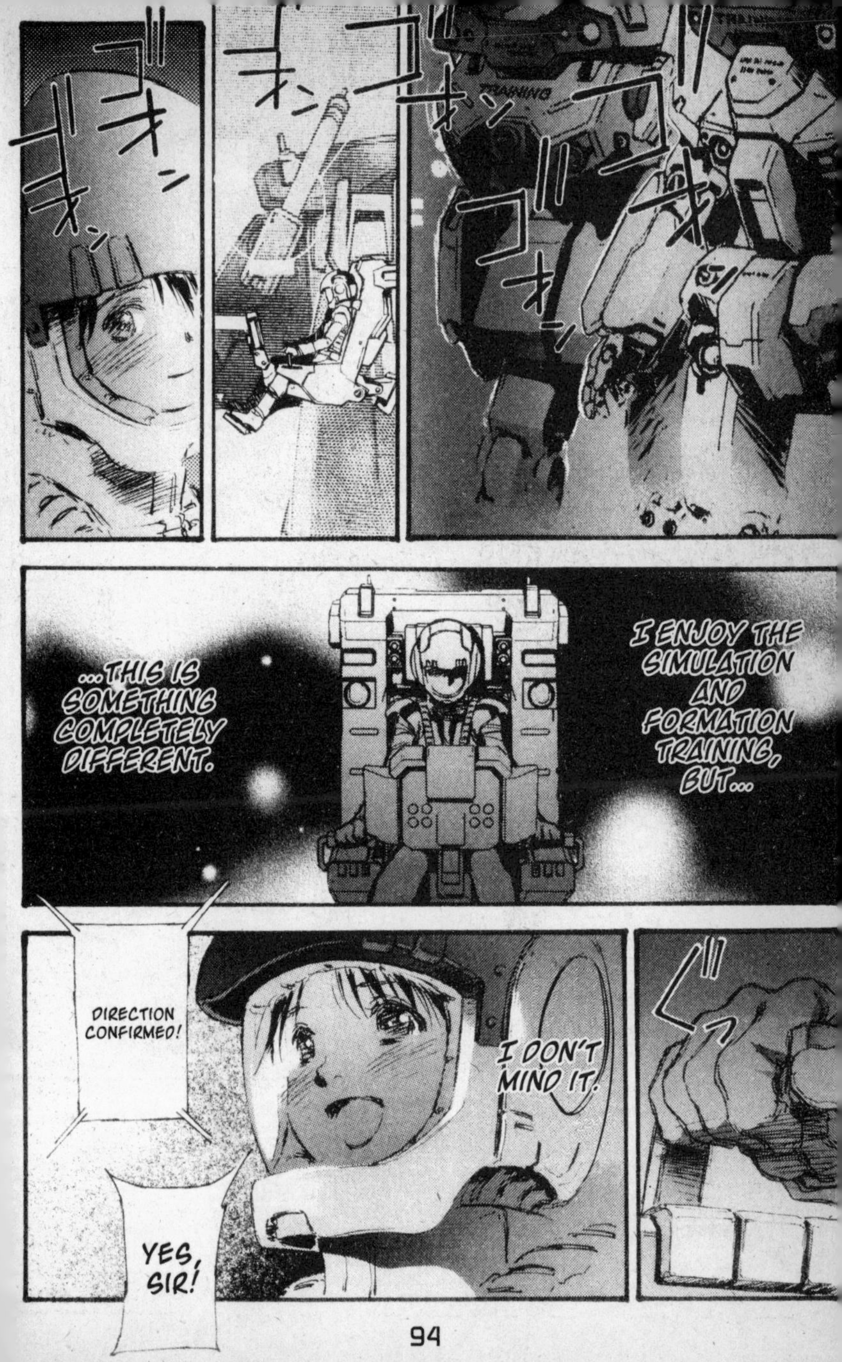
TRAINING
I ENJOY THE SIMULATION AND FORMATION TRAINING, BUT...
...THIS IS SOMETHING COMPLETELY DIFFERENT.
I DON'T MIND IT.
DIRECTION CONFIRMED!
YES, SIR!

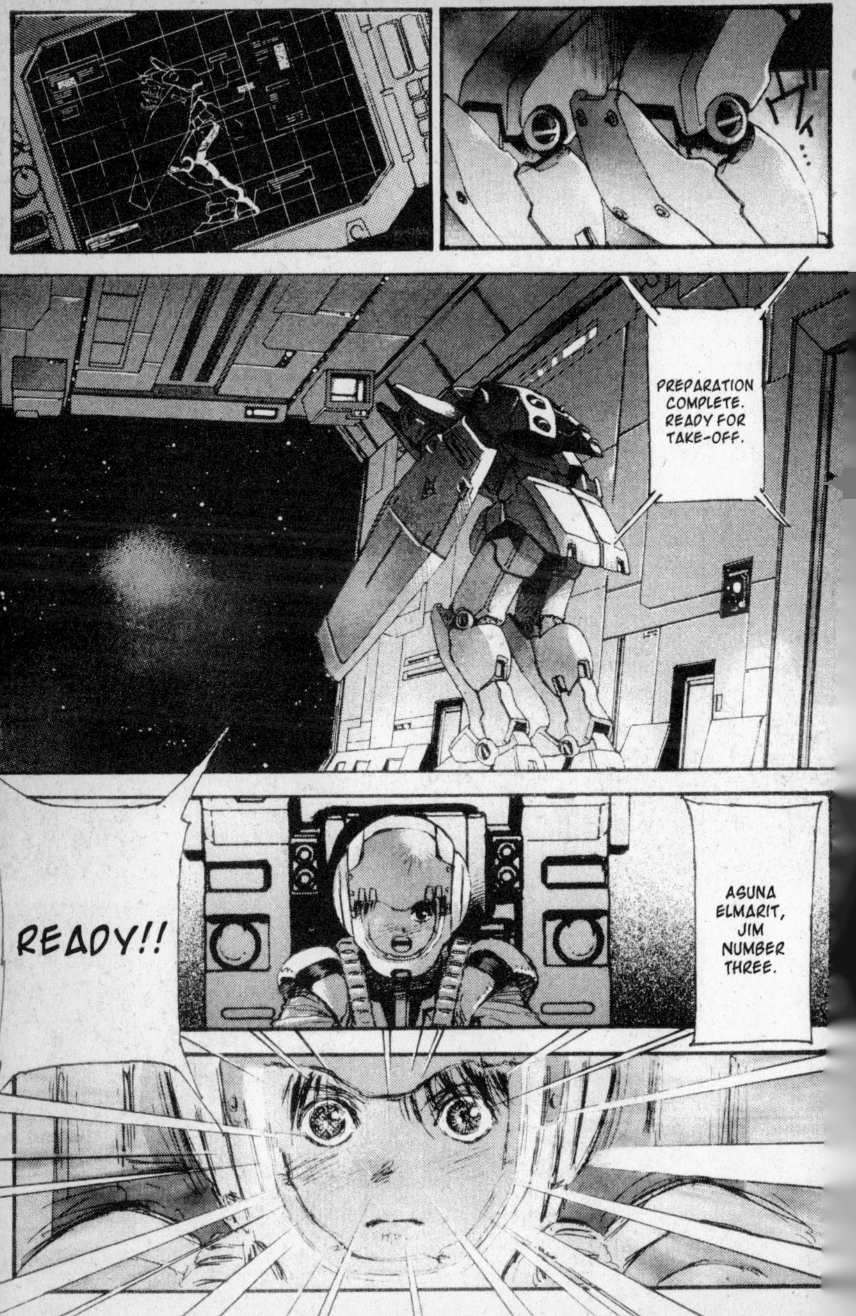
PREPARATION COMPLETE. READY FOR TAKE-OFF.
ASUNA ELMARIT, JIM NUMBER THREE.
READY!!

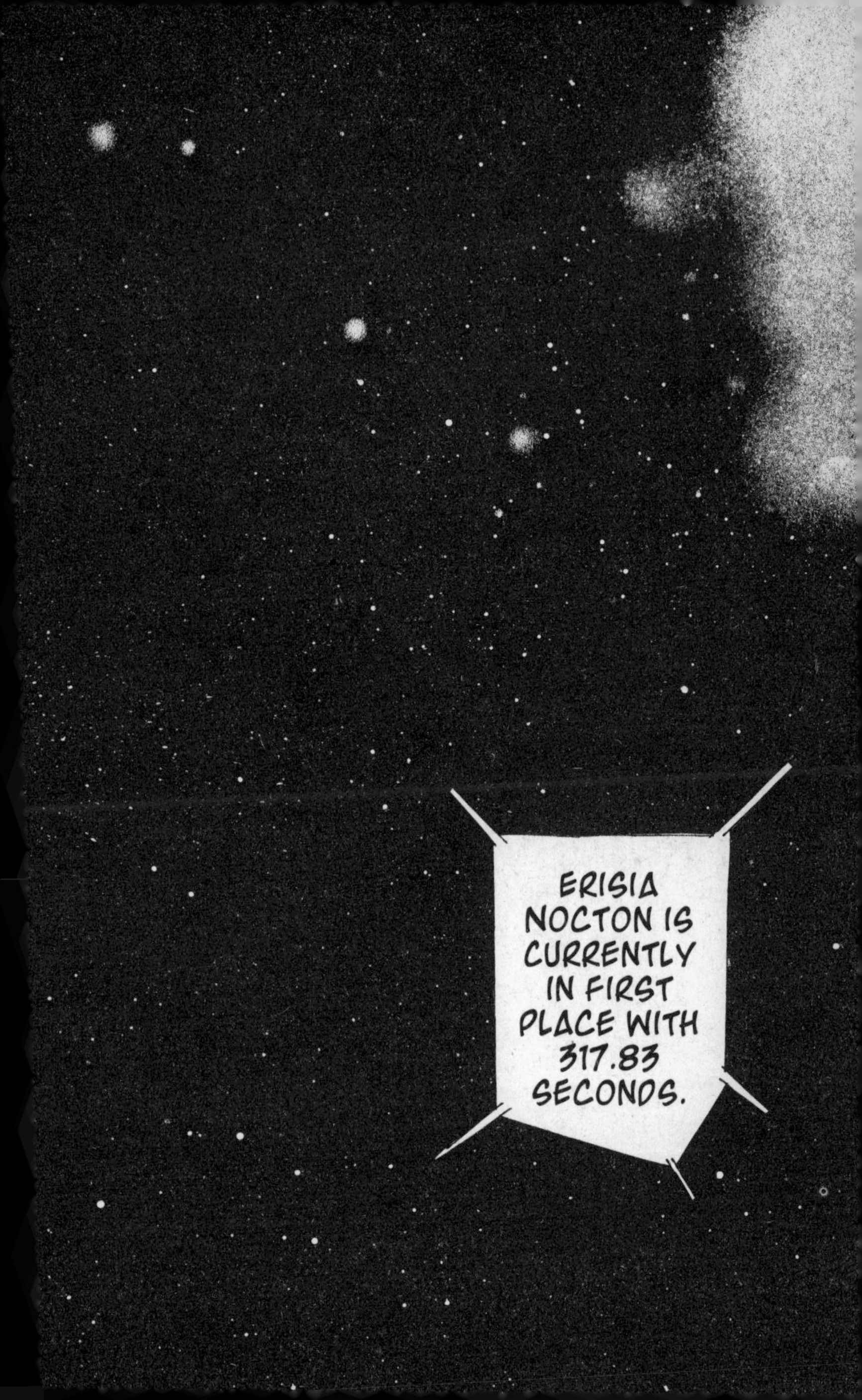
ERISIA NOCTON IS CURRENTLY IN FIRST PLACE WITH 317.83 SECONDS.

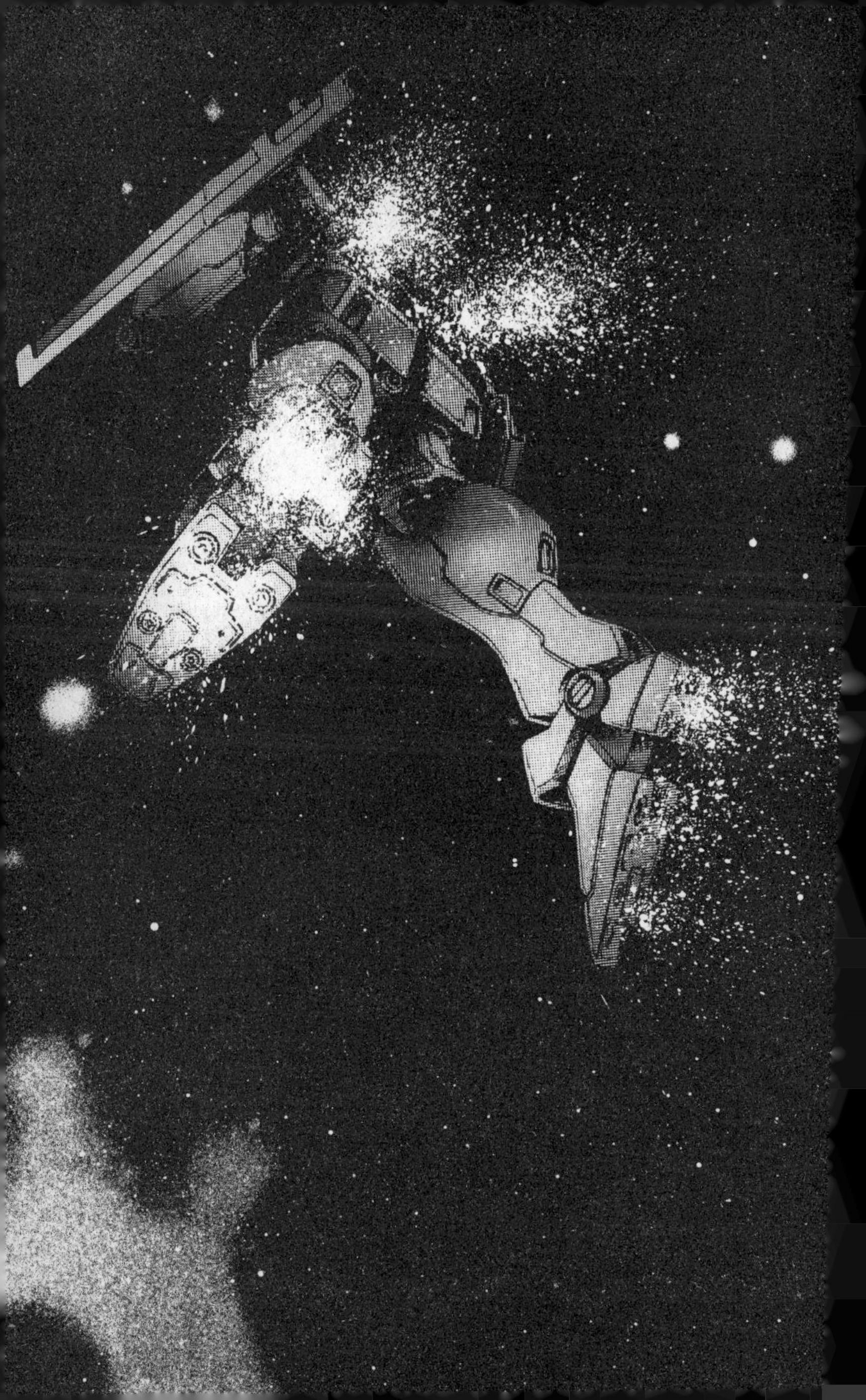

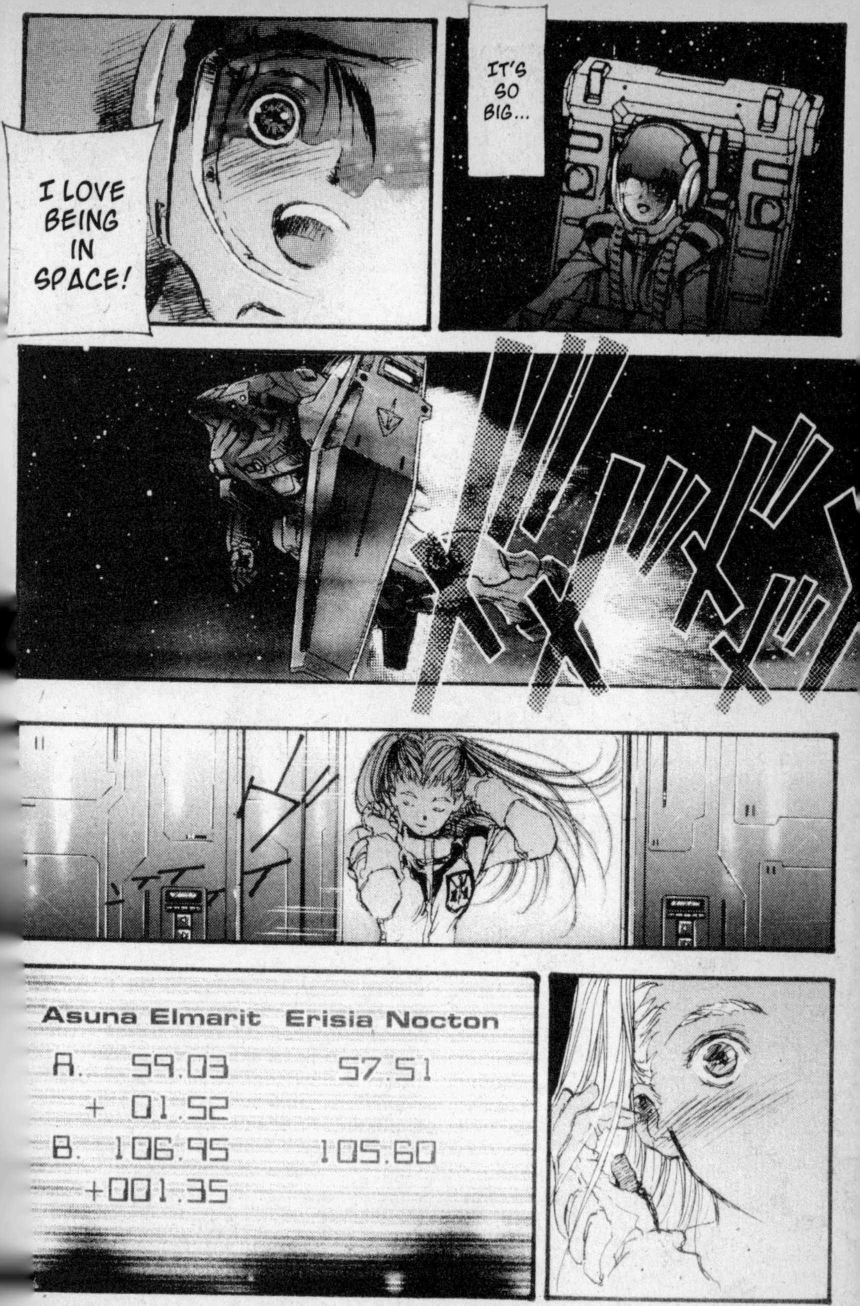
IT'S SO BIG...
I LOVE BEING IN SPACE!
Asuna Elmarit
Erisia Nocton
A. 59.03
57.51
+ 01.52
B. 106.95
105.60
+001.35

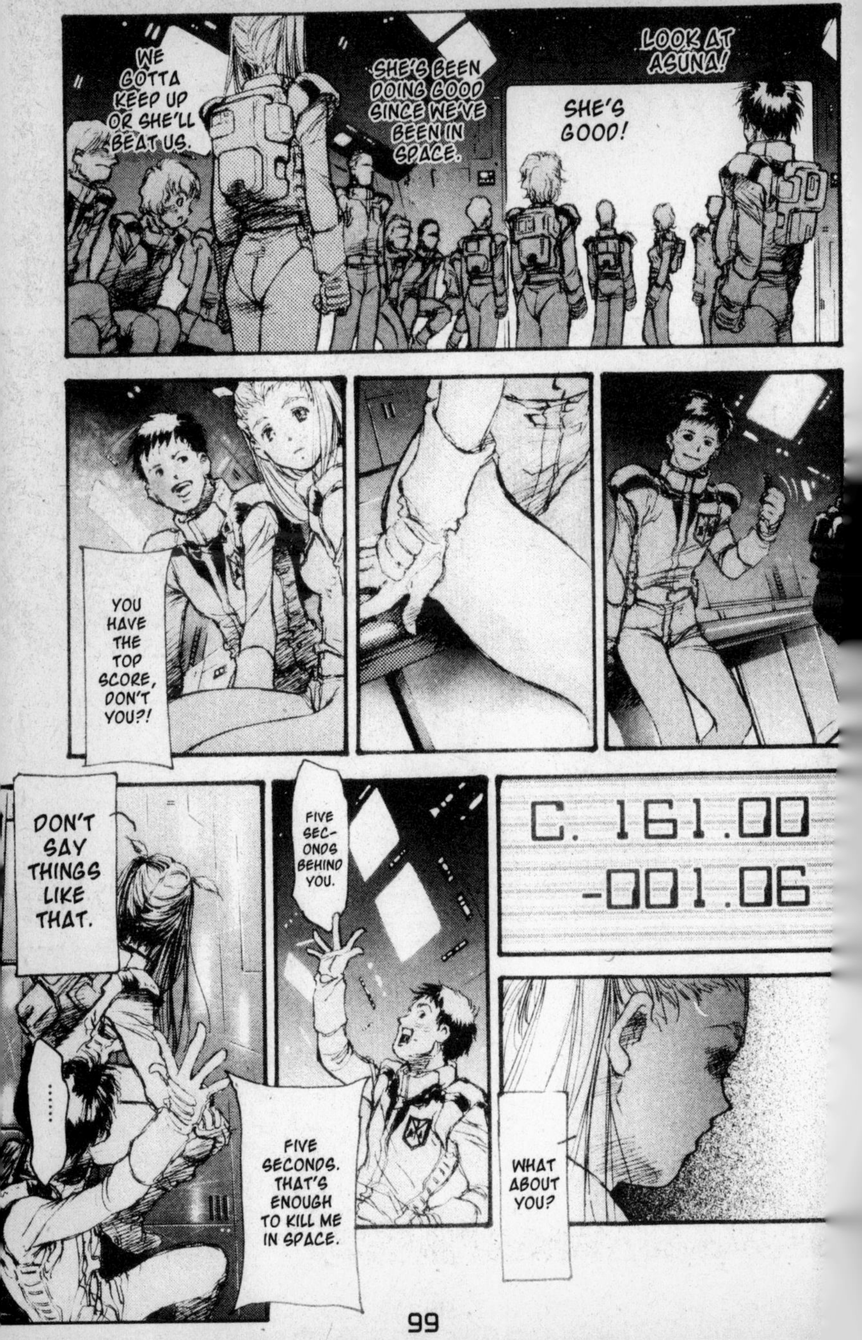
LOOK AT ASUNA!
SHE'S GOOD!
SHE'S BEEN DOING GOOD SINCE WE'VE BEEN IN SPACE.
WE GOTTA KEEP UP OR SHE'LL BEAT US.
YOU HAVE THE TOP SCORE, DON'T YOU?!
C. 161.00
-001.06
WHAT ABOUT YOU?
FIVE SECONDS BEHIND YOU.
FIVE SECONDS. THAT'S ENOUGH TO KILL ME IN SPACE.
DON'T SAY THINGS LIKE THAT.
......

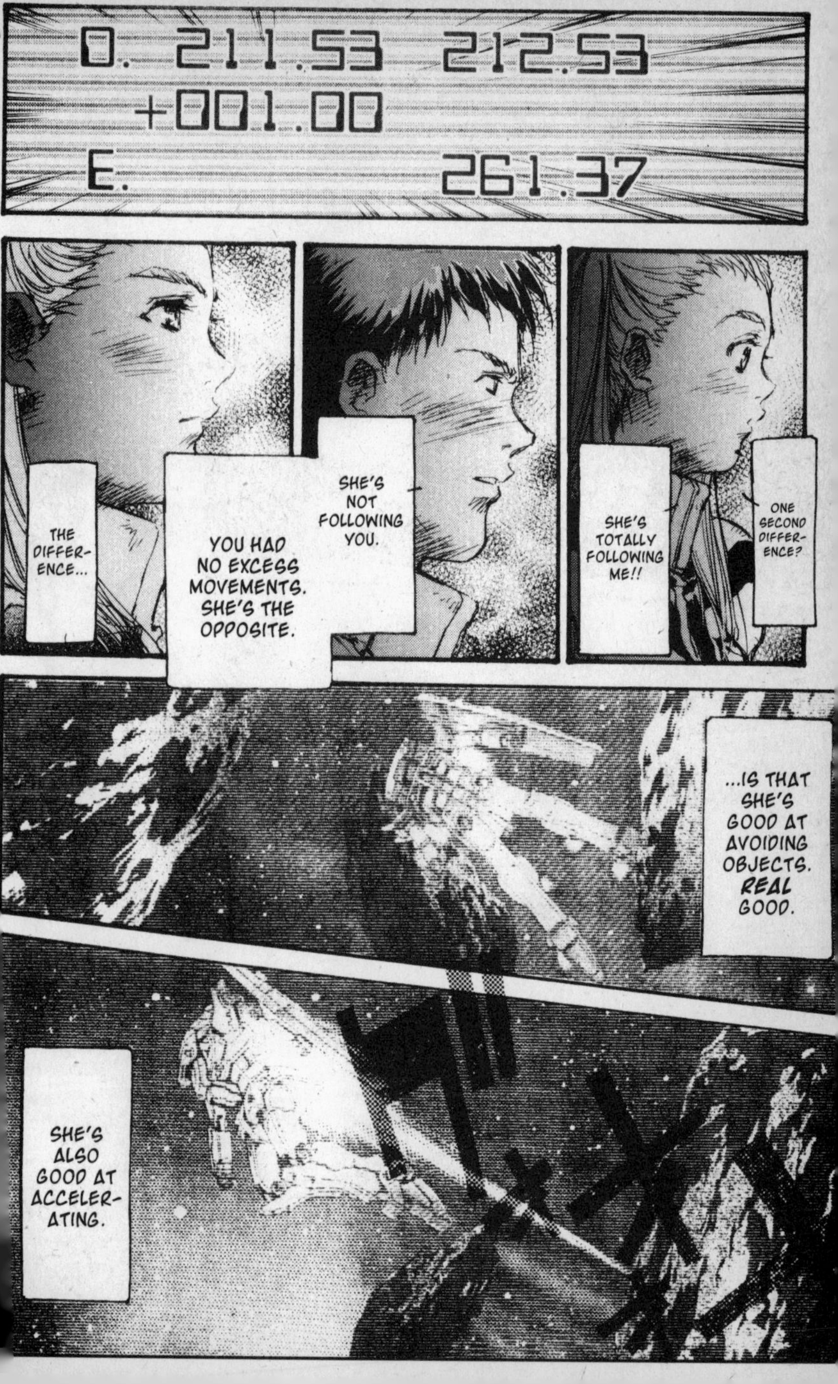

O. 211.53 212.53
+001.00
E. 261.37
ONE SECOND DIFFER-ENCE?
SHE'S TOTALLY FOLLOWING ME!!
SHE'S NOT FOLLOWING YOU.
YOU HAD NO EXCESS MOVEMENTS. SHE'S THE OPPOSITE.
THE DIFFER-ENCE...
...IS THAT SHE'S GOOD AT AVOIDING OBJECTS. REAL GOOD.
SHE'S ALSO GOOD AT ACCELER-ATING.

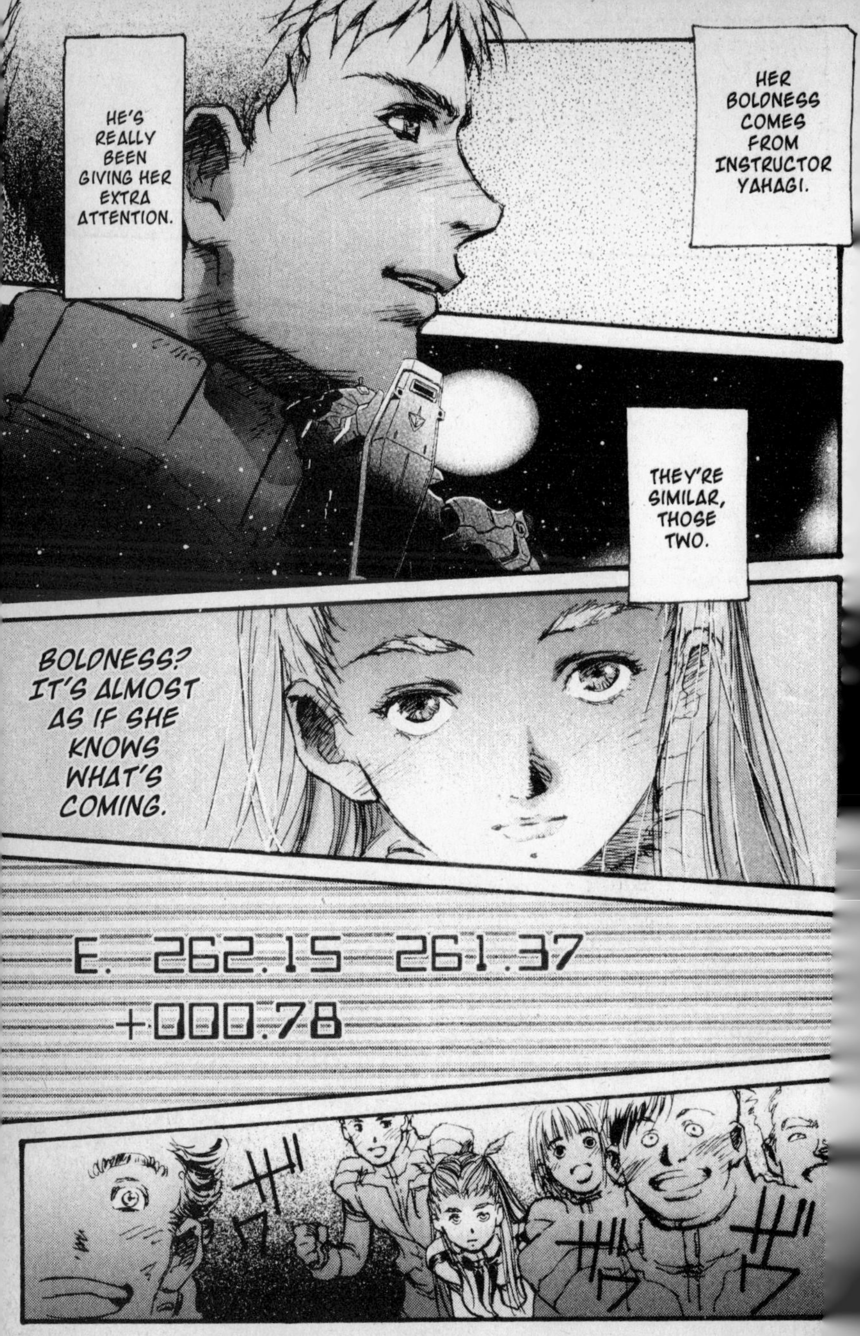
HER BOLDNESS COMES FROM INSTRUCTOR YAHAGI.
HE'S REALLY BEEN GIVING HER EXTRA ATTENTION.
THEY'RE SIMILAR, THOSE TWO.
BOLDNESS? IT'S ALMOST AS IF SHE KNOWS WHAT'S COMING.
E. 262.15 261.37
+000.78

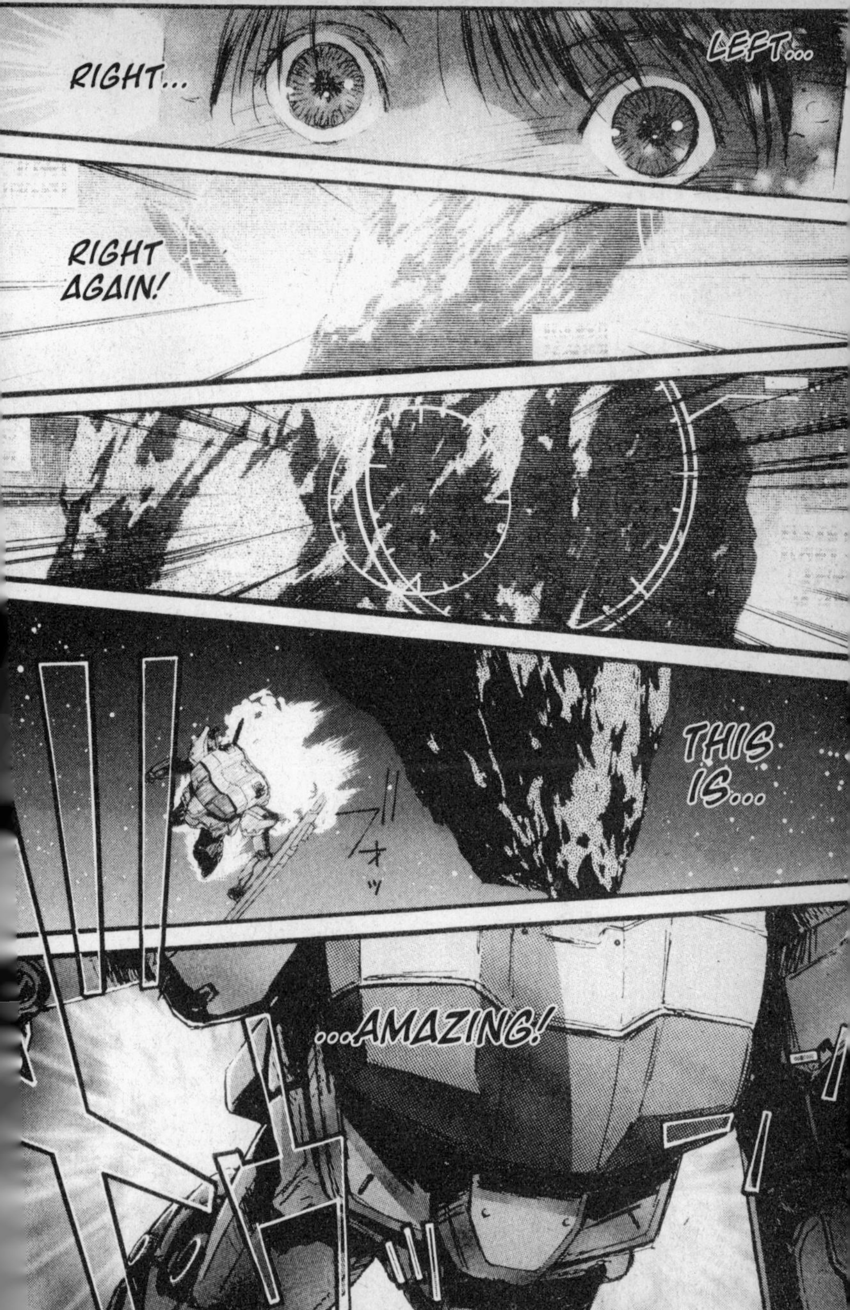
LEFT...
RIGHT...
RIGHT AGAIN!
THIS IS...
...AMAZING!

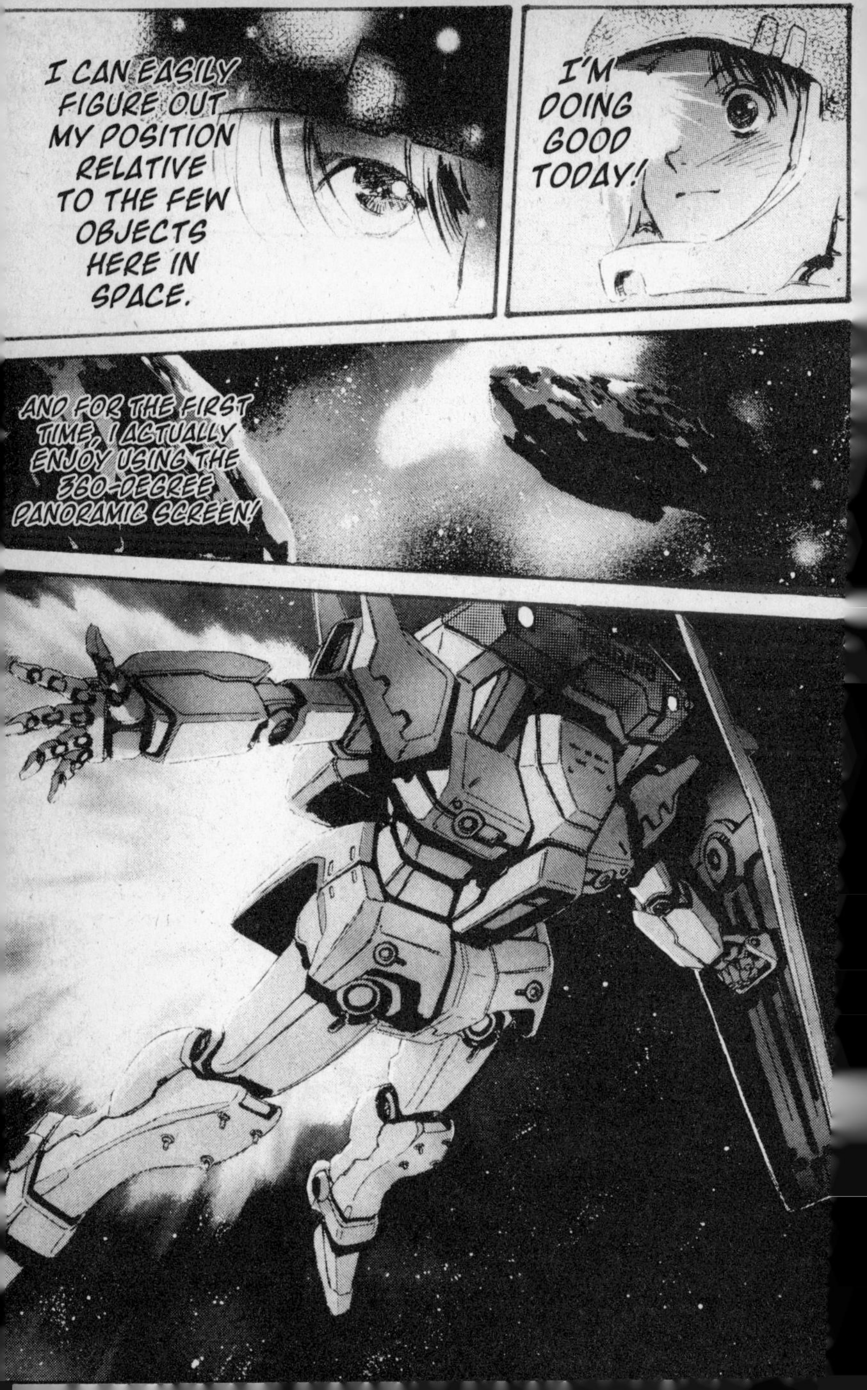
I'M DOING GOOD TODAY!
I CAN EASILY FIGURE OUT MY POSITION RELATIVE TO THE FEW OBJECTS HERE IN SPACE.
AND FOR THE FIRST TIME, I ACTUALLY ENJOY USING THE 360-DEGREE PANORAMIC SCREEN!

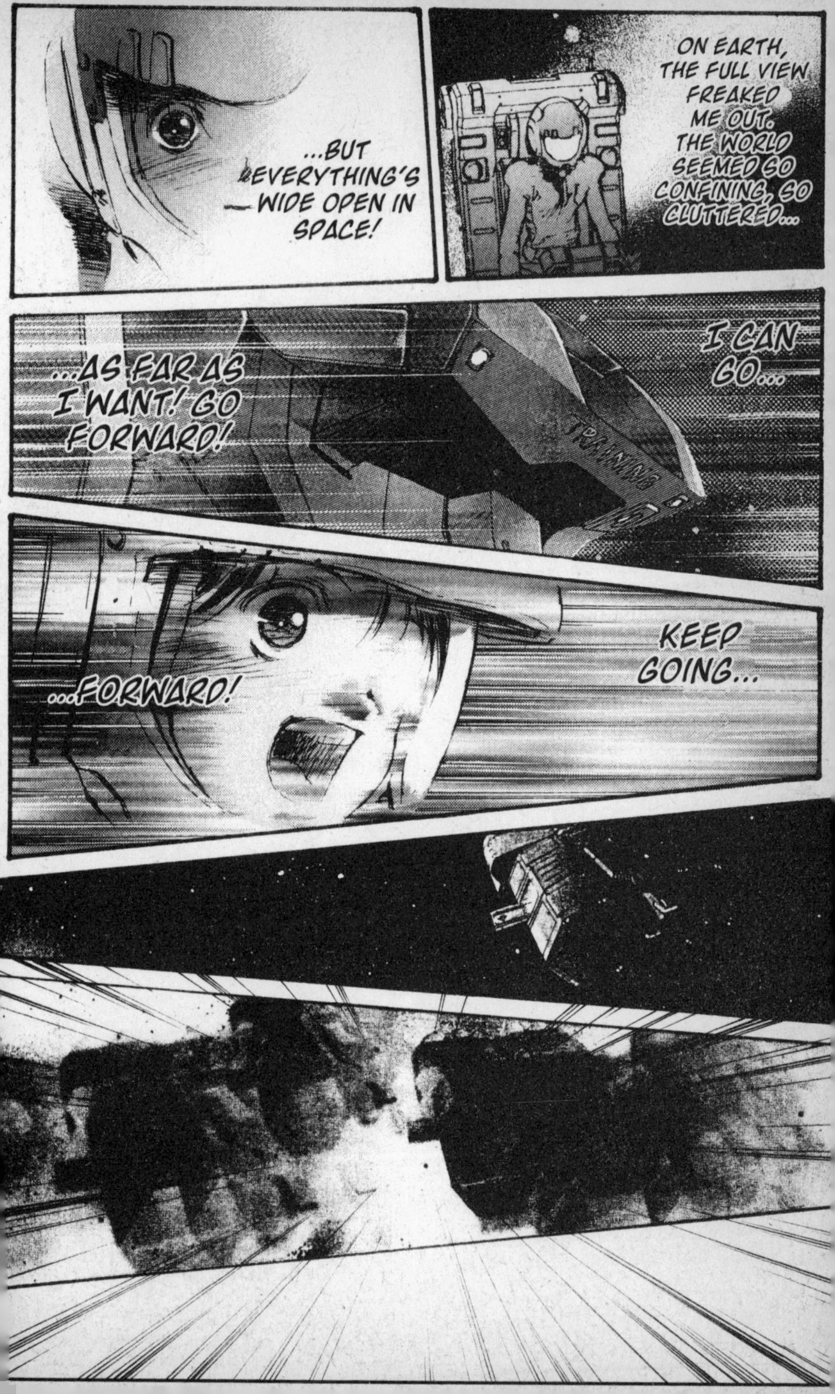
ON EARTH, THE FULL VIEW FREAKED ME OUT. THE WORLD SEEMED SO CONFINING, SO CLUTTERED...
...BUT EVERYTHING'S WIDE OPEN IN SPACE!
I CAN GO...
...AS FAR AS I WANT! GO FORWARD!
TRAINING
KEEP GOING...
...FORWARD!

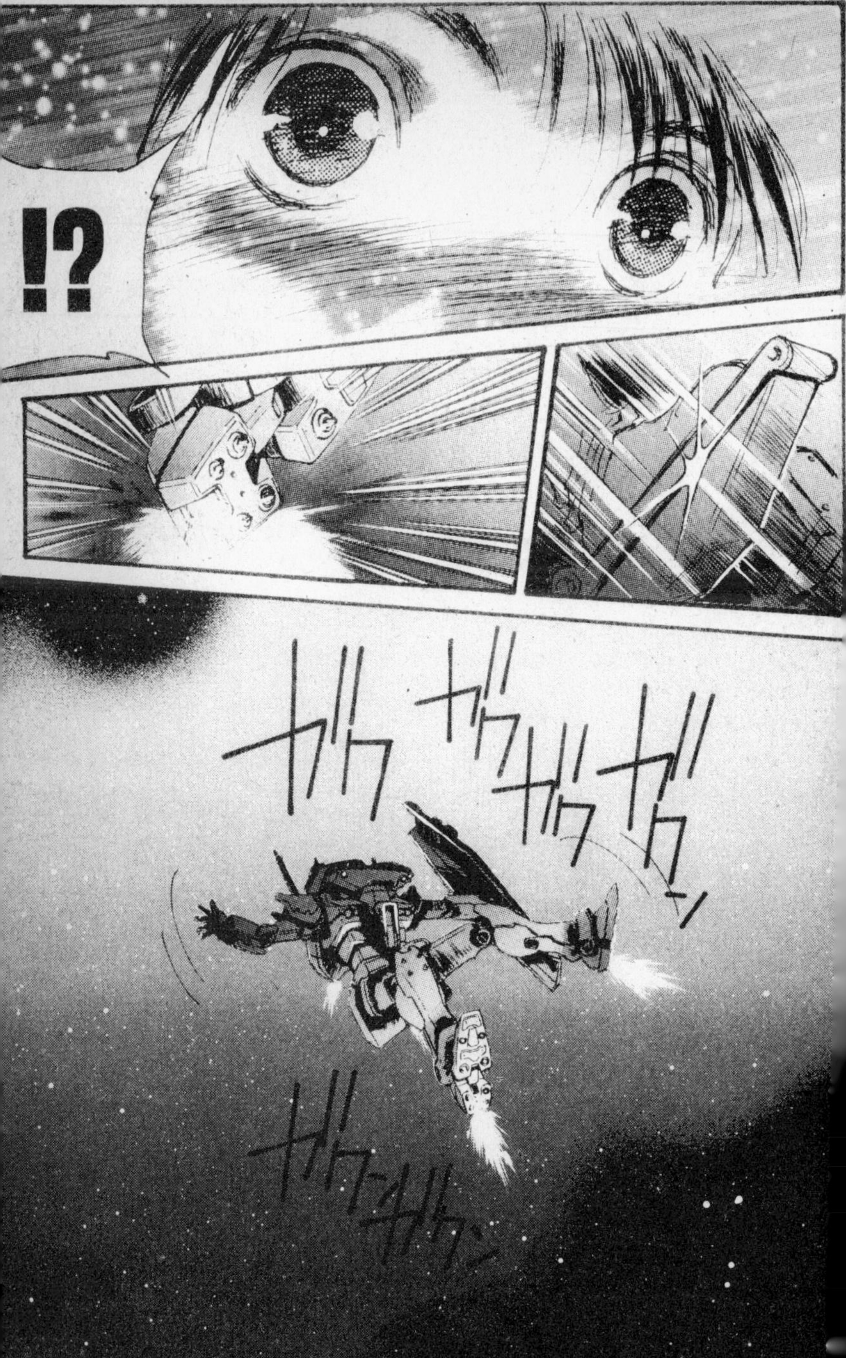
!?

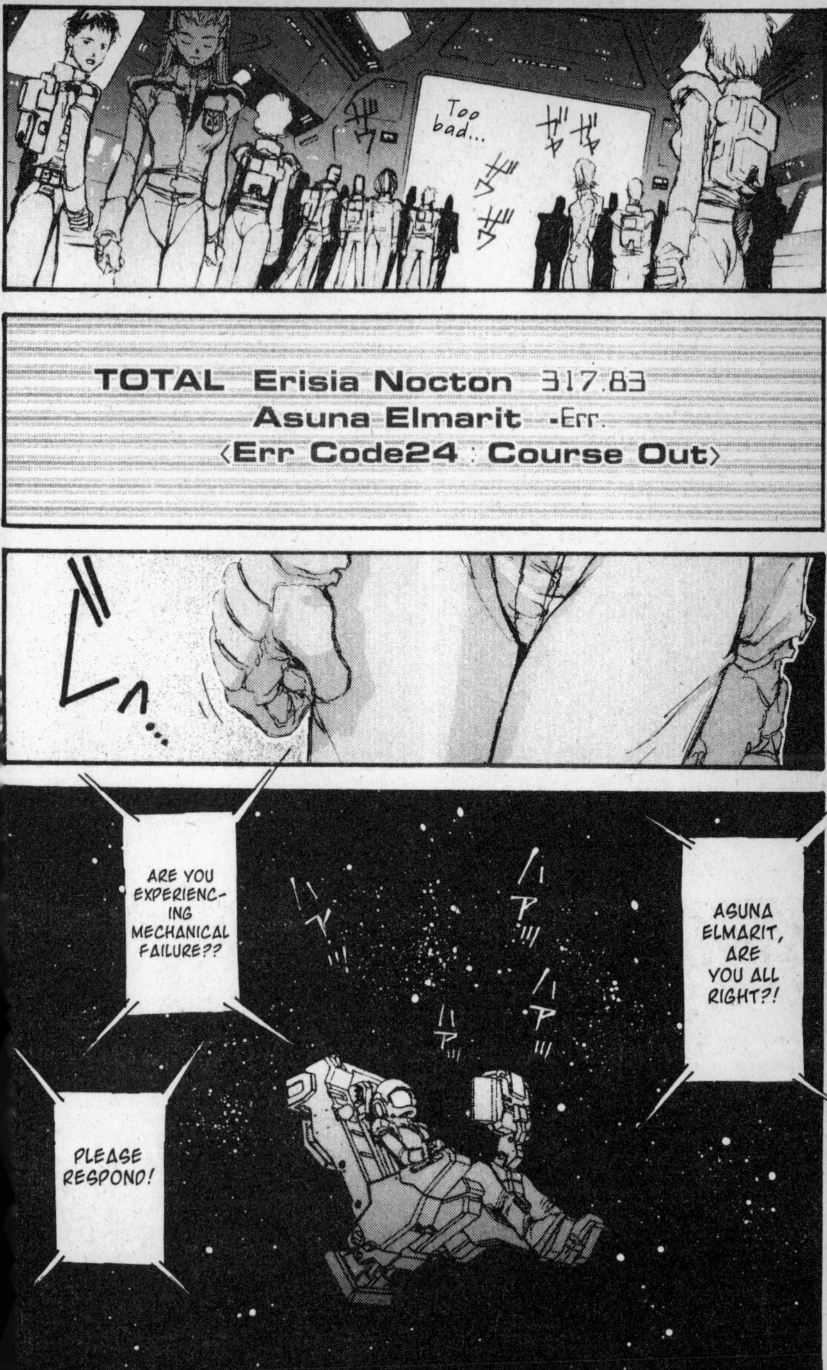

Too bad...
TOTAL Erisia Nocton 317.83
Asuna Elmarit -Err.
〈Err Code24 : Course Out〉
ASUNA ELMARIT, ARE YOU ALL RIGHT?!
ARE YOU EXPERIENC-ING MECHANICAL FAILURE??
PLEASE RESPOND!

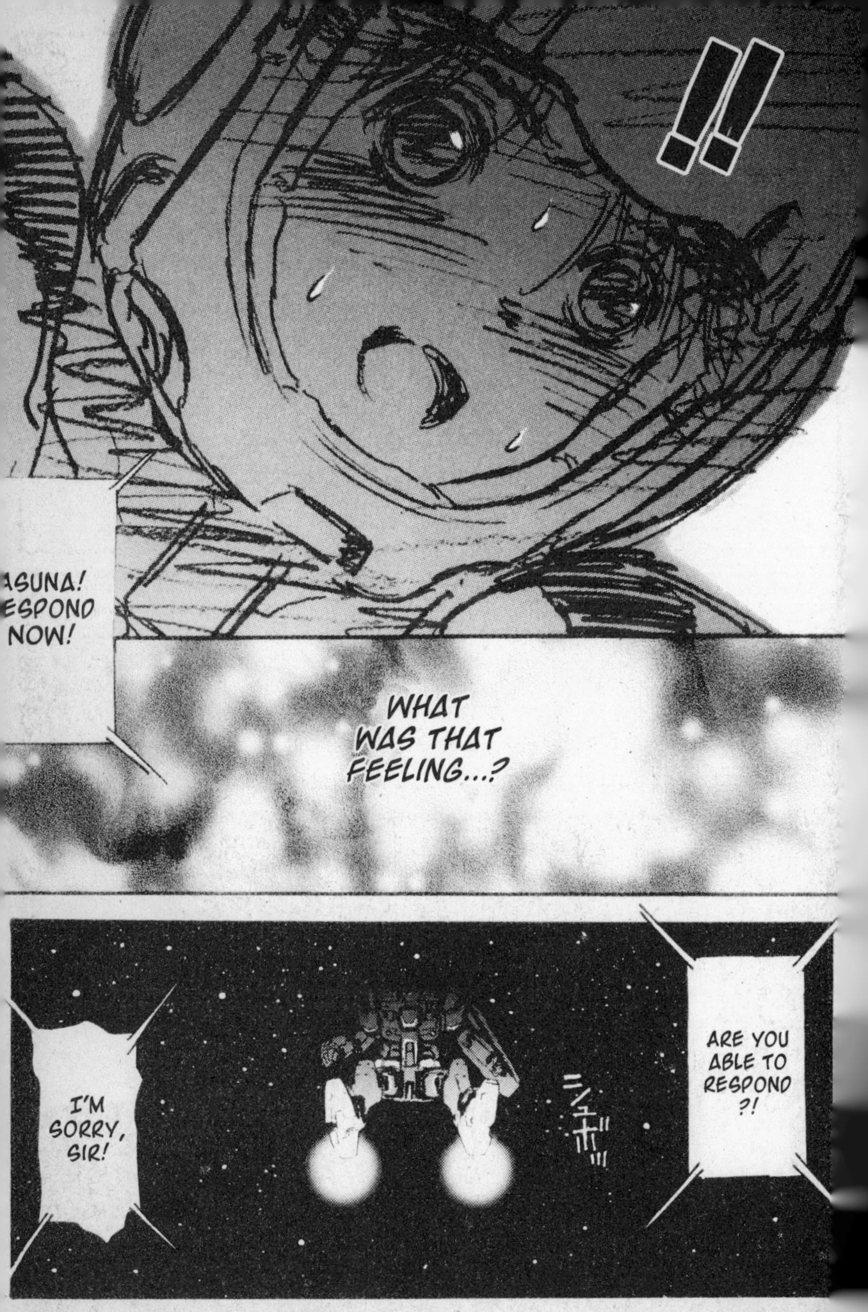
!!
ASUNA! ESPOND NOW!
WHAT WAS THAT FEELING...?
ARE YOU ABLE TO RESPOND ?!
シュボッ
I'M SORRY, SIR!

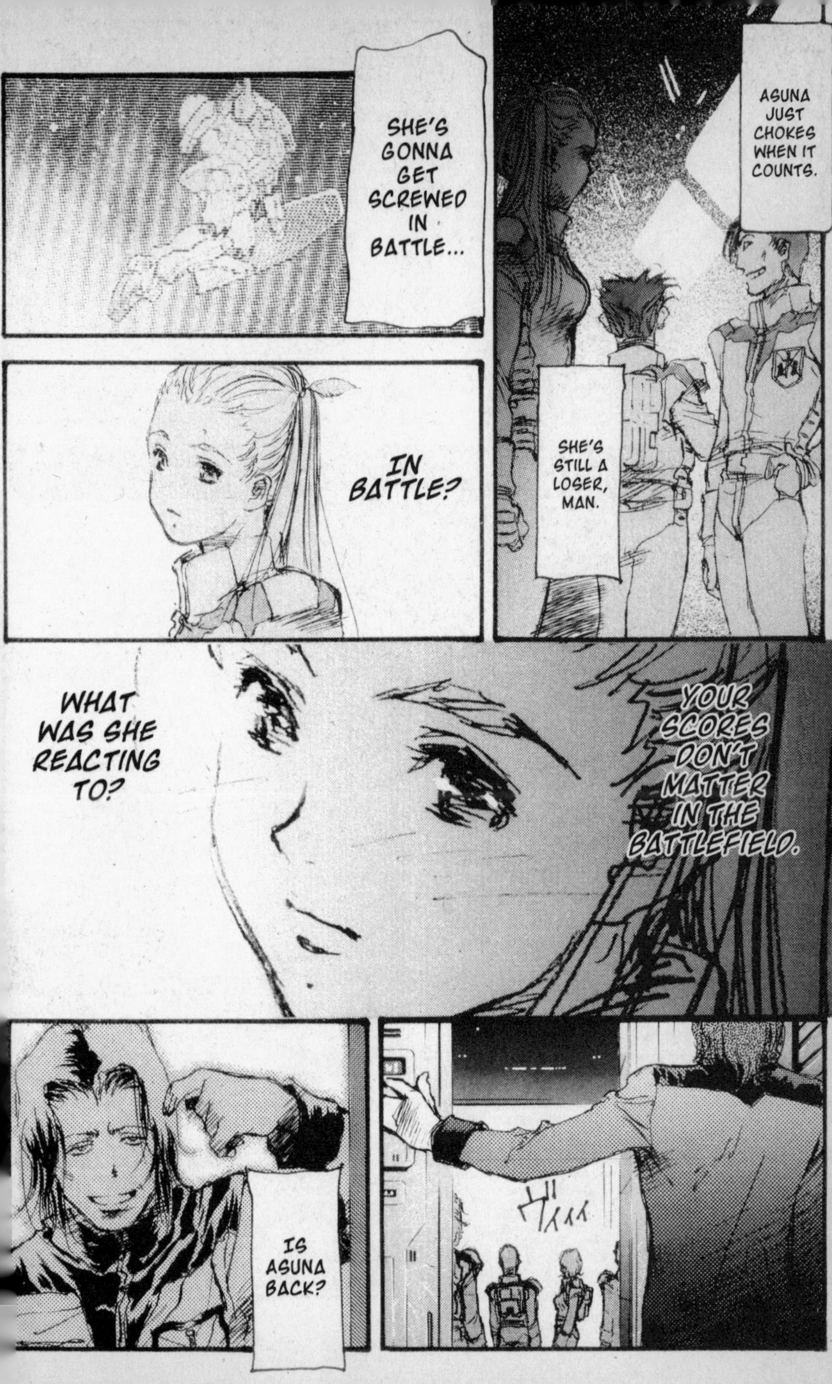
ASUNA JUST CHOKES WHEN IT COUNTS.
SHE'S STILL A LOSER, MAN.
SHE'S GONNA GET SCREWED IN BATTLE...
IN BATTLE?
YOUR SCORES DON'T MATTER IN THE BATTLEFIELD.
WHAT WAS SHE REACTING TO?
ヴィイイ
IS ASUNA BACK?

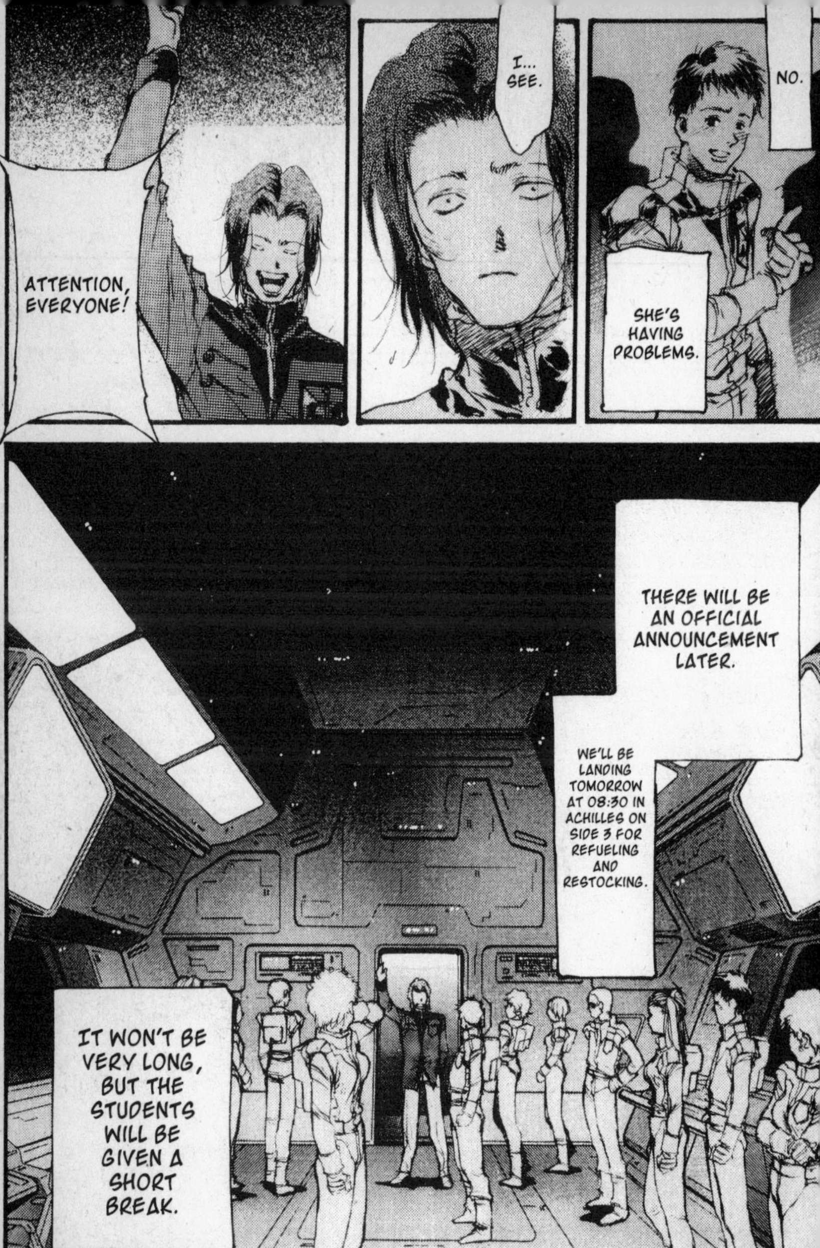
NO.
SHE'S HAVING PROBLEMS.
I... SEE.
ATTENTION, EVERYONE!
THERE WILL BE AN OFFICIAL ANNOUNCEMENT LATER.
WE'LL BE LANDING TOMORROW AT 08:30 IN ACHILLES ON SIDE 3 FOR REFUELING AND RESTOCKING.
IT WON'T BE VERY LONG, BUT THE STUDENTS WILL BE GIVEN A SHORT BREAK.

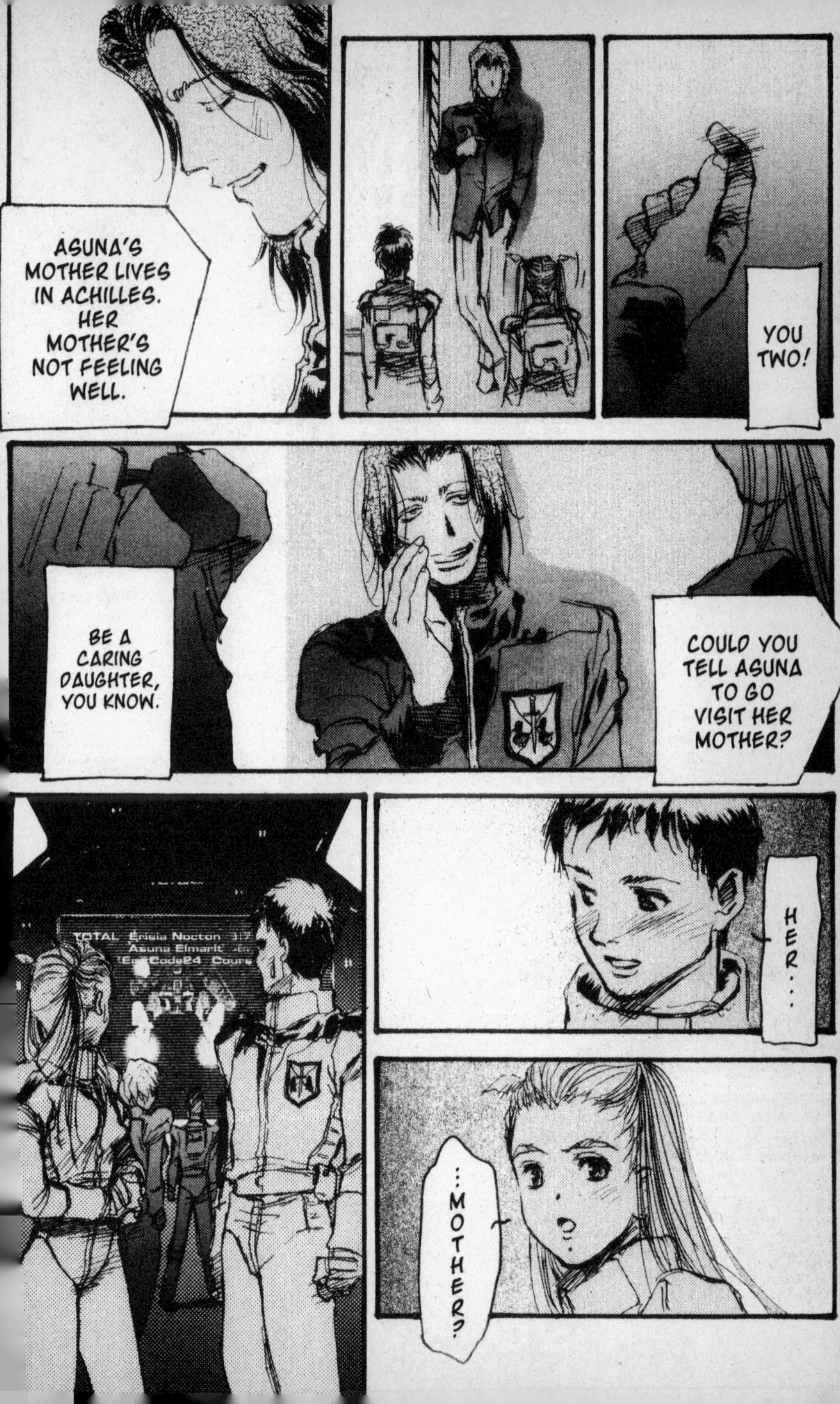
YOU TWO!
ASUNA'S MOTHER LIVES IN ACHILLES. HER MOTHER'S NOT FEELING WELL.
COULD YOU TELL ASUNA TO GO VISIT HER MOTHER?
BE A CARING DAUGHTER, YOU KNOW.
HER...
...MOTHER?
TOTAL Erisia Nocton
Asuna Elmarit

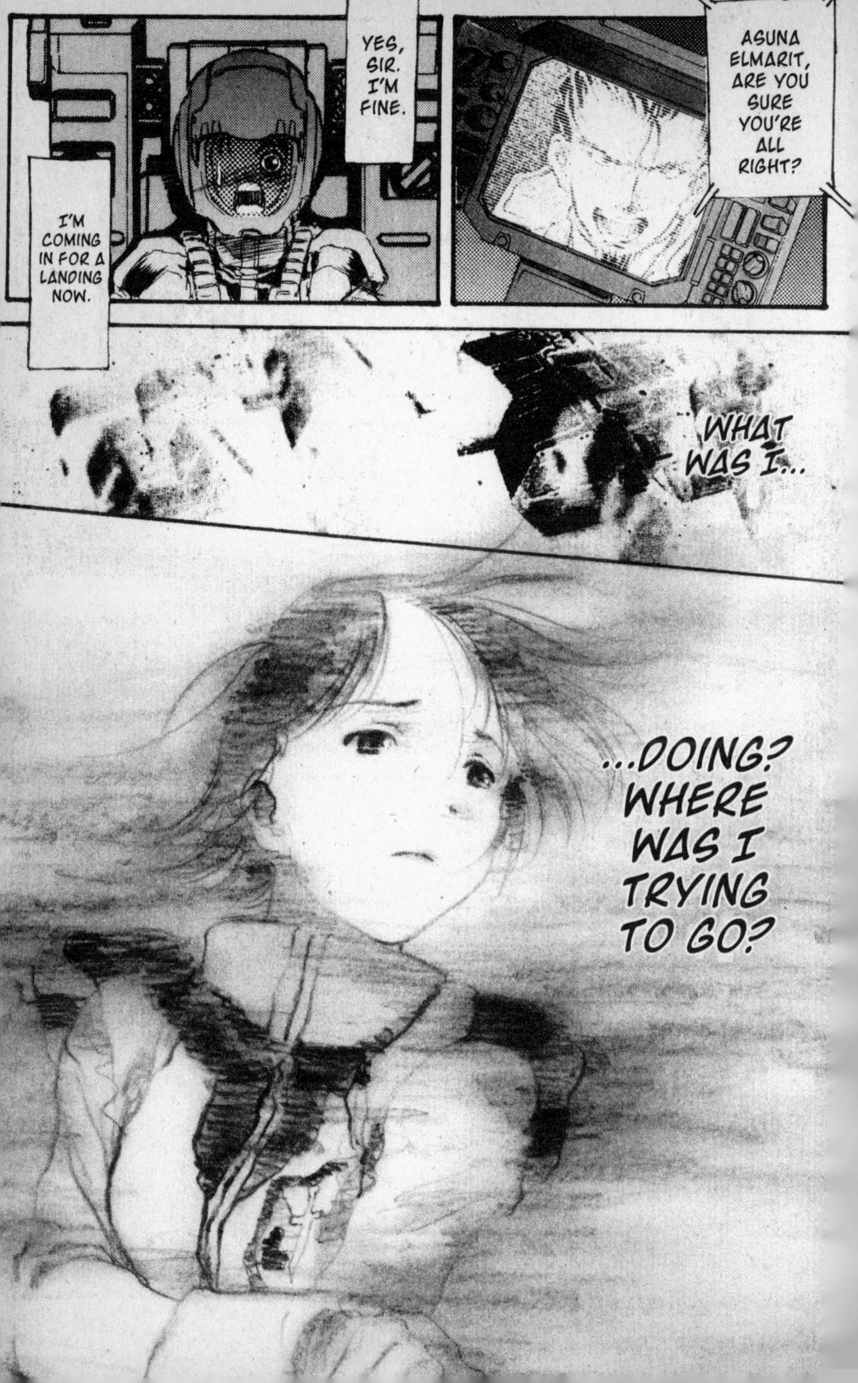
ASUNA ELMARIT, ARE YOU SURE YOU'RE ALL RIGHT?
YES, SIR. I'M FINE.
I'M COMING IN FOR A LANDING NOW.
WHAT WAS I...
...DOING? WHERE WAS I TRYING TO GO?

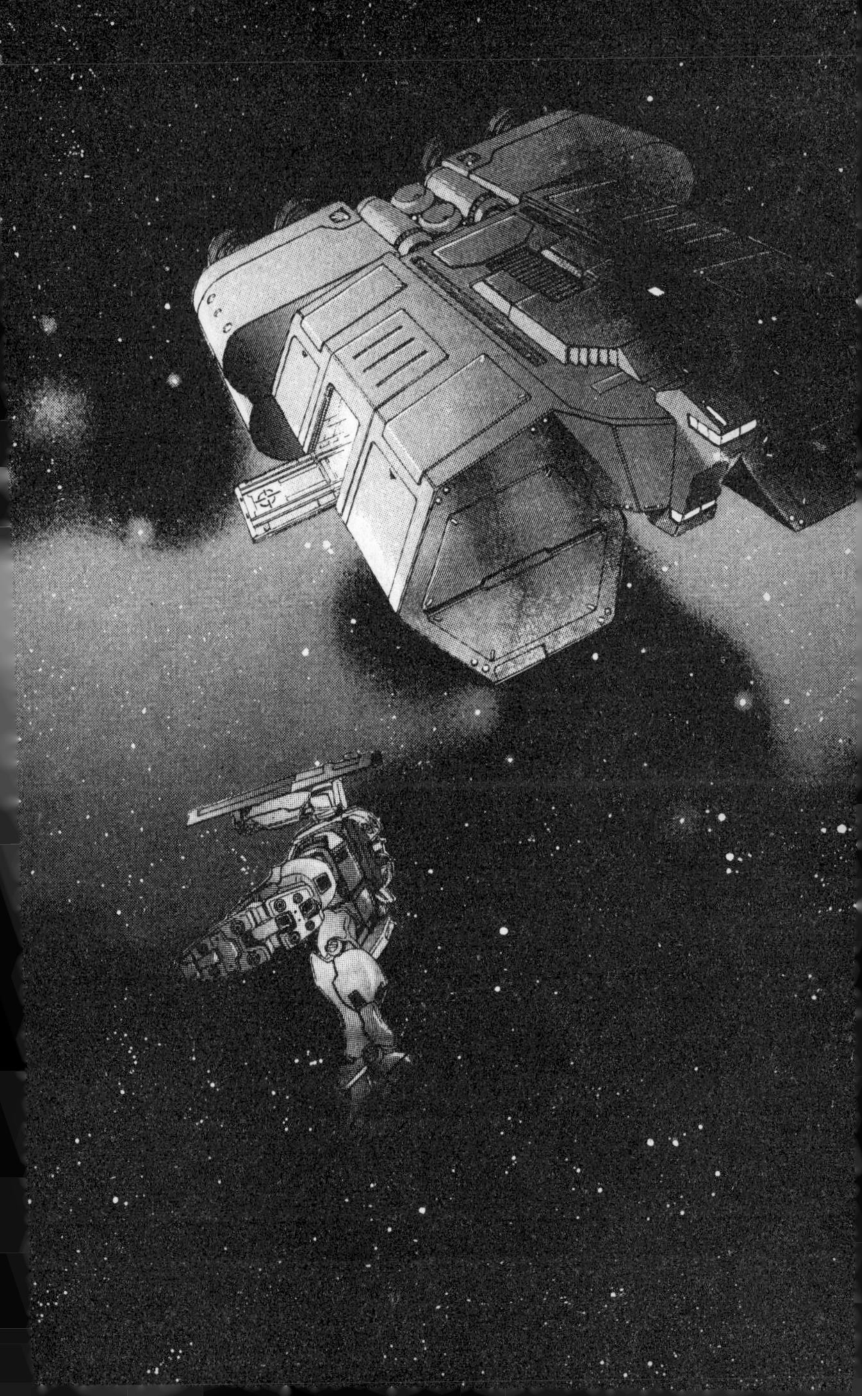

CHARACTER FILE:04

Shinn Barnack

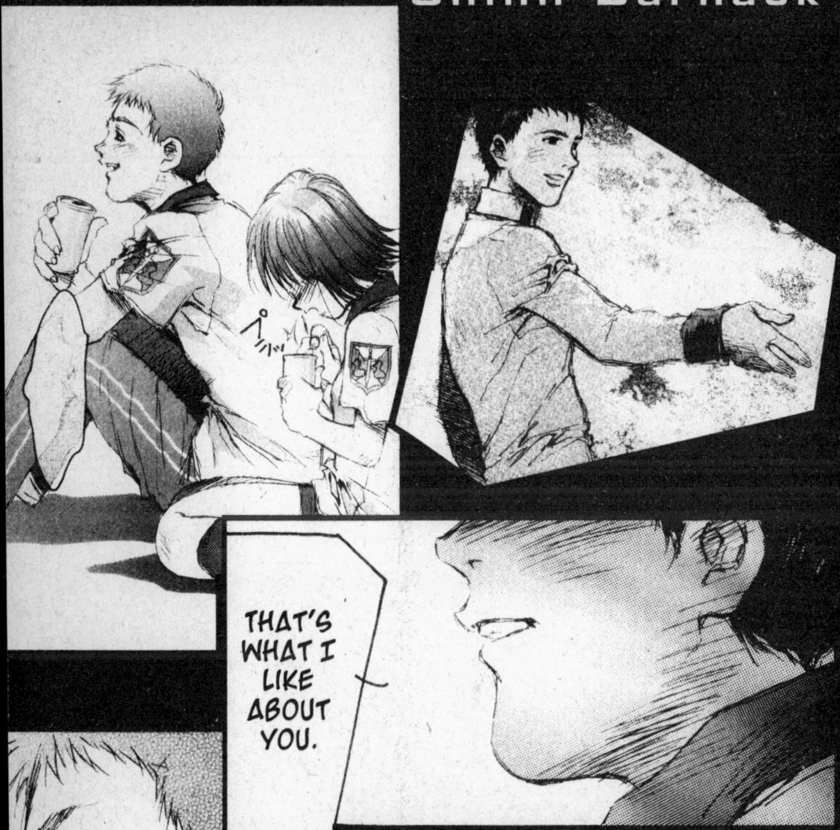
THAT'S WHAT I LIKE ABOUT YOU.

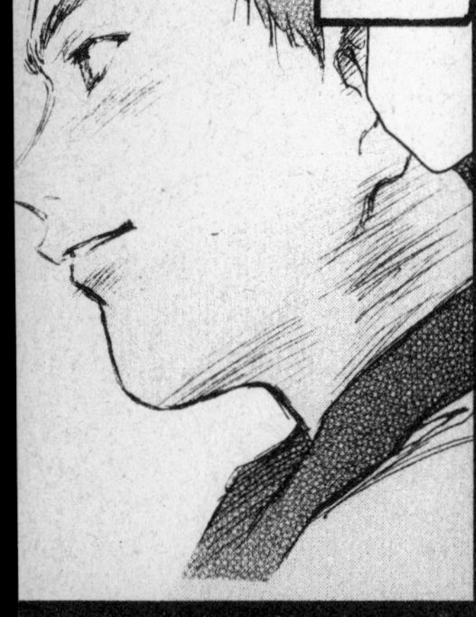

SHINN BARNACK

ASUNA'S CLASSMATE. HE'S FROM THE COAST, BUT HE JOINED ÉCOLE DU CIEL TO TRAIN AS A MOBILE SUIT PILOT. HE COMFORTS ASUNA WHEN SHE'S DOWN (WHICH IS COMMON) BY TELLING HER ABOUT HIS EXPERIENCES AND THOUGHTS. ON THE SIMULATION MACHINES, HE FOUGHT AGAINST ASUNA USING A ZAKU (MOBILE SUIT-06J). HE AGGRESSIVELY DOMINATED HER, BUT IN THE END, ASUNA BEAT HIM BY THROWING HIM. HE'S SWEET TO EVERYONE, AND ASUNA HAS A BIG CRUSH ON HIM. HOWEVER, ERISIA SEEMS TO HAVE FEELINGS FOR HIM AS WELL. WHILE HE'S IN THE SAME GRADE AS ASUNA, DUE TO HIS TRANSFER FROM THE COAST, HE IS ACTUALLY THREE YEARS OLDER.

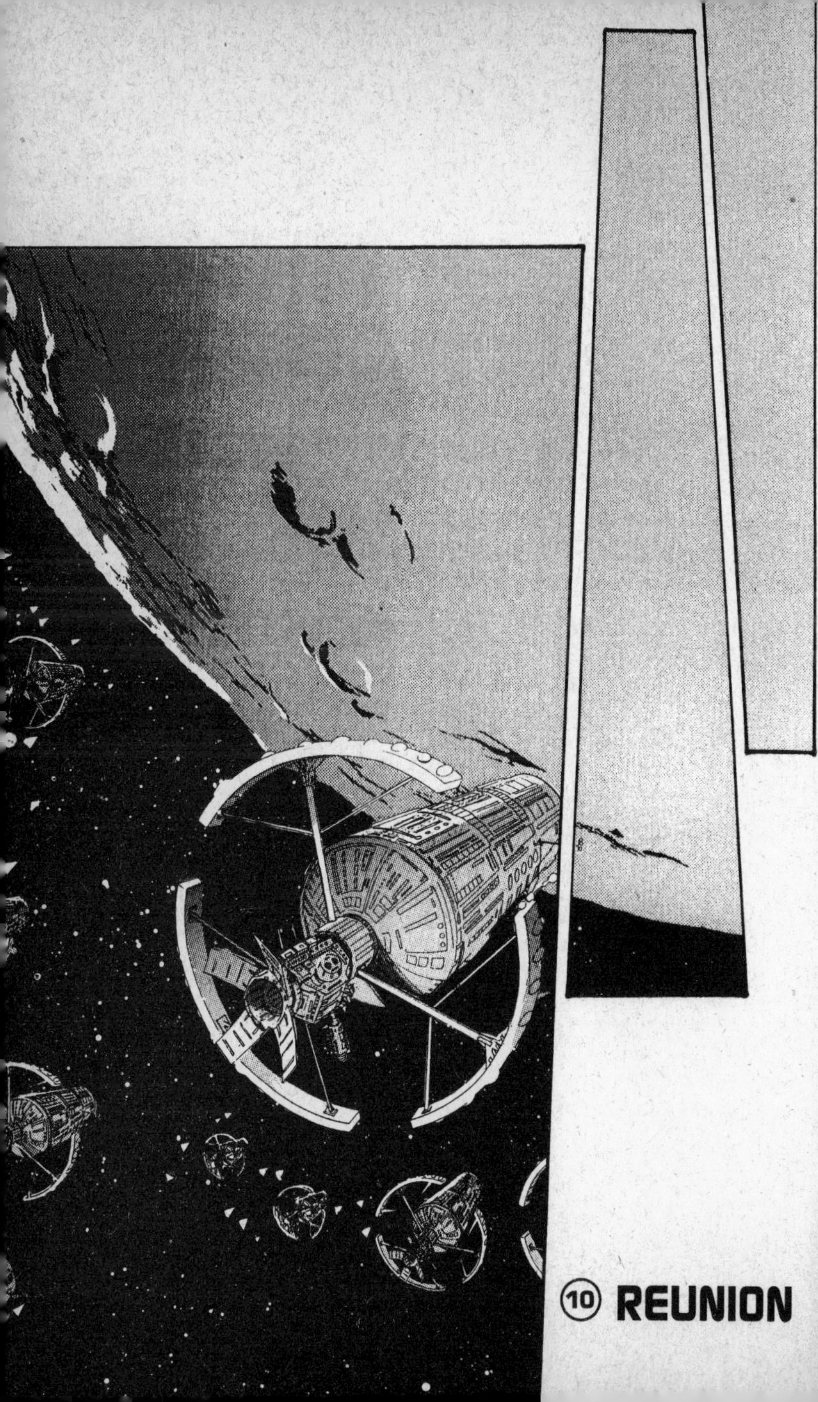

⑩ REUNION

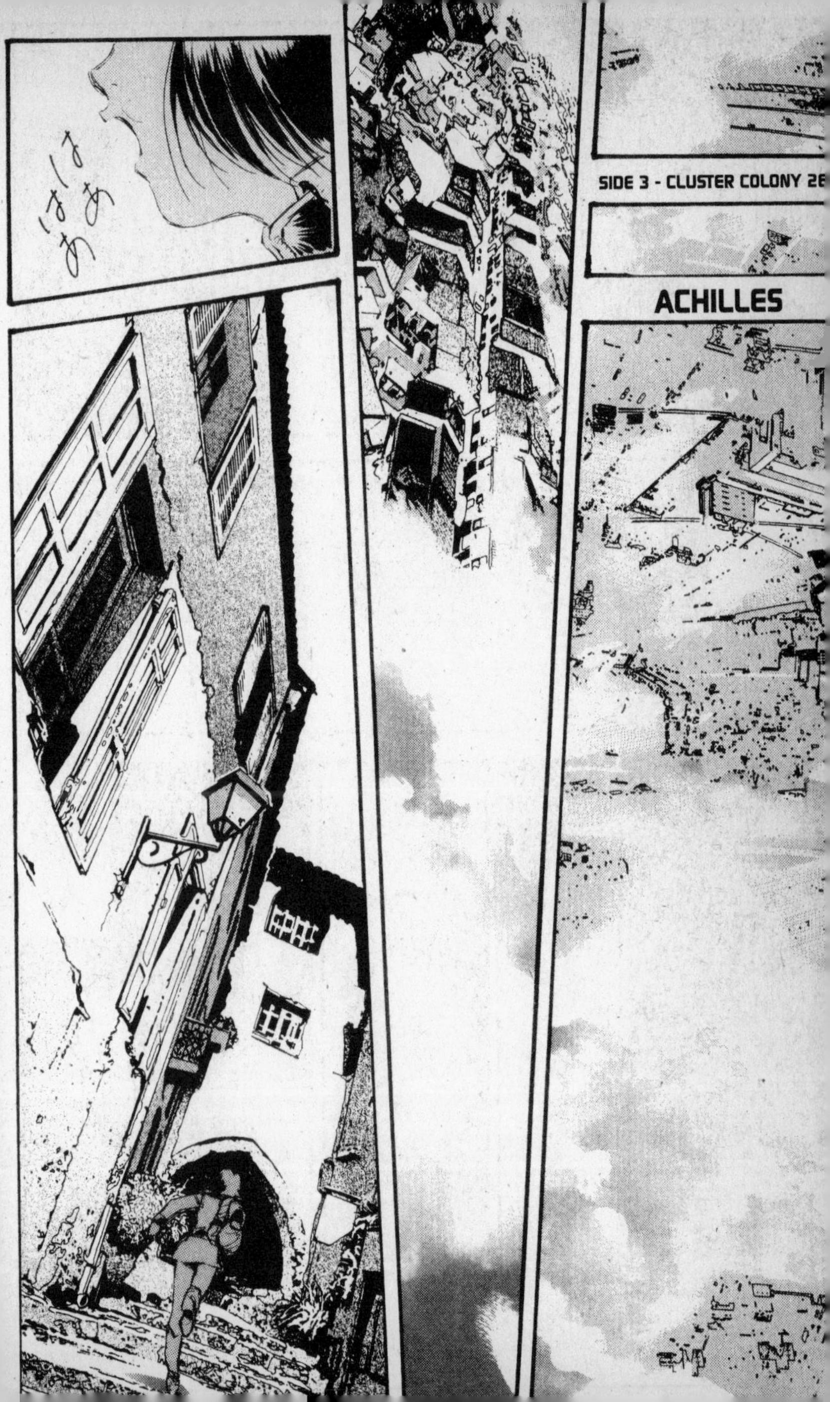
SIDE 3 - CLUSTER COLONY 26
ACHILLES
はあ
はあ

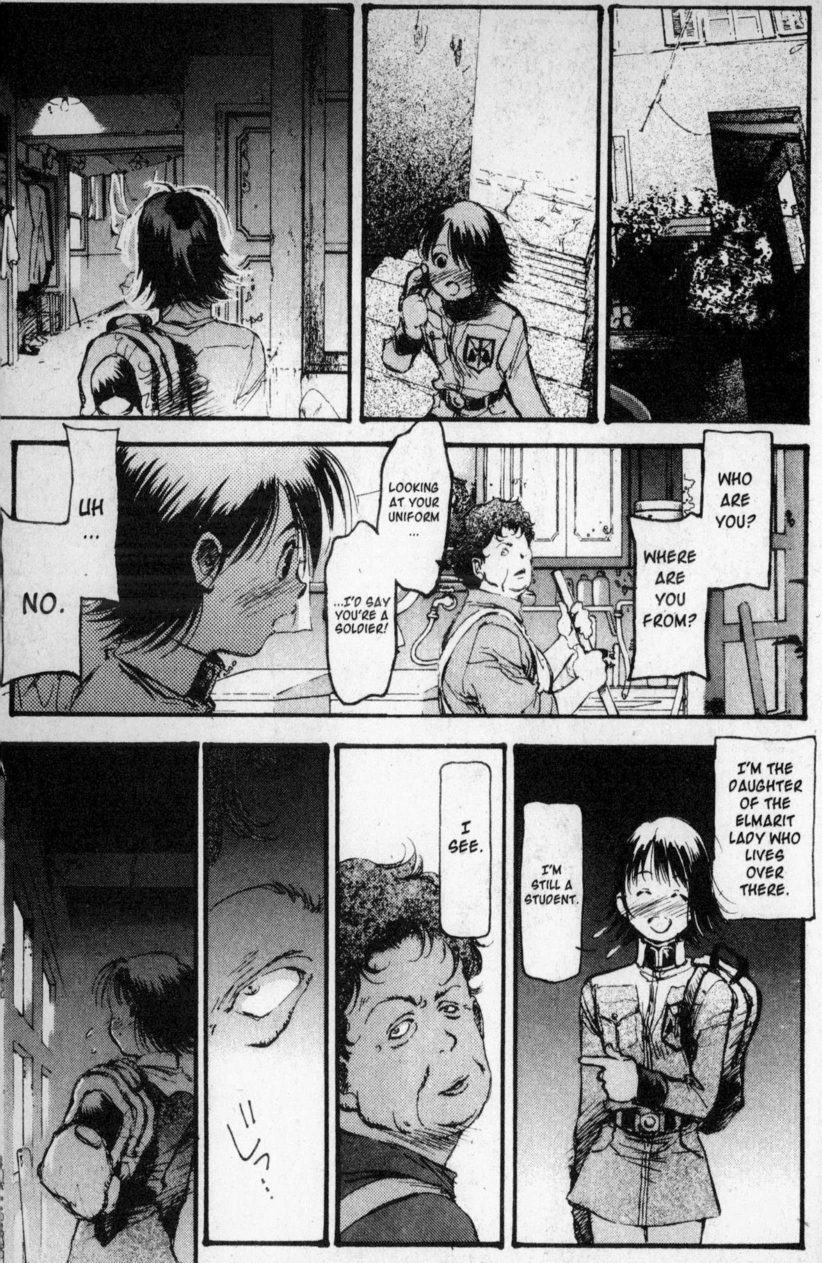
WHO ARE YOU?
WHERE ARE YOU FROM?
LOOKING AT YOUR UNIFORM ...
...I'D SAY YOU'RE A SOLDIER!
UH ...
NO.
I'M THE DAUGHTER OF THE ELMARIT LADY WHO LIVES OVER THERE.
I'M STILL A STUDENT.
I SEE.

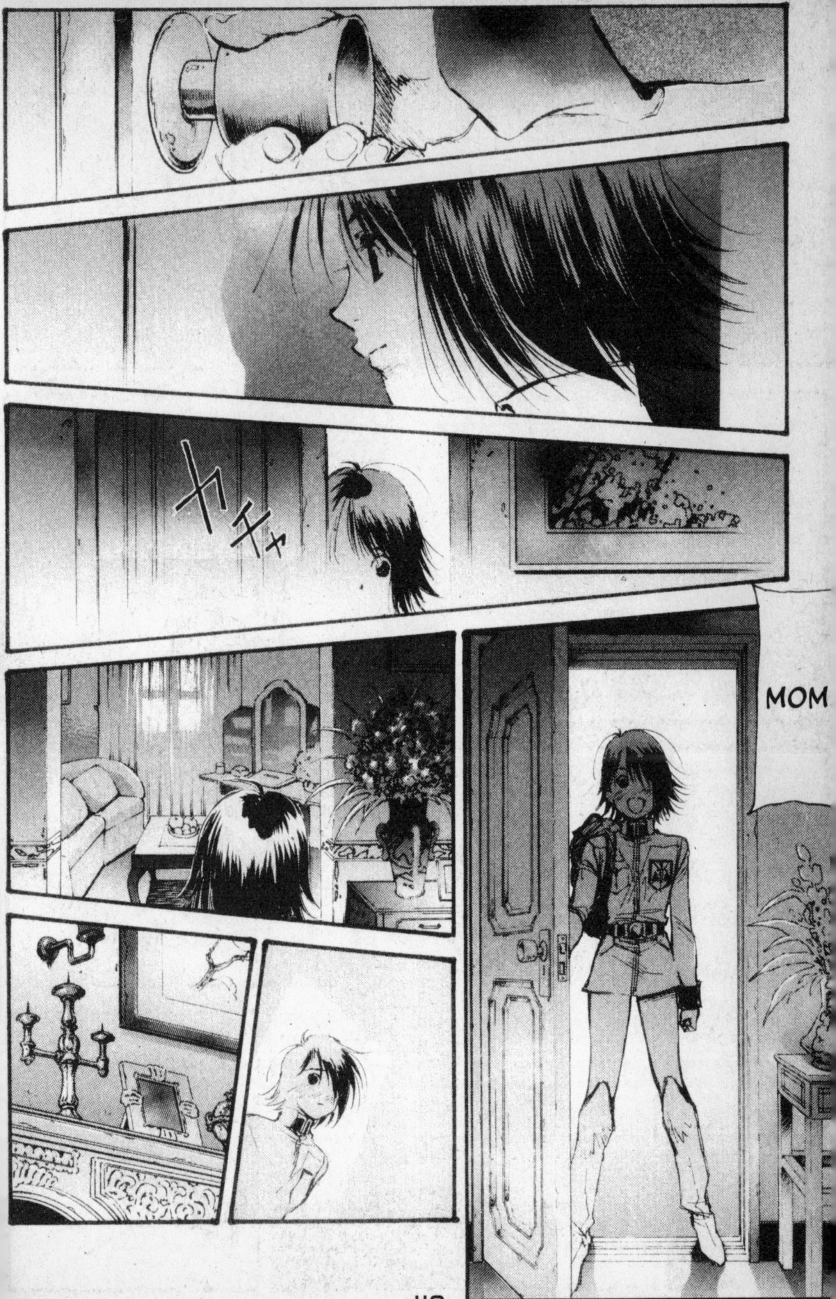
カチャ
MOM

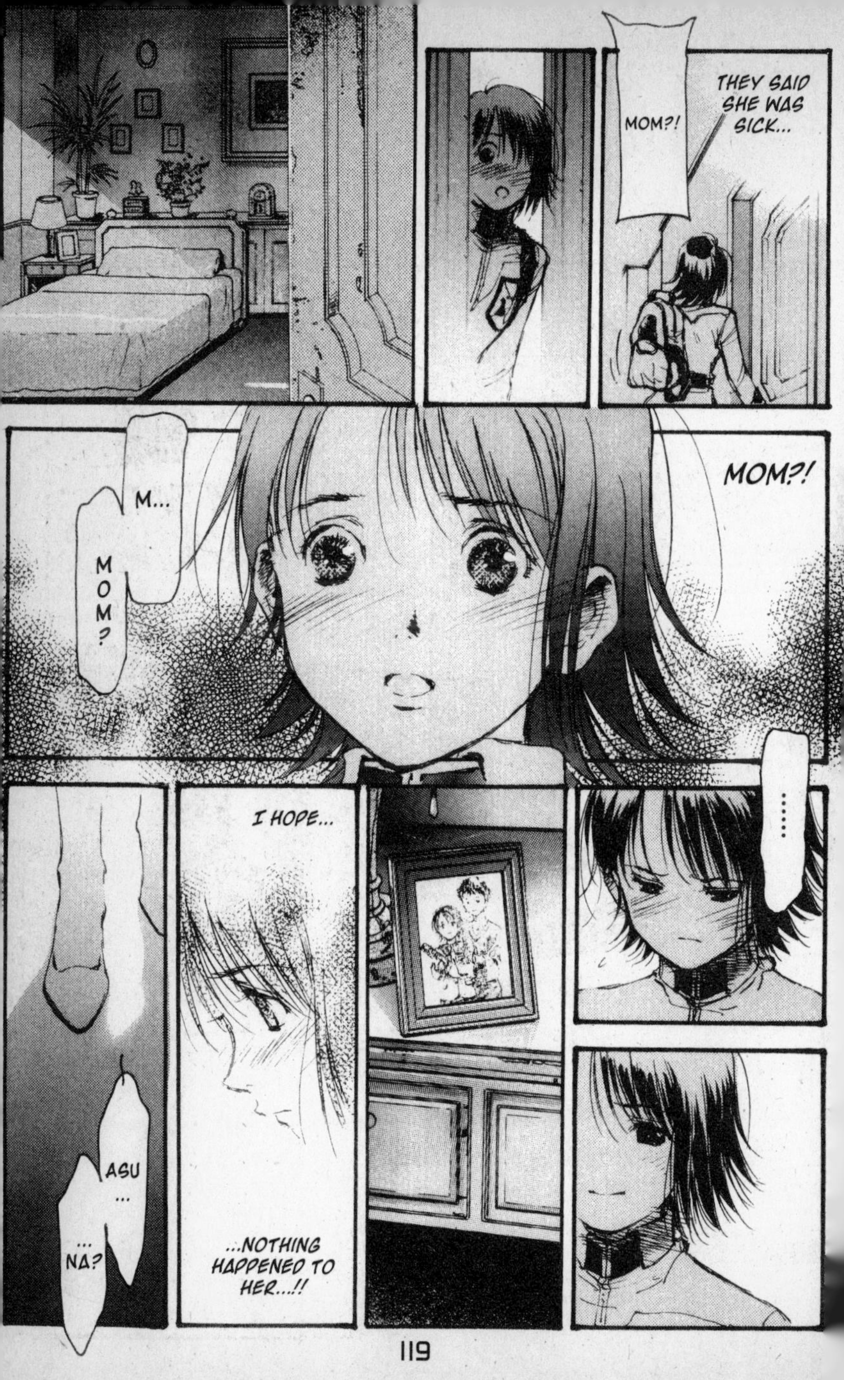
MOM?!
THEY SAID SHE WAS SICK...
MOM?!
M... MOM?
......
I HOPE...
...NOTHING HAPPENED TO HER...!!
ASU... ...NA?

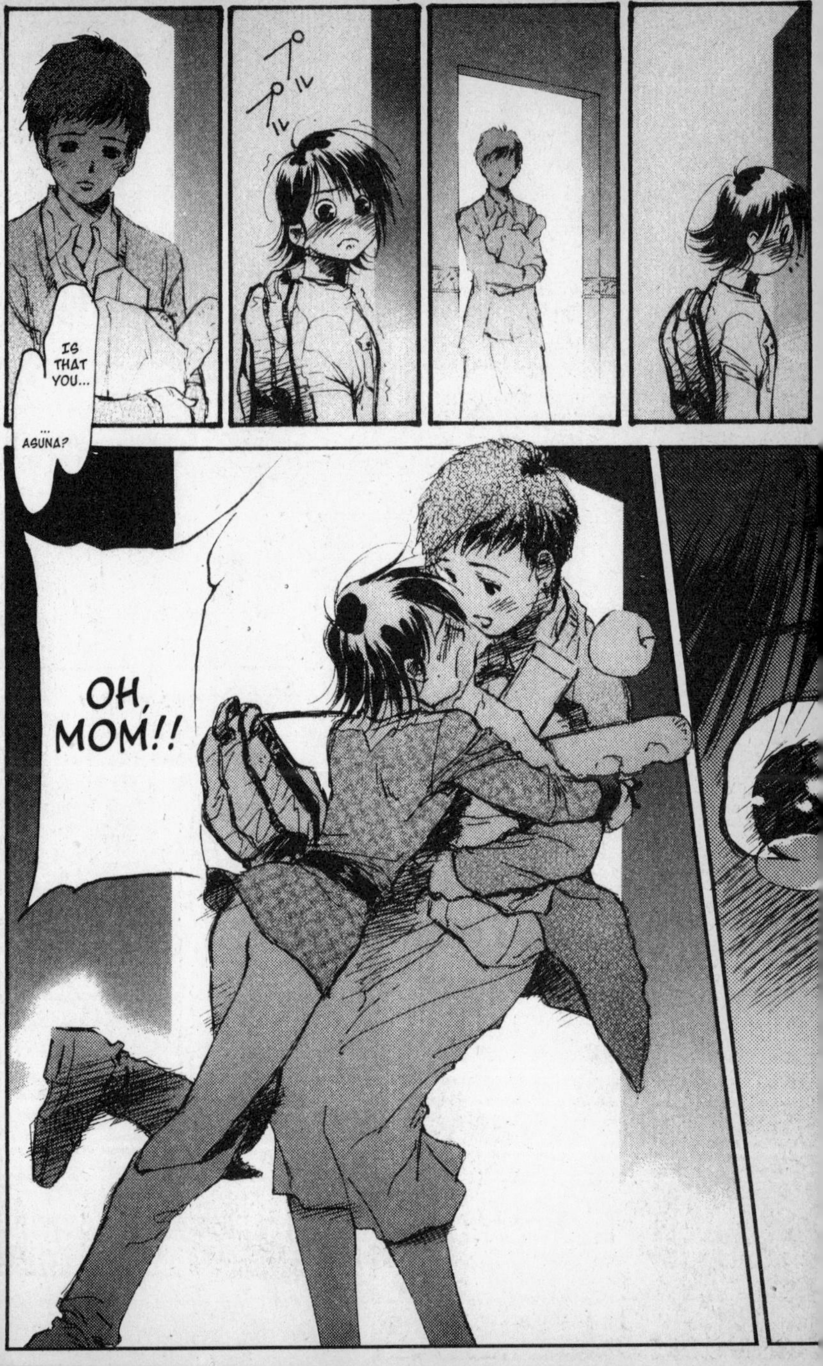

プル
プル
IS THAT YOU...
... ASUNA?
OH, MOM!!

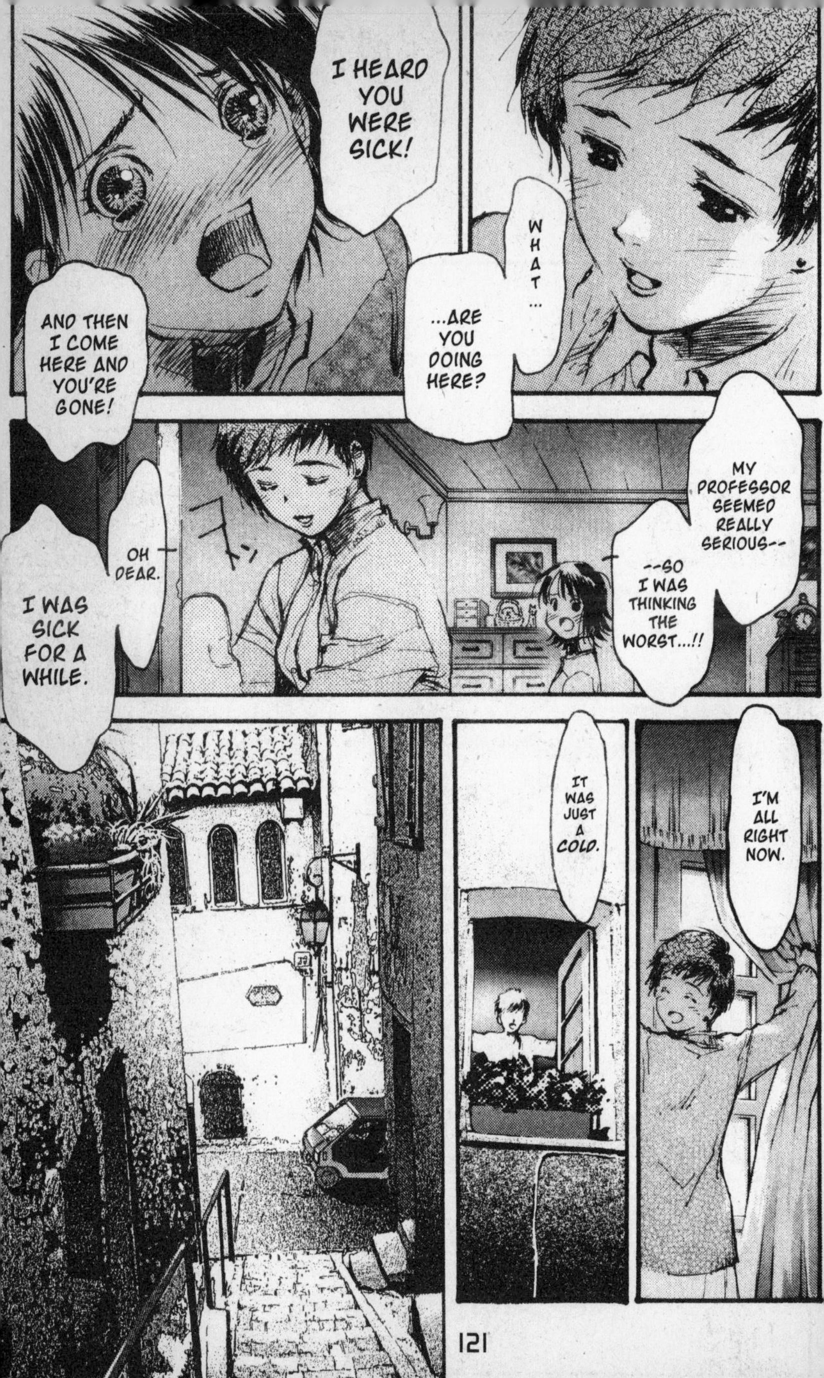

WHAT...
...ARE YOU DOING HERE?
I HEARD YOU WERE SICK!
AND THEN I COME HERE AND YOU'RE GONE!
MY PROFESSOR SEEMED REALLY SERIOUS--
--SO I WAS THINKING THE WORST...!!
OH DEAR.
I WAS SICK FOR A WHILE.
I'M ALL RIGHT NOW.
IT WAS JUST A COLD.

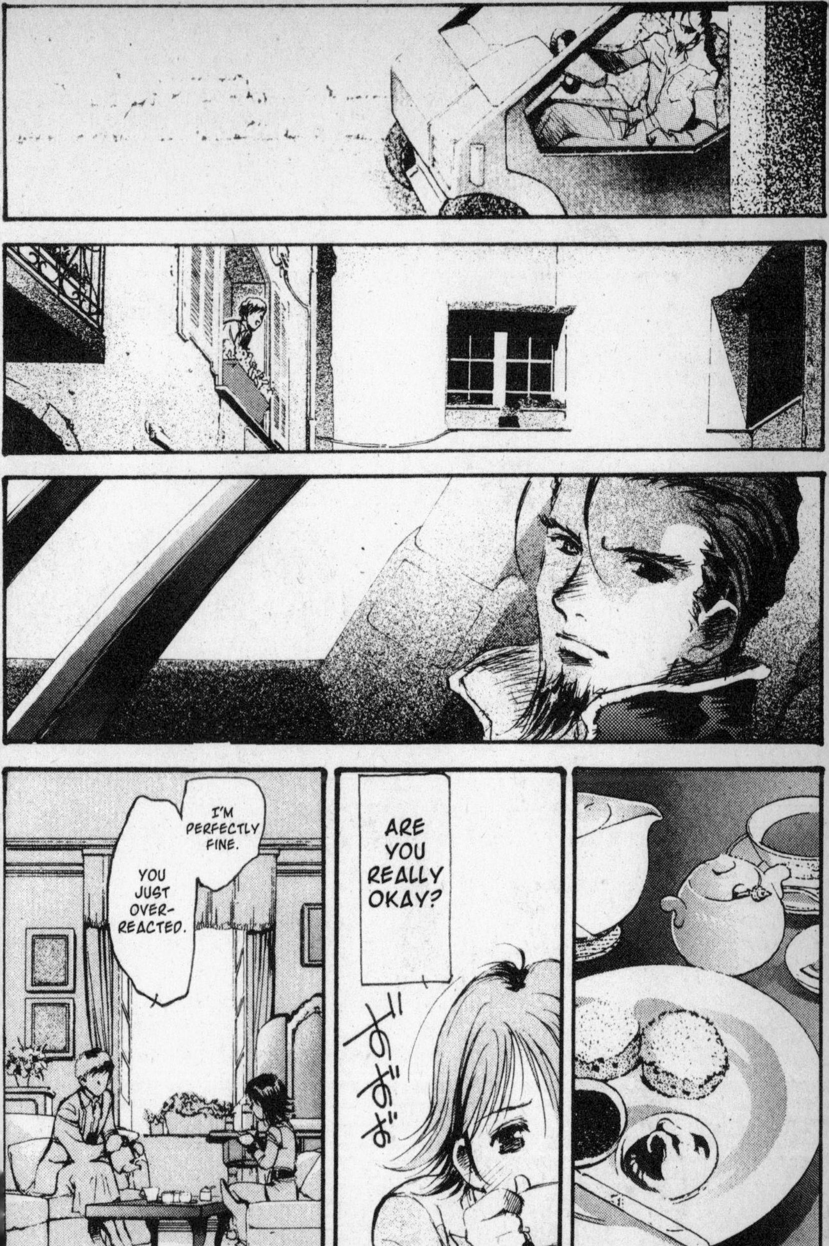
ARE YOU REALLY OKAY?
おずおず
I'M PERFECTLY FINE.
YOU JUST OVER-REACTED.

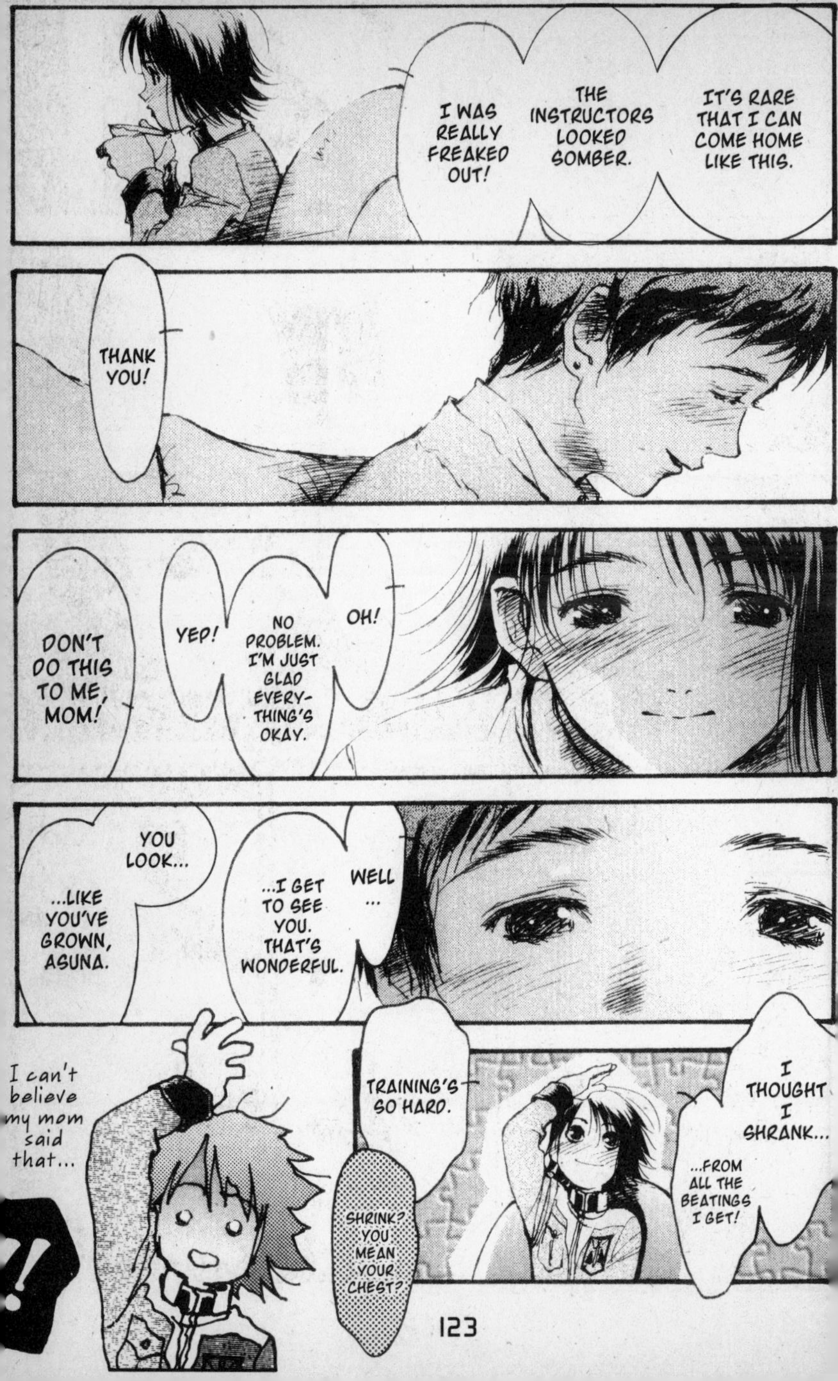
IT'S RARE THAT I CAN COME HOME LIKE THIS.
THE INSTRUCTORS LOOKED SOMBER.
I WAS REALLY FREAKED OUT!
THANK YOU!
OH!
NO PROBLEM. I'M JUST GLAD EVERY-THING'S OKAY.
YEP!
DON'T DO THIS TO ME, MOM!
WELL...
...I GET TO SEE YOU. THAT'S WONDERFUL.
YOU LOOK...
...LIKE YOU'VE GROWN, ASUNA.
I THOUGHT I SHRANK...
...FROM ALL THE BEATINGS I GET!
TRAINING'S SO HARD.
SHRINK? YOU MEAN YOUR CHEST?
I can't believe my mom said that...
?!

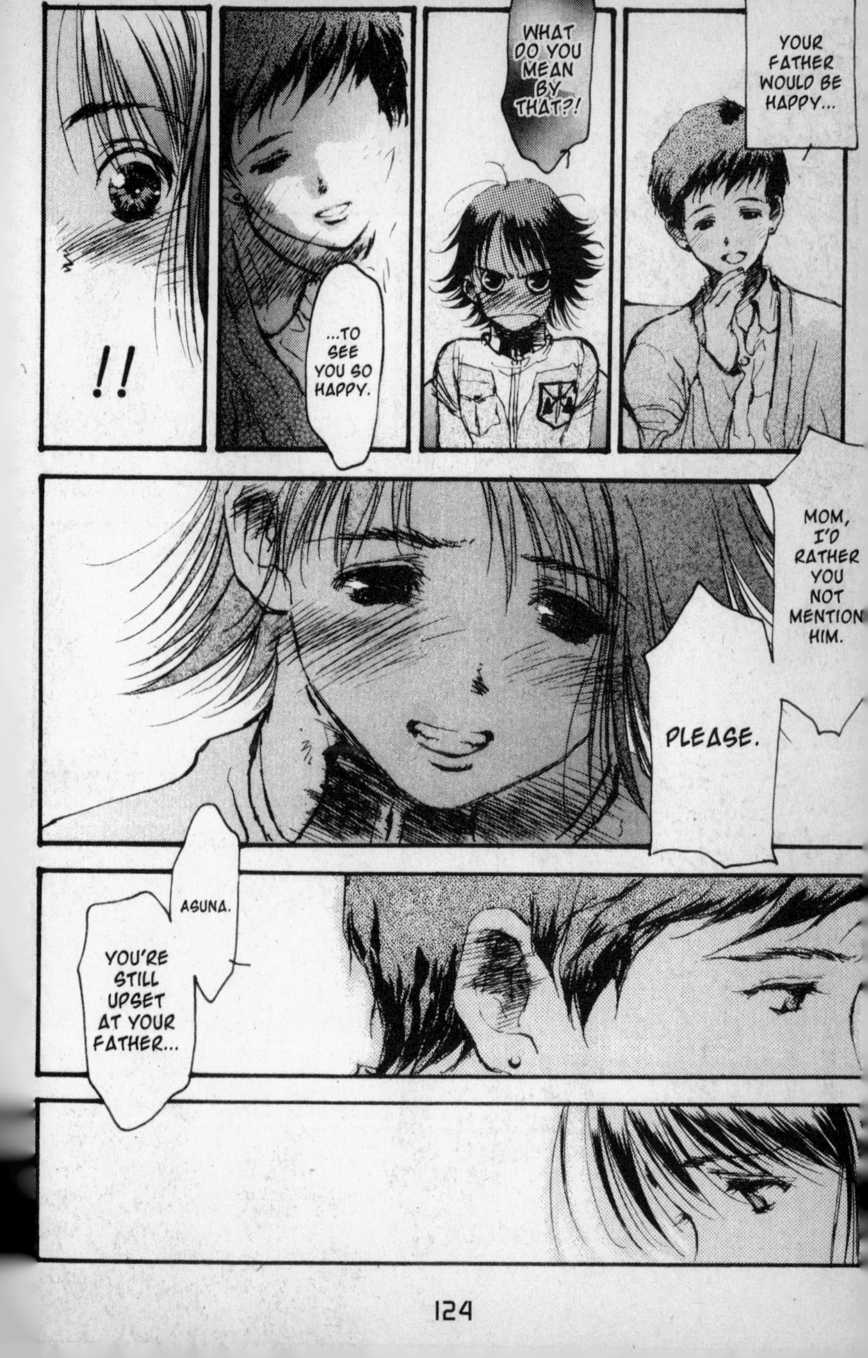
YOUR FATHER WOULD BE HAPPY...
WHAT DO YOU MEAN BY THAT?!
...TO SEE YOU SO HAPPY.
!!
MOM, I'D RATHER YOU NOT MENTION HIM.
PLEASE.
ASUNA.
YOU'RE STILL UPSET AT YOUR FATHER...

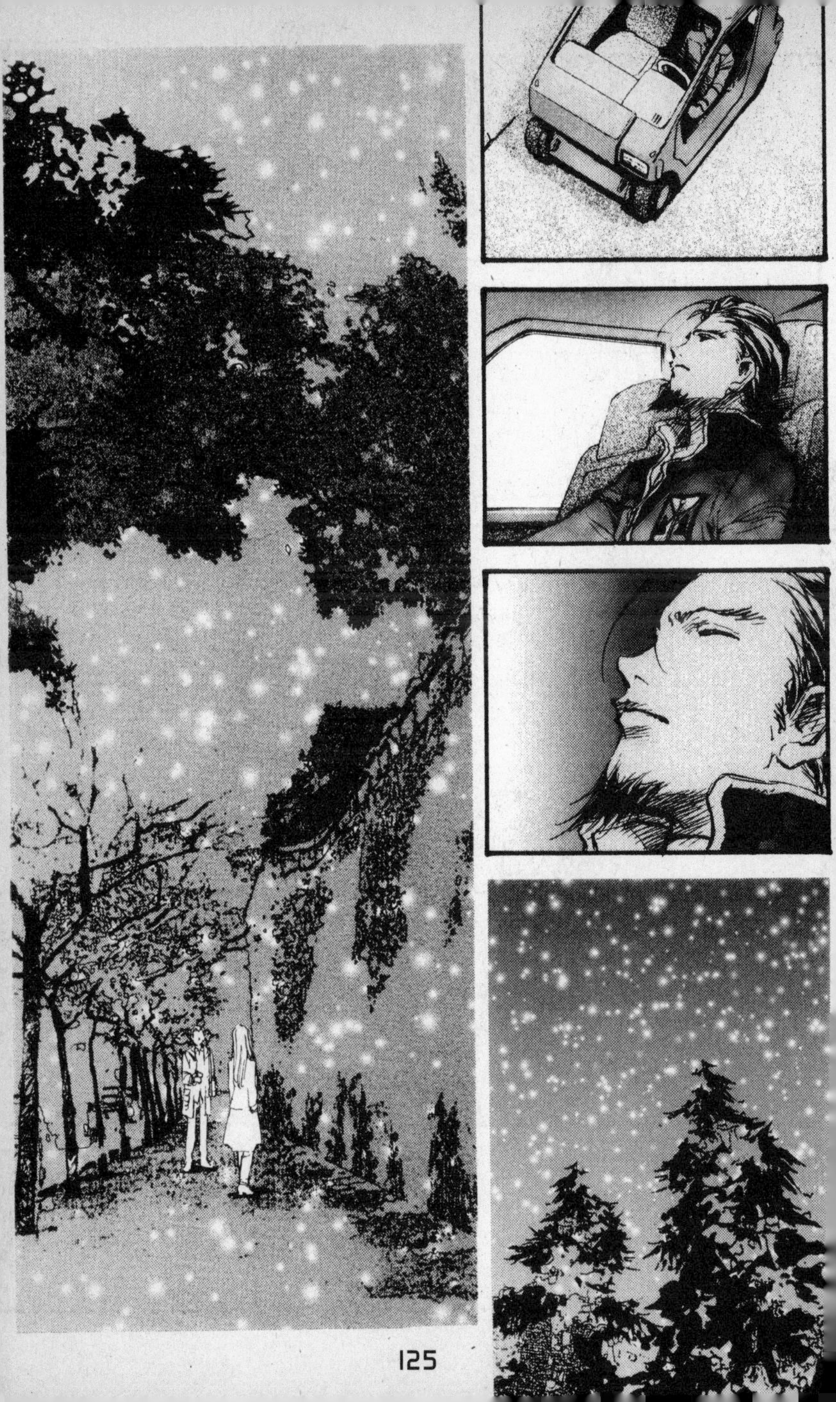

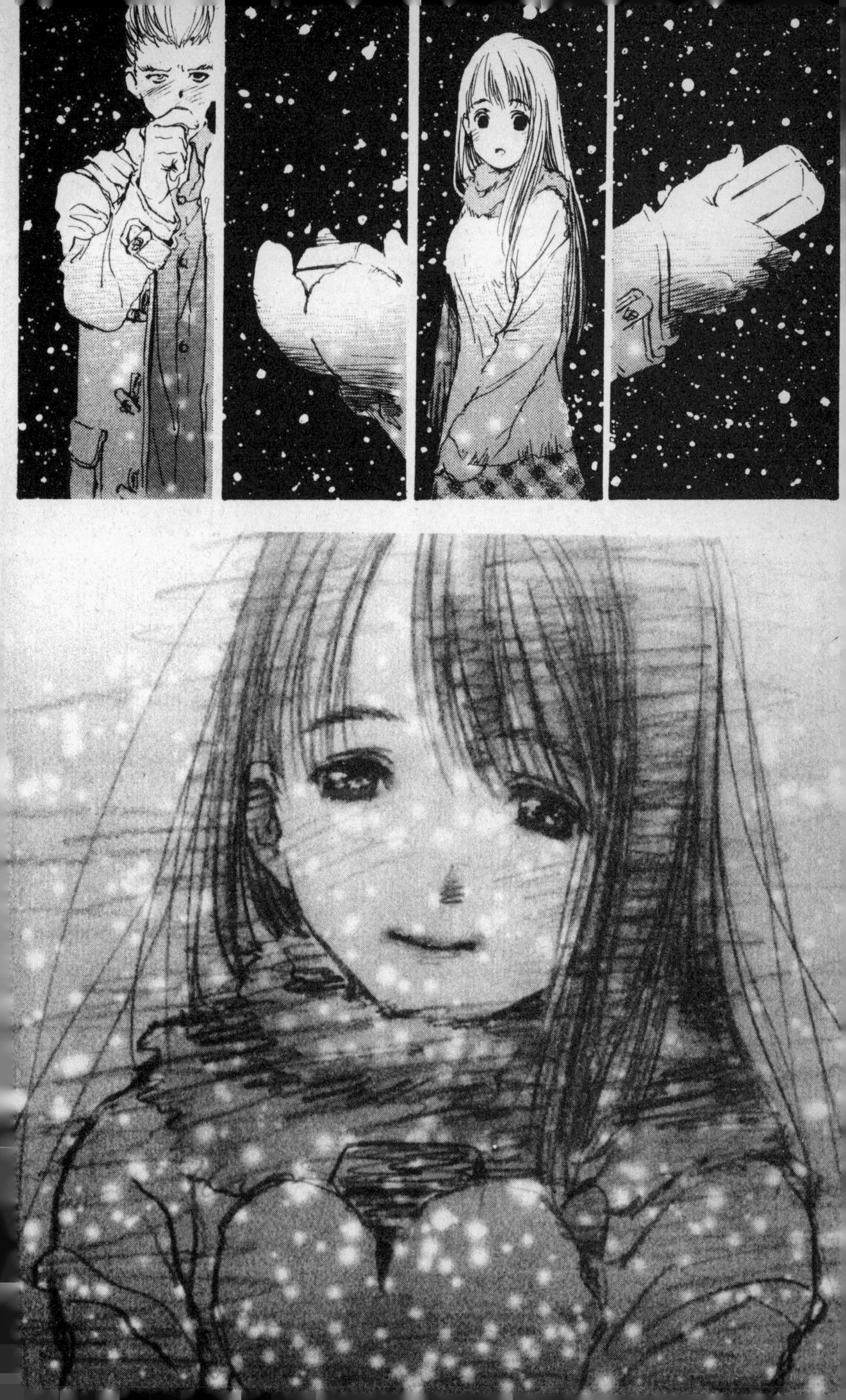

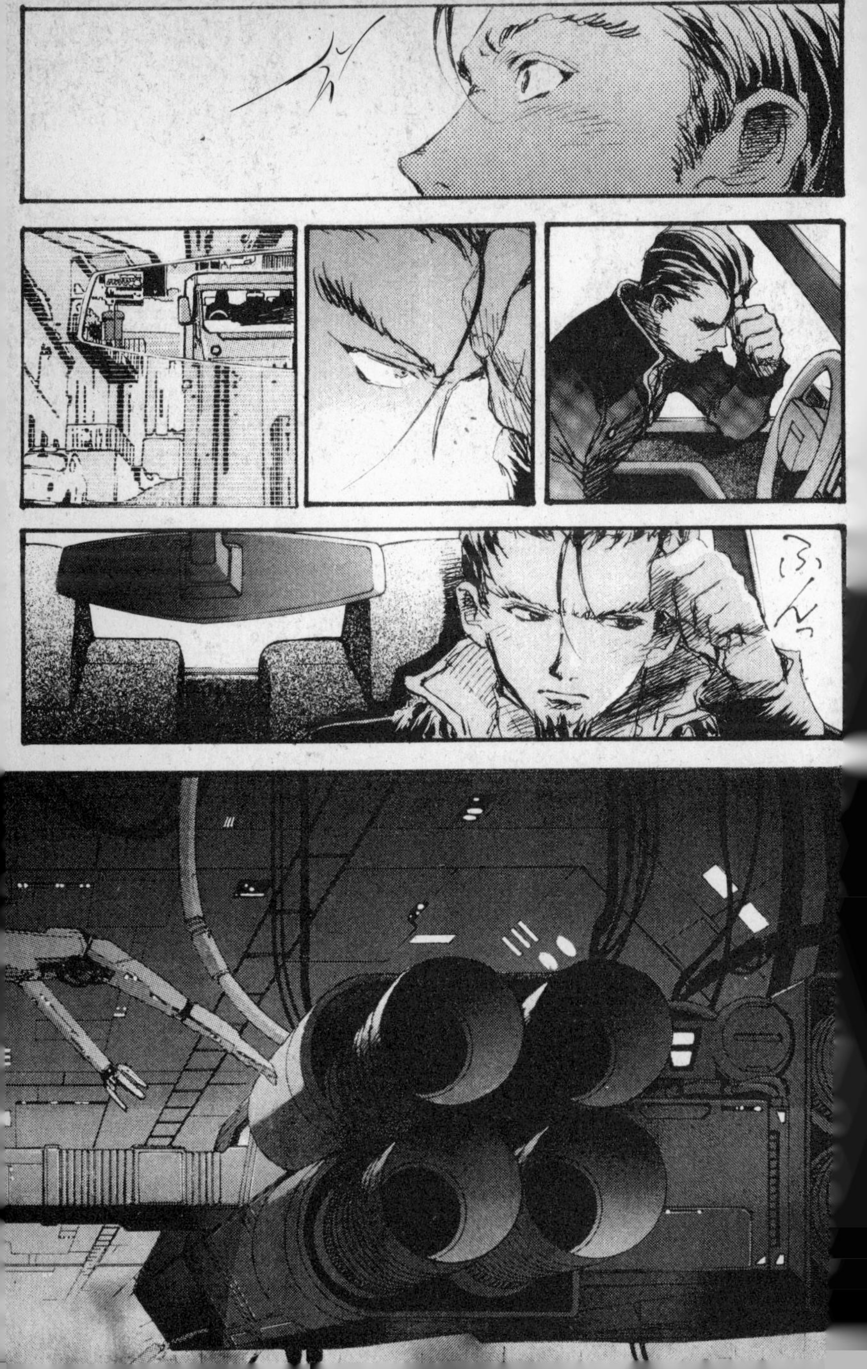
ふんっ

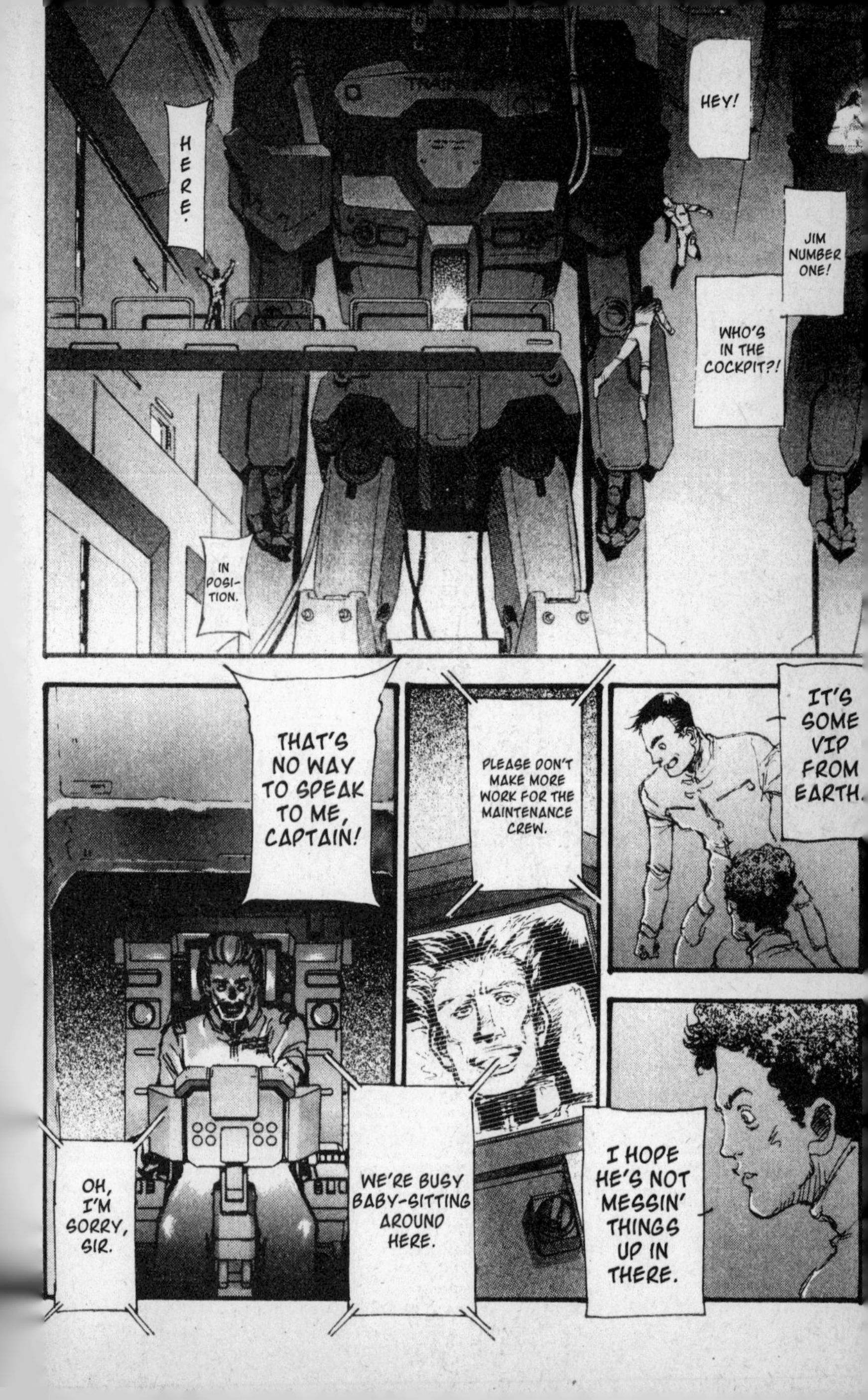
HEY!
JIM NUMBER ONE!
WHO'S IN THE COCKPIT?!
HERE.
IN POSITION.
IT'S SOME VIP FROM EARTH.
I HOPE HE'S NOT MESSIN' THINGS UP IN THERE.
PLEASE DON'T MAKE MORE WORK FOR THE MAINTENANCE CREW.
WE'RE BUSY BABY-SITTING AROUND HERE.
THAT'S NO WAY TO SPEAK TO ME, CAPTAIN!
OH, I'M SORRY, SIR.

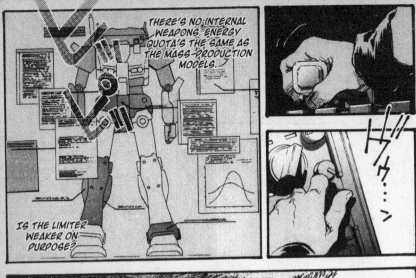

ドゥ…ン
THERE'S NO INTERNAL WEAPONS. ENERGY QUOTA'S THE SAME AS THE MASS-PRODUCTION MODELS.
IS THE LIMITER WEAKER ON PURPOSE?
IT'S BEEN THOROUGHLY PREPARED, BUT...
...TO THINK THEY'LL ACTUALLY FIGHT USING THIS MACHINE...!!
MARIE ALBELTIA.

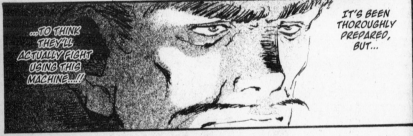

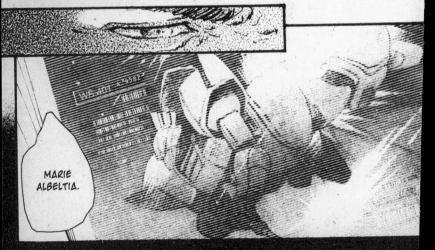

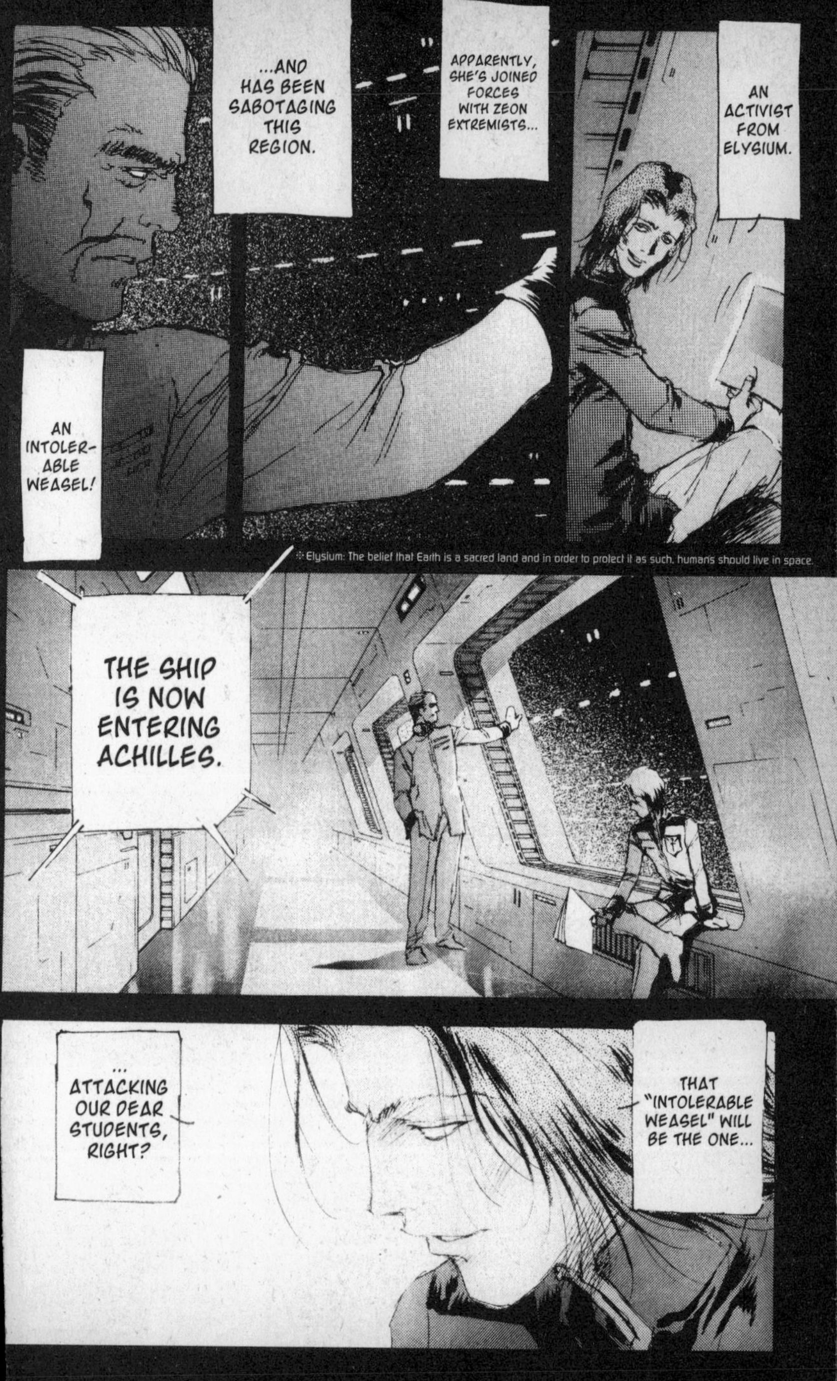
AN ACTIVIST FROM ELYSIUM.
APPARENTLY, SHE'S JOINED FORCES WITH ZEON EXTREMISTS...
...AND HAS BEEN SABOTAGING THIS REGION.
AN INTOLERABLE WEASEL!
THE SHIP IS NOW ENTERING ACHILLES.
THAT "INTOLERABLE WEASEL" WILL BE THE ONE...
...ATTACKING OUR DEAR STUDENTS, RIGHT?

※ Elysium: The belief that Earth is a sacred land and in order to protect it as such, humans should live in space.

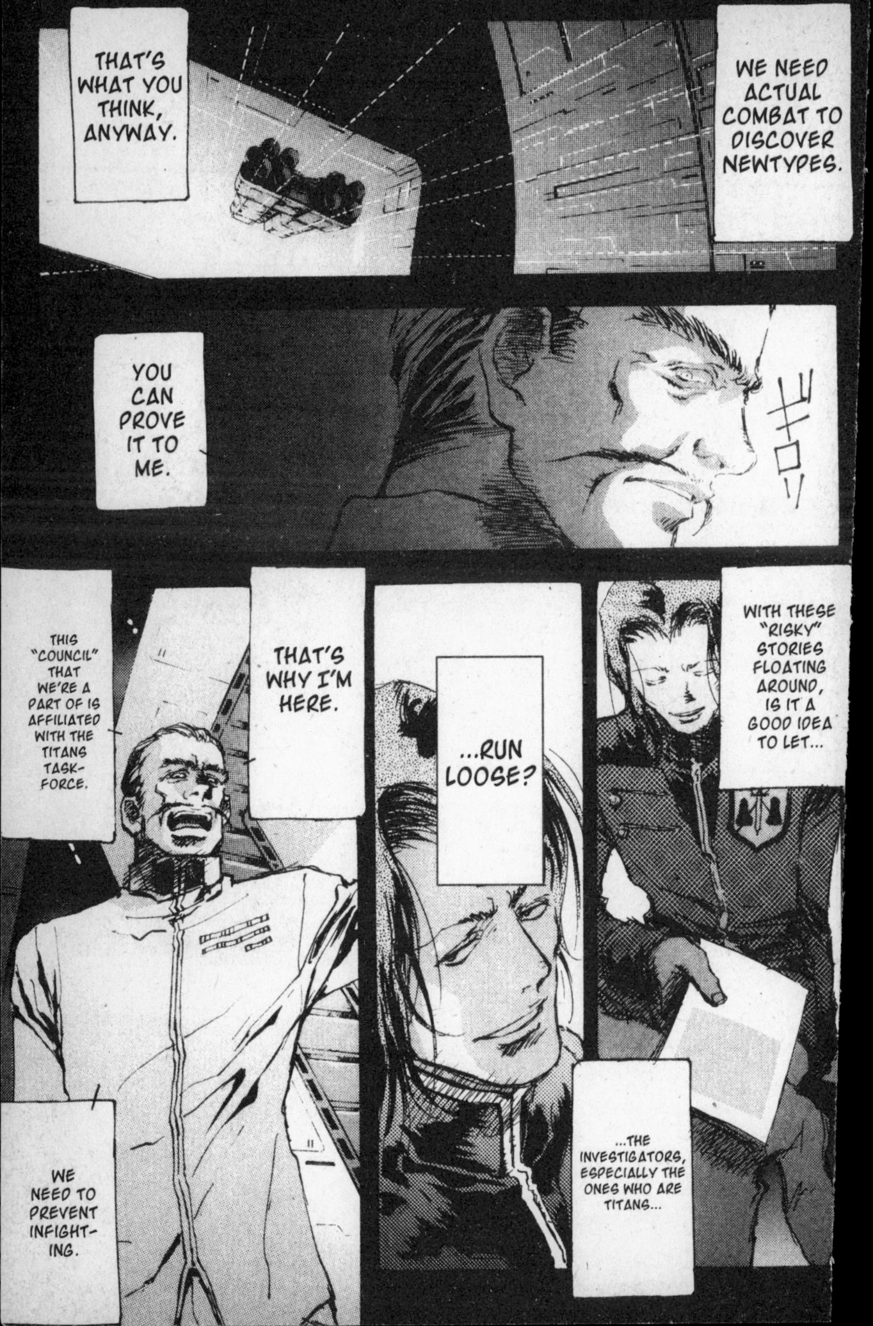
WE NEED ACTUAL COMBAT TO DISCOVER NEWTYPES.
THAT'S WHAT YOU THINK, ANYWAY.
YOU CAN PROVE IT TO ME.
ギロリ
WITH THESE "RISKY" STORIES FLOATING AROUND, IS IT A GOOD IDEA TO LET...
...THE INVESTIGATORS, ESPECIALLY THE ONES WHO ARE TITANS...
...RUN LOOSE?
THAT'S WHY I'M HERE.
THIS "COUNCIL" THAT WE'RE A PART OF IS AFFILIATED WITH THE TITANS TASK-FORCE.
WE NEED TO PREVENT INFIGHTING.

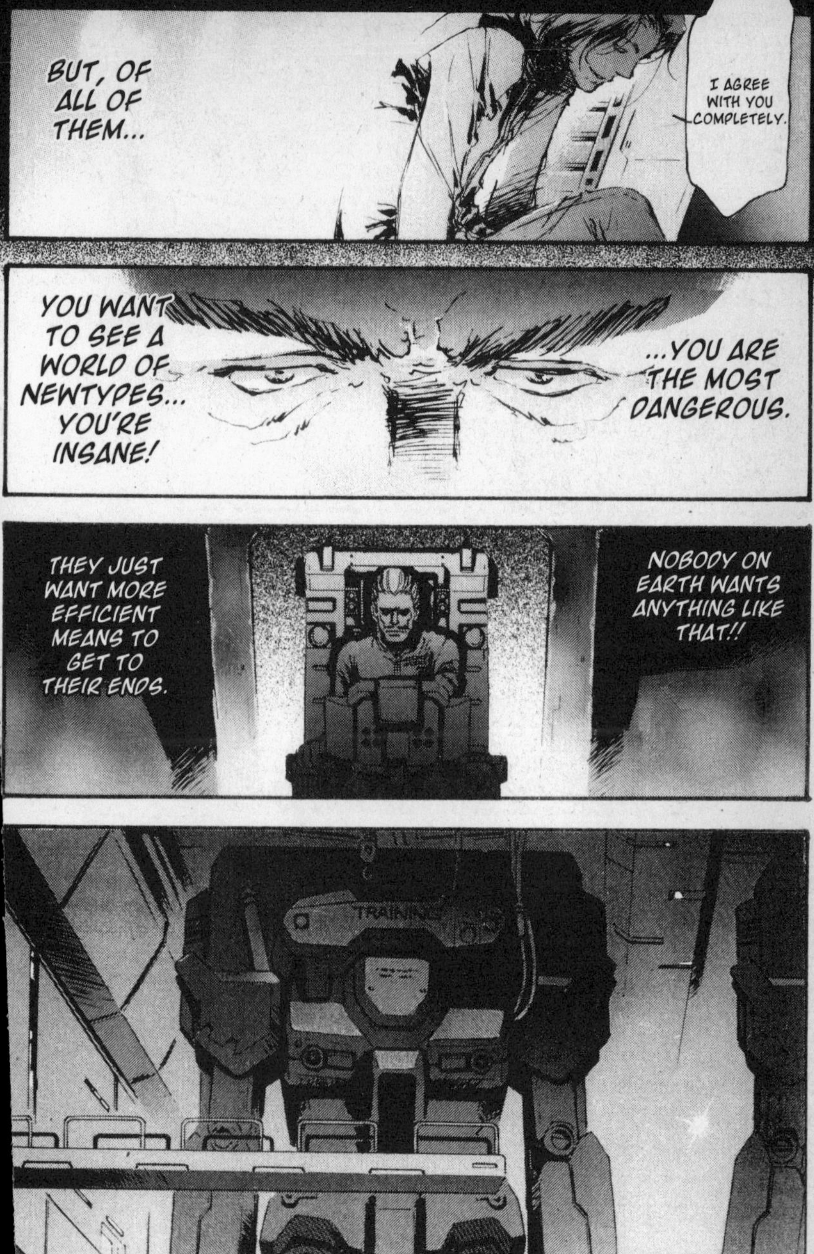
I AGREE WITH YOU COMPLETELY.
BUT, OF ALL OF THEM...
...YOU ARE THE MOST DANGEROUS.
YOU WANT TO SEE A WORLD OF NEWTYPES... YOU'RE INSANE!
NOBODY ON EARTH WANTS ANYTHING LIKE THAT!!
THEY JUST WANT MORE EFFICIENT MEANS TO GET TO THEIR ENDS.

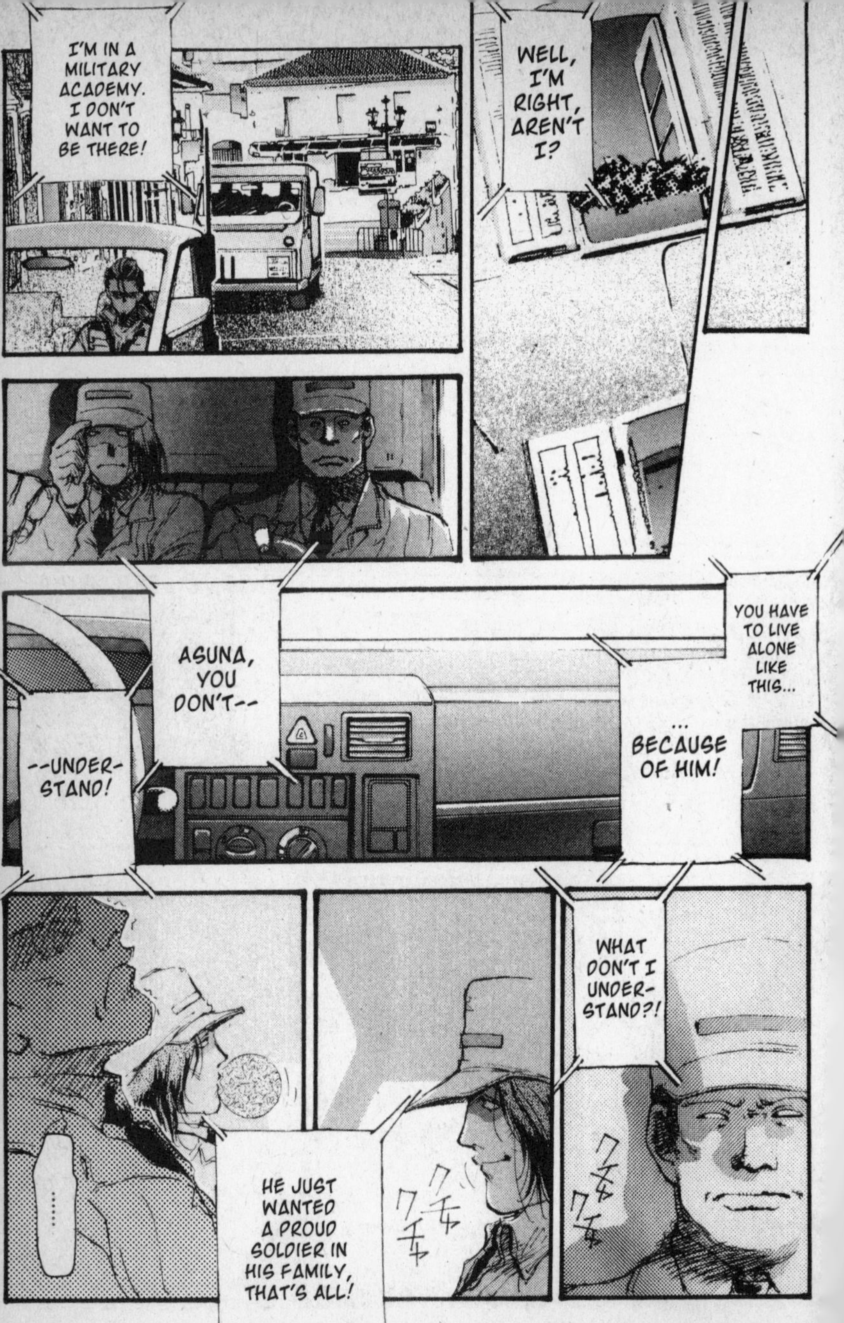
WELL, I'M RIGHT, AREN'T I?
I'M IN A MILITARY ACADEMY. I DON'T WANT TO BE THERE!
YOU HAVE TO LIVE ALONE LIKE THIS...
...BECAUSE OF HIM!
ASUNA, YOU DON'T--
--UNDER-STAND!
WHAT DON'T I UNDER-STAND?!
クチャ クチャ
クチャ クチャ
HE JUST WANTED A PROUD SOLDIER IN HIS FAMILY, THAT'S ALL!
......

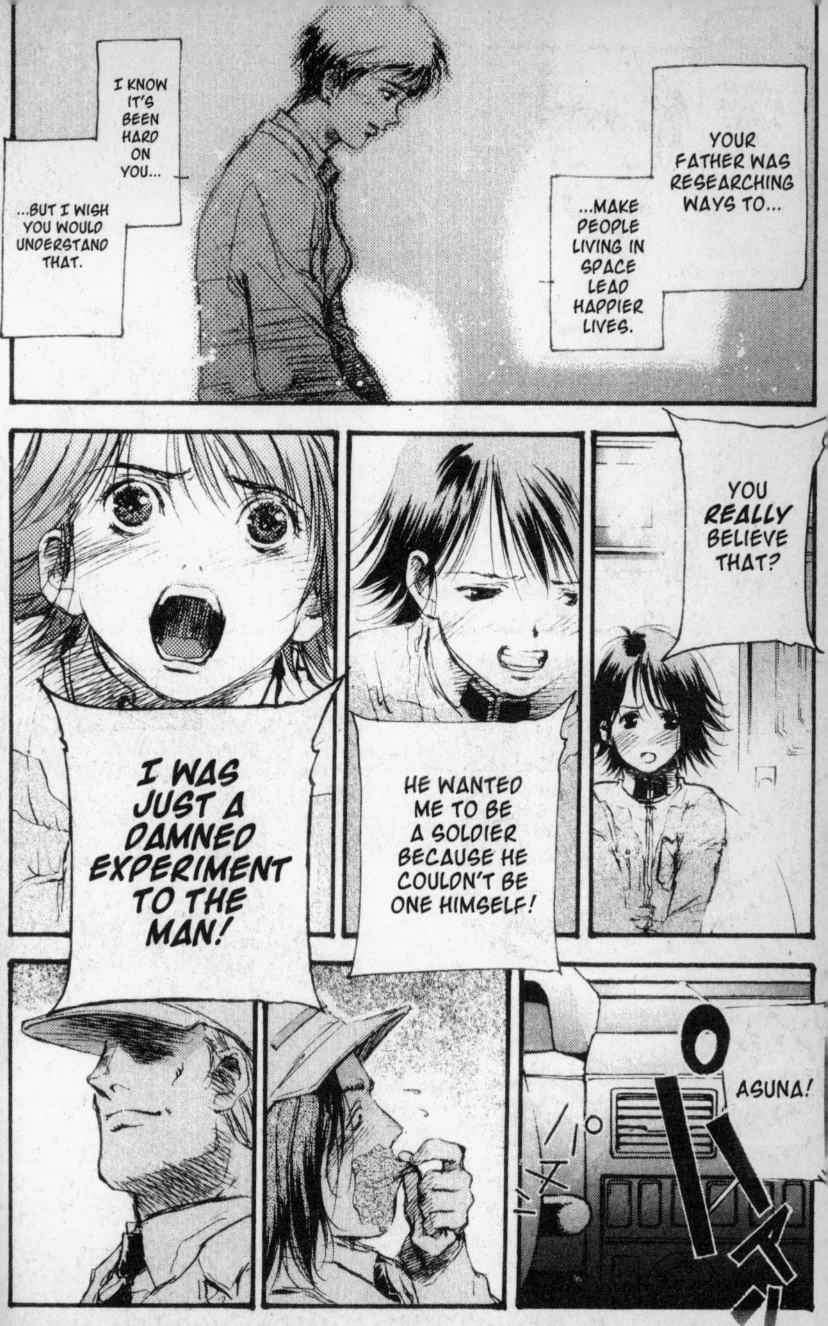

YOUR FATHER WAS RESEARCHING WAYS TO...
...MAKE PEOPLE LIVING IN SPACE LEAD HAPPIER LIVES.
I KNOW IT'S BEEN HARD ON YOU...
...BUT I WISH YOU WOULD UNDERSTAND THAT.
YOU REALLY BELIEVE THAT?
HE WANTED ME TO BE A SOLDIER BECAUSE HE COULDN'T BE ONE HIMSELF!
I WAS JUST A DAMNED EXPERIMENT TO THE MAN!
ASUNA!

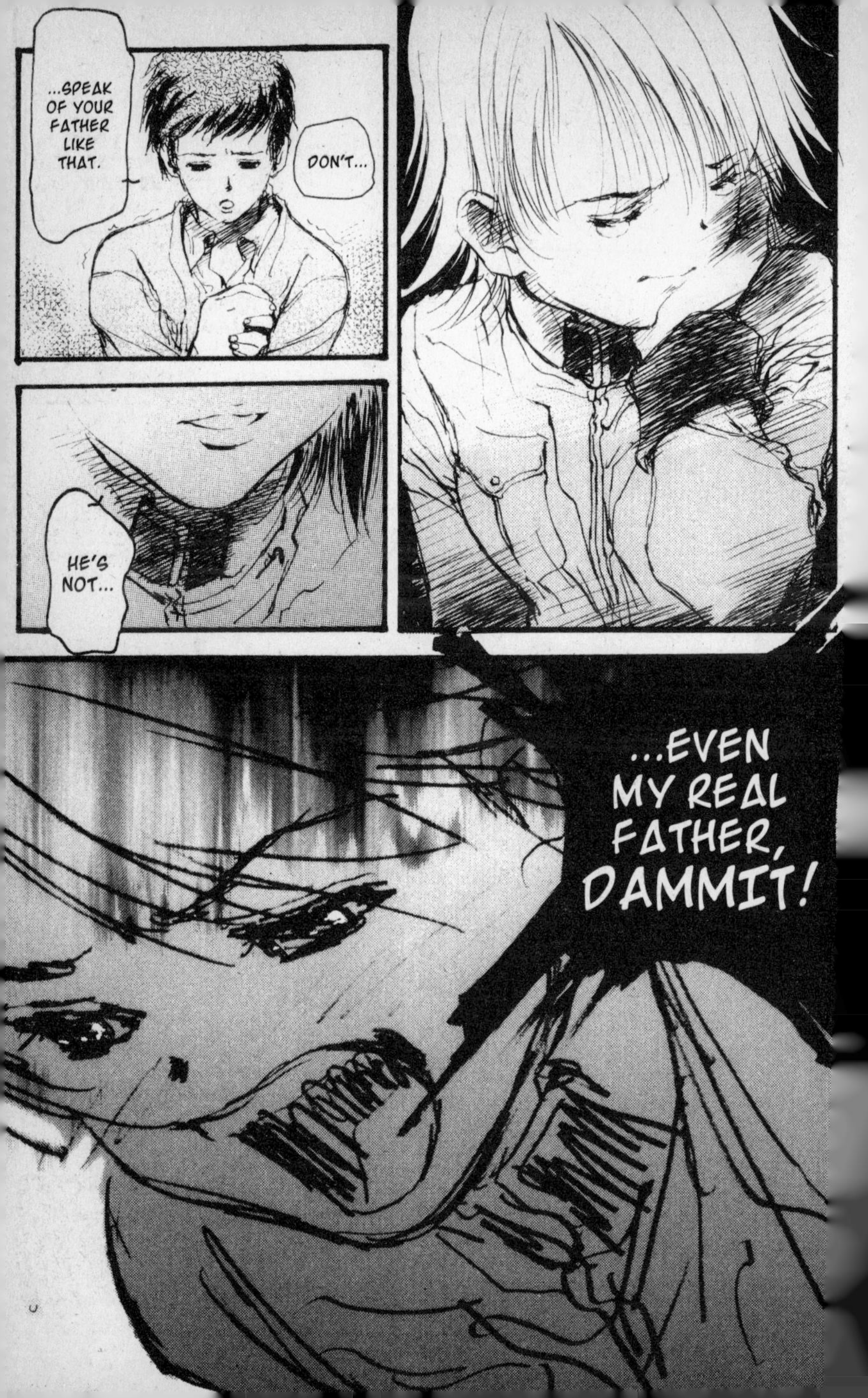
DON'T...
...SPEAK OF YOUR FATHER LIKE THAT.
HE'S NOT...
...EVEN MY REAL FATHER, DAMMIT!

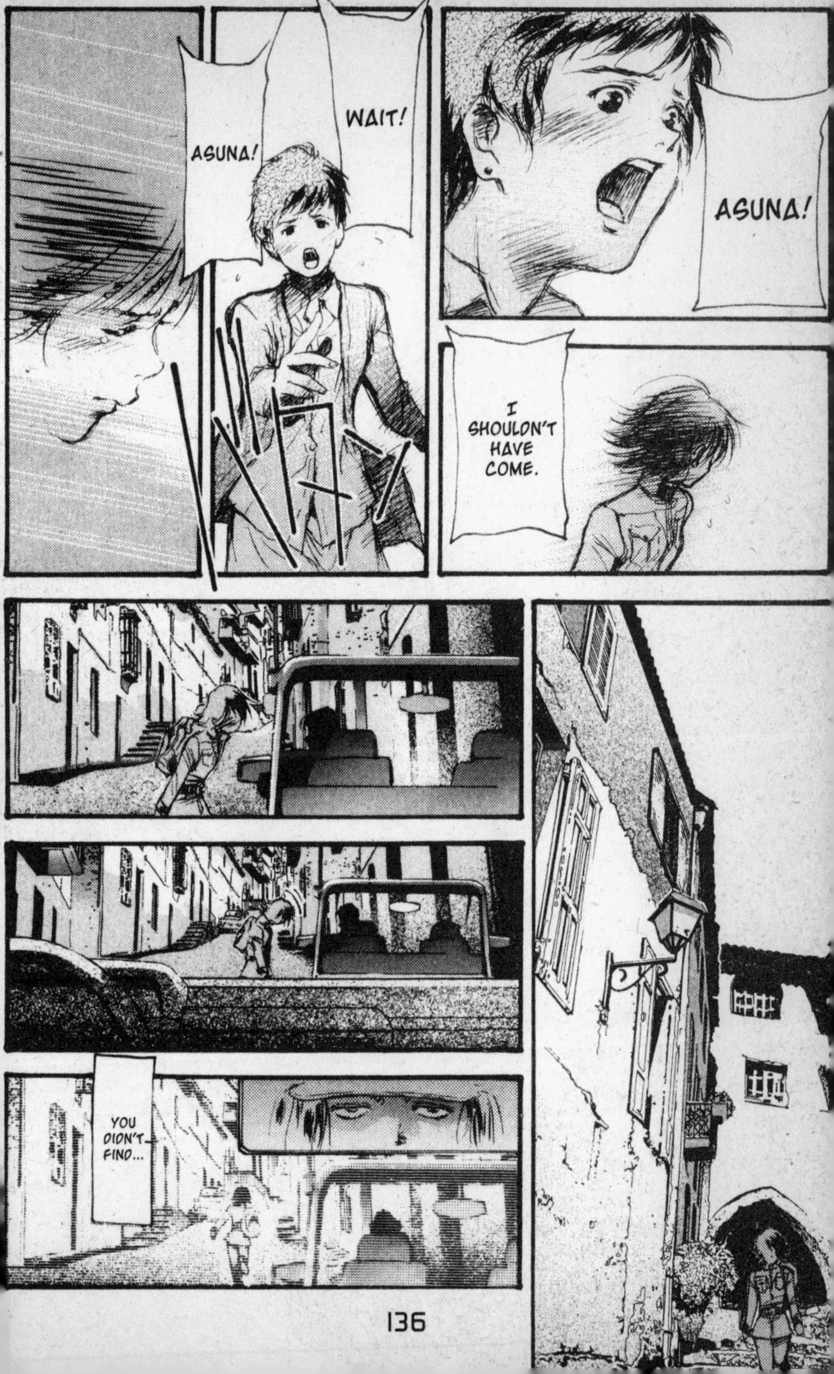
ASUNA!
I SHOULDN'T HAVE COME.
WAIT!
ASUNA!
YOU DIDN'T FIND...

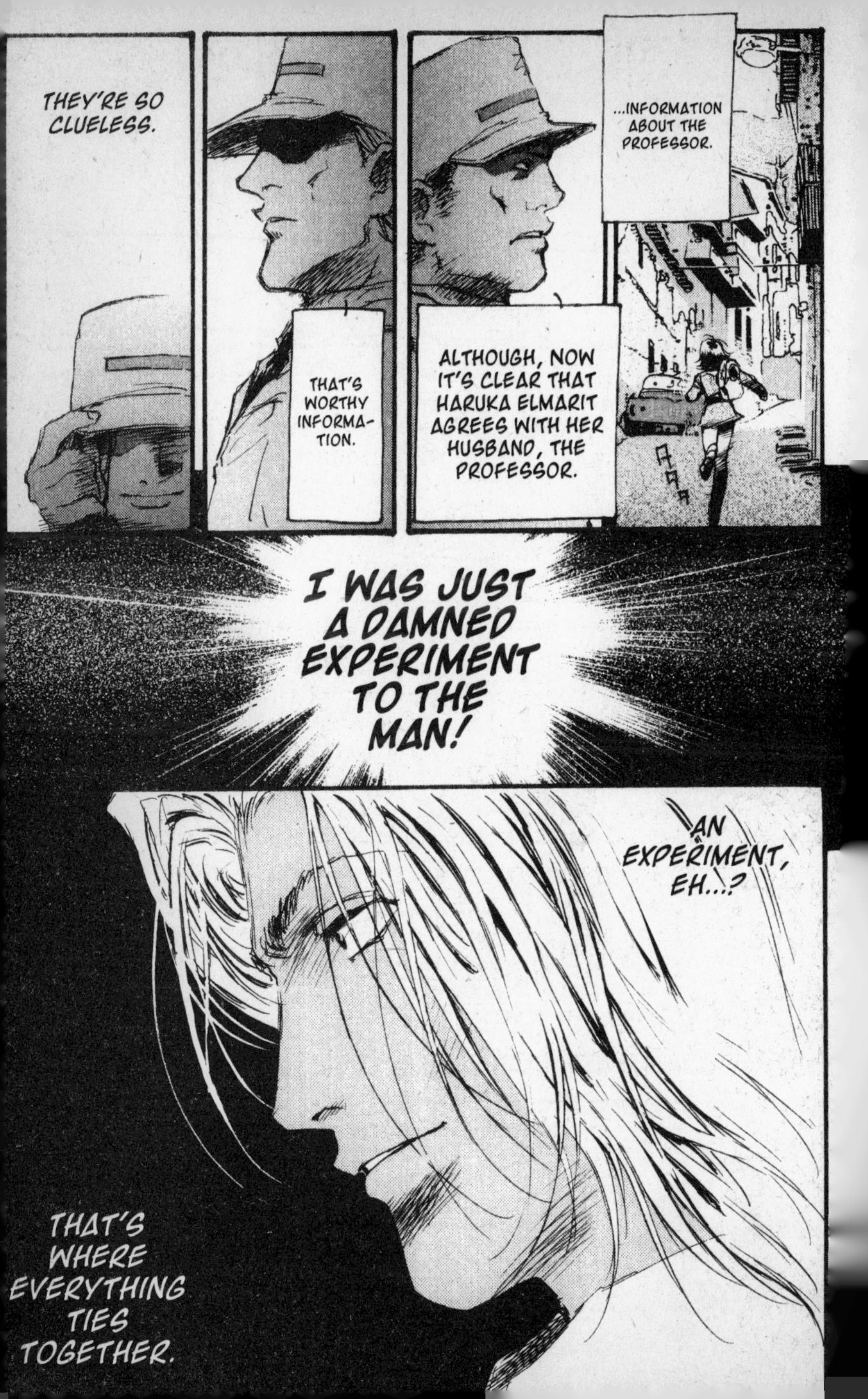
...INFORMATION ABOUT THE PROFESSOR.
ALTHOUGH, NOW IT'S CLEAR THAT HARUKA ELMARIT AGREES WITH HER HUSBAND, THE PROFESSOR.
THAT'S WORTHY INFORMATION.
THEY'RE SO CLUELESS.
I WAS JUST A DAMNED EXPERIMENT TO THE MAN!
AN EXPERIMENT, EH...?
THAT'S WHERE EVERYTHING TIES TOGETHER.

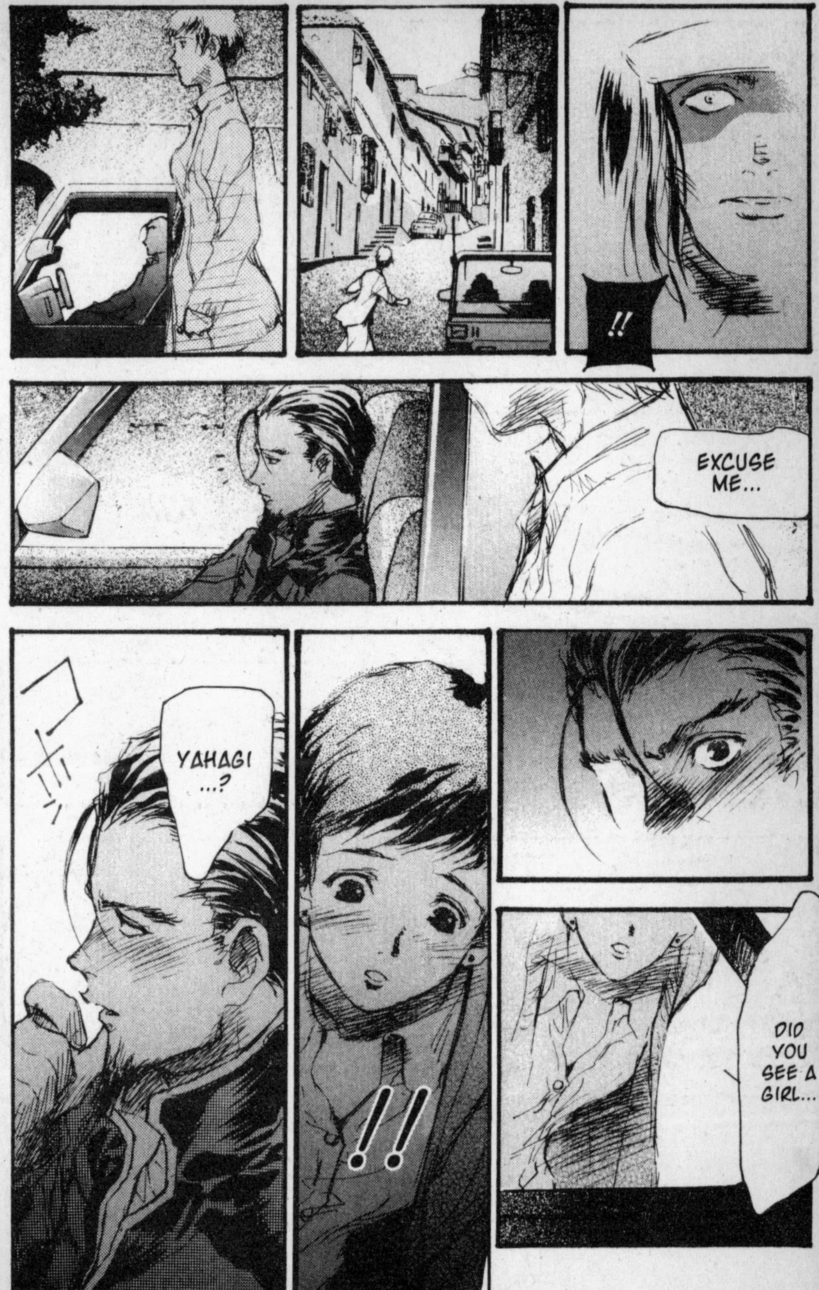
!!
EXCUSE ME...
DID YOU SEE A GIRL...
!!
YAHAGI ...?

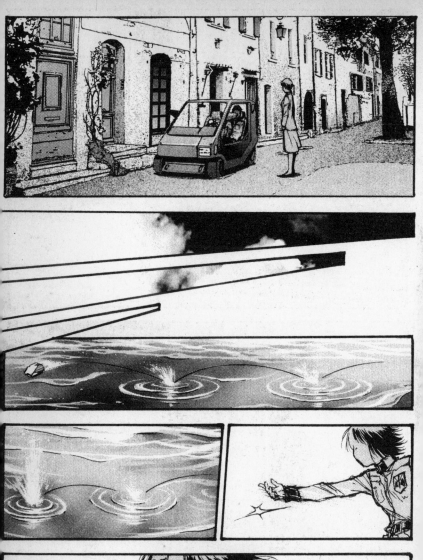

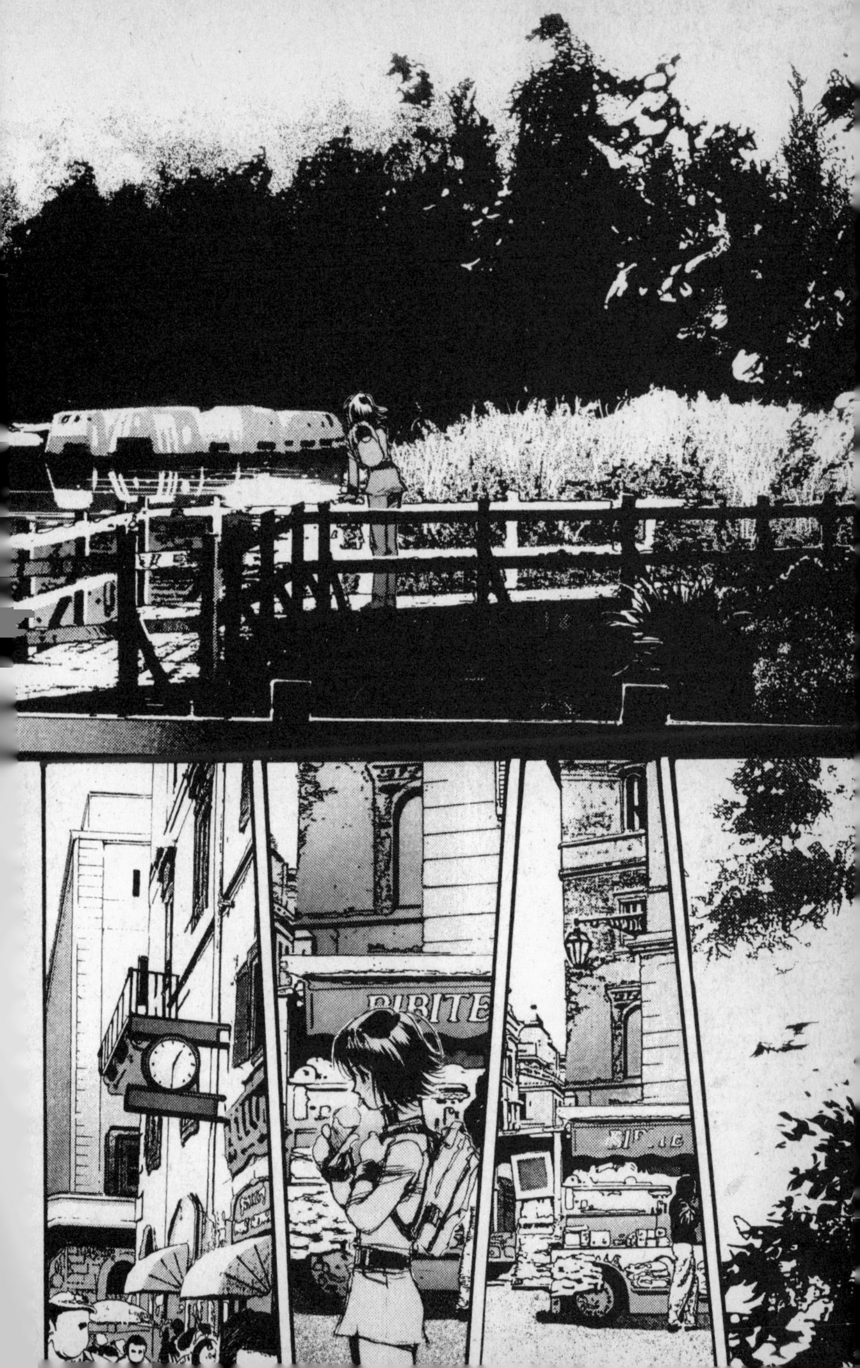

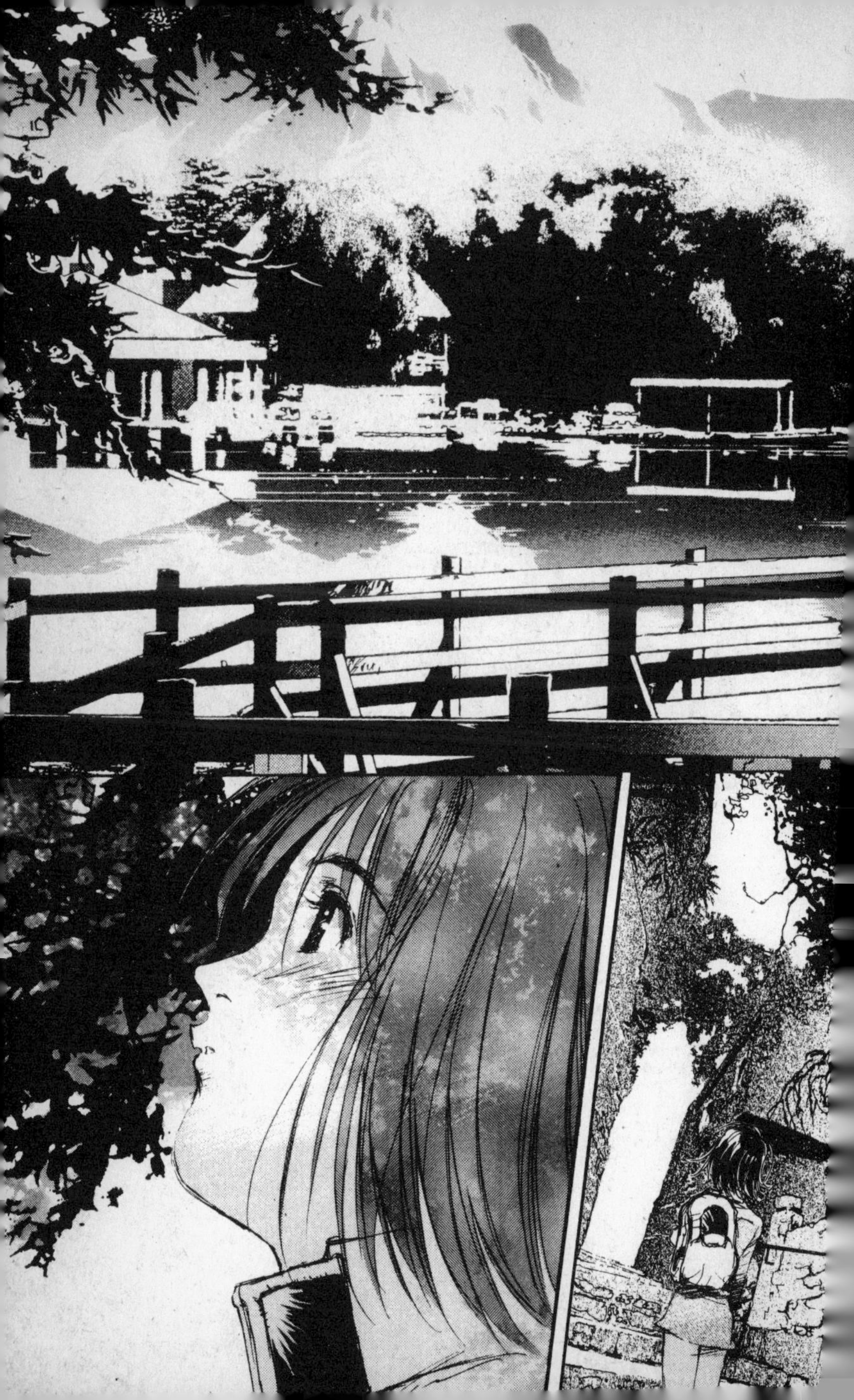

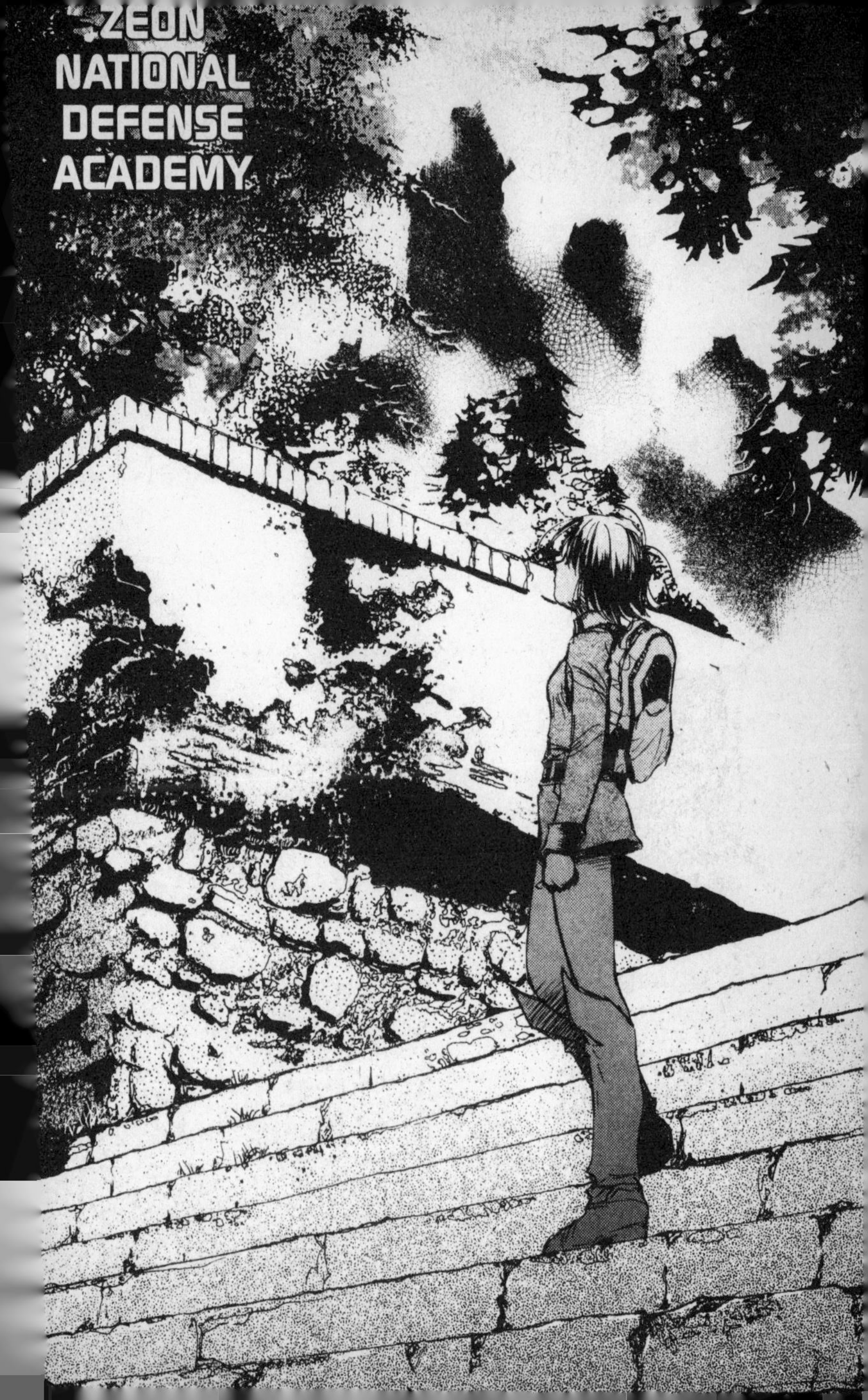
ZEON NATIONAL DEFENSE ACADEMY

CHARACTER FILE:05

Yahagi Franziback

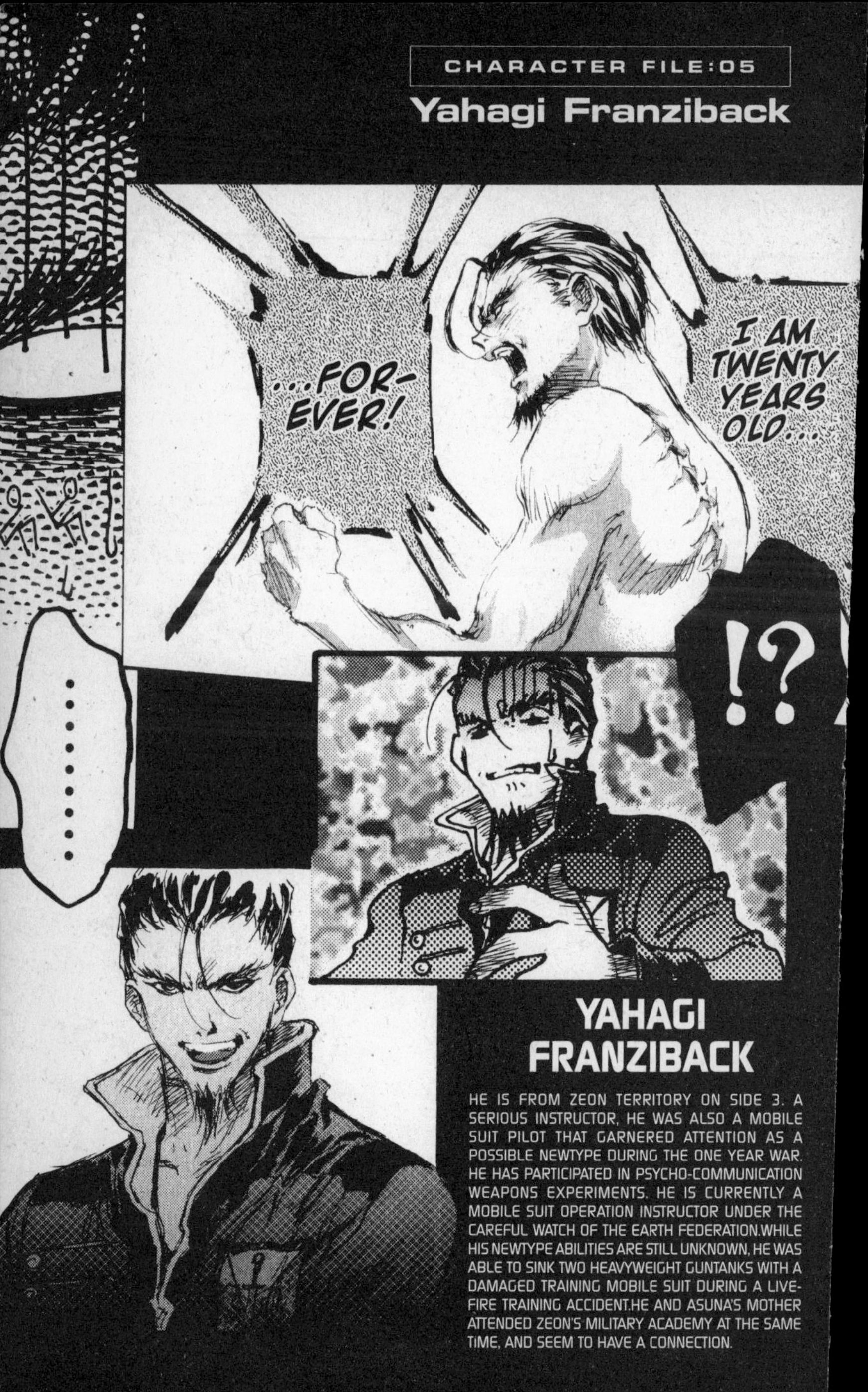
I AM TWENTY YEARS OLD...
...FOR-EVER!
!?
......

YAHAGI FRANZIBACK

HE IS FROM ZEON TERRITORY ON SIDE 3. A SERIOUS INSTRUCTOR, HE WAS ALSO A MOBILE SUIT PILOT THAT GARNERED ATTENTION AS A POSSIBLE NEWTYPE DURING THE ONE YEAR WAR. HE HAS PARTICIPATED IN PSYCHO-COMMUNICATION WEAPONS EXPERIMENTS. HE IS CURRENTLY A MOBILE SUIT OPERATION INSTRUCTOR UNDER THE CAREFUL WATCH OF THE EARTH FEDERATION.WHILE HIS NEWTYPE ABILITIES ARE STILL UNKNOWN, HE WAS ABLE TO SINK TWO HEAVYWEIGHT GUNTANKS WITH A DAMAGED TRAINING MOBILE SUIT DURING A LIVE-FIRE TRAINING ACCIDENT.HE AND ASUNA'S MOTHER ATTENDED ZEON'S MILITARY ACADEMY AT THE SAME TIME, AND SEEM TO HAVE A CONNECTION.

SPECIAL CHAPTER: ASUNA ENTERS THE ACADEMY

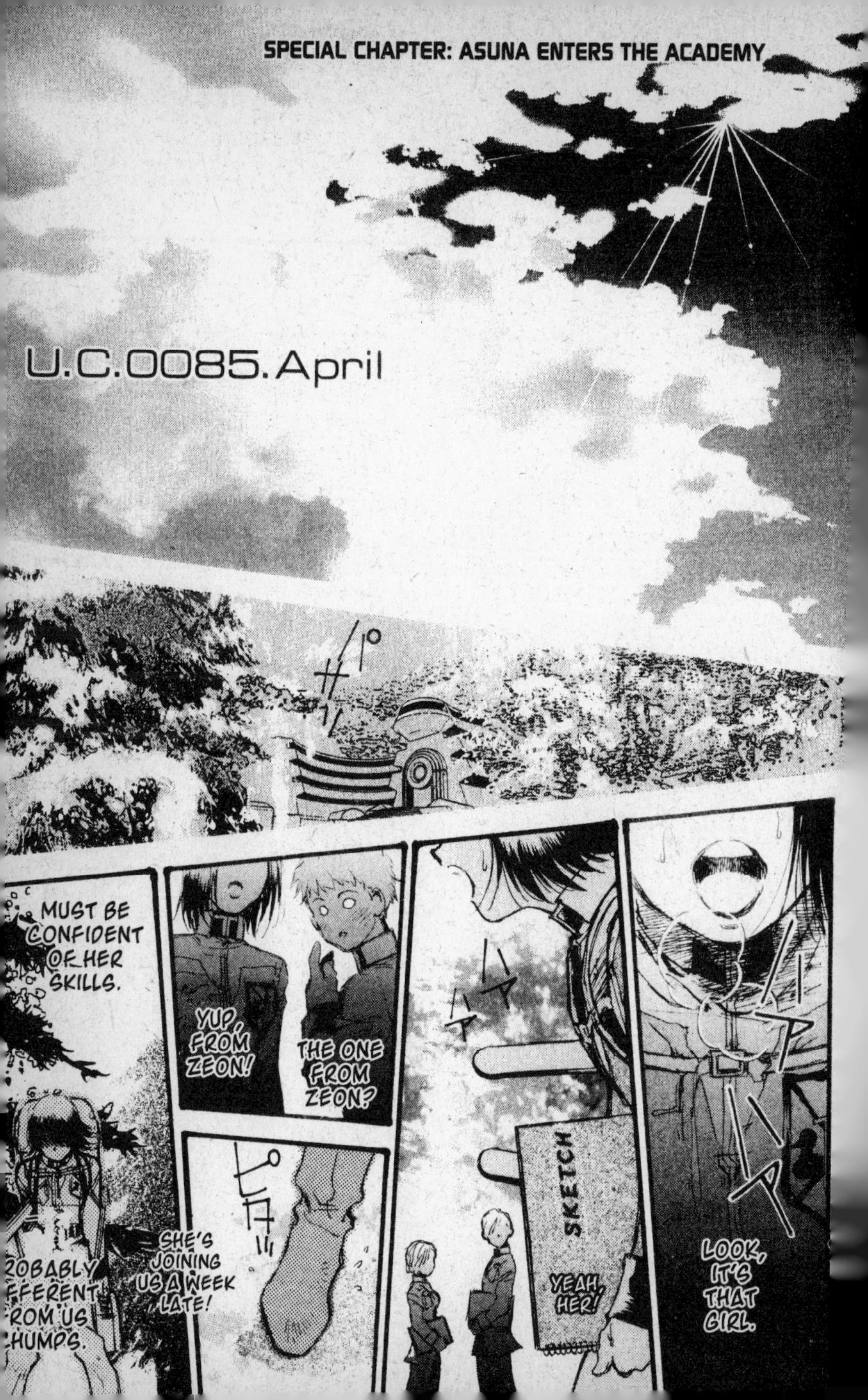
U.C.0085. April
LOOK, IT'S THAT GIRL.
YEAH, HER!
SKETCH
THE ONE FROM ZEON?
YUP, FROM ZEON!
SHE'S JOINING US A WEEK LATE!
MUST BE CONFIDENT OF HER SKILLS.
ROBABLY FFERENT ROM US HUMPS.

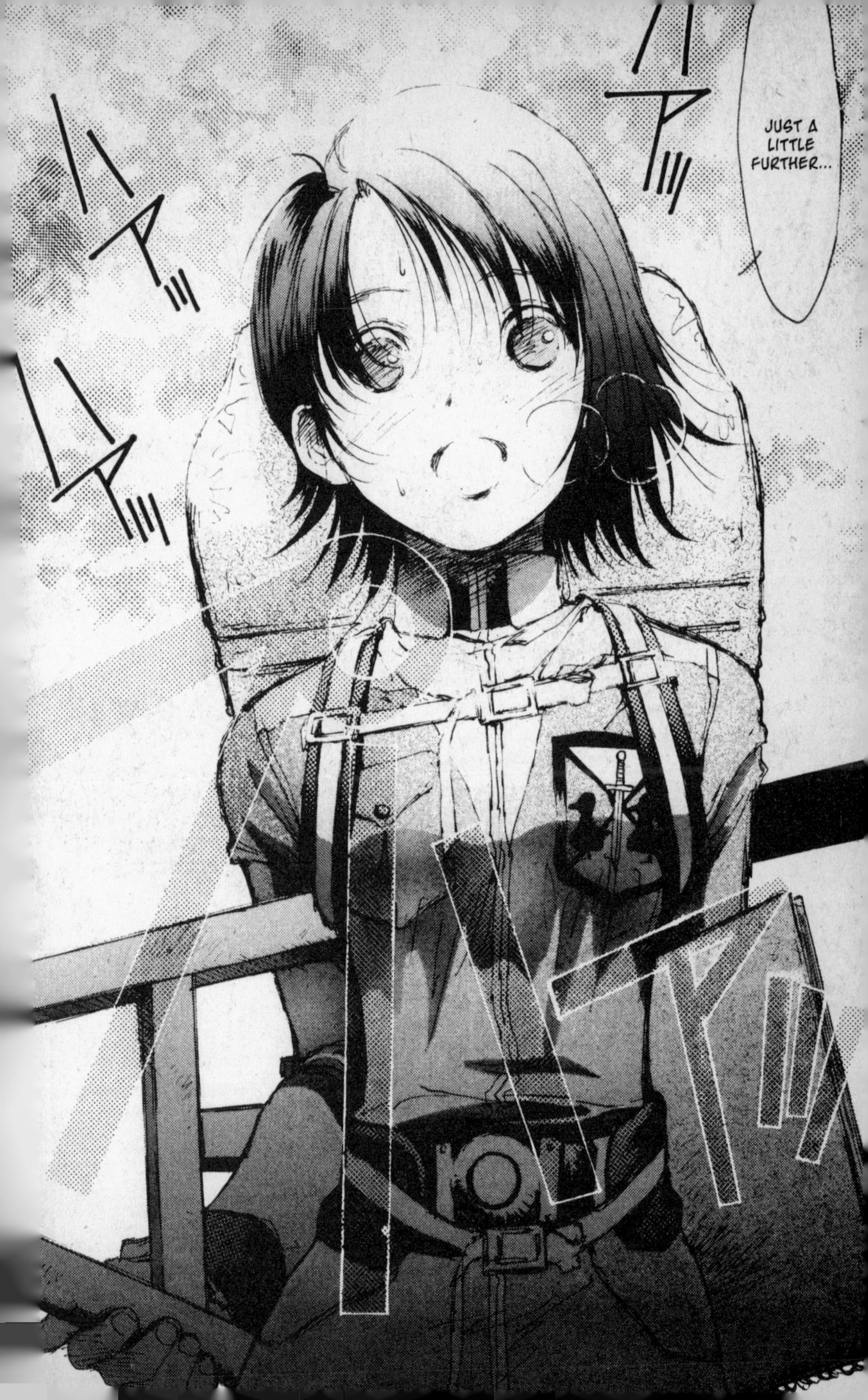
JUST A LITTLE FURTHER...

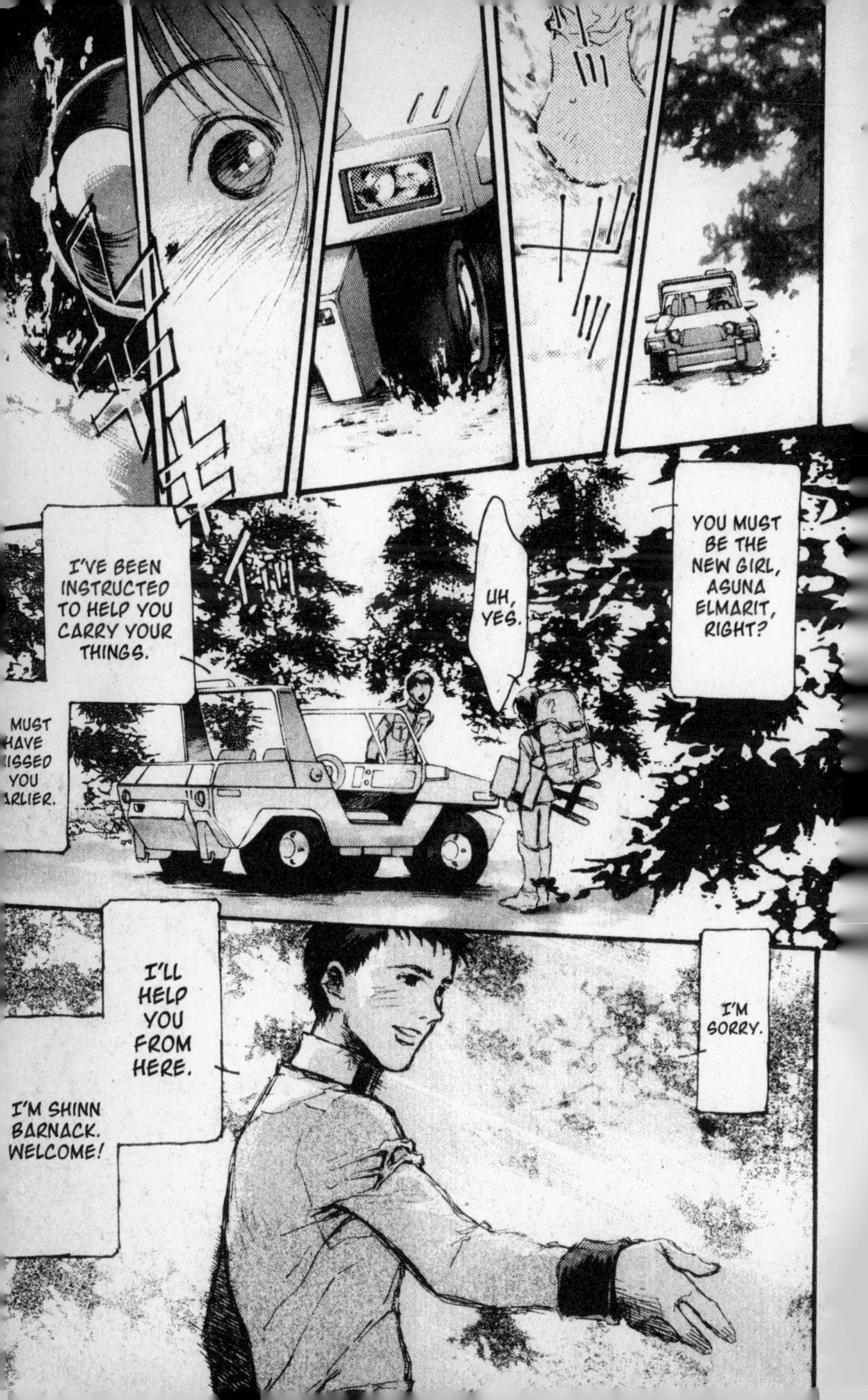
YOU MUST BE THE NEW GIRL, ASUNA ELMARIT, RIGHT?
UH, YES.
I'VE BEEN INSTRUCTED TO HELP YOU CARRY YOUR THINGS.
MUST HAVE ISSED YOU ARLIER.
I'M SORRY.
I'LL HELP YOU FROM HERE.
I'M SHINN BARNACK. WELCOME!

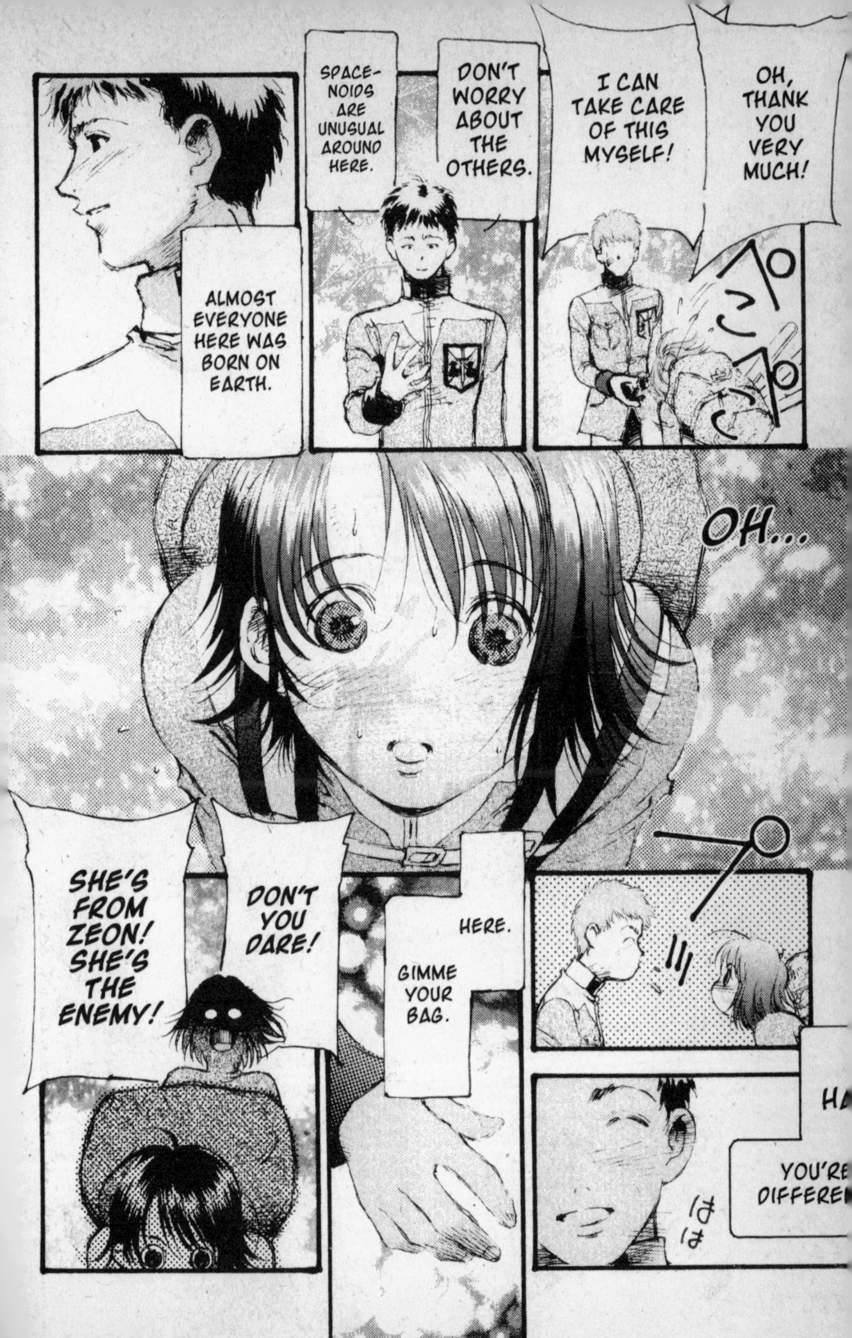

OH, THANK YOU VERY MUCH!
I CAN TAKE CARE OF THIS MYSELF!
ぺこ ぺこ
DON'T WORRY ABOUT THE OTHERS.
SPACE-NOIDS ARE UNUSUAL AROUND HERE.
ALMOST EVERYONE HERE WAS BORN ON EARTH.
OH...
HA
YOU'RE DIFFERE
はは
HERE.
GIMME YOUR BAG.
DON'T YOU DARE!
SHE'S FROM ZEON! SHE'S THE ENEMY!

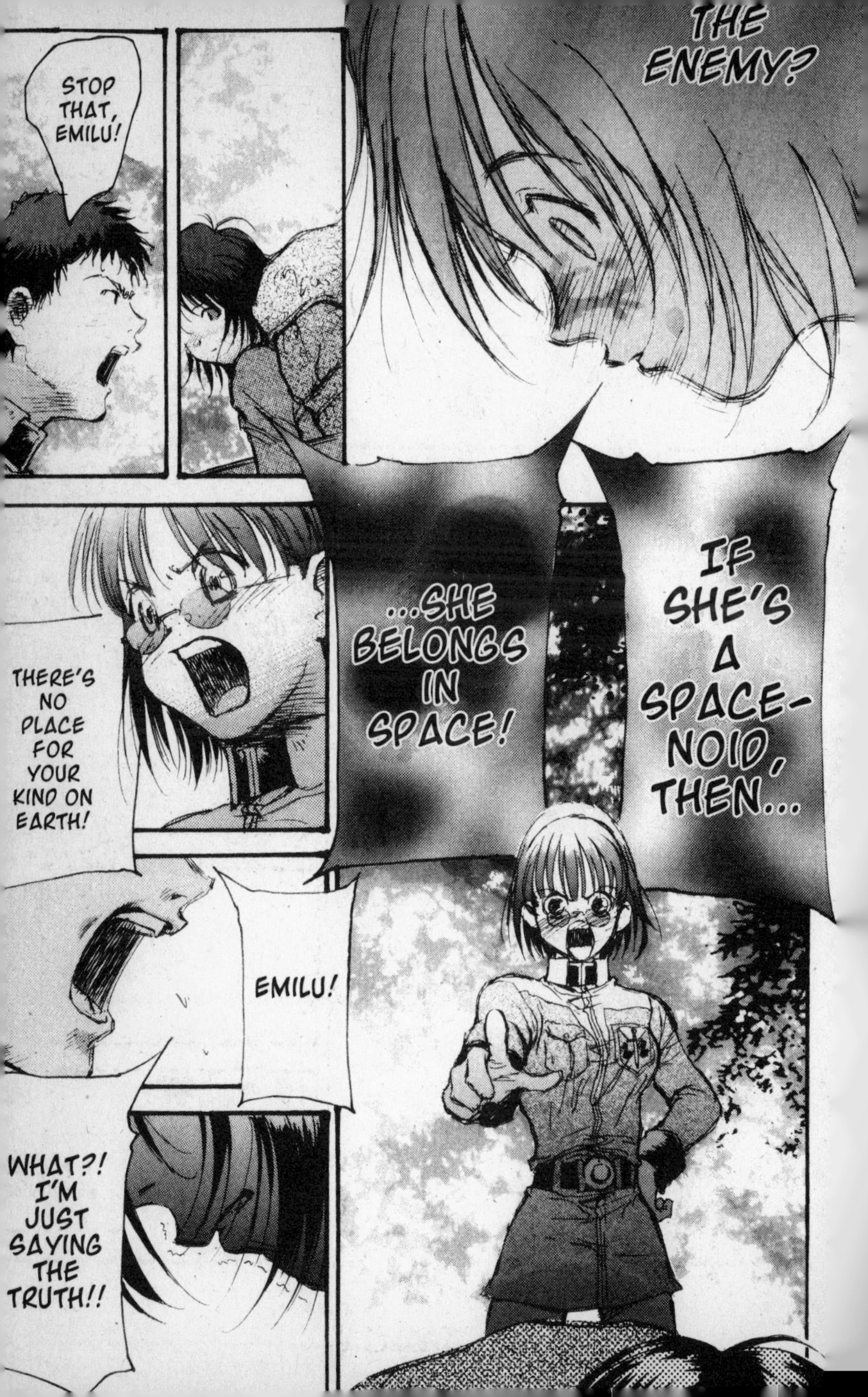

THE ENEMY?
STOP THAT, EMILU!
IF SHE'S A SPACE-NOID, THEN...
...SHE BELONGS IN SPACE!
THERE'S NO PLACE FOR YOUR KIND ON EARTH!
EMILU!
WHAT?! I'M JUST SAYING THE TRUTH!!

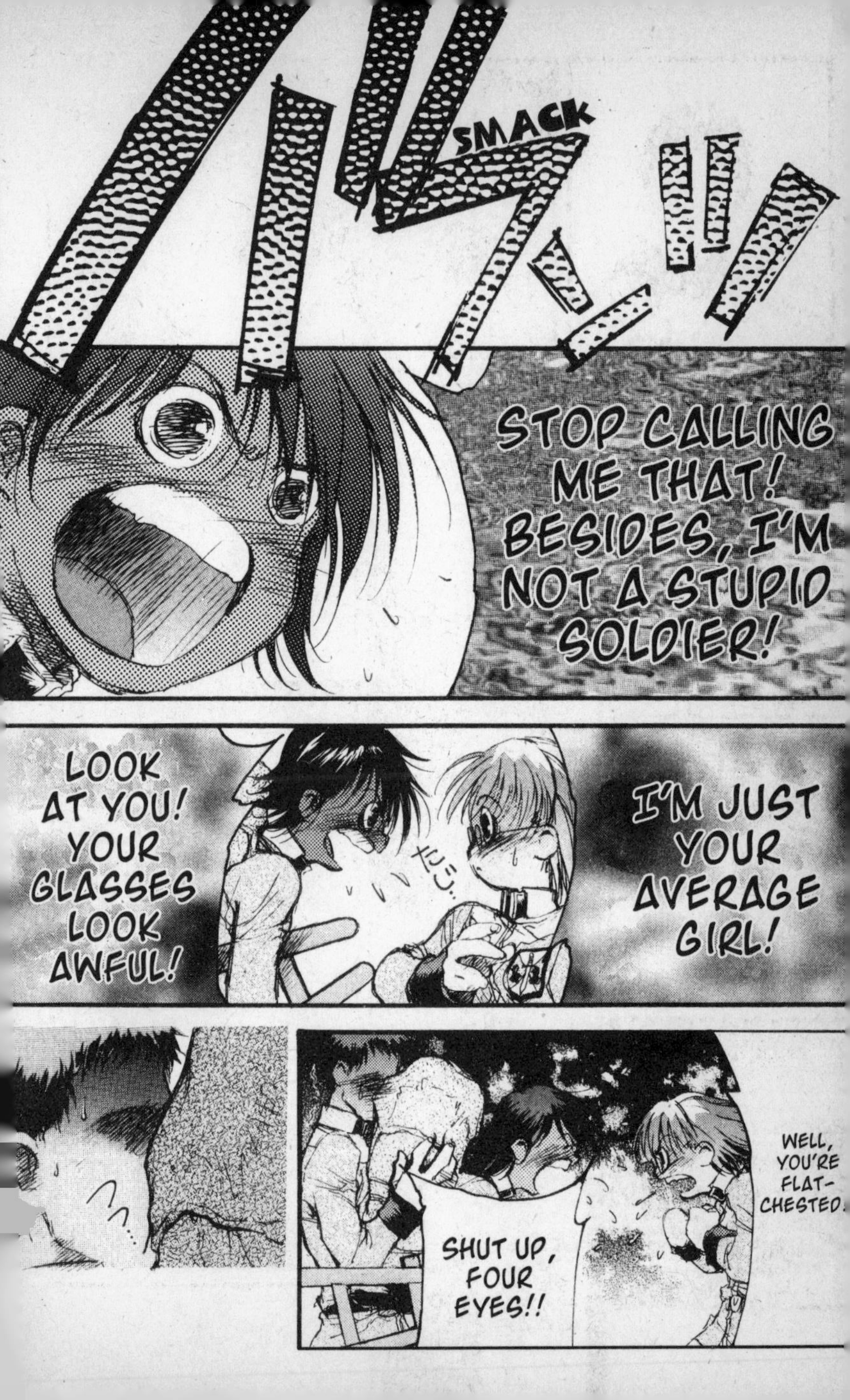
SMACK
STOP CALLING ME THAT! BESIDES, I'M NOT A STUPID SOLDIER!
I'M JUST YOUR AVERAGE GIRL!
LOOK AT YOU! YOUR GLASSES LOOK AWFUL!
WELL, YOU'RE FLAT-CHESTED.
SHUT UP, FOUR EYES!!

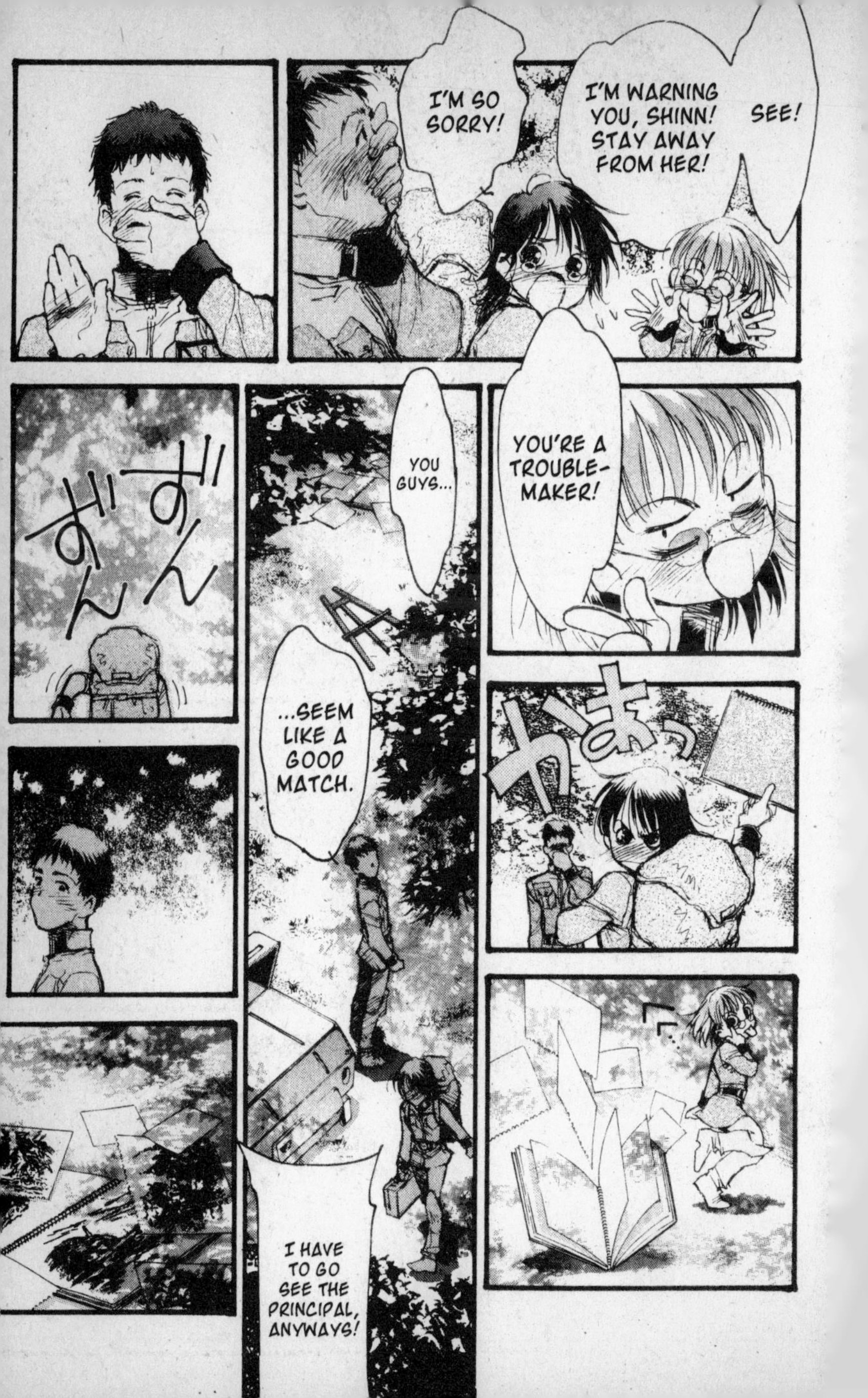
SEE!
I'M WARNING YOU, SHINN! STAY AWAY FROM HER!
I'M SO SORRY!
YOU'RE A TROUBLE-MAKER!
やあっ
YOU GUYS...
...SEEM LIKE A GOOD MATCH.
I HAVE TO GO SEE THE PRINCIPAL, ANYWAYS!
ずん ずん

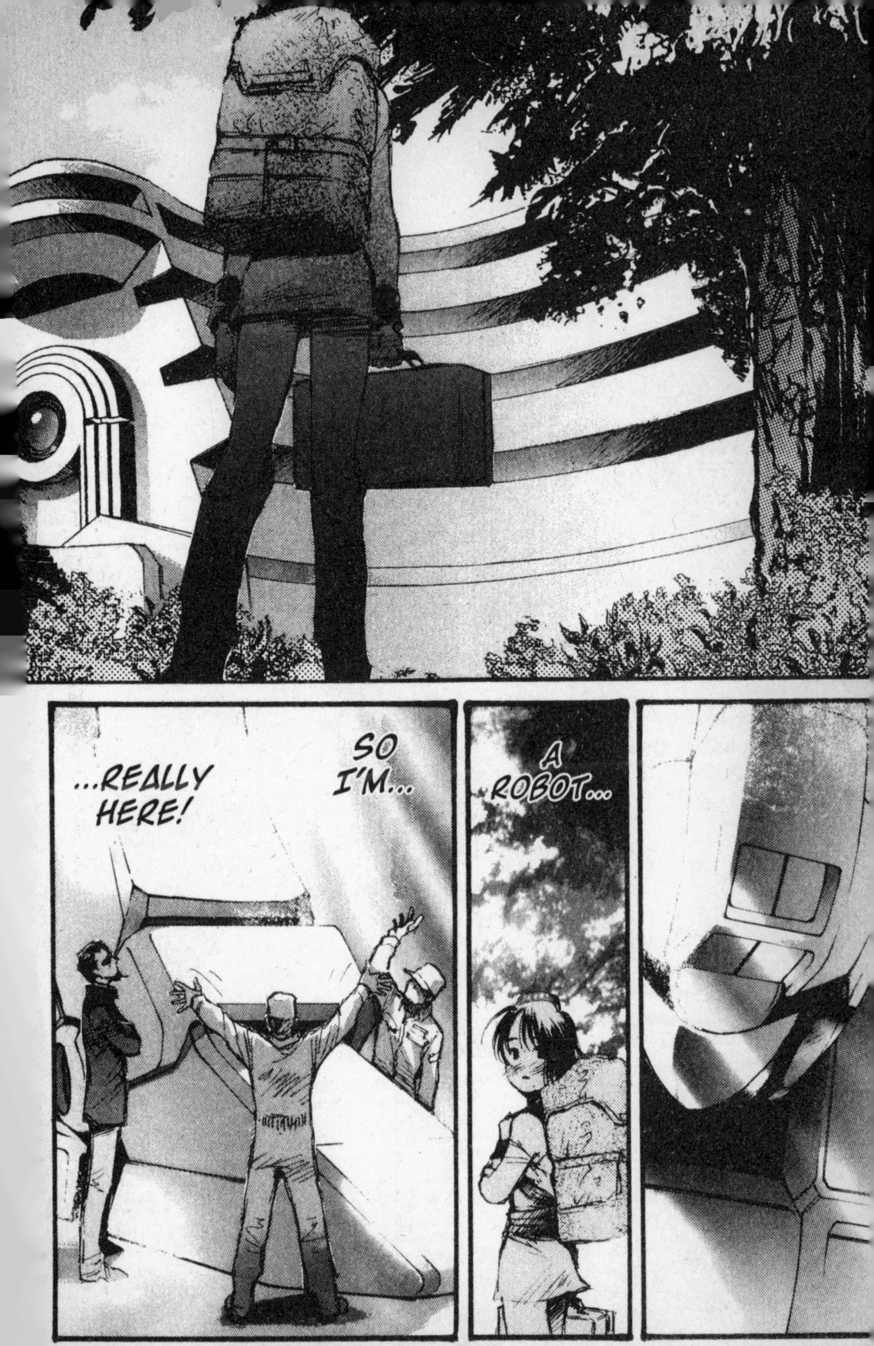
A ROBOT...
SO I'M...
...REALLY HERE!

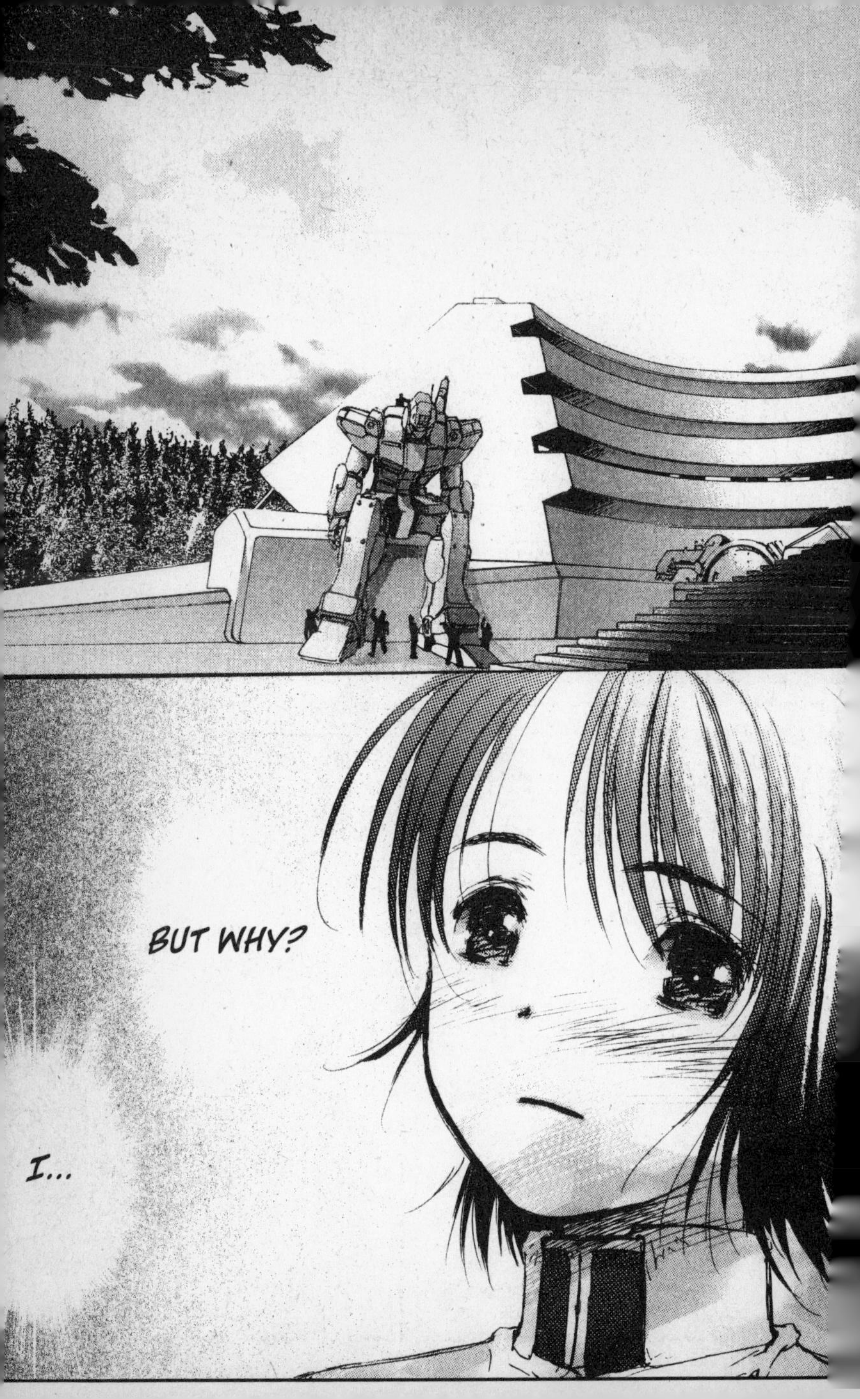
BUT WHY?
I...

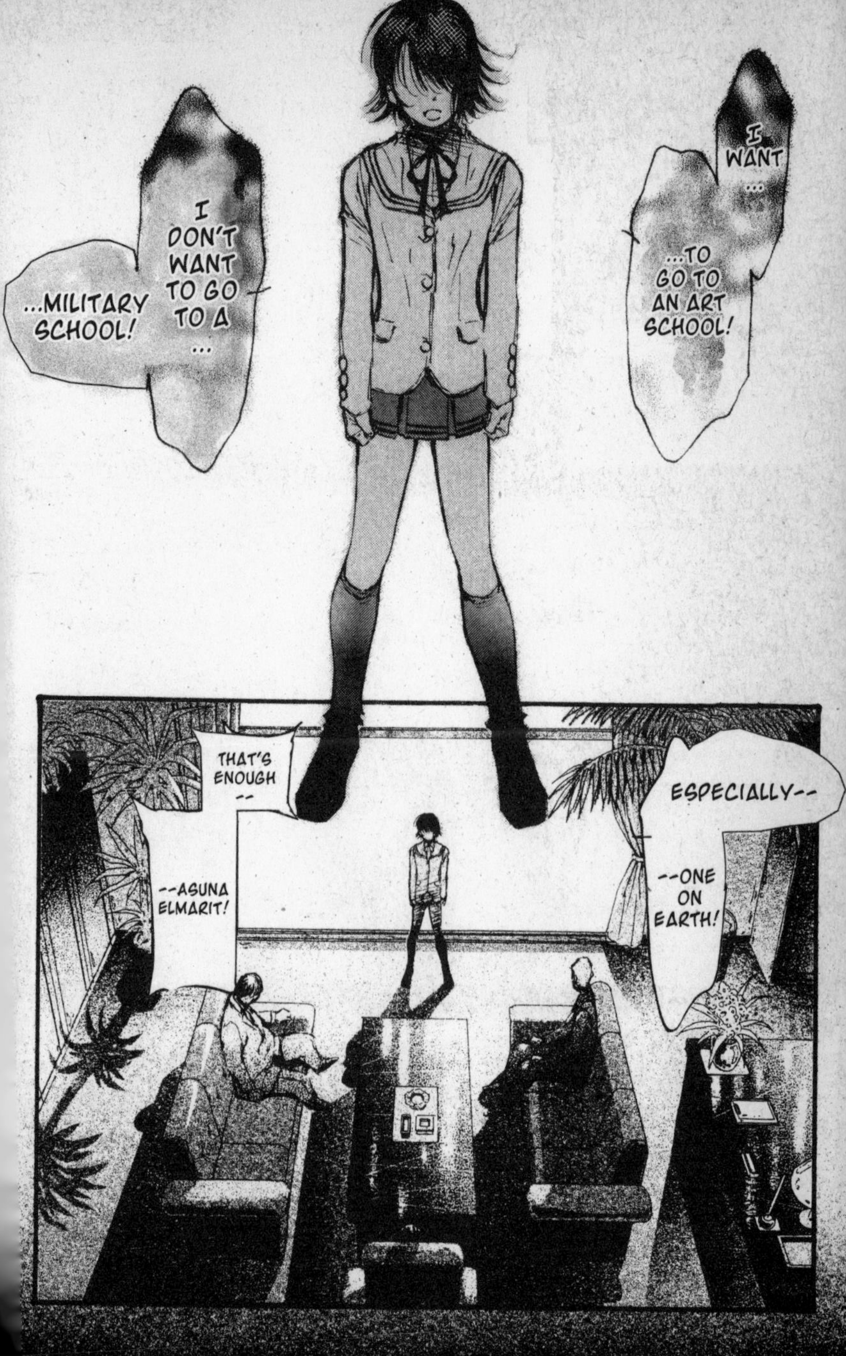
I WANT ...
...TO GO TO AN ART SCHOOL!
I DON'T WANT TO GO TO A ...
...MILITARY SCHOOL!
ESPECIALLY--
--ONE ON EARTH!
THAT'S ENOUGH --
--ASUNA ELMARIT!

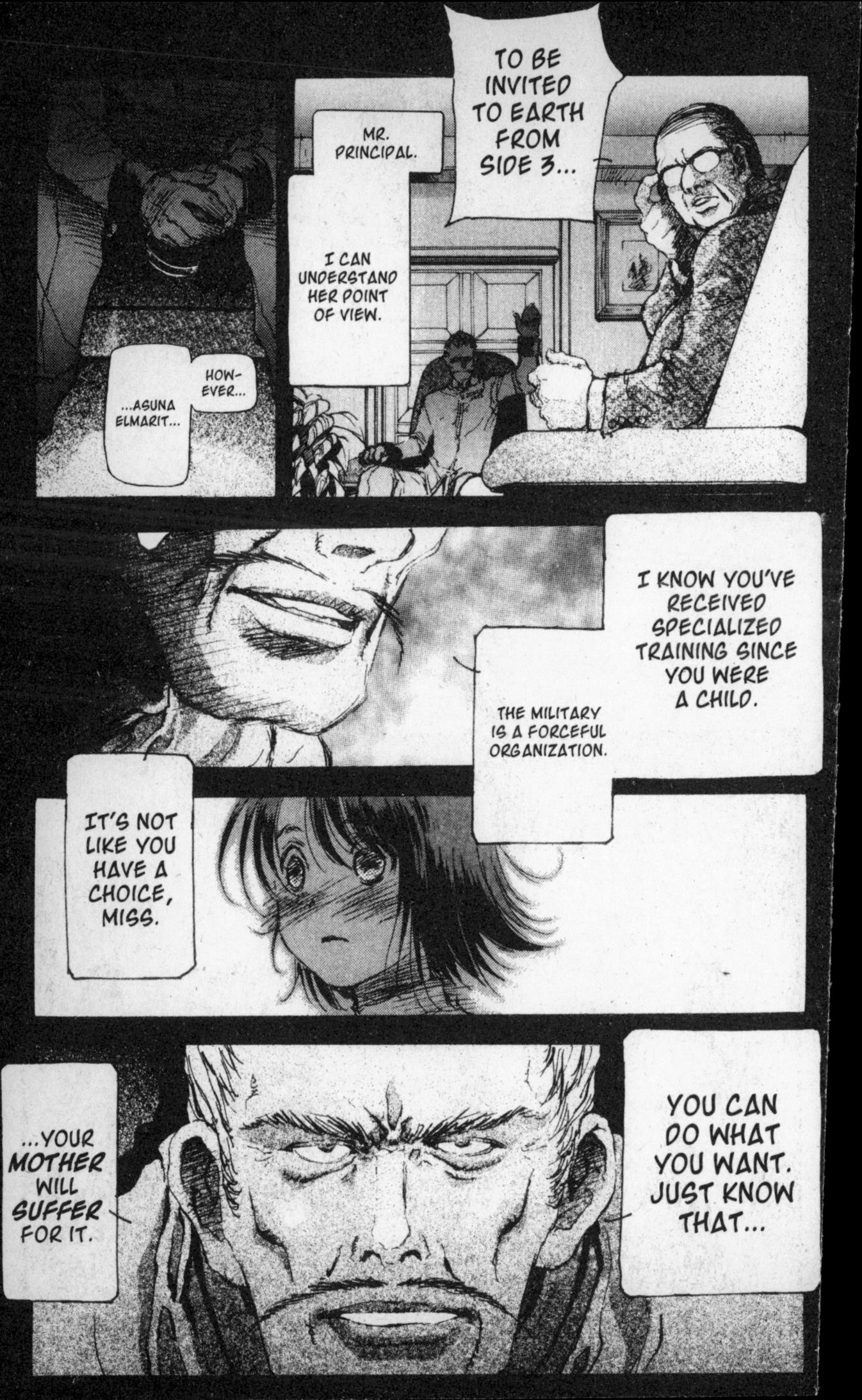
TO BE INVITED TO EARTH FROM SIDE 3...
MR. PRINCIPAL.
I CAN UNDERSTAND HER POINT OF VIEW.
HOW-EVER...
...ASUNA ELMARIT...
I KNOW YOU'VE RECEIVED SPECIALIZED TRAINING SINCE YOU WERE A CHILD.
THE MILITARY IS A FORCEFUL ORGANIZATION.
IT'S NOT LIKE YOU HAVE A CHOICE, MISS.
YOU CAN DO WHAT YOU WANT. JUST KNOW THAT...
...YOUR MOTHER WILL SUFFER FOR IT.

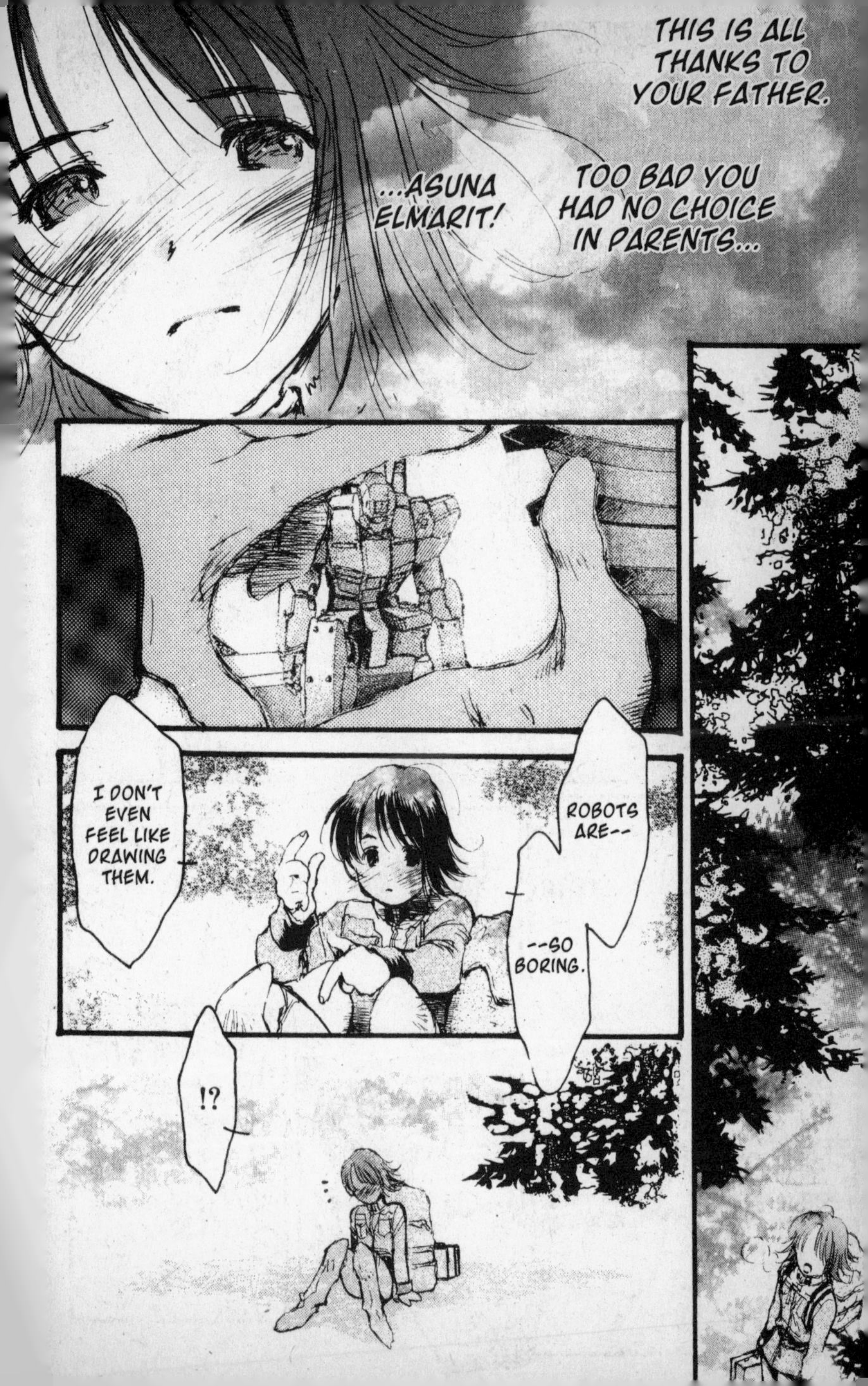
THIS IS ALL THANKS TO YOUR FATHER.
TOO BAD YOU HAD NO CHOICE IN PARENTS...
...ASUNA ELMARIT!
ROBOTS ARE--
--SO BORING.
I DON'T EVEN FEEL LIKE DRAWING THEM.
!?

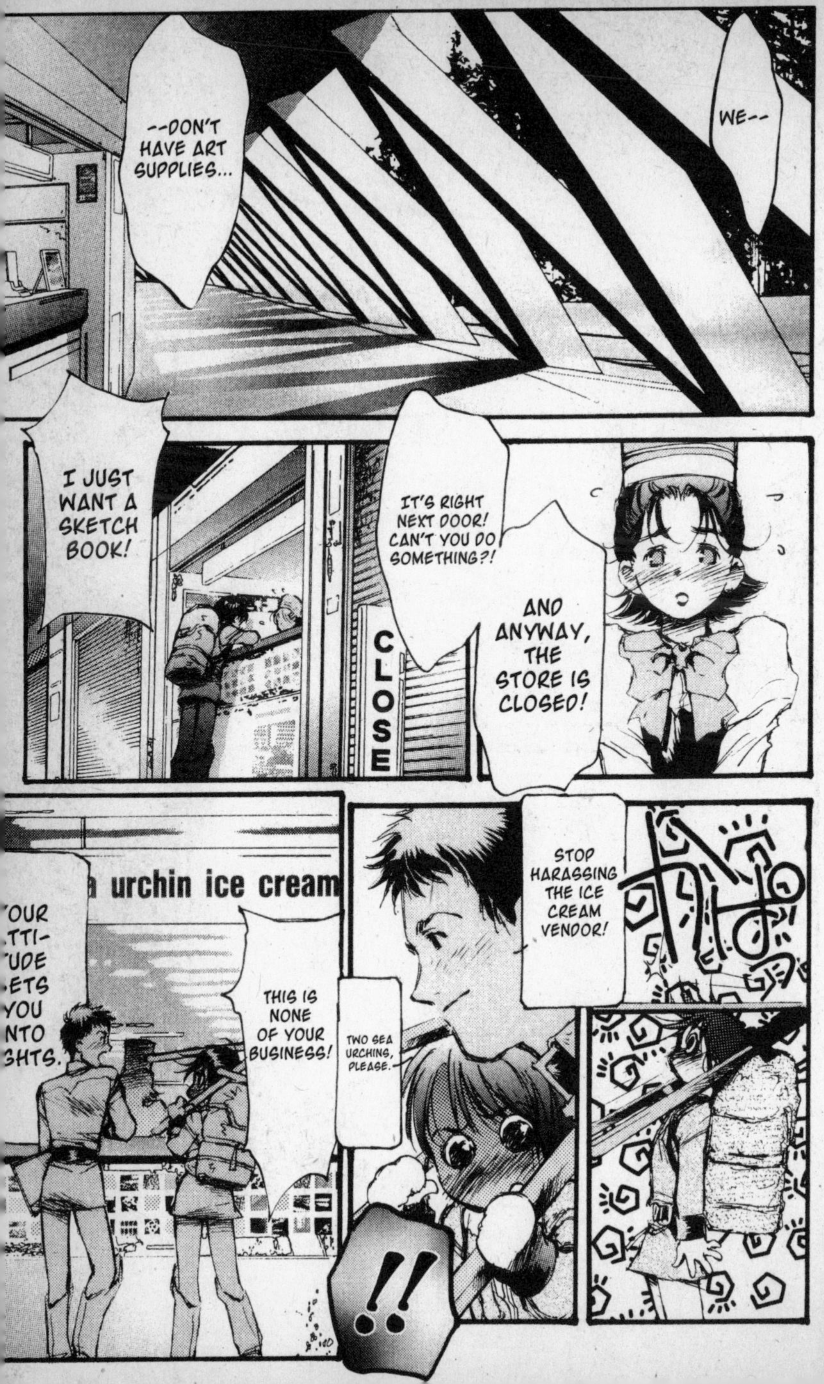
WE--
--DON'T HAVE ART SUPPLIES...
I JUST WANT A SKETCH BOOK!
IT'S RIGHT NEXT DOOR! CAN'T YOU DO SOMETHING?!
AND ANYWAY, THE STORE IS CLOSED!
STOP HARASSING THE ICE CREAM VENDOR!
TWO SEA URCHINS, PLEASE.
!!
THIS IS NONE OF YOUR BUSINESS!
a urchin ice cream
OUR TTI- TUDE ETS YOU NTO GHTS.

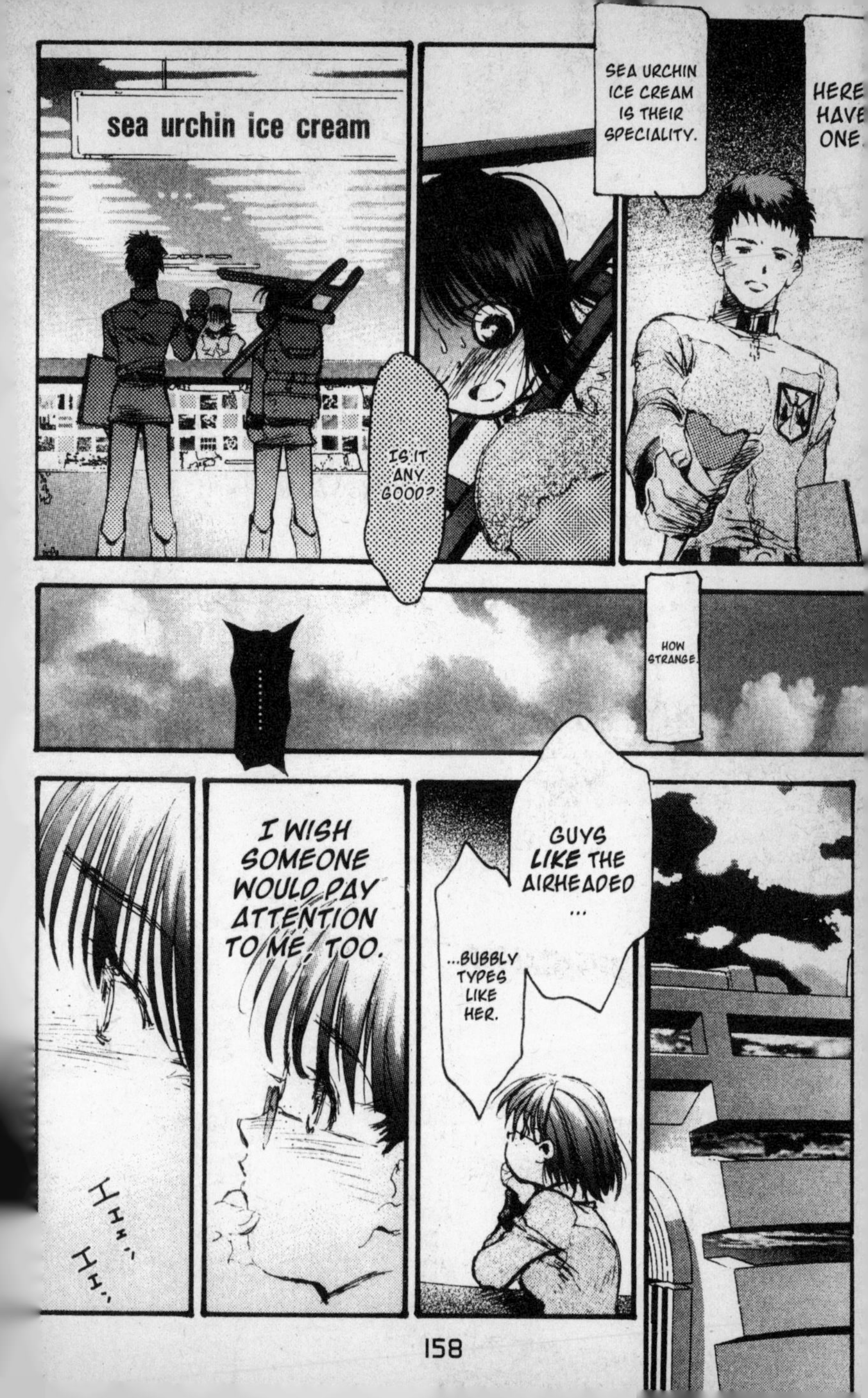
HERE HAVE ONE.
SEA URCHIN ICE CREAM IS THEIR SPECIALITY.
IS IT ANY GOOD?
sea urchin ice cream
HOW STRANGE.
......
GUYS LIKE THE AIRHEADED ...
...BUBBLY TYPES LIKE HER.
I WISH SOMEONE WOULD PAY ATTENTION TO ME, TOO.
HI... HI...

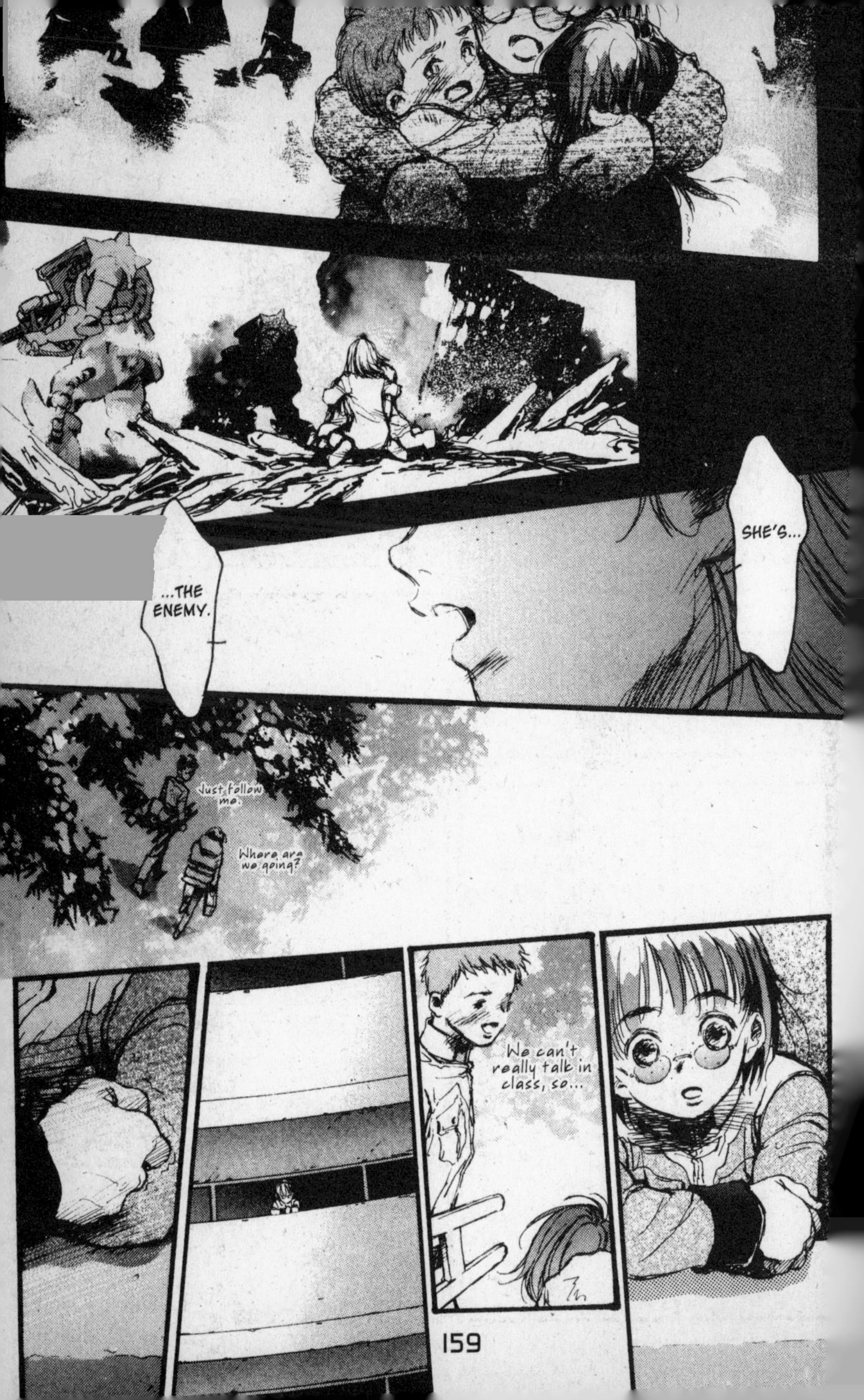
SHE'S...
...THE ENEMY.
Just follow me.
Where are we going?
We can't really talk in class, so...

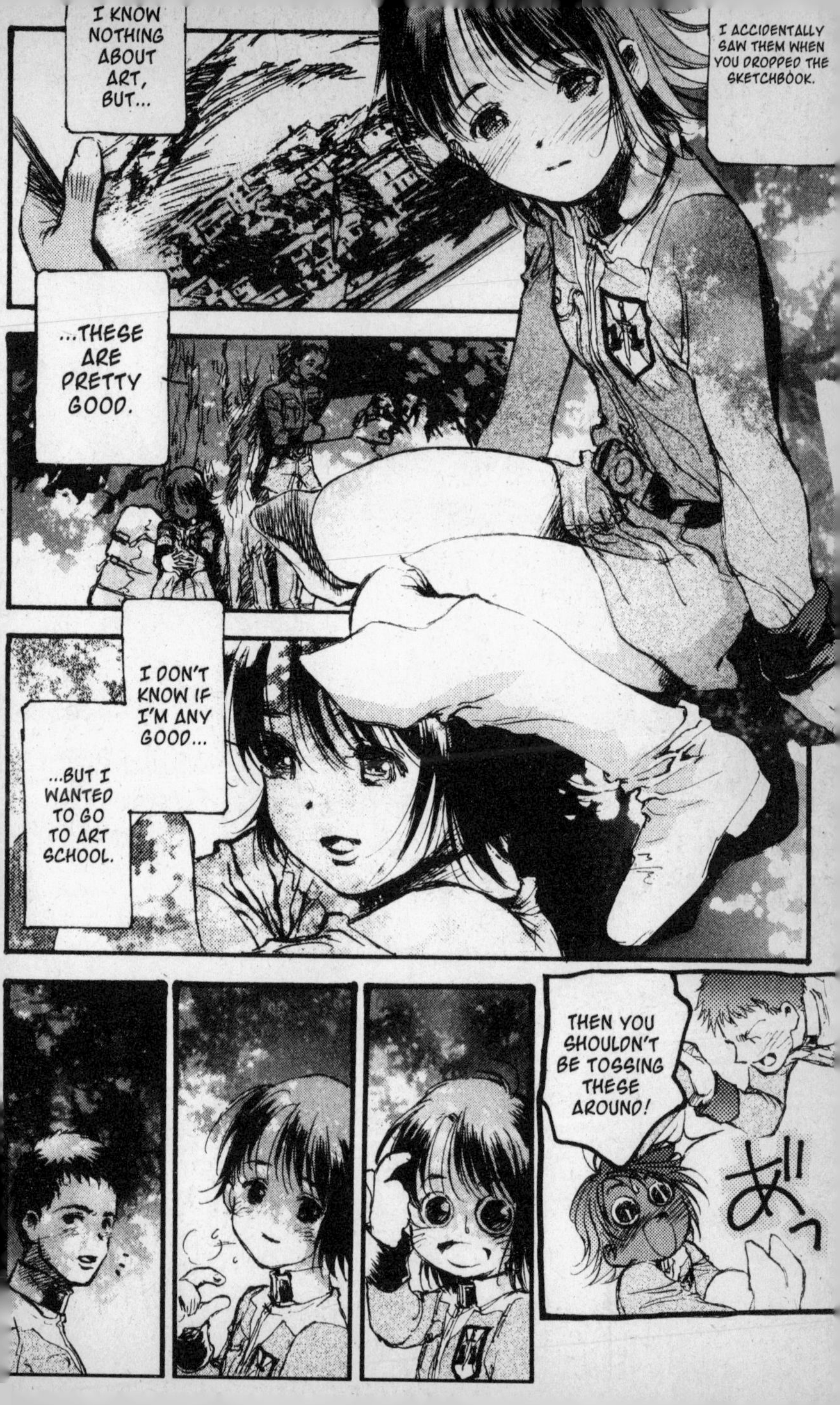
I ACCIDENTALLY SAW THEM WHEN YOU DROPPED THE SKETCHBOOK.
I KNOW NOTHING ABOUT ART, BUT...
...THESE ARE PRETTY GOOD.
I DON'T KNOW IF I'M ANY GOOD...
...BUT I WANTED TO GO TO ART SCHOOL.
THEN YOU SHOULDN'T BE TOSSING THESE AROUND!
あっ

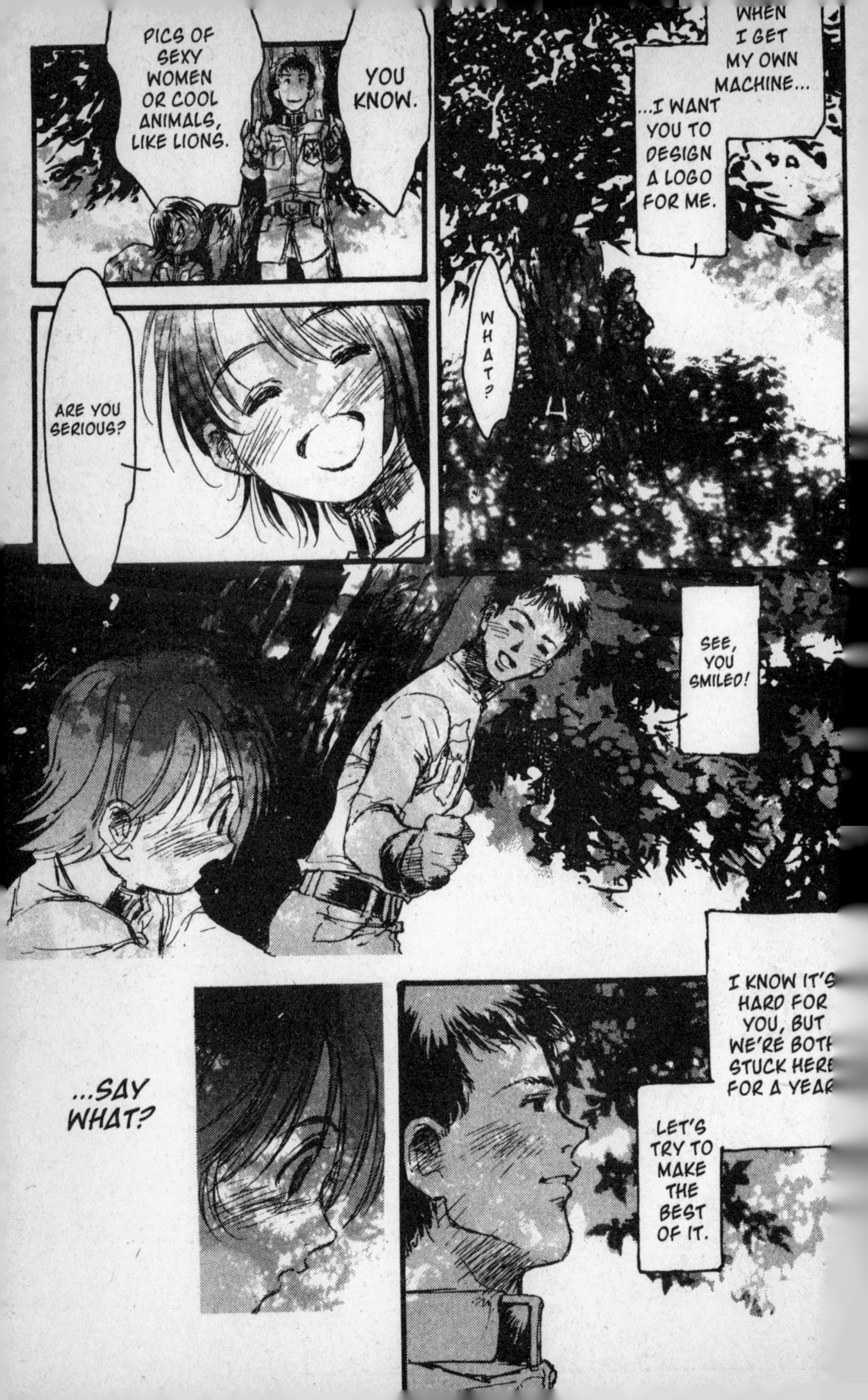
WHEN I GET MY OWN MACHINE...
...I WANT YOU TO DESIGN A LOGO FOR ME.
WHAT?
PICS OF SEXY WOMEN OR COOL ANIMALS, LIKE LIONS.
YOU KNOW.
ARE YOU SERIOUS?
SEE, YOU SMILED!
I KNOW IT'S HARD FOR YOU, BUT WE'RE BOTH STUCK HERE FOR A YEAR
LET'S TRY TO MAKE THE BEST OF IT.
...SAY WHAT?

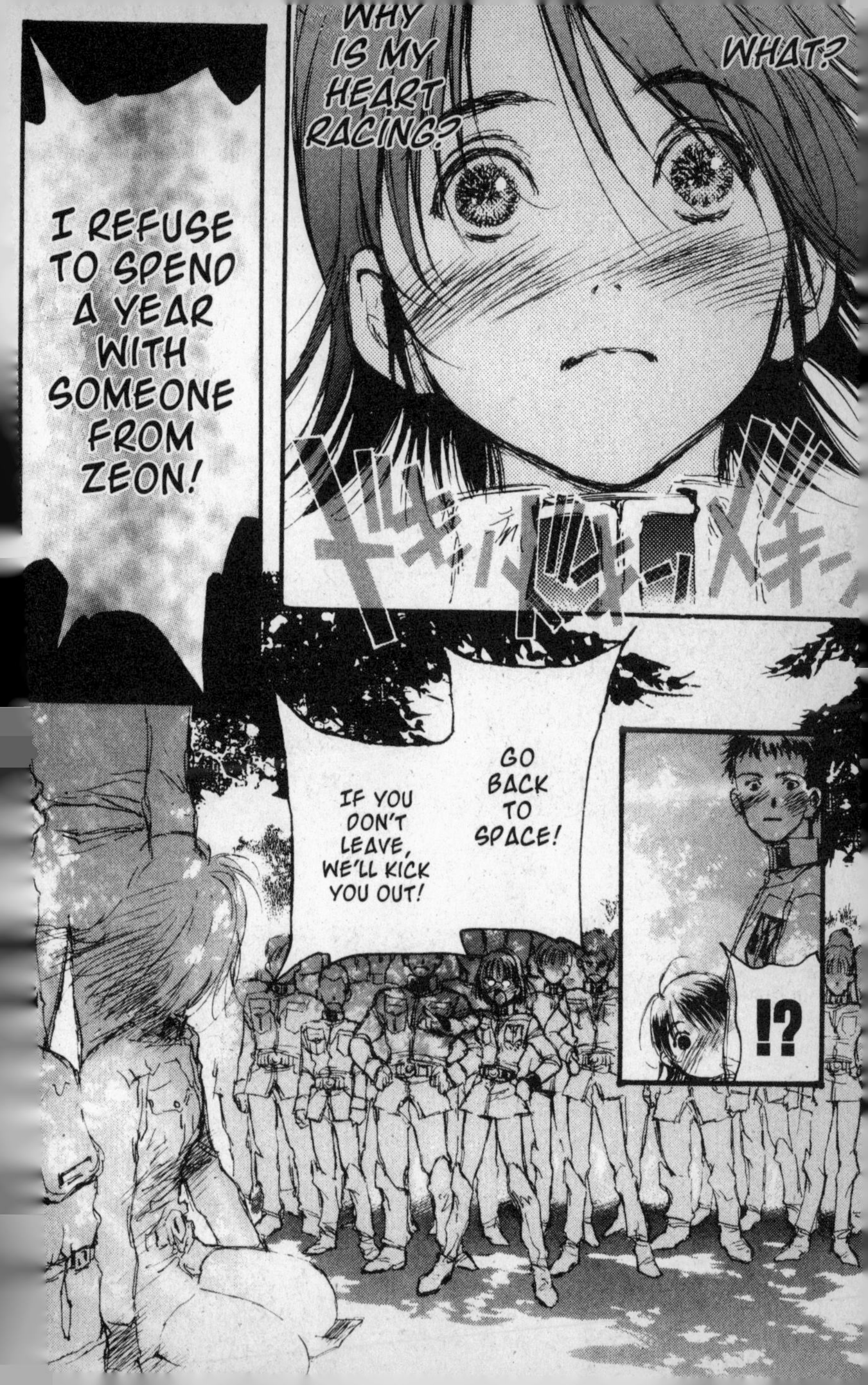
WHAT?
WHY IS MY HEART RACING?
I REFUSE TO SPEND A YEAR WITH SOMEONE FROM ZEON!
!?
GO BACK TO SPACE!
IF YOU DON'T LEAVE, WE'LL KICK YOU OUT!

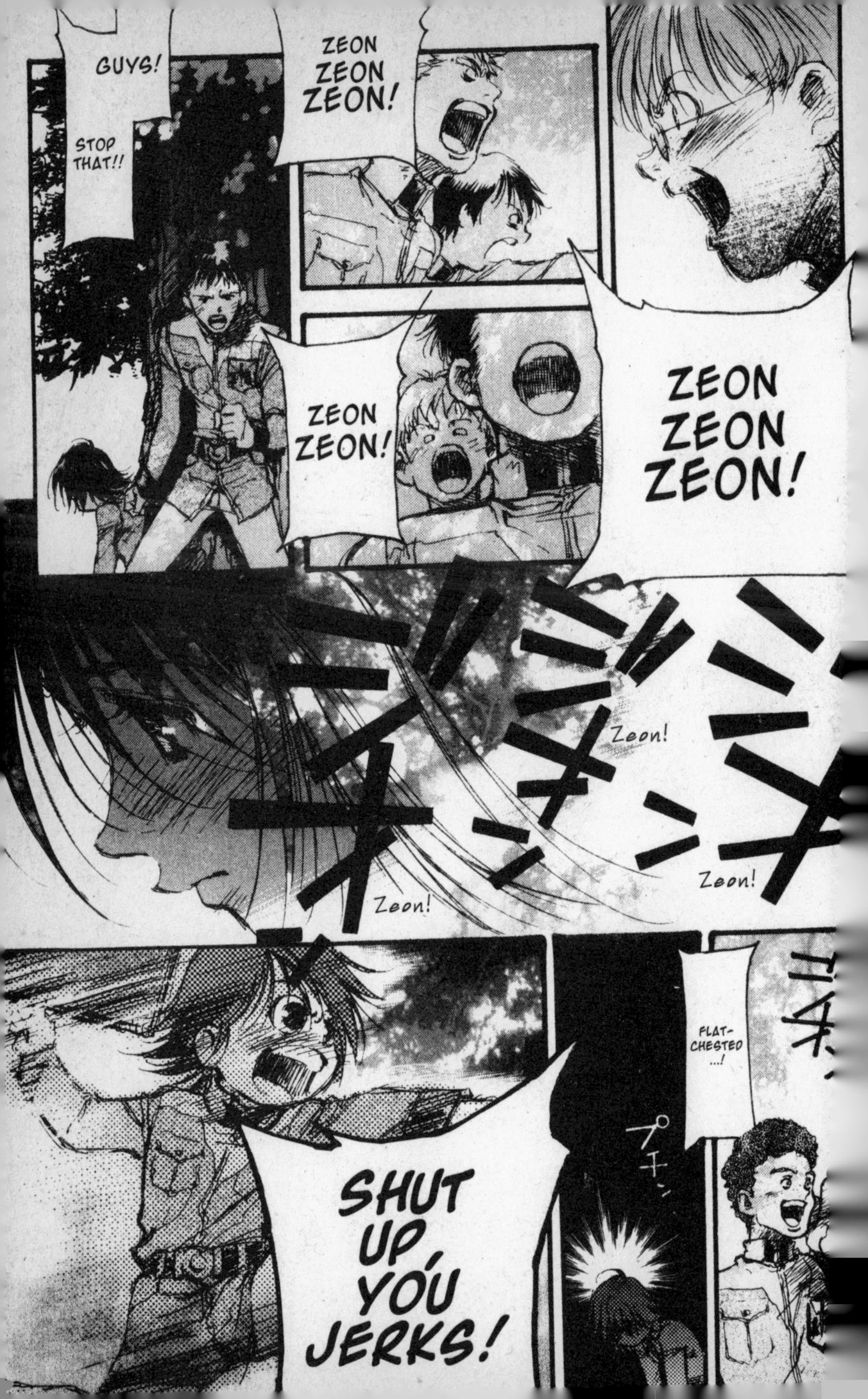
ZEON ZEON ZEON!
ZEON ZEON ZEON!
ZEON ZEON!
GUYS!
STOP THAT!!
Zeon!
Zeon!
Zeon!
FLAT-CHESTED ...!
SHUT UP, YOU JERKS!

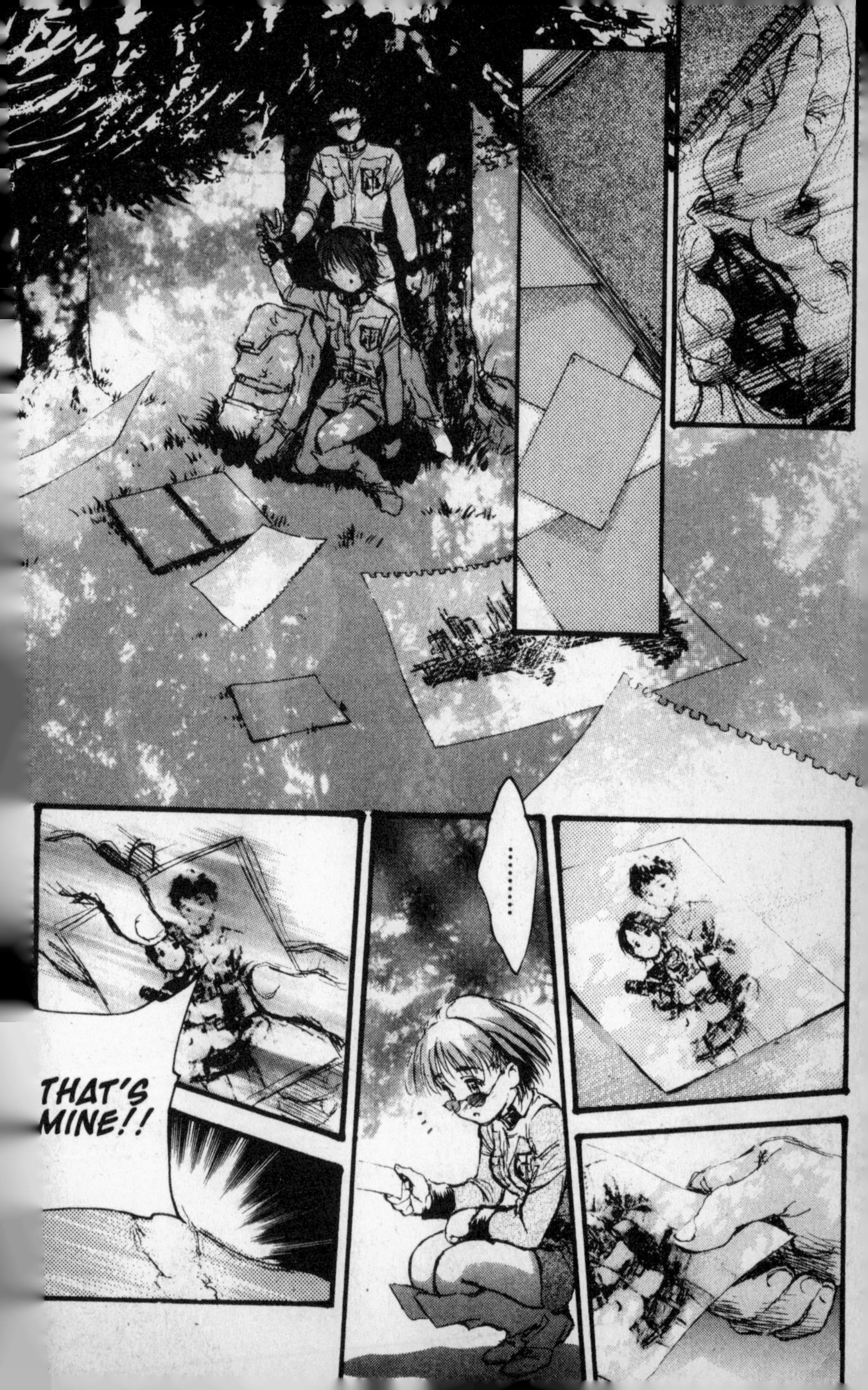
……
THAT'S MINE!!

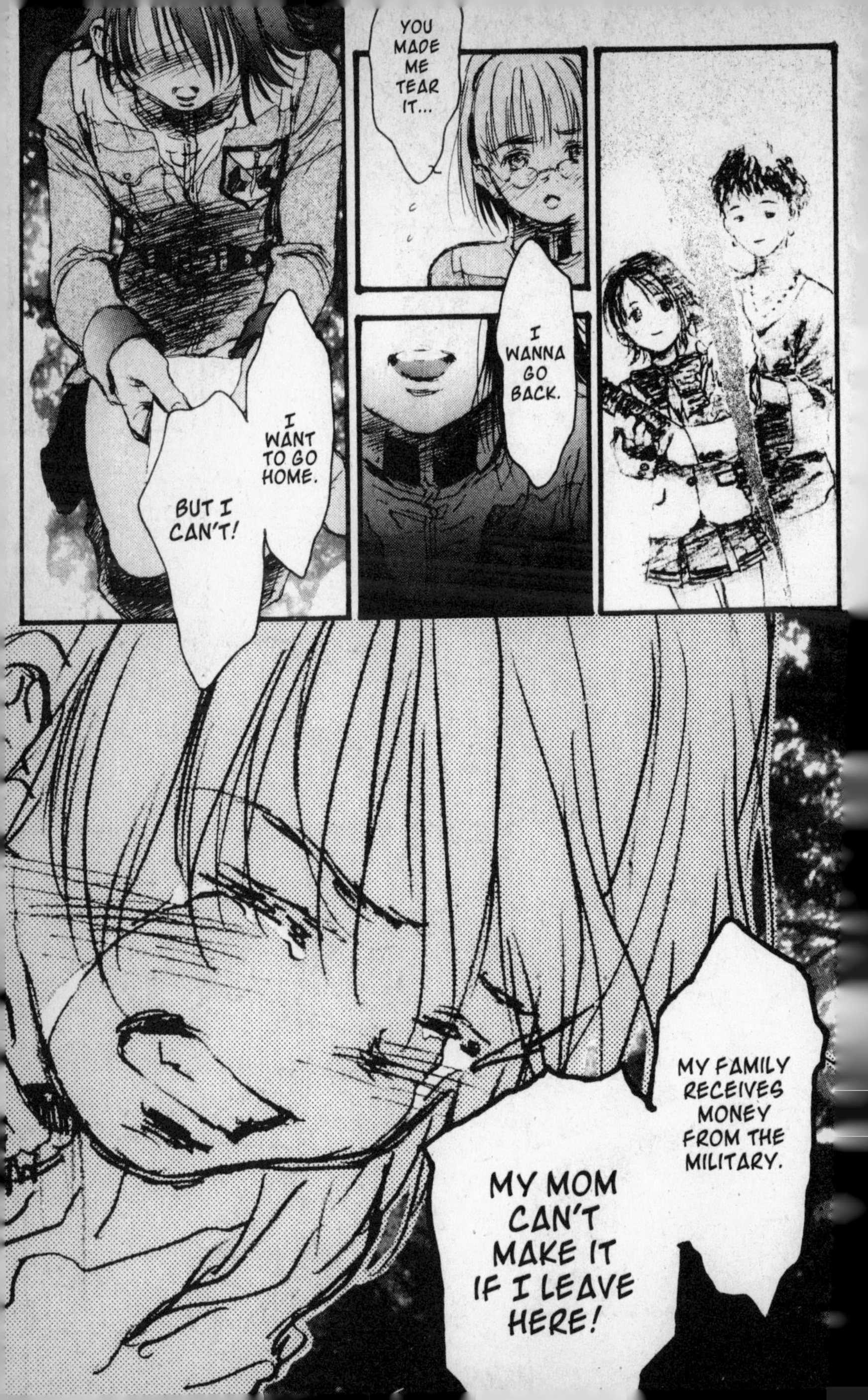
YOU MADE ME TEAR IT...
I WANNA GO BACK.
I WANT TO GO HOME.
BUT I CAN'T!
MY FAMILY RECEIVES MONEY FROM THE MILITARY.
MY MOM CAN'T MAKE IT IF I LEAVE HERE!

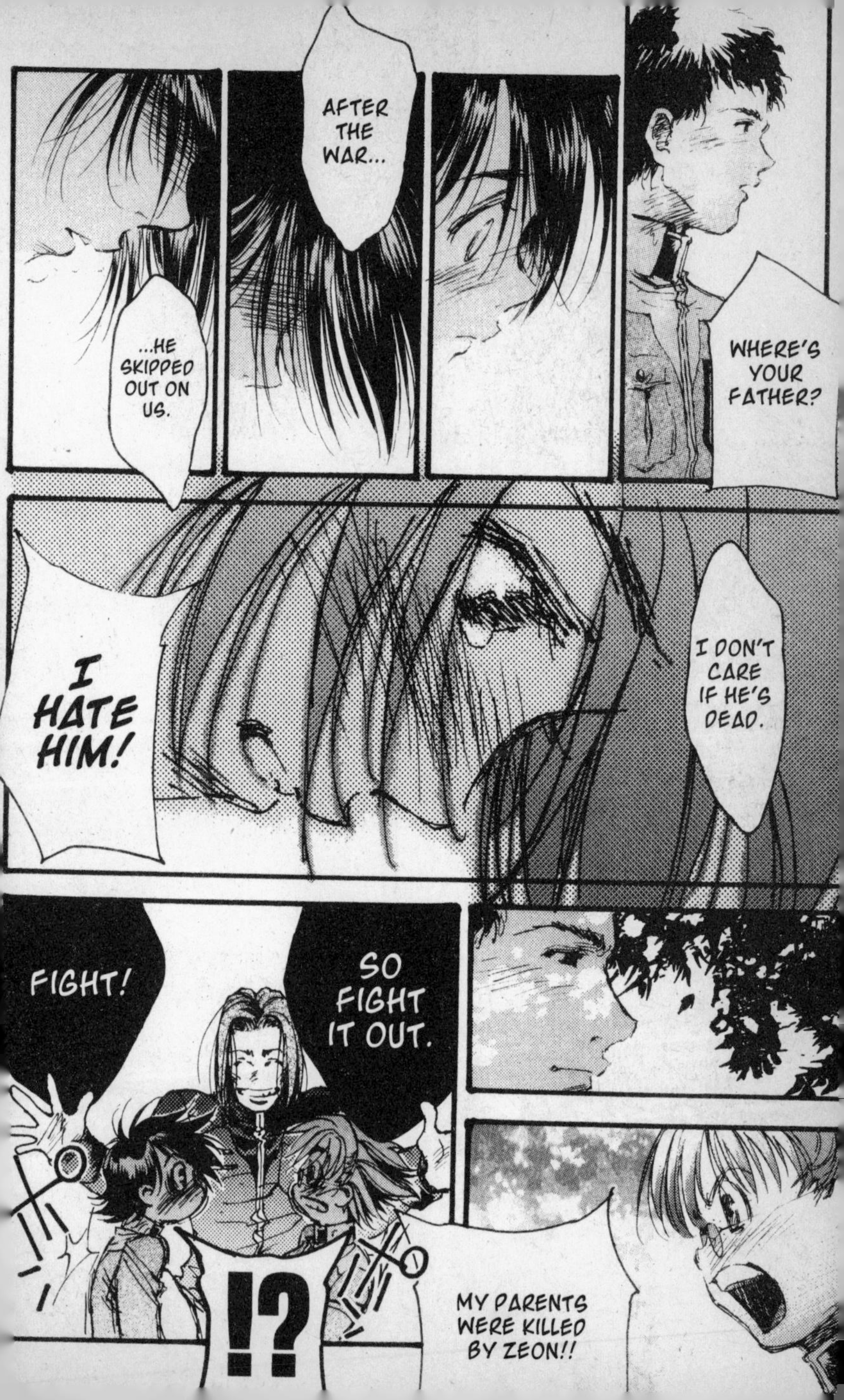
WHERE'S YOUR FATHER?
AFTER THE WAR...
...HE SKIPPED OUT ON US.
I DON'T CARE IF HE'S DEAD.
I HATE HIM!
MY PARENTS WERE KILLED BY ZEON!!
SO FIGHT IT OUT.
FIGHT!
!?

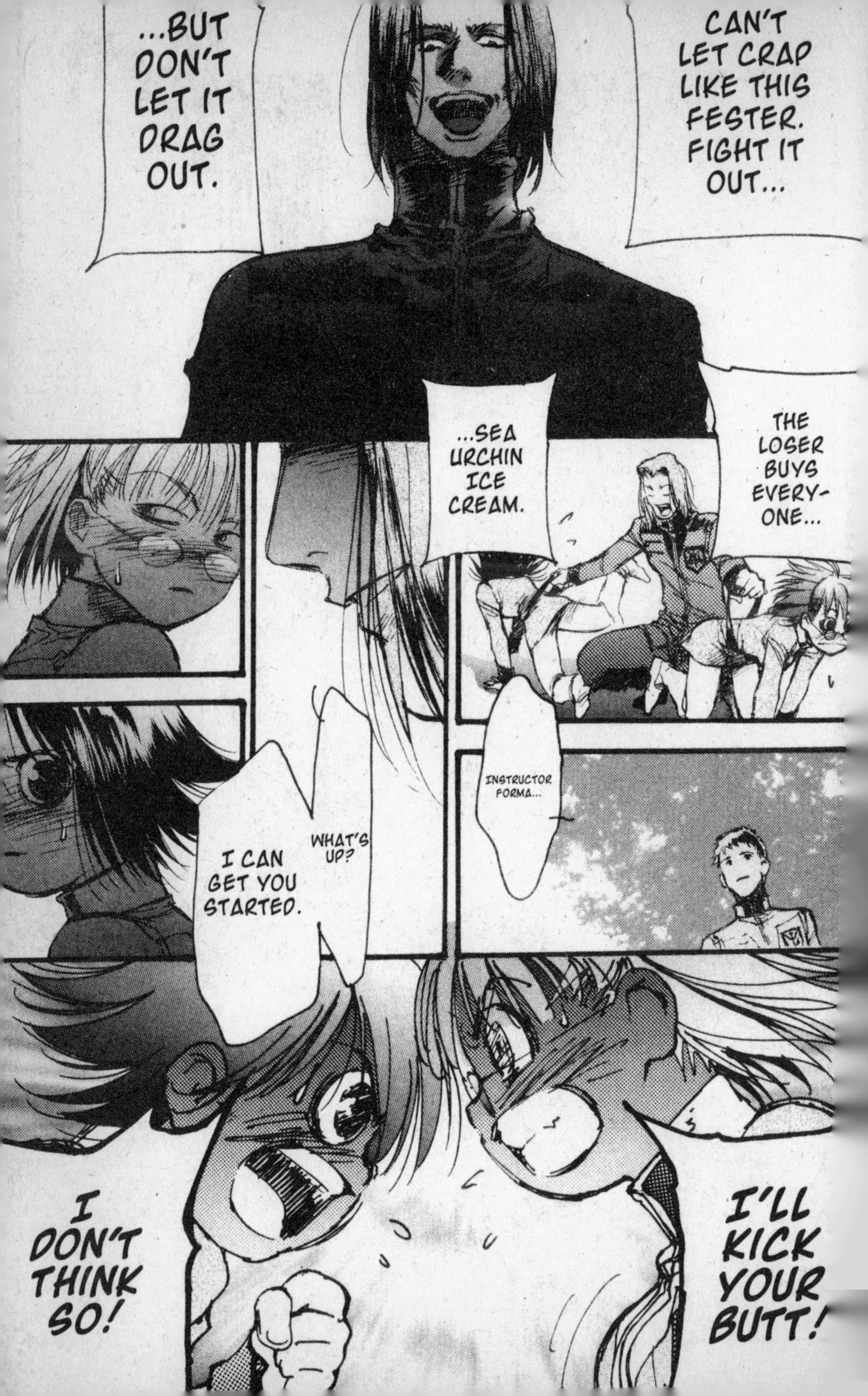
CAN'T LET CRAP LIKE THIS FESTER. FIGHT IT OUT...
...BUT DON'T LET IT DRAG OUT.
THE LOSER BUYS EVERY-ONE...
...SEA URCHIN ICE CREAM.
INSTRUCTOR FORMA...
WHAT'S UP?
I CAN GET YOU STARTED.
I'LL KICK YOUR BUTT!
I DON'T THINK SO!

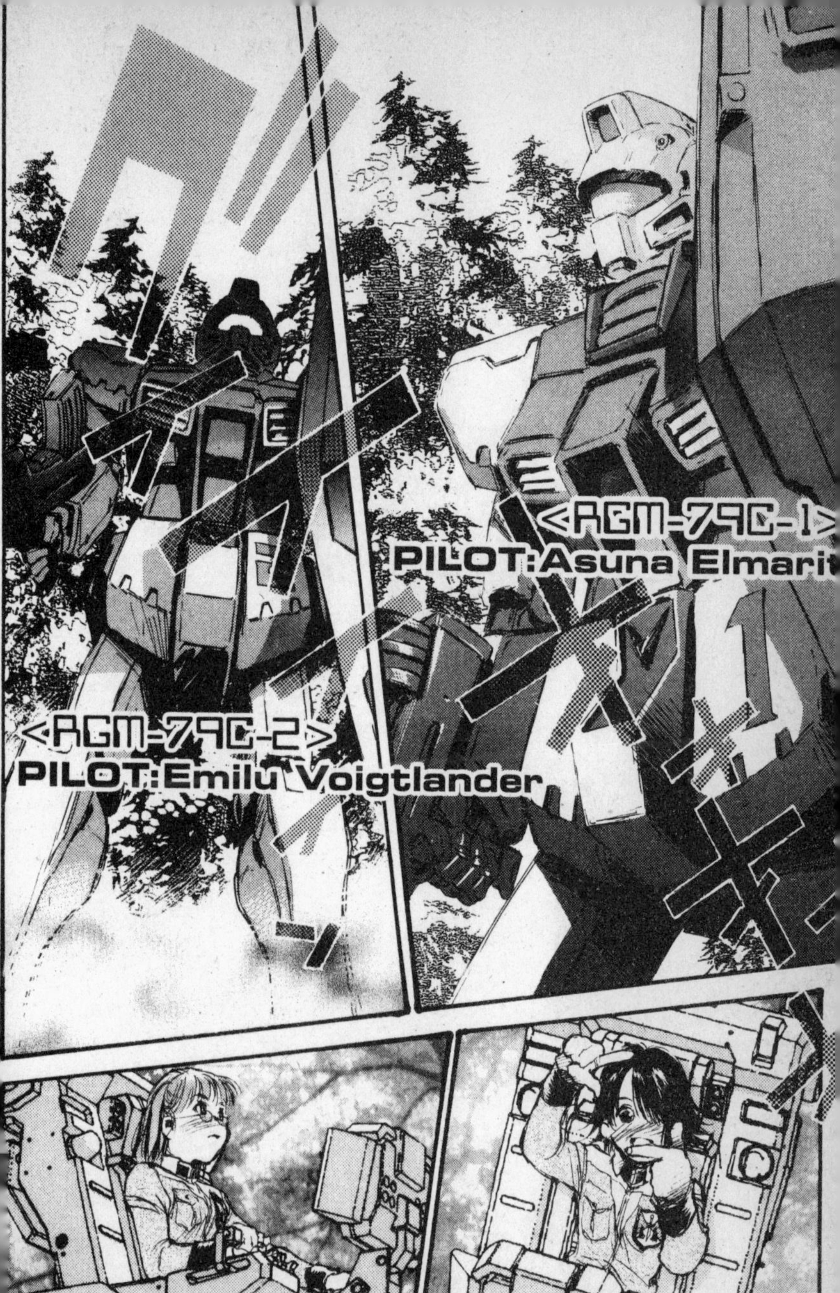
<RGM-79C-1>
PILOT:Asuna Elmarit
<RGM-79C-2>
PILOT:Emilu Voigtlander

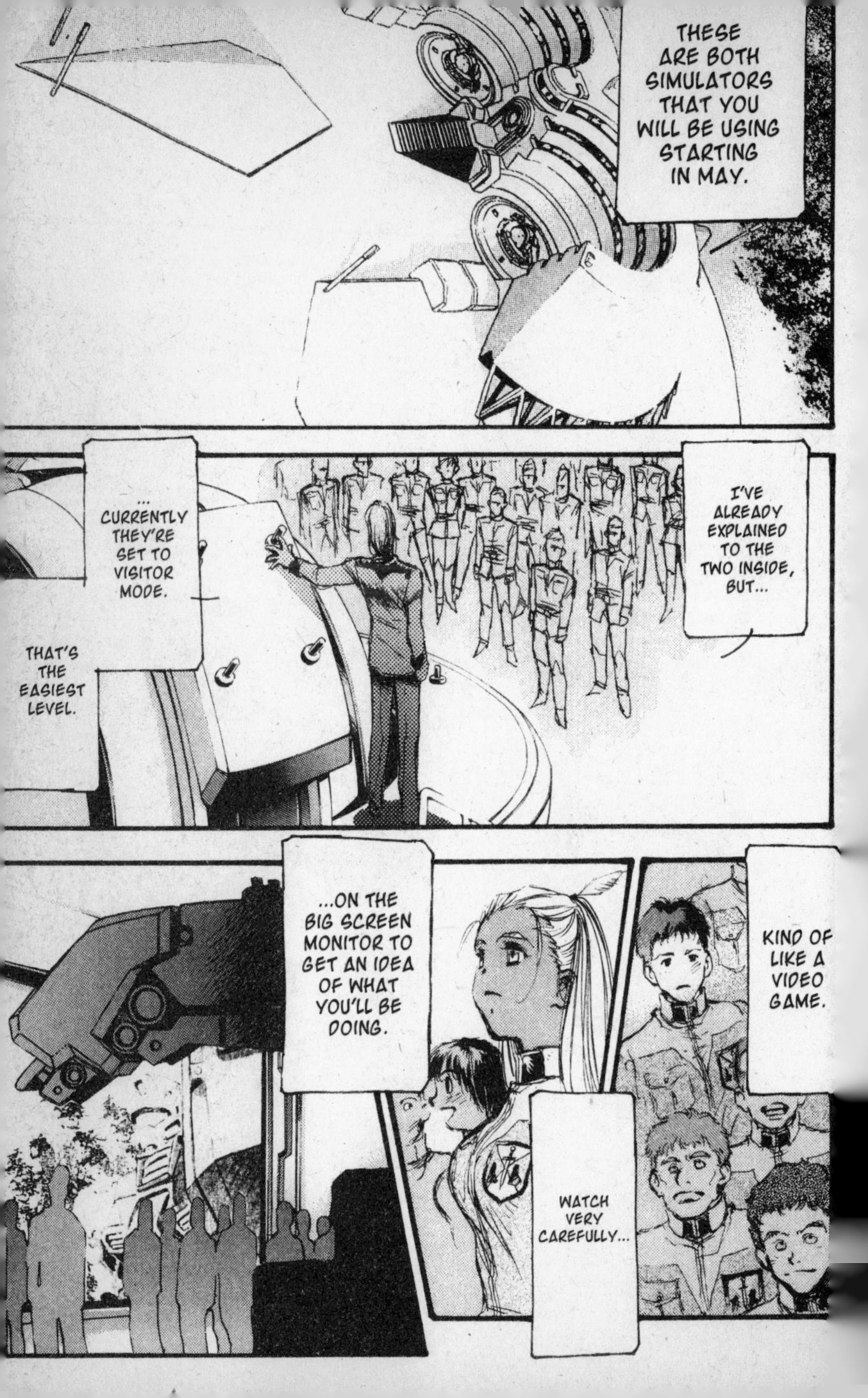
THESE ARE BOTH SIMULATORS THAT YOU WILL BE USING STARTING IN MAY.
I'VE ALREADY EXPLAINED TO THE TWO INSIDE, BUT...
...CURRENTLY THEY'RE SET TO VISITOR MODE.
THAT'S THE EASIEST LEVEL.
KIND OF LIKE A VIDEO GAME.
WATCH VERY CAREFULLY...
...ON THE BIG SCREEN MONITOR TO GET AN IDEA OF WHAT YOU'LL BE DOING.

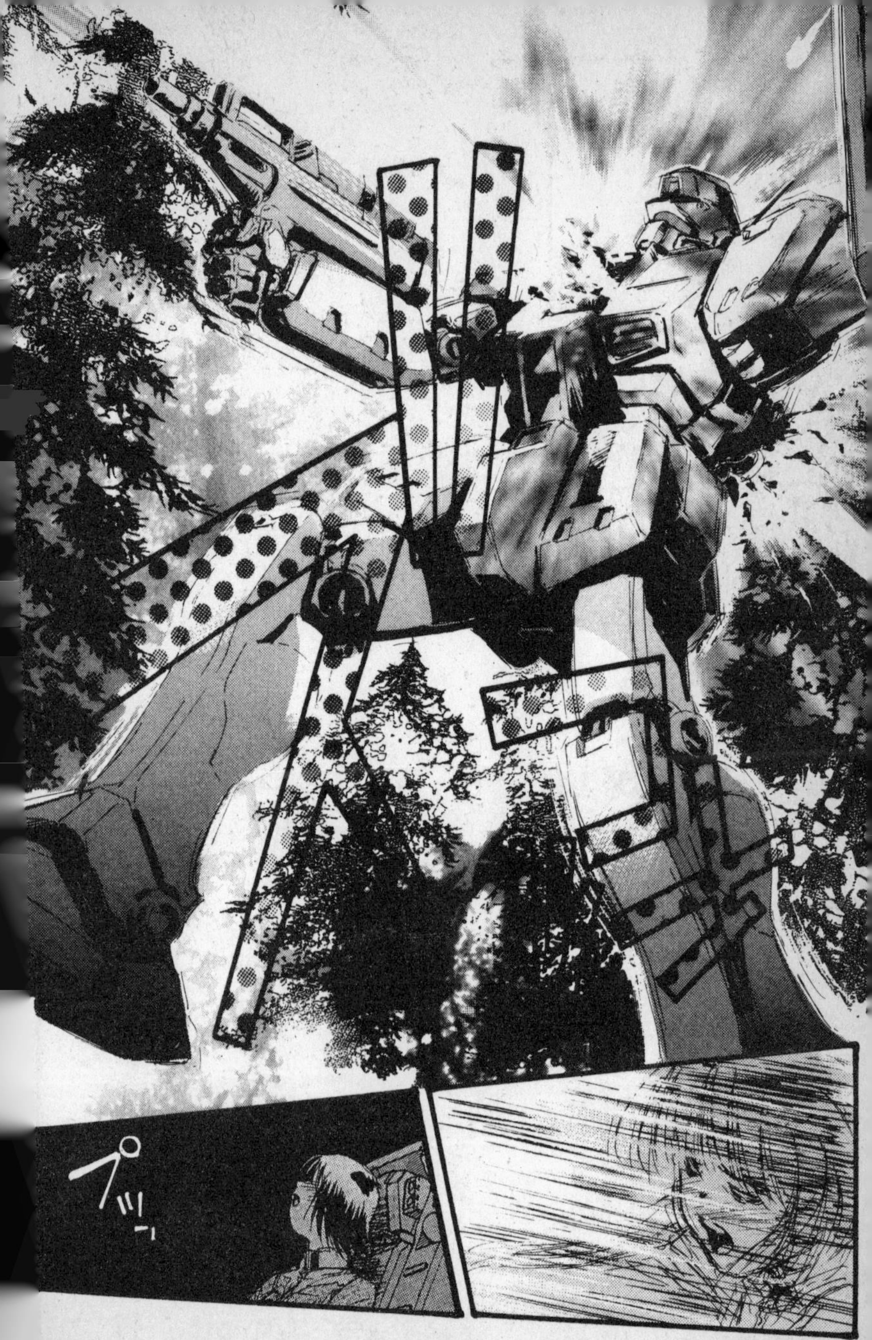

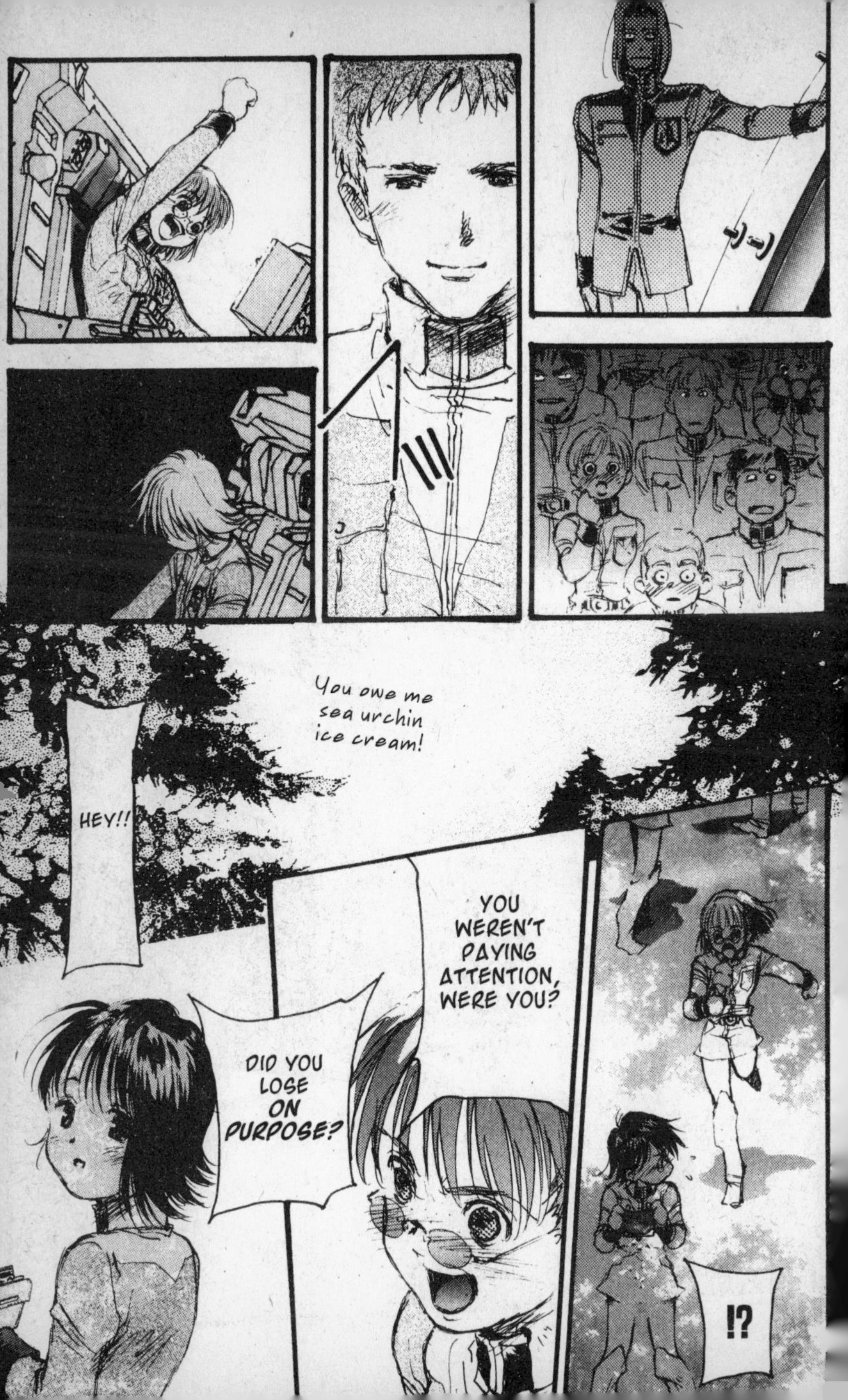
You owe me sea urchin ice cream!
HEY!!
!?
YOU WEREN'T PAYING ATTENTION, WERE YOU?
DID YOU LOSE ON PURPOSE?

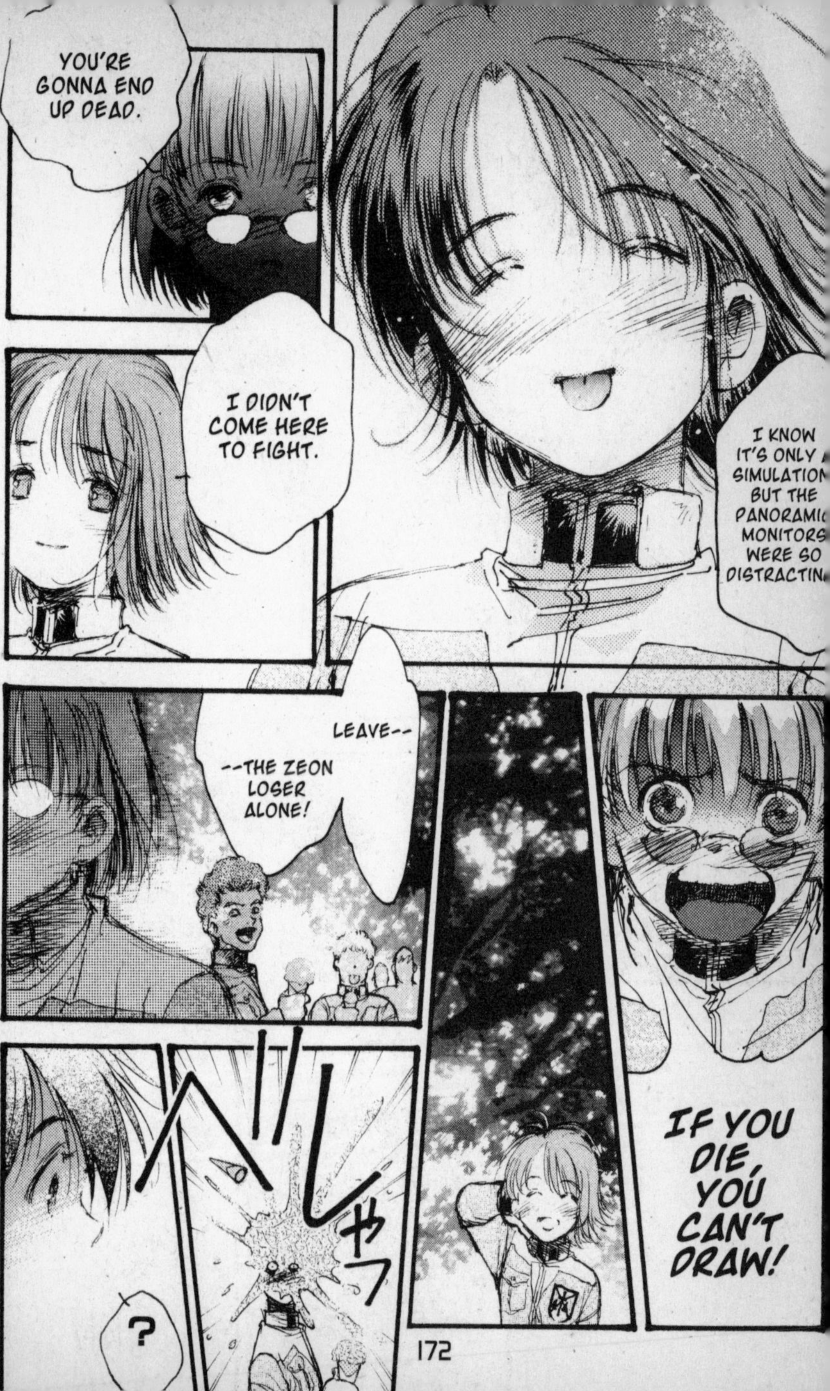
I KNOW IT'S ONLY SIMULATIO BUT THE PANORAMI MONITORS WERE SO DISTRACTIN
YOU'RE GONNA END UP DEAD.
I DIDN'T COME HERE TO FIGHT.
IF YOU DIE, YOU CAN'T DRAW!
LEAVE--
--THE ZEON LOSER ALONE!
ベリしゃっ
?

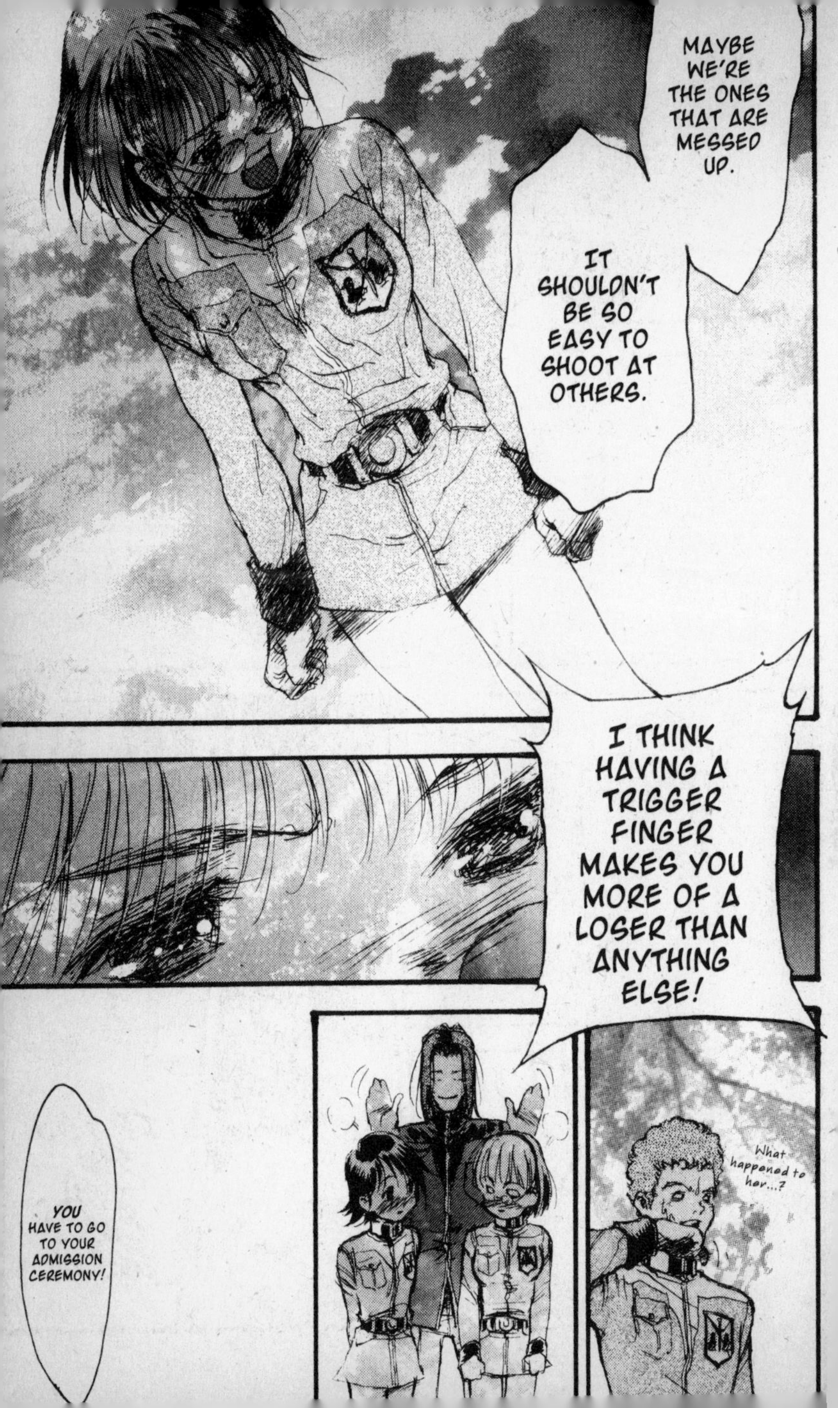
MAYBE WE'RE THE ONES THAT ARE MESSED UP.
IT SHOULDN'T BE SO EASY TO SHOOT AT OTHERS.
I THINK HAVING A TRIGGER FINGER MAKES YOU MORE OF A LOSER THAN ANYTHING ELSE!
What happened to her...?
YOU HAVE TO GO TO YOUR ADMISSION CEREMONY!

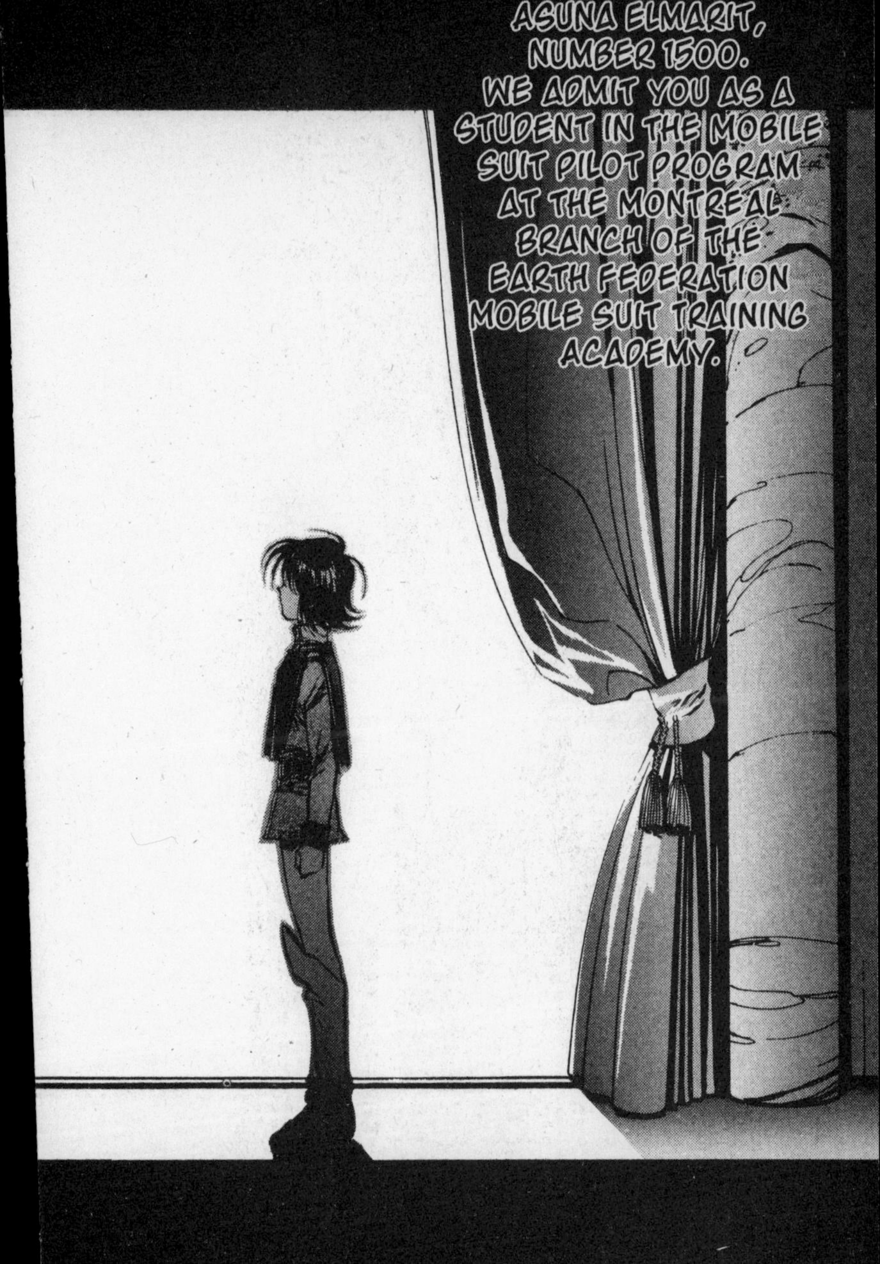
ASUNA ELMARIT, NUMBER 1500. WE ADMIT YOU AS A STUDENT IN THE MOBILE SUIT PILOT PROGRAM AT THE MONTREAL BRANCH OF THE EARTH FEDERATION MOBILE SUIT TRAINING ACADEMY.

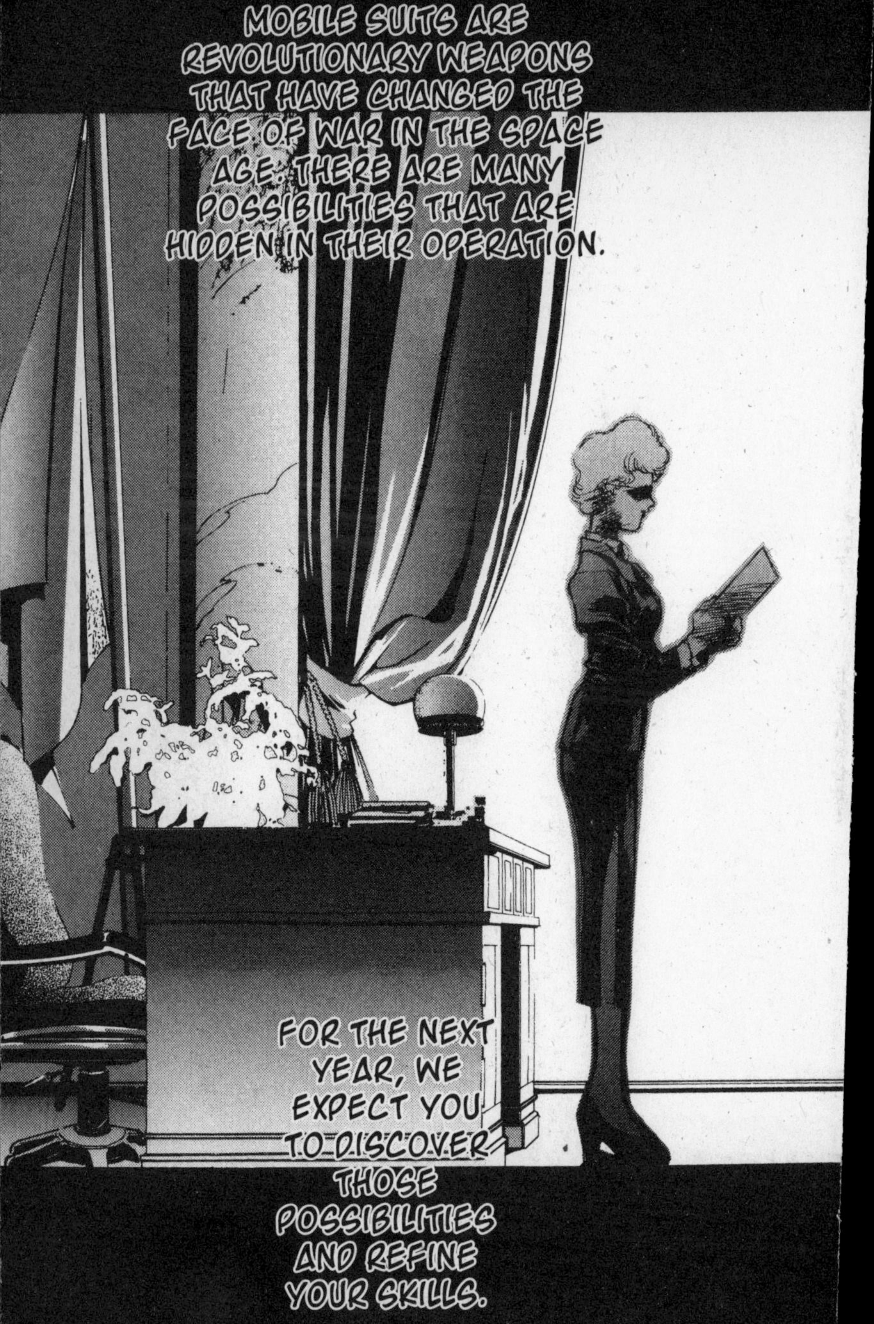
MOBILE SUITS ARE REVOLUTIONARY WEAPONS THAT HAVE CHANGED THE FACE OF WAR IN THE SPACE AGE. THERE ARE MANY POSSIBILITIES THAT ARE HIDDEN IN THEIR OPERATION.
FOR THE NEXT YEAR, WE EXPECT YOU TO DISCOVER THOSE POSSIBILITIES AND REFINE YOUR SKILLS.

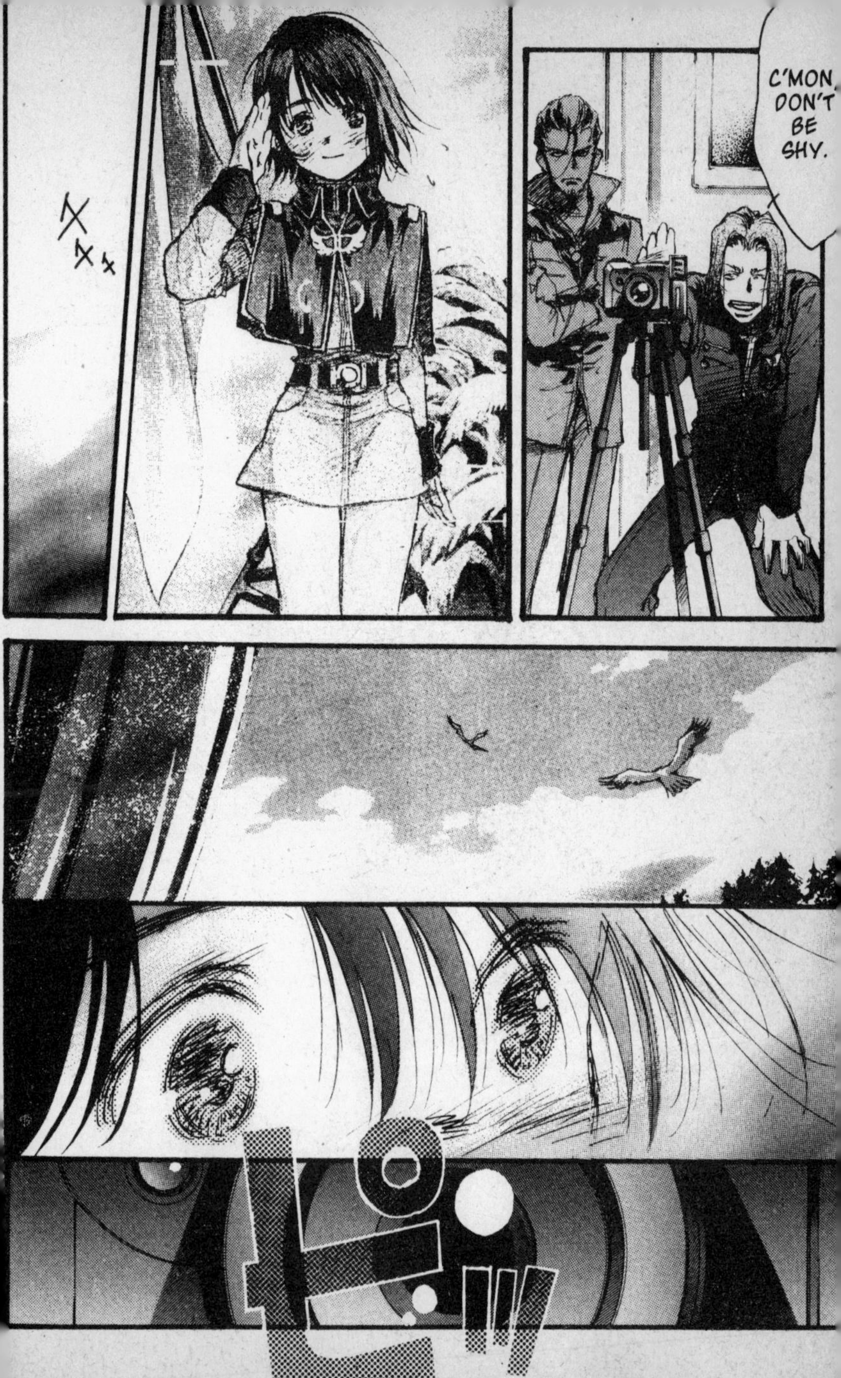
C'MON, DON'T BE SHY.

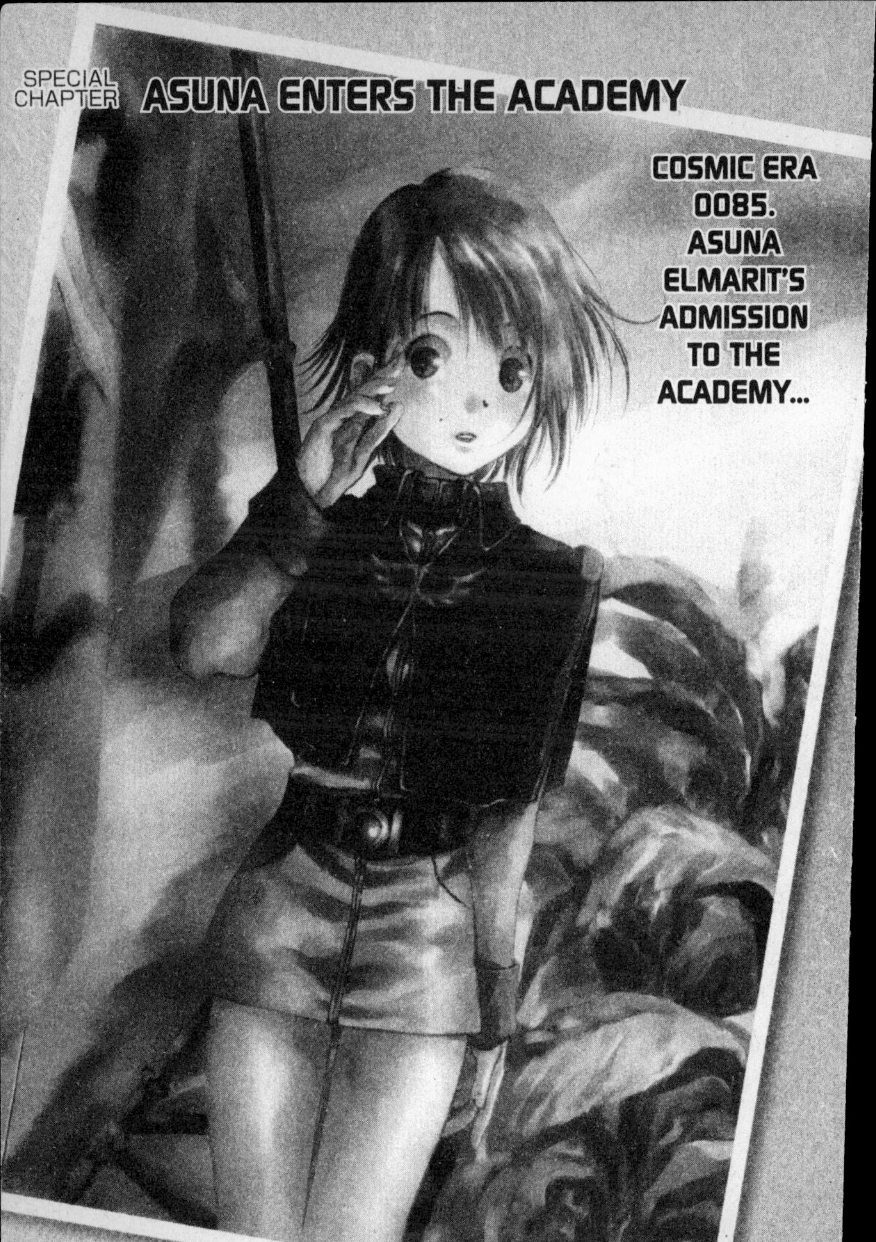
SPECIAL CHAPTER
ASUNA ENTERS THE ACADEMY
COSMIC ERA 0085. ASUNA ELMARIT'S ADMISSION TO THE ACADEMY...

TO BE CONTINUED...

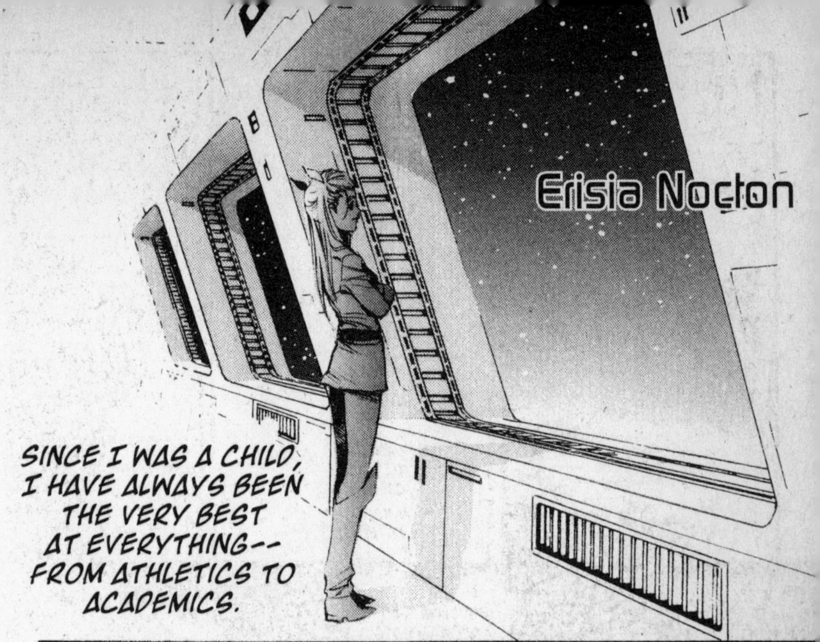
Erisia Nocton
SINCE I WAS A CHILD, I HAVE ALWAYS BEEN THE VERY BEST AT EVERYTHING--FROM ATHLETICS TO ACADEMICS.

MY PERSONAL NOTES ON A SERIOUS TURN OF EVENTS

ERISIA'S DEPRESSION

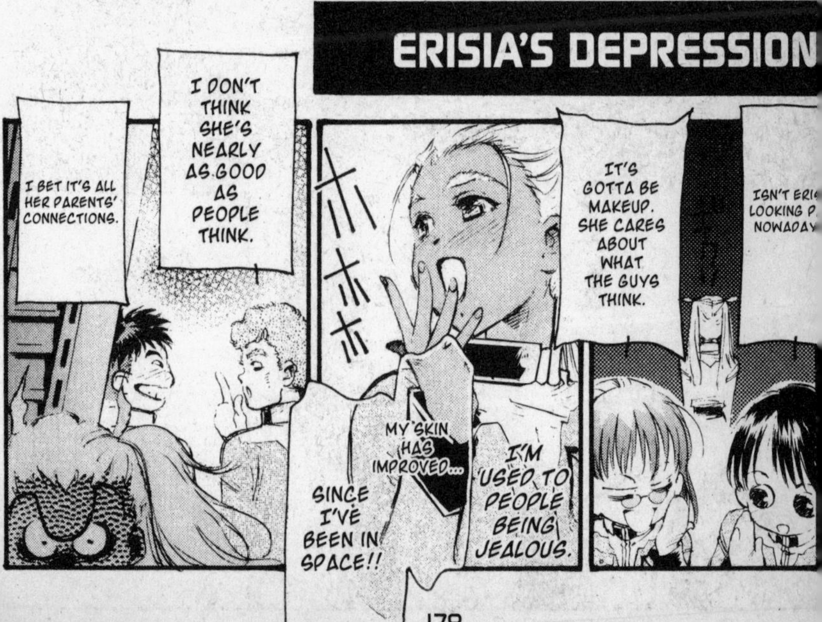
ISN'T ERI
LOOKING P
NOWADAY
IT'S GOTTA BE MAKEUP. SHE CARES ABOUT WHAT THE GUYS THINK.
I'M USED TO PEOPLE BEING JEALOUS.
MY SKIN HAS IMPROVED... SINCE I'VE BEEN IN SPACE!!
ホホホ
I DON'T THINK SHE'S NEARLY AS GOOD AS PEOPLE THINK.
I BET IT'S ALL HER PARENTS' CONNECTIONS.

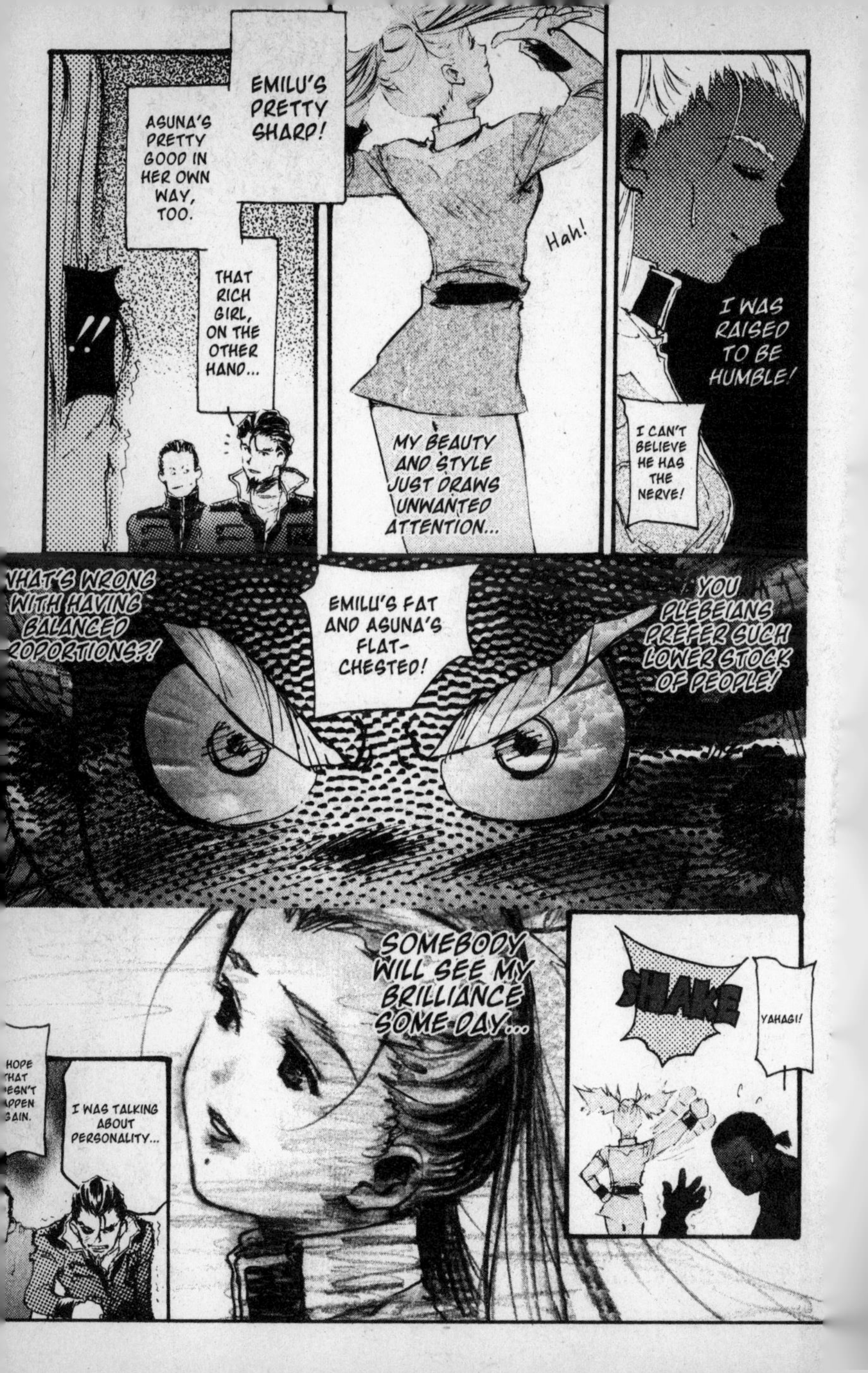
I WAS RAISED TO BE HUMBLE!
I CAN'T BELIEVE HE HAS THE NERVE!
Hah!
MY BEAUTY AND STYLE JUST DRAWS UNWANTED ATTENTION...
EMILU'S PRETTY SHARP!
ASUNA'S PRETTY GOOD IN HER OWN WAY, TOO.
THAT RICH GIRL, ON THE OTHER HAND...
!!
YOU PLEBEIANS PREFER SUCH LOWER STOCK OF PEOPLE!
EMILU'S FAT AND ASUNA'S FLAT-CHESTED!
HAT'S WRONG WITH HAVING BALANCED ROPORTIONS?!
SHAKE
YAHAGI!
SOMEBODY WILL SEE MY BRILLIANCE SOME DAY...
I WAS TALKING ABOUT PERSONALITY...
HOPE THAT ESN'T PPEN GAIN.

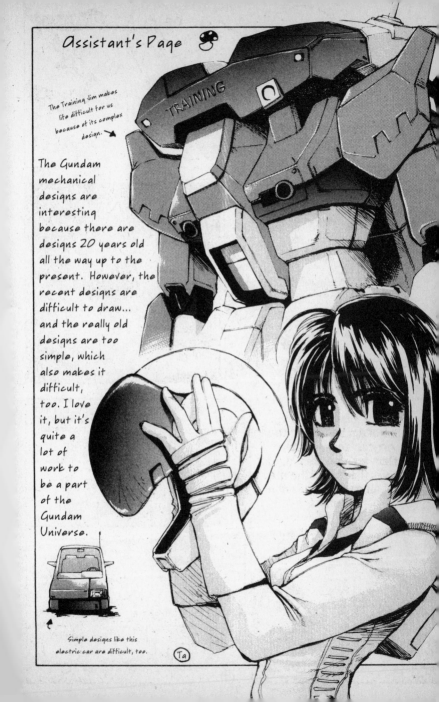

Assistant's Page

The Training Jim makes life difficult for us because of its complex design.

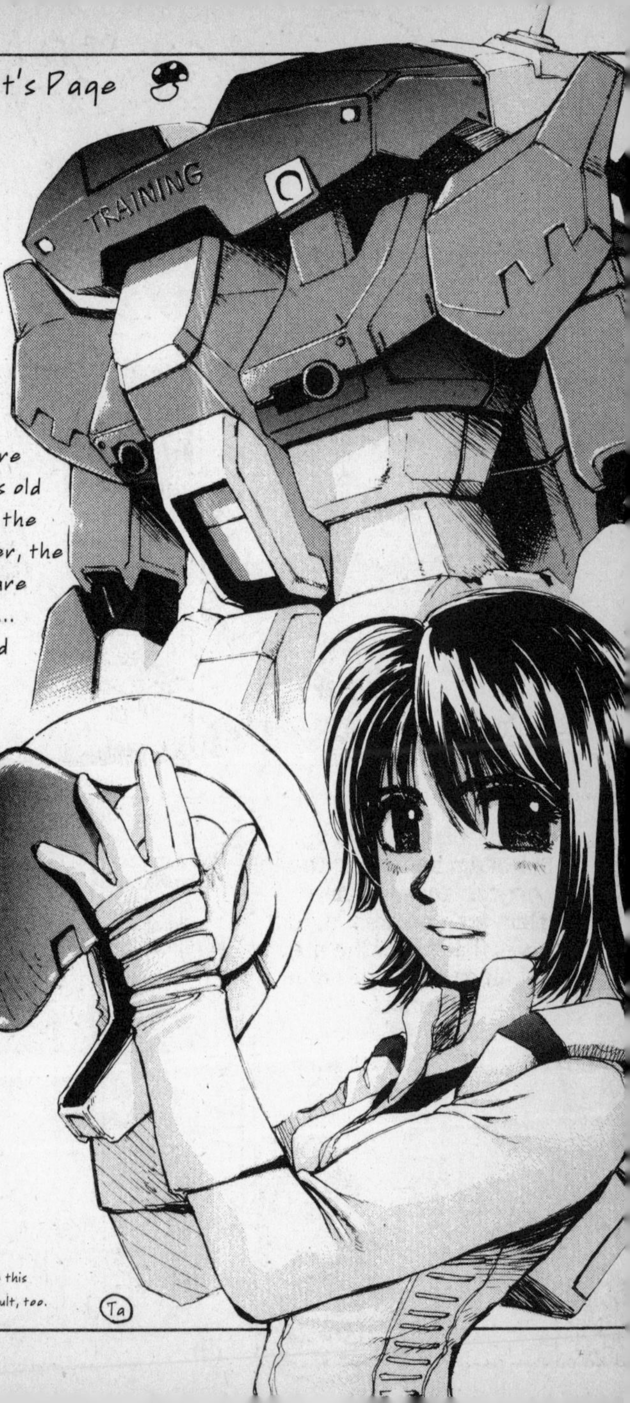
TRAINING

The Gundam mechanical designs are interesting because there are designs 20 years old all the way up to the present. However, the recent designs are difficult to draw... and the really old designs are too simple, which also makes it difficult, too. I love it, but it's quite a lot of work to be a part of the Gundam Universe.

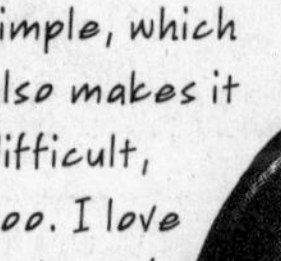

Simple designs like this electric car are difficult, too.

Ta

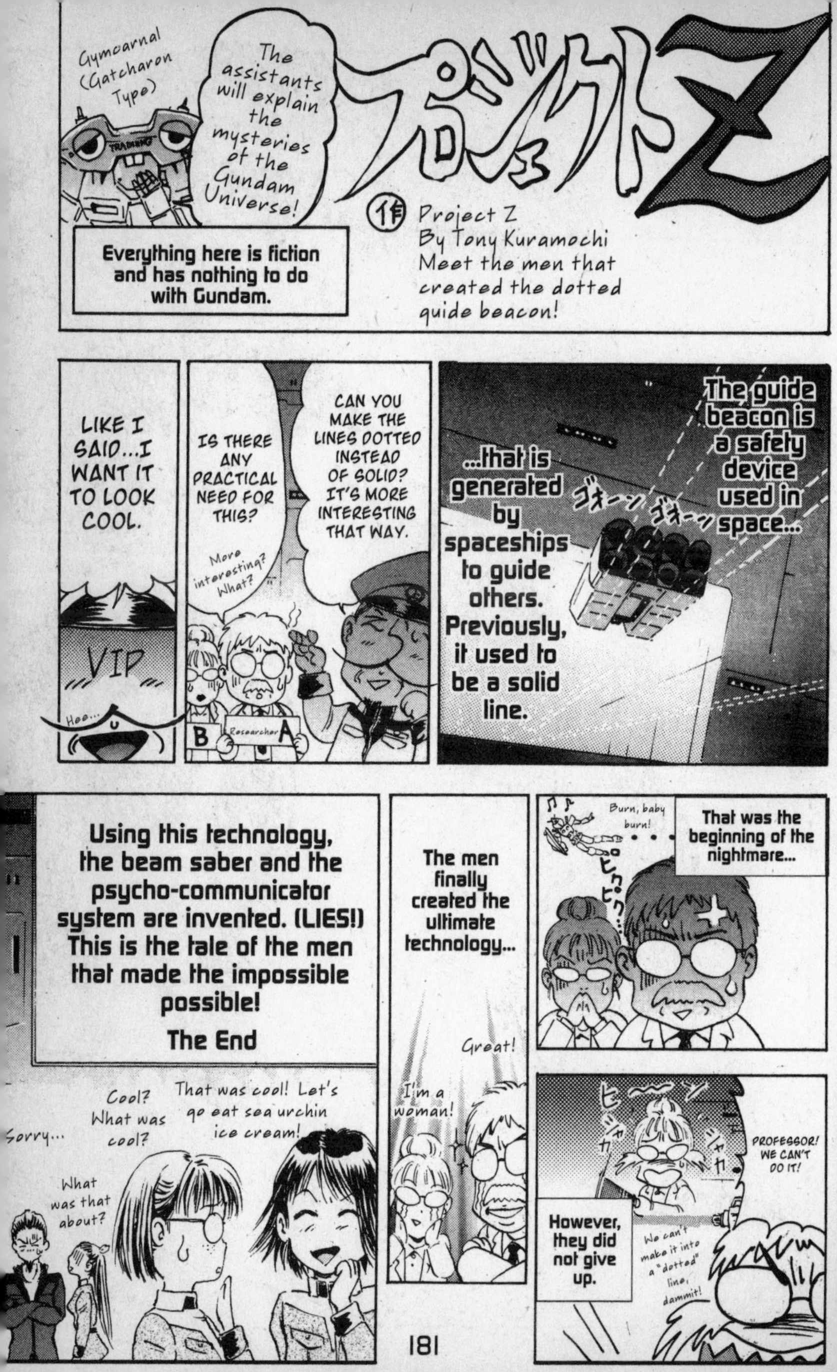
プロジェクトZ
作
Project Z
By Tony Kuramochi
Meet the men that created the dotted guide beacon!
The assistants will explain the mysteries of the Gundam Universe!
Gymoarnal (Gatcharon Type)
Everything here is fiction and has nothing to do with Gundam.
The guide beacon is a safety device used in space...
...that is generated by spaceships to guide others. Previously, it used to be a solid line.
ゴォーン ゴォーン
CAN YOU MAKE THE LINES DOTTED INSTEAD OF SOLID? IT'S MORE INTERESTING THAT WAY.
IS THERE ANY PRACTICAL NEED FOR THIS?
More interesting? What?
Researcher A
B
LIKE I SAID...I WANT IT TO LOOK COOL.
VIP
Hee...
That was the beginning of the nightmare...
Burn, baby burn!
ピクピク
PROFESSOR! WE CAN'T DO IT!
However, they did not give up.
We can't make it into a "dotted" line, dammit!
The men finally created the ultimate technology...
Great!
I'm a woman!
Using this technology, the beam saber and the psycho-communicator system are invented. (LIES!) This is the tale of the men that made the impossible possible!
The End
That was cool! Let's go eat sea urchin ice cream!
Cool? What was cool?
Sorry...
What was that about?

In the next Volume of...

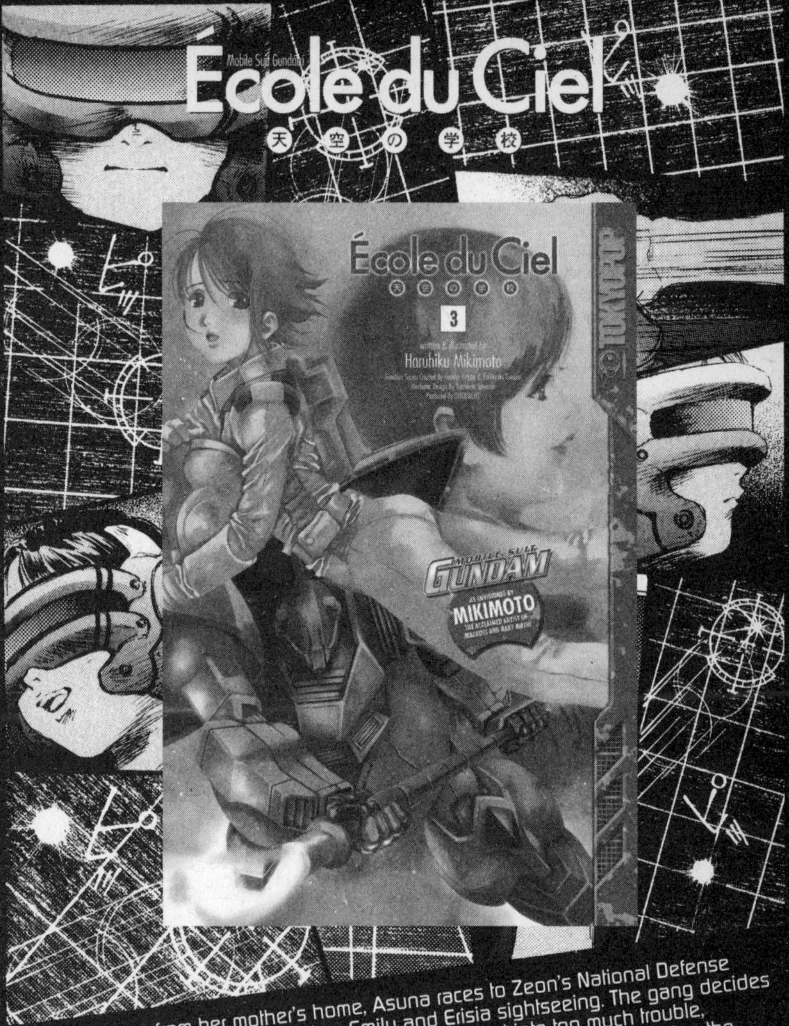
Mobile Suit Gundam
École du Ciel
天空の学校
École du Ciel
3
Haruhiko Mikimoto
MOBILE SUIT GUNDAM
AS ENVISIONED BY
MIKIMOTO

After fleeing from her mother's home, Asuna races to Zeon's National Defense Academy, where she finds Shinn, Emilu and Erisia sightseeing. The gang decides to sneak into the Academy. But before they can get into too much trouble, combat breaks out in space, and an evacuation signal is given, returning the students to their school ship.

Later, Asuna encounters a mysterious boy named Akira, who reveals that they were born and raised together--as experiments for a "superior hybrid breeding project." Meanwhile, Professor Forma discovers another shocking part of Asuna's past--the identity of her true father...

Vol. 3 Available May 2006!

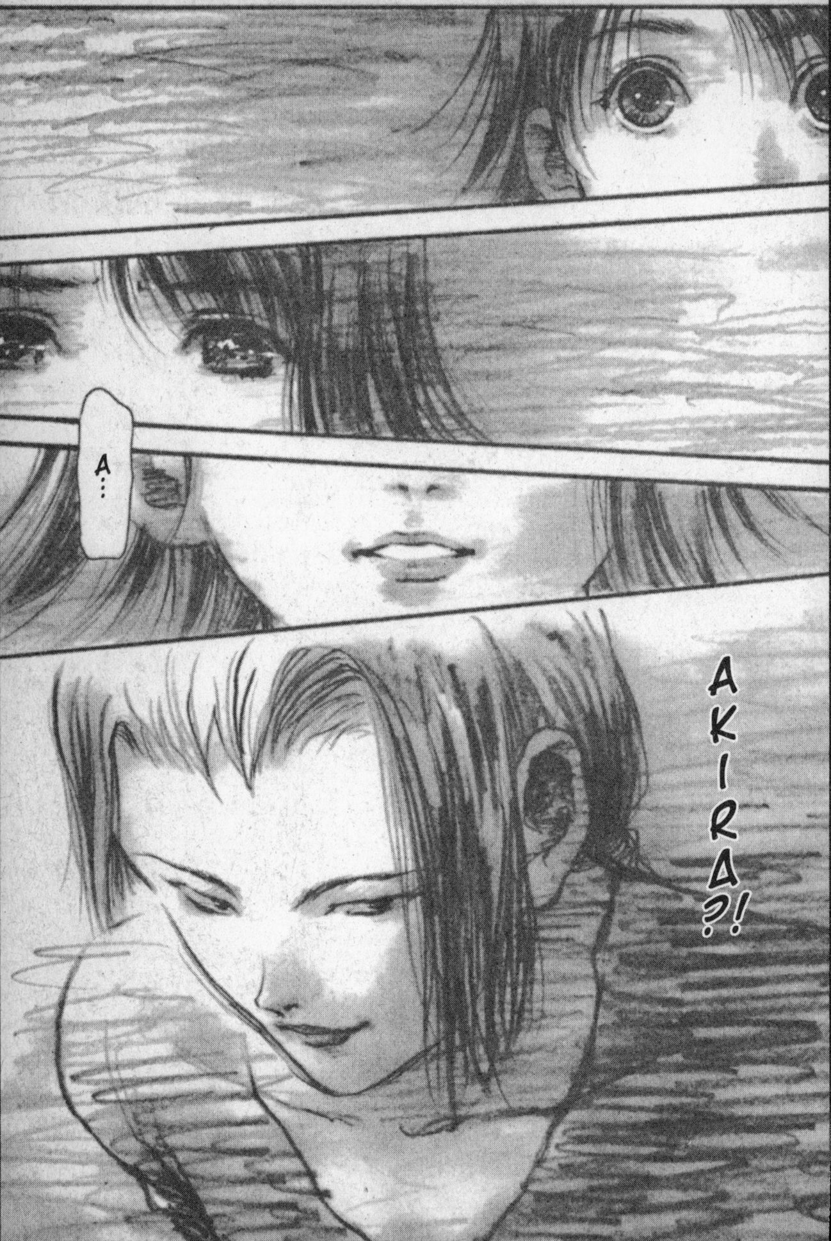
A...
AKIRA?!

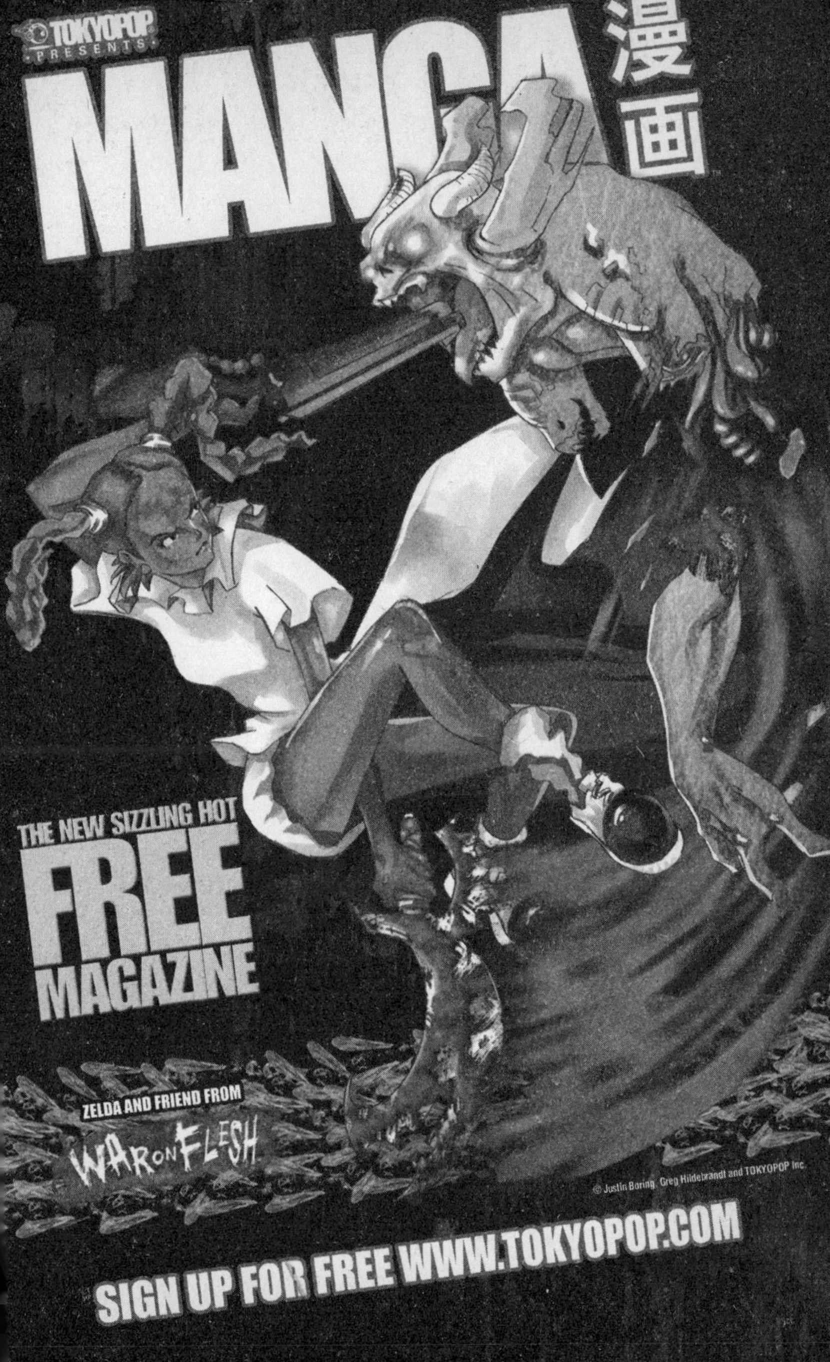
TOKYOPOP
PRESENTS
MANGA 漫画
THE NEW SIZZLING HOT
FREE
MAGAZINE
ZELDA AND FRIEND FROM
WAR ON FLESH
© Justin Boring, Greg Hildebrandt and TOKYOPOP Inc.
SIGN UP FOR FREE WWW.TOKYOPOP.COM

TOKYOPOP SHOP

WWW.TOKYOPOP.COM/SHOP

HOT NEWS!

Check out the TOKYOPOP SHOP! The world's best collection of manga in English is now available online in one place!

Ark Angels and other hot titles are available at the store that never closes!

THE DREAMING

PITA-TEN OFFICIAL FAN BOOK

WWW.TOKYOPOP.COM/SHOP

0 00000 00000 0

ARK ANGELS

- LOOK FOR SPECIAL OFFERS
- PRE-ORDER UPCOMING RELEASES
- COMPLETE YOUR COLLECTIONS

Ark Angels © Sang-Sun Park and TOKYOPOP K.K. The Dreaming © Queenie Chan and TOKYOPOP Inc. Pita Ten Official Fan Book © Koge-Donbo.

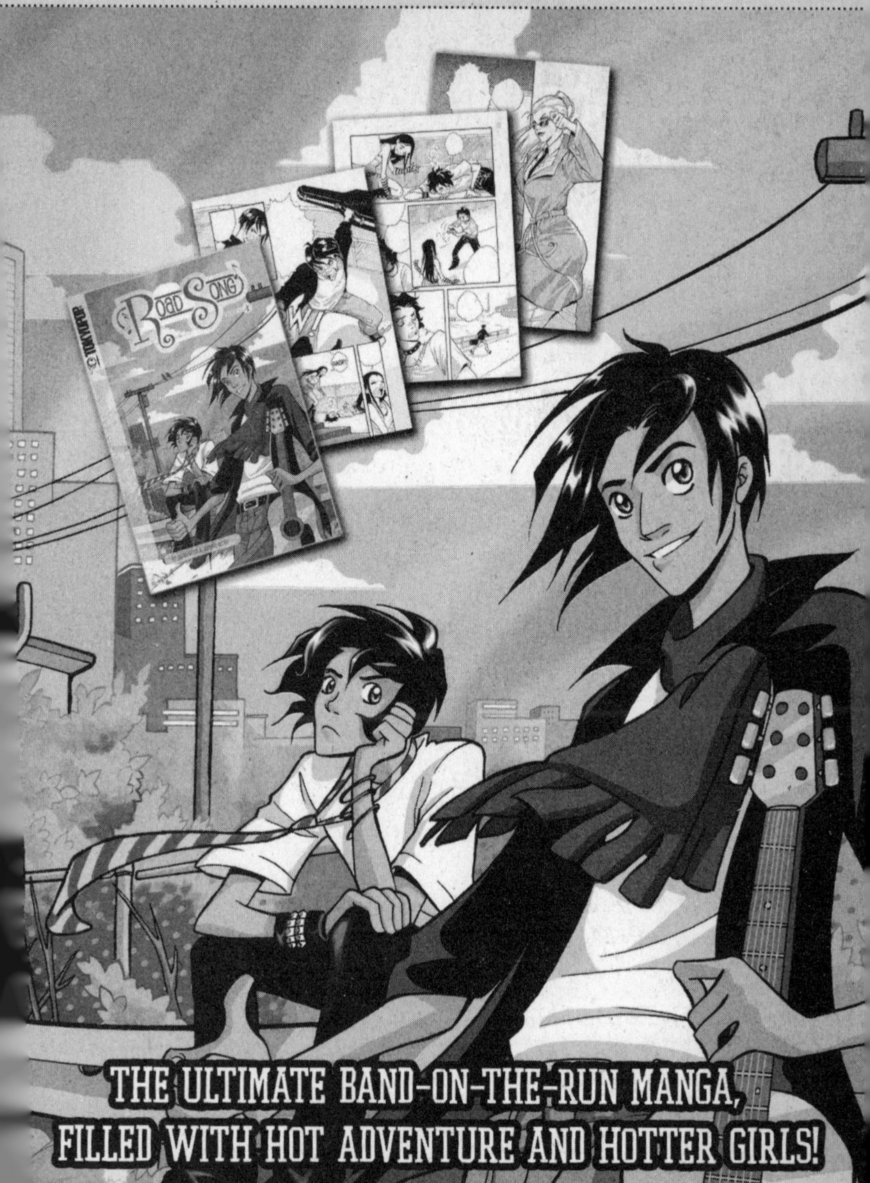
ROAD SONG
TOKYOPOP
THE ULTIMATE BAND-ON-THE-RUN MANGA,
FILLED WITH HOT ADVENTURE AND HOTTER GIRLS!

Music...mystery...and Murder!

RoadSong

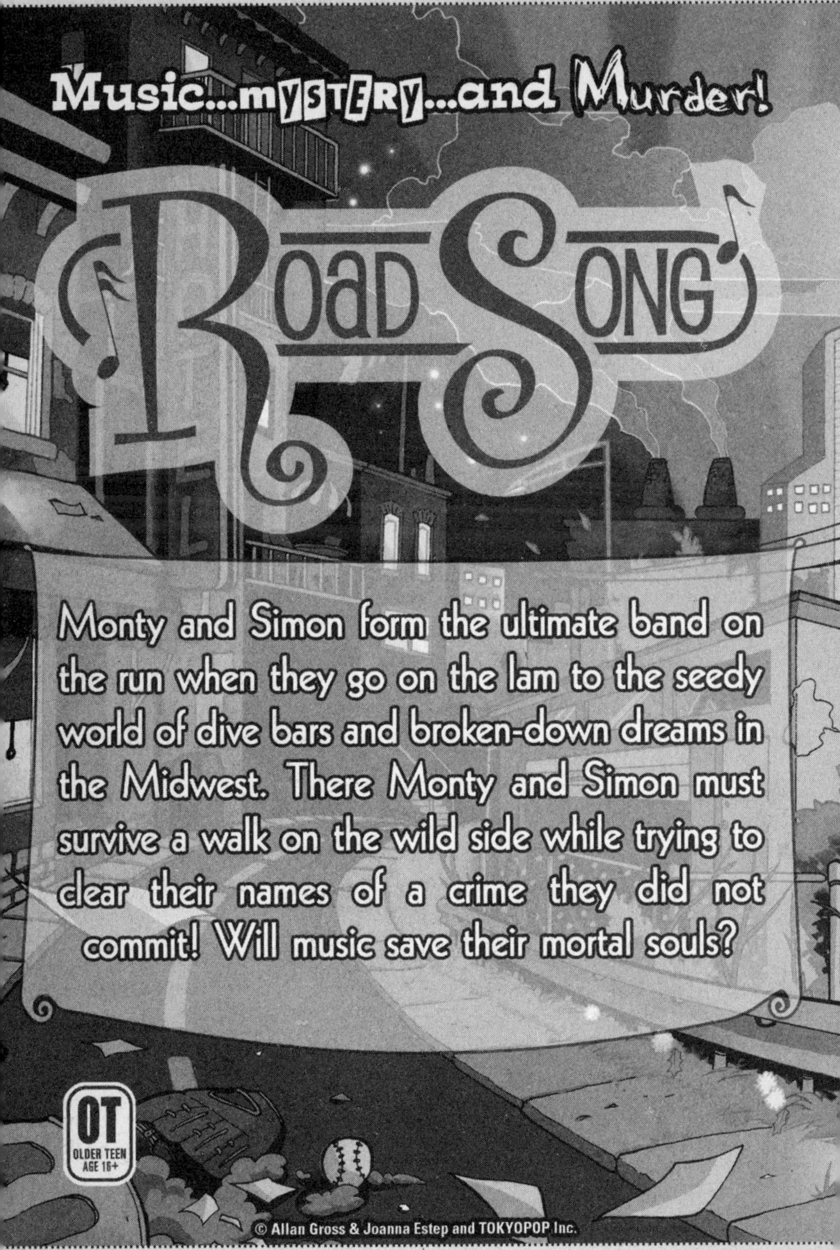

Monty and Simon form the ultimate band on the run when they go on the lam to the seedy world of dive bars and broken-down dreams in the Midwest. There Monty and Simon must survive a walk on the wild side while trying to clear their names of a crime they did not commit! Will music save their mortal souls?

OT
OLDER TEEN
AGE 16+

© Allan Gross & Joanna Estep and TOKYOPOP Inc.

READ A CHAPTER OF THE MANGA ONLINE FOR FREE:

SPOTLIGHT

TOKYOPOP MANGA SUPPLEMENT

LOVELESS
BY YUN KOUGA

The mystery behind the death of his older brother was only the beginning...

THE WAIT IS OVER — THE FAN-FAVORITE MANGA IS FINALLY HERE!

LOVELESS
by Yun Kouga

LOVELESS™

After discovering a posthumous message from his brother indicating he was murdered, twelve-year-old Ritsuka becomes involved in a shadowy world of spell battles and secret names. Together with the mysterious Soubi, Ritsuka begins the search to uncover the truth behind the murder! But in a world where mere words have unbelievable power, how can you find true friendship when your very name is Loveless?

OT OLDER TEEN AGE 16+

© Yun Kouga / ICHIJINSHA

FOR MORE INFORMATION VISIT: WWW.TOKYOPOP.COM/LOVELESS

© Minari Endoh/ICHIJINSHA

DAZZLE
BY MINARI ENDOH

When a young girl named Rahzel sets out to see the world, she meets Alzeid, a mysterious loner on a mission to find his father's killer. Although the two share similar magical abilities, they don't exactly see eye-to-eye...but they will need each other to survive their journey!

An epic coming-of-age story from an accomplished manga artist!

T TEEN AGE 13+

© CHIHO SAITOU and IKUNI & Be-PaPas

THE WORLD EXISTS FOR ME
BY BE-PAPAS AND CHIHO SAITOU

Once upon a time, the source of the devil R's invincible powers was *The Book of S & M*. But one day, a young man stole the book without knowing what it was, cut it into strips and used it to create a girl doll named "S" and a boy doll named "M." With that act, the unimaginable power that the devil held from the book was unleashed upon the world!

From the creators of the manga classic *Revolutionary Girl Utena!*

T TEEN AGE 13+

© Keitaro Arima

TSUKUYOMI: MOON PHASE
BY KEITARO ARIMA

Cameraman Kouhei Midou is researching Schwarz Quelle Castle. When he steps inside the castle's great walls, he discovers a mysterious little girl, Hazuki, who's been trapped there for years. Utilizing her controlling charm, Hazuki tries to get Kouhei to set her free. But this sweet little girl isn't everything she appears to be...

The manga that launched the popular anime!

T TEEN AGE 13+

BY HO-KYUNG YEO

HONEY MUSTARD

I'm often asked about the title of *Honey Mustard*. What does a condiment have to do with romance and teen angst? One might ask the same thing about a basket of fruits, but I digress. Honey mustard is sweet with a good dose of bite, and I'd say that sums up this series pretty darn well, too. Ho-Kyung Yeo does a marvelous job of balancing the painful situations of adolescence with plenty of whacked-out humor to keep the mood from getting *too* heavy. It's a good, solid romantic comedy...and come to think of it, it'd go great with that sandwich.

~Carol Fox, Editor

BY YURIKO NISHIYAMA

REBOUND

At first glance, *Rebound* may seem like a simple sports manga. But on closer inspection, you'll find that the real drama takes place off the court. While the kids of the Johnan basketball team play and grow as a team, they learn valuable life lessons as well. By fusing the raw energy of basketball with the apple pie earnestness of an afterschool special, Yuriko Nishiyama has created a unique and heartfelt manga that appeals to all readers, male and female.

~Troy Lewter, Editor

Honey Mustard © Ho-Kyung Yeo, HAKSAN PUBLISHING CO., LTD. Rebound © Yuriko Nishiyama.

TOKYOPOP®
· P R E S E N T S ·

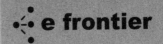
e frontier

MANGA STUDIO™ 3.0

WHAT WILL *YOU* CREATE?

The Best Software For Digital Manga Creation

e frontier's Manga Studio lets you draw, ink, tone and letter your manga in the computer. A library of **1800 digital tones** uses vector technology for moiré-free results. Automated drawing tools speed the process of creating your sequential art. Twelve types of layers keep your work organized and easy to edit. Scan in existing artwork and finish it in the computer, saving time and money on materials. Manga Studio's 1200-dpi resolution ensures professional-quality files that can be saved in several popular formats.

For more information or to purchase, visit:
www.e-frontier.com/go/tokyopop

SPECIAL INTRODUCTORY PRICE FOR MANGA STUDIO 3.0 DEBUT:
$49.99

CALL OFF YOUR MONSTERS, ADONETTE.

VAN VON HUNTER™

VAN VON HUNTER
MANGA CREATED WITH MANGA STUDIO.

Copyright © 2005 e frontier America, Inc. and © 2003-2005 CelSys, Inc. Manga images from Van Von Hunter © 2005 Pseudomé Studio LLC. TOKYOPOP is a registered trademark and Van Von Hunter is a trademark of TOKYOPOP Inc. All other logos, product names and company names are trademarks or registered trademarks of their respective owners.

STOP!

This is the back of the book.
You wouldn't want to spoil a great ending!

This book is printed "manga-style," in the authentic Japanese right-to-left format. Since none of the artwork has been flipped or altered, readers get to experience the story just as the creator intended. You've been asking for it, so TOKYOPOP® delivered: authentic, hot-off-the-press, and far more fun!

DIRECTIONS

If this is your first time reading manga-style, here's a quick guide to help you understand how it works.

It's easy... just start in the top right panel and follow the numbers. Have fun, and look for more 100% authentic manga from TOKYOPOP®!